CW00486108

Organising Poetry

ORGANISING POETRY

The Coleridge Circle, 1790–1798

DAVID FAIRER

OXFORD
UNIVERSITY PRESS

*This book has been printed digitally and produced in a standard specification
in order to ensure its continuing availability*

OXFORD
UNIVERSITY PRESS

Great Clarendon Street, Oxford OX2 6DP
United Kingdom

Oxford University Press is a department of the University of Oxford.
It furthers the University's objective of excellence in research, scholarship,
and education by publishing worldwide. Oxford is a registered trade mark of
Oxford University Press in the UK and in certain other countries

© David Fairer 2009

The moral rights of the author have been asserted

First published 2009
Reprinted 2012

All rights reserved. No part of this publication may be reproduced, stored in
a retrieval system, or transmitted, in any form or by any means, without the
prior permission in writing of Oxford University Press, or as expressly permitted
by law, by licence or under terms agreed with the appropriate reprographics
rights organization. Enquiries concerning reproduction outside the scope of the
above should be sent to the Rights Department, Oxford University Press, at the
address above

You must not circulate this book in any other binding or cover
And you must impose this same condition on any acquirer

British Library Cataloguing in Publication Data
Data available

Library of Congress Cataloging in Publication Data
Data available

ISBN 978-0-19-929616-3

For ADAM

Acknowledgements

I GRATEFULLY ACKNOWLEDGE the permission of the following publishers and editors to include material that has appeared in an earlier form elsewhere: a version of Chapter 4 first appeared as a tribute to Roger Lonsdale in *Tradition in Transition: Women Writers, Marginal Texts, and the Eighteenth-Century Canon*, ed. Alvaro Ribeiro and James G. Basker (Oxford University Press, 1996), 314–38; Chapter 5 is extended from the essay in *Robert Southey and the Contexts of English Romanticism*, ed. Lynda Pratt (Ashgate, 2006), 1–17; Chapter 6 has been developed from the essay in *Thomas Chatterton and Romantic Culture*, ed. Nick Groom (Macmillan, 1999), 228–52; Chapter 8 originally appeared in *Studies in Romanticism*, 41 (Winter 2002), 585–604, and is here reproduced by permission of the Trustees of Boston University; parts of Chapters 10 and 11 were published respectively in *The Coleridge Bulletin*, NS 21 (Spring 2003), 20–33, and *The Charles Lamb Bulletin*, NS 131 (July 2005), 62–75; a substantial part of Chapter 3 was included in 'Gaps and Tracings: Gothic Lines in the 1790s', delivered as the inaugural Landor Lecture, University of Aberystwyth, and was printed in their pamphlet monograph series. My warm thanks to all. Parts of many chapters were first tested out in lectures and papers delivered to the Wordsworth Summer Conference, Grasmere; the International Coleridge Conference, Cannington, Somerset; the Friends of Coleridge Weekend, Kilve; the Charles Lamb Society; the Eighteenth-Century Seminar, Smith College, Northampton, MA; the American Society for Eighteenth-Century Studies Annual Meetings, at Austin, Montreal, and Atlanta; the Eighteenth-Century Worlds Seminar, University of Liverpool; the Eighteenth-Century/Romantic Research group, University of Exeter; the Romantic Realignments Seminar, University of Oxford; and the Midlands Romantic seminar, University of Nottingham. I am grateful for permissions to reproduce material, obtained as follows: three plates from Piranesi's *Prima Parte di Architteture* and *Carceri d'Invenzione* (Ashmolean Museum, Oxford); chart from Joseph Priestley's *A Description of a New Chart of History* (Bodleian Library, Oxford); a page from Laurence Sterne's *Tristram Shandy* (Leeds University Library); the engraved drawing of Cowper's Oak (Leeds University Library); John Flaxman's drawing, 'Thomas Chatterton Taking the Bowl of Poison from the Spirit of Despair' (Department of Prints and Drawings, British Museum); the Chatterton Handkerchief (British Library); and the painting 'Monastery Ruins at Eldena' by C. D. Friedrich (Alte Nationalgalerie, Berlin). I thank the staff of the Brotherton Collection and

Special Collections, University of Leeds, especially Chris Sheppard and Oliver Pickering, for their generous research support of various kinds over the years. The library's excellent resources have been a great asset.

No study of the 'organic', as re-conceptualised here, can fail to be aware of how other texts of all kinds have fed into it. Over the years the most helpful critics have often been those from whom I have differed most markedly, and in the notes I have tried to acknowledge my critical debts and divergences. But the influence of some scholars has reverberated more widely through this book, and I am conscious of having pursued further (perhaps further than they would go themselves) the implications of their ideas and methods. In this way I am indebted to the late Paul Magnuson's focus on the immediate contexts of 'Romantic' texts; to Nicholas Roe's alertness to the subtle political languages of the 1790s; to Michael O'Neill's close readings of 'self-conscious poems'; and to Lucy Newlyn's handling of poetic allusion and the emergence of more communal meanings. In attempting to free this 1790s poetry, especially Coleridge's, from the formal demands of unity and system, and to recover a concept of 'form' that is more various, dynamic, and accommodating, I have been heartened by the examples of Seamus Perry writing on Coleridge's creative 'double-mindedness', and of Susan Wolfson on Coleridge and the simile.

In bringing this study to completion I owe a huge thank you to Andrew McNeillie of Oxford University Press, who first welcomed proposals for a book of this kind, and who has ever since given it his unstinting support. My warm acknowledgements are due to the School of English, University of Leeds, for supporting the project as it has developed: much of the writing was done during a year's research leave in 2007–8 awarded by the School and the Faculty of Arts combined. Colleagues have been generous with their help: John Whale has been a thoughtful and inspirational guide at every stage, and a rigorous critic of several chapters; and other parts of the book have benefited from the advice and expertise of Shirley Chew, Robert Jones, and Simon Swift. Discussing Coleridge and his friends over several years with Gurion Taussig was a delight, and his *Coleridge and the Idea of Friendship*, developed from his Leeds Ph.D., has had a formative influence on my own study. I shall always be indebted to Nicholas Roe, who first encouraged me to extend my sights to the 1790s, and drew a recalcitrant eighteenth-century scholar to Wordsworth and Coleridge. The late Reggie Watters first invited me to speak on Coleridge and Chatterton, and since then the Friends of Coleridge have provided the most congenial context for hard scholarly thought about all aspects of STC's work: Paul Cheshire's knowledge of Coleridge's manuscripts has been of real help, as has Graham Davidson's humane and committed understanding of the more metaphysical Coleridge. Other friends have been a direct intellectual stimulus: Juan Christian Pellicer on the georgic; Nick Groom on Chatterton; Lynda Pratt on Southey; and Felicity James on Lamb and Lloyd. I'm especially grateful to Jane Stabler for years of encouragement and critical guidance, and for commenting on and improving much of this material in typescript. Adam Bray has been my ideal reader and 'best prop' while the book has taken shape. Because this is a study of (albeit very late) eighteenth-century poetry it is appropriate to record that Paul Hunter, Roger Lonsdale, John Sitter, and Howard Weinbrot continue to be the best kind of scholarly models. I also thank, for help of various kinds, Kelly Grovier, Jeffrey Hipolito, Sarah Poynting, Wolfram Schmidgen, and Colin Winborn. For O.U.P., the thoughtfulness and expertise of Claire Thompson, Charles Lauder, and Andrew Hawkey have guided the book through its later stages. Certainly not the least of these acknowledgements must finally be to J. C. C. Mays, whose comprehensive scholarship on Coleridge's poems in the great Bollingen edition has been invaluable.

Contents

List of Illustrations

List of Abbreviations

Biog. Lit.	*Biographia Literaria*, ed. James Engell and W. Jackson Bate, 2 vols. (London: Routledge and Kegan Paul, 1983). *Collected Works*, vol. 7
BL	British Library
CB	*Coleridge Bulletin*
CL	*Comparative Literature*
CLB *Charles Lamb Bulletin*	
Collected Works	*The Collected Works of Samuel Taylor Coleridge*, gen. ed. Kathleen Coburn. Bollingen Series LXXV, 16 vols. (London: Routledge and Kegan Paul; Princeton: Princeton University Press, 1969–2002)
Early Recollections	Joseph Cottle, *Early Recollections; Chiefly Relating to the Late Samuel Taylor Coleridge*, 2 vols. (London: Longman, etc., 1837)
EC	*Essays in Criticism*
ELH	*ELH: Journal of English Literary History*
GM	*The Gentleman's Magazine*
Griggs	*Collected Letters of Samuel Taylor Coleridge*, vols. 1–2 (1785–1806), ed. Earl Leslie Griggs (Oxford: Clarendon Press,1956). Continuously paginated.
JAAC	*Journal of Aesthetics and Art Criticism*
Marrs	*The Letters of Charles and Mary Anne Lamb*, vol. 1: *Letters of Charles Lamb, 1796–1801*, ed. Edwin W. Marrs, Jr. (Ithaca and London: Cornell University Press, 1975)
Mays	S. T. Coleridge, *Poetical Works*, ed. J. C. C. Mays, 3 vols. (Princeton: Princeton University Press, 2001). *Collected Works*, vol. 16
MLQ	*Modern Language Quarterly*
MLR	*Modern Language Review*
N&Q	*Notes & Queries*
Notebooks	*The Notebooks of Samuel Taylor Coleridge*, vols. 1–3, ed. Kathleen Coburn (London: Routledge and Kegan Paul, 1957–73)
OED	*Oxford English Dictionary*

1796 *Poems*	*Poems on Various Subjects, by S. T. Coleridge, Late of Jesus College, Cambridge* (London: G. G. and J. Robinson; Bristol: J. Cottle, 1796)
1797 *Poems*	*Poems, by S. T. Coleridge, Second Edition. To which are now added Poems By Charles Lamb, and Charles Lloyd* (Bristol: J. Cottle; London: Messrs. Robinsons, 1797)
PMLA	*Publications of the Modern Language Association of America*
PQ	*Philological Quarterly*
RES	*Review of English Studies*
SEL	*Studies in English Literature*
SiR	*Studies in Romanticism*
SP	*Studies in Philology*
The Spectator	*The Spectator*, ed. Donald F. Bond, 5 vols. (Oxford: Clarendon Press, 1965).
TLS	*Times Literary Supplement*
UTQ	*University of Toronto Quarterly*
The Watchman	*The Watchman*, ed. Lewis Patton (Princeton: Princeton University Press, 1970). *Collected Works*, vol. 2
WC	*The Wordsworth Circle*

Introduction: 'one common life'

> That being then one plant which has such an organization of parts in one coherent body, partaking of one common life, it continues to be the same plant as long as it partakes of the same life, though that life be communicated to new particles of matter vitally united to the living plant, in a like continued organization.
>
> —John Locke, *An Essay Concerning Human Understanding*
> (2nd edn., 1694), II.xxvii.4

ORGANISING POETRY IS a book about continuities and connectedness during a decade in which these related concepts were at the centre of public debate and were being privately tested in many different ways. In the wake of the dramatic political events in France in 1789 it seemed that anything might be reorganised on entirely new principles and all continuities broken. Any institution, body or system—the clergy or the calendar—could by law be dissolved and constituted afresh. If *Year One* had officially commenced on 22 September 1792, it was possible to think that History was capable of being disconnected from the present; and with the unit of the revolutionary week extended to ten days, Time itself might be regularised and fitted to a metric frame. In light of such easy inaugurations and performative decrees, any mode of continuity or connection was placed under strain. Against this background, the vocabularies of structure and growth, foundation and root, principle and system, marked out a disputed language of change that was at the heart of the 'Revolution Controversy', a term that can hardly do justice to the fundamental nature of the questions being raised. Across the scale of embodied ideas, from the nation and its institutions to a human mind or a poem, how things were organised, and what might constitute their continuing identity, could no longer be taken for granted. Much has been written on the poetry of Wordsworth, Coleridge, and their friends within the revolutionary context; but I hope this book will find its own winding path by focusing on how these issues of continuity and connectedness impinged on the organisation of their poems.

The emphasis of this study is not on the wider reorganisation of the political world. Only at the end does a national picture begin to form, and I hope that by then the issues involved at the local and personal level for the poets I discuss will help to illuminate the state of Britain in April 1798, a time when individual critical questions were reverberating across the landscape to become a national voice. I suggest a series of individual localised settings for the bigger picture—in this case not only the scene of national politics but also the literary history of the 1790s, a decade that can be thought of as the eighteenth-century *fin de siècle*.

The poetry of the 'revolutionary decade' (to use a more traditional term) has often been celebrated for fresh beginnings, as expressing a 'moment' when the poetic landscape changed and a new generation of poets found their voice; but this book argues that there is another story running through those years, one in which the voices of these men are in creative dialogue not only with each other, but with the poets of the previous decades, an engagement that in itself raises questions of continuity through influence and absorption. This is a study of how these writers in the 1790s contributed to the 'continued organization' of poetry at a time when all continuities, and the meanings and values they expressed, were being challenged. Focused on the work of Coleridge and his male circle (Wordsworth, Southey, Lamb, Lloyd, and Thelwall) it sets out to investigate the fraught topic of connectedness in its many forms (spatial and temporal) during this period, and to trace some of the issues that arise when radically minded young poets come to embrace ideas of inheritance, retrospect, revisitings, recoveries, and friendly 'converse', and engage themselves with various organic geographies (streams, paths, cottages) and organic histories (national and local, literary and personal). In many ways this is a strange thing for a group of young radicals to do.

Perhaps inevitably, then, the key term of this study is the *organic*; but here it carries a sense and a set of associations at odds with those traditionally exploited in criticism of Coleridge and his associates. It is a term which has become freighted with a set of formal expectations that work against the spirit of the organic as I conceive it, and in the opening chapter I aim to clarify my use of the word as distinguished from the organic of German idealist theory. Because the Coleridge of the 1790s is at the centre of the discussion, I do not want to anticipate his later intense interest in, and commitment to, the 'organische Form' of A. W. Schlegel, a crucial development that did not occur until his thirties. Instead, what is relevant to my purposes is a home-grown eighteenth-century organic of markedly different character, an empirical concept with very different critical implications. Chapters 2 and 3 attempt to establish this earlier tradition and to map out two related fields in which the possibility of making connections and finding continuities is crucial: identity and history.

Locke's extremely influential chapter on 'Identity and Diversity' provides my epigraph, and his ideas of continuing consciousness and vital communication, discussed in Chapter 2, help to provide the dynamics of this book. The poets of the Coleridge circle in the 1790s were 'vitally united', by both friendship and antagonism; but they also sensed that they were part of some developing narrative of the time. By wishing 'to begin the world over again',[1] Thomas Paine and the revolutionaries in France challenged the

---

[1] Thomas Paine, 'Appendix' to *Common Sense; Addressed to the Inhabitants of America... A New Edition, with several Additions* (London: J. Ridgway, 1791), 76.

value, even the validity, of history as a connected narrative; yet these English poets were aware of how their identities, their own personal histories, were taking shape within wider fraternal, local, and national histories. Conscious of themselves as being caught between past and future at a time of revolutionary disorganisation, they were fascinated by the notion of organisation—whether forming bonds among themselves, or in organising their individual poems or volumes of poems.

Locke's chapter can remind us that beneath the 'one life' concept developed by Coleridge and Wordsworth is an earlier more embodied principle, which directly confronts the problem of time and change, and which raises difficult questions about how identity can be sustained through a period of repeated loss and replacement. This study therefore challenges the belief that the concept of an organic 'one life' was essentially a formation of the 'Romantic period', a premise that has underpinned so much criticism of the poetry of the 1790s.[2] This study is not concerned to characterise or in any way validate a category of the 'Romantic'.

But my argument also involves a reassessment of the 'one life' idea itself. In place of theories of organic unity, the book traces a less idealised and rarefied principle of sustainability, which is embedded in physical change, decay, and corruption, and which struggles against ideas of entropy, fragmentation, disjunction, and loss. During the 1790s an idealist concept of 'organic unity' was less useful than a recognition of the practical human struggle to find life within diurnal materials and sustain it through time. As my eleventh chapter aims to show in relation to Wordsworth's 'Ruined Cottage' and poems in *Lyrical Ballads*, these were the dynamics of the mid-century blank-verse georgic, and by the 1780s they had become subsumed into a genre of topographical poetry in which Nature is less a transcendent unifier than a mixed economy. An unsettled Virgilian context of mutability and insecurity provides an uncanny anticipation of the poetry of uprootedness in the 1790s. Both offer a scenario in which the human struggle to survive is informed by nature's ambivalent powers. These poets of the 1790s, I argue, engage with an eighteenth-century georgic tradition that casts nature in a more recalcitrant role challenging human commitments and energies. Not far behind narratives of spiritual growth are lurking intimations of ruination and decay; but the 'life of things' in a more ecological sense can be nourished by organic matter of many kinds, and nature's model has its human equivalent, as Locke suggests. His 'one common life' is a dynamic principle grounded in the idea that individual 'particles' can form a common identity that is able to incorporate change. His image is one of vital sustenance linking past and future, a continual newness that possesses at the same time a continuous meaning. That, he suggests, is how organisms

---

[2] See Chapter 11, n. 1.

survive. In the 1790s it was a principle that was being tested in many different ways.

Instead of looking for new beginnings this book interests itself in the challenges posed by continuities during the decade. The nature of the historical is therefore at issue, particularly the role history plays in articulating meaning through time. Such a history is 'organic' in the terms set out in this book: not a unifying power but a process of making experience coherent, while registering and understanding change. Linked to the concept of identity explored in the second chapter, this empirical, antiquarian history raises questions about how narratives—including biographical ones—are pieced together out of what we know, learn, and remember. Chapter 3 is concerned with characterising an eighteenth-century tradition of organic history, which is aggregative and associative, a mixed mode that confronts disjunctive experiences, while tracing lines of connection across them. It does not run smoothly, nor filter out what is awkward or inconvenient, but acknowledges compromise and bias, failure and prejudice. The chapter features texts as diverse as Sterne's *Tristram Shandy*, Warton's *History of English Poetry*, and Burke's *Reflections*, arguing that Burke's conception of his organic constitution (unwritten because always in the act of being written) is indebted to an eighteenth-century tradition in which unifying theory bends before the stubborn exigencies of experience; emphasis shifts from the ideal to the pragmatic, and all teleologies are frustrated. Seen in this light, a 'system' does not function as a containing order, inherent or imposed; instead it negotiates disparateness while expressing living continuities. Walter Shandy's schematic *Tristrapaedia* is forever outrun by Tristram's life, just as Warton's progressive, ordered narrative is repeatedly compromised by new materials; both texts, like Burke's constitution, are in process, adaptive, full of odd turnings and details that bear the imprint of a persisting identity. And both are open-ended and accommodating narratives, not completed structures but ongoing organisations.

Coleridge and his friends were beginning their careers towards the end of a century that had seen the emergence of a national literary history, and Chapters 4 and 5 (focused respectively on Wordsworth and Southey), argue that they were aware of being part of a poetic story. In the work of the Warton School in the 1780s (a group of poets who formed round the figure of Thomas Warton, author of the first narrative history of English poetry) I offer not only a model for the early poetry of the Coleridge circle, but suggest that poets of the 1790s appreciated the Wartonian tradition ('the true English school' as Southey later called it) and valued the idea of sharing a 'native stream' from which they could draw. An awareness of literary history (as opposed to a consciousness of great poetic 'models'—a very different thing indeed) involves understanding one's own creativity within a continuing inheritance. Southey's acute sense of literary history as a story of loss and recovery, disruption and continuity, forms the core of Chapter 5.

The writers on whom the book focuses are those popularly called the 'first generation Romantics'; but that term is predicated on certain assumptions about priority and innovation—and the 'Romantic'—that this study seeks to challenge. My preferred term 'the Coleridge circle' recognises the extent to which STC perhaps inevitably made himself the most important figure in the book. He is, however, not being used here to exemplify anything, let alone the 'organic' as I am using the term. Where Wordsworth, for example, appears to sit more comfortably within this notion during the 1790s, Coleridge is forever disrupting and testing it, challenging those bonds of sympathy and shared endeavour that he also values, and at moments reaching out to an idealist, seraphic plane. The role Coleridge plays in this book is a disturbed and disturbing one: sometimes he is longing to be grounded and collaborative, at others he wants to seize and embody the Idea itself. As Seamus Perry has shown, he is a writer who raises complex questions about the struggle for coherence;[3] and, as we shall see, it is clear that how Coleridge as an individual was organised usually had implications well beyond himself. In the sympathies, tensions, and antagonisms that characterise his friendships during the 1790s continuous commitments are repeatedly put to the test. The poetry of his circle becomes a channel for exploring and gauging lines of connection; and their poetic converse can be seen as having a familial character, one which often finds meaning through echoes and responses. To use Locke's phrase, it 'partakes of the same life'.

The Coleridge circle was also conscious of representing the life of the nation at a time when all Europe was debating how states should constitute themselves. These men seem to have understood how their poetic organisations might be implicated in wider questions of political organisation. This has often been acknowledged; but the track of Coleridge, Wordsworth, and Southey through the 1790s has been persistently seen as a retreat from principle, as representing a loss of the radical dynamic that drove their work during the years immediately following the events of 1789. It has been told by E. P. Thompson as a narrative of 'disenchantment or default' when these poets lost faith in the possibility of revolutionary change and found a refuge in nature, home, and reassuring friendships.[4] More recently some scholars, notably Nicholas Roe, have challenged this picture by recovering the intricate political contexts of their work and allowing the texts to speak with an allusive eloquence. As Roe remarks, the poetry of the 1790s did not sink into 'an aesthetic retreat or escape', but continued to 'address and answer the most pressing issues of the day'.[5] This study is driven by a

[3] Seamus Perry, *Coleridge and the Uses of Division* (Oxford: Oxford University Press, 1999).
[4] See E. P. Thompson, 'Disenchantment or Default? A Lay Sermon', in C. C. O'Brien and W. D. Vanech (eds.), *Power and Consciousness* (New York: New York University Press, 1969), 149–81. See especially 163.
[5] Nicholas Roe, *The Politics of Nature: William Wordsworth and Some Contemporaries*, 2nd edn. (Houndmills: Palgrave, 2002), 3, xi.

similar dissatisfaction with the old narrative of retreat and loss of principle, and with the more recent accounts of poetic 'suppression' and 'evasion' developed in some new historicist approaches, which invoke an equivalent poetic bad faith.[6]

Nevertheless, at first sight this book might appear to be characterising an impulse that was inherently reactionary, which valued the history that Paine wished to erase and cherished the personal experience and emotional local ties that he and Godwin distrusted.[7] But a binary of revolutionary radicalism versus nostalgic conservatism oversimplifies the pressures felt within intelligent reforming minds during the decade, when figures like John Adams, Richard Price, and Jean-Joseph Mounier could press for a reformed constitution based on empirical principles, one that worked with the grain of human nature and reflected practical experience and historical precedents aplenty.[8] As Eleanor Shaffer has argued in relation to *Lyrical Ballads* (1798), Wordsworth and Coleridge were deeply concerned about the continuing constitutional organisation of society, and with balancing 'their ardent wish for reform, on the one hand, and their hope for the preservation of the fabric of society, on the other'. It was certainly possible, as she shows, to integrate Burke's organic constitution with arguments from 'Commonwealth' theory.[9] My book proposes that the eighteenth-century organic is not a reactionary idea, but one in which continuities can direct and further change. My context is a spatiotemporal one, and I want to counter the assumption that an acceptance of temporality is necessarily a reactionary move.[10] Compensation for loss can be found, not by seeking refuge, but by opening up new channels for life to continue. This, I suggest, is the positive aspect of those instances where poetic *retreat* has been diagnosed as a withdrawal from activity, a surrendering of principle: Thelwall's 'Lines, written at Bridgewater', Wordsworth's 'Tintern Abbey', or Coleridge's 'Fears in Solitude'. But in 1797–8, seeking to avoid imprisonment, declining to advocate the violent overthrow of the state, and fearing a French invasion

---

[6] See, for example, Marjorie Levinson, *Wordsworth's Great Period Poems: Four Essays* (Cambridge: Cambridge University Press, 1986), and Alan Liu, *Wordsworth: The Sense of History* (Stanford: Stanford University Press, 1989).

[7] The popularity of 'organic' in conservative social thought is noted by Raymond Williams, *Keywords: A Vocabulary of Culture and Society*, rev. edn (New York: Oxford University Press, 1983), 228–9.

[8] Don Herzog challenges the binary of empirical conservatism vs metaphysical radicalism, and offers a more subtle account of 'conservatism' during the 1790s. See *Poisoning the Minds of the Lower Orders* (Princeton: Princeton University Press, 1998), 13–49.

[9] Eleanor Shaffer, 'Myths of Community in the *Lyrical Ballads* 1798–1998: The Commonwealth and the Constitution', in Nicholas Roe (ed.), *Samuel Taylor Coleridge and the Sciences of Life* (Oxford: Oxford University Press, 2001), 25–46 (46).

[10] John Axcelson has spoken of Coleridge's and Wordsworth's 'common efforts throughout the 1790s and into the next decade to realign temporal experience with liberal politics' ('Timing the Apocalypse: The Career of *Religious Musings*', *European Romantic Review*, 16 (2005), 439–54 (441)).

were not conservative positions. During these disturbed years, to keep meanings alive and truths fresh was the challenge; and at a time of extreme crisis a retrenchment might imply a determination to locate and preserve one's core values. An element of withdrawal might bring a degree of concentration that could equally unsettle authority. The organic, in its resistance to structure and hierarchy, always has the promise of becoming a radical seed whose germination poses a threat to the status quo. Certainly in the pages of the *Anti-Jacobin* during 1798 the poets of Coleridge's circle, even Lamb and Lloyd, are pronounced dangerous: a cell of personal integrity might mutate into a Jacobinical cell of social disaffection.[11] In the suspicious eyes of the state a language of domestic innocence, fraternal ties, and the vital force of nature could be seen as insidiously primal and also worryingly patient—its very disengagement might be a radical retrenchment waiting for a change in the political weather. There are phases when the exertion of power is less threatening than a renewing of potential.

As has already been said, this is not a book about unity, but about organising diversity. It is centred on how poetic texts are shaped, but never, I hope, without an awareness of how other modes of organisation might be implicated in the process. During this decade of argument over constitutional texts (American, British, and French), how texts were themselves constituted, and how values might be embodied in them, became a living issue. Whether a text's language was declaratory and performative, or reflective and suggestive, might mark a political divide, and the nature of meaning itself be fought over. The largest issues could have localised effects, and (as those who debated constitutional niceties well understood) a single verbal detail might impact on a national scale. For good or ill, the pressures on a public text could come from any quarter at any moment; and its words had to be sanctioned, resilient, ready to bear weight and hold their place. But a constitution is not, of course, a poem. In the poetical context of this book, it is important to recognise that a word is not a single, unitary Idea, freshly minted for use, but is instead a much handled, always potentially debased currency drawing on many experiences and a long and varied past. To appreciate this organic dimension of English vocabulary is to recognise that our language has an identity shaped by history. The Logos gives way to a rich verbal mixture, in which meaning is never merely 'contained' by the individual words, but is created amongst them. At this organic level, human communication, not the Idea, is the key, and the model is once again an empirical and associative one. The passages of close reading offered in this book assume that meaning is a form of intricate interconnection, of reading across and between.

---

[11] E. P. Thompson describes the democrats in 1797 as 'being driven into small and personal survival groups' ('Disenchantment or Default?', 162).

The poetic texts discussed here do have gaps and discontinuities, but these are seen not as marks of bad faith (or bad politics) or as inevitable deconstructive *aporiai*, but in terms of an ethically conceived problem of self-consciousness and self-representation that lies at the heart of eighteenth-century empiricism. Running through the book's various episodes, as it does through Locke's passage about the oak tree, is a question about what constitutes a persisting human identity sufficient to sanction demands of commitment and responsibility.[12] The focus of interest for this study is therefore not organic unity, but what might be thought of as an organic integrity—a concept that repeatedly tests itself through experience, and extends itself in time. Emphasis shifts from matters of structure and harmony to those of character and durability—Goethe's 'Dauer im Wechsel' ('endurance through change').[13] Locke's theorising of 'consciousness' allows it to override inevitable interruption and discontinuity, 'this consciousness', he remarks, 'being interrupted always by forgetfulness, there being no moment of our lives wherein we have the whole train of our past actions before our eyes in one view, but even the best memories losing the sight of one part whilst they are viewing another' (*Essay*, II.xxvii.10). Bearing these sobering words in mind, it is clear that empirical continuities cannot be continuous: their commitment is to the continu*al*, to repeated testings and confirmations. They depend on bridging gaps and compensating for loss. It should be stressed that empiricism offers an inherently dynamic understanding of the mind's operations. The temporal and spatial dimensions are vital, and in my analyses of the poetic texts, whether single poems, groups of poems, or complete volumes, I want to make ideas of temporal succession and spatial superimposition key features of my readings. In an empirical context, the *successive* and the *superimposed* are crucial to the way meanings are formed.

The motif of the *return* is therefore important to this study because it combines the two ideas in ways that recall a philosophical crux about the temporal dimension of personal identity.[14] For these poets, to revisit a place and its associations is to gain a sharper understanding of oneself in the present, with the implication that, rather than being preserved despite discontinuities, personal identity is confirmed and strengthened by them.

---

[12] '[I]t is', Locke remarks, 'by the consciousness it has of its present thoughts and actions, that it is *self to itself* now, and so will be the same self, as far as the same consciousness can extend to actions past or to come; and would be by distance of time, or change of substance, no more two persons, than a man be two men by wearing other clothes today than he did yesterday...the same consciousness uniting those distant actions into the same person' (*Essay*, II.xxvii.10).

[13] Goethe's lyric poem of 1803 was written under the influence of Johann Christian Reil's theory of personal identity, which (like Locke's) stressed 'consciousness of the continuity of our personality'. See John R. Williams, *The Life of Goethe: A Critical Biography* (Oxford: Blackwell, 1998), 103–4.

[14] See Chapter 2.

Understood within an eighteenth-century tradition of Lockean 'consciousness', acts of revisiting are thus not nostalgic in implication, but represent the testing of individual identity across time.[15] Resistant to the notion of memory as mere fading and loss, poetic retrospects can become markers for an extended self with dialogic potential. Returns—to the Wye valley or a ruined cottage—can be subtle relocations of a self, which allow differences to be felt and therefore permit continuities to be traced. As the *now* and *here* is superimposed, repeated displacement shades into incremental replacement, just as in georgic writing the soil subsumes ruination and decay.

The eighteenth-century organic celebrates mixture, not purity: it evades binaries, preferring juxtaposition and superimposition as being truer reflections of human experience, because meaning forms at those points where ideas join or overlap—points of articulation that allow experience to be articulated.[16] Intriguingly, by locating identity in consciousness rather than substance, Locke opened up the possibility of its becoming communal, 'different substances, by the same consciousness (where they do partake in it) being united into one person' (*Essay*, II.xxvii.10). For Coleridge and his circle during the 1790s this Lockean line of thought, partly mediated through the work of Hartley and Priestley, encouraged them to explore modes of connectedness in which ideas of association and organisation might converge.

But the struggle to organise ideas in material form, especially for Coleridge himself, proved a constant challenge, and poetry carried the imprint of these difficulties. Conversely, real life felt the impress of poetic commitment and debate, whether in Coleridge's testing relationships with Lamb, Lloyd, and Thelwall (the subjects of Chapters 9 and 10), or in the generic uncertainty of the Pantisocracy scheme, an organisational failure that swung uneasily between idealised pastoral and practical georgic—and could be conceived as accommodating a dead but convivial Chatterton. In Chapter 6, Coleridge's early reworkings of the Chatterton 'Monody' bear the strain of the poet's irresolute sense of his own identity. Caught in a negotiation between Idea and its embodiment, the elusive spirit and the suffering body, eternal youth and manly experience, the figure of the poet becomes infused with Coleridge's own tensions. At the same time the poem raises related questions about continuities in literary history, how to make the old new. Chapter 7 suggests that similar dynamics operate throughout Coleridge's earliest published volume of poems, his first presentation of the

---

[15] In this I develop a point made by Richard Cronin about 'making the fact of change the proof not that we are separated from our former selves, but that we are bound to what we have been by a process of personal development' (*The Politics of Romantic Poetry: In Search of the Pure Commonwealth* (Basingstoke: Macmillan; New York: St Martin's Press, 2000), 11).

[16] To be 'articulate' is to have jointed limbs, distinct parts that function coherently together, 'vitally united', just as articulate speech depends on its discrete, individually identifiable, sounds. See *OED*, s.v. 'articulate', 1, 6.

'body' of his work before a reading public. In the 1796 *Poems* a dynamic impulse is repeatedly checked, renewed, blasted, and revived. There is no easy progress here, but an unsettling negotiation with his poetic materials, and with his own past, present, and future.

Following on from the tactical incorporation of Lamb into his 1796 volume, Chapter 8 looks at how a Coleridgean text could be compiled from the individual voices of others. Coleridge's *Sonnets from Various Authors*, his privately printed pamphlet of twenty-eight sonnets by twelve poets (with four sonnets each by Southey, Lamb, Lloyd, and himself), was designed to be bound up with the sonnets of Bowles; and this chapter argues that it represents an attempt to engage with the fraught domestic and personal problems of his friends Lamb and Lloyd, who were both in crisis that autumn, and suggests how isolation and trauma could be subsumed into a potentially healing communal identity. I suggest that the result is virtually a lost conversation poem, a dramatic 'converse' meditating on themes of self and society, friendship and social action, and moving from single lonely thoughts to a more integrated sense of 'one common life'.

The organisation of individual friendships is an important part of my story, and Chapter 9 traces Coleridge's developing poetic intimacies with Lamb and Lloyd, whose identities sympathetically overlapped with each other, and whose tendency to idealism, especially their idealising of Coleridge himself, almost inevitably brought a critical reaction from him. Their poetic pledges and mementoes became vulnerable to treachery and violation; secret meanings were caught up in questions of trust and betrayal. Rather than being negotiated in a more open and organic way, through elements of adaptability and compromise, their friendships with Coleridge tended to be freighted with idealistic hopes in which poetic incompatibilities were symptomatic of personal ones. These finally proved decisive, and in each case moved to a moment of crisis that was simultaneously biographical and textual.

The texts—individual and composite—discussed in this book are seen as 'living', not in a vague metaphorical way but in the specific terms of their organisation, their manifestation of empirical consciousness and its complexities. I approach them with an interest in *coherence*, not as unified structure or metaphysical Idea but as literally *making* sense, often through or within mixture and variety. The long established 'vitalist analogy' of creativity (an inner principle fulfilling itself through outward form) has led to a concept of organic*ism* that privileges the holistic. It has become difficult to disengage the organic from this analogical sense of fulfilment, with inevitable implications for poetic form. My aim throughout has been to preserve an awareness of process without the teleological dimension, and a sense of coherence without favouring harmony and structural unity.

There is much matter for debate here, and some of the implications of vitalism come into focus in Chapter 10, where the poetic disagreement

between Coleridge and Thelwall reveals how political and religious prin-
ciples could assert themselves through the minutiae of the poetic craft.
Questions of rhythm and verbal emphasis might be bound up with the
nature of the life force itself. Their disagreement centred on Coleridge's
'heart-honour'd' Bowles, whose verse in Thelwall's opinion exemplified
the debilitating melancholy 'into which persons sink from contemplating
nothing but their own sensations'. In place of this retrospective organicism
Thelwall celebrated his own materialist principle of 'animal vitality', an
electric stimulus to thought and action that animates human life. It was a
clash between two opposed views of the human organism. It is ironic that
the poems Thelwall himself began writing in late summer 1797 (his 'Effu-
sions of Social and Relative Affection') expressed his need for settling into
a life of 'kindred sympathies' and 'sweet converse', and the nature of
their dialogue with Coleridge's 'conversation' poetry suggests that within
Thelwall too there were tensions and contradictions.

The motif of the *return* comes to the fore again when Chapter 11 stages its
own return to Wordsworth, to the 'wild green landscape' of 'Tintern Abbey',
and to 'The Old Cumberland Beggar' and 'The Ruined Cottage', three texts,
I argue, that prompt thoughts about what a 'green' language might be in
1798 at a time of hardship and vagrancy. The differences in implication
between pastoral nature and georgic nature are significant, and I suggest that
in his poems of the late 1790s Wordsworth negotiates the distinction
thoughtfully. This chapter considers how growth and decay in nature can
function as a means of tracing continuity across the hiatuses of a narrative.
In Wordsworth's 'Ruined Cottage' tragic event is subsumed into organic
history. The text's successive returnings allow change to be registered eco-
logically as continuity, and death as endurance and survival.

In the book's final chapter Britain itself is uneasily waiting and wondering,
and during the invasion threat of 1797–8 the concept of 'one common life'
becomes a public discourse bound up with the identity and survival of the
nation. The renewed crisis of April 1798 brought calls for a pragmatic
recognition of shared interests and commitments that would embody the
Kingdom; and pamphlets instructed the populace on how to organise them-
selves against the threat. People became conscious of the duality of a vul-
nerable sea-coast and an inland haven, of outfacing the enemy while
confronting threats from within; and in this final chapter the politics of
looking 'homeward', in its various senses, is explored. With the cause of
reform postponed, the call for national unity sat uneasily alongside a com-
mitment to personal integrity; and Coleridge's response in his composite
volume combining 'Fears in Solitude' with 'France. An Ode' and 'Frost at
Midnight' highlights the national dimension of several themes that run
through this book.

Organising Poetry, then, aims to offer a fresh critical vocabulary for
thinking about the poetry of Wordsworth, Coleridge, and their friends

during the 1790s. The book suggests that instead of seeking to identify and
characterise 'the Romantic', by celebrating imaginative truth, symbolic
unity, creative genius, and transformative Idea—and assuming an equivalent
poetic 'revolution'—we might recognise how genius, in its eighteenth-
century sense, is rooted in the *genial*, the creatively sustaining climate, the
fertile poetic soil. In this more discursive context, meanings are pieced
together from the bits and pieces of knowledge we call ideas—in the Lock-
ean sense.[17] In moving the emphasis away from the language of idealist
'Romantic' theory towards an empirical stress on how identities are devel-
oped and enriched through time, *Organising Poetry* traces these poets'
struggles to find meaning not in vision and symbol but through connection
and dialogue. For them during these testing years, the concept of a continued
organisation 'partaking of one common life' offered not only a model for a
much-needed reformed constitution but also an opportunity for negotiating
the self, poetry, and friendship in a creatively sustaining way. In the chapters
that follow I offer some new perspectives for looking at poetic 'creativity'
during this period which recognise its more communal and collaborative
aspects, and the degree to which poetic meanings drew from—and in turn
articulated—wider responsibilities.

---

[17] Throughout the book I have used upper case 'Idea' for meanings of a more idealist or
Platonic kind, and lower case for other uses, including Lockean ideas.

I

1 Organicism: The Idealist Tradition

'WHAT ON EARTH has happened to organicism?' asks Charles Armstrong in the first paragraph of his book, *Romantic Organicism: From Idealist Origins to Ambivalent Afterlife* (2003), ' "Whither is fled the visionary gleam?" '[1] Not often does a critical work begin by contemplating elegiacally the demise of its subject; but Armstrong is conscious that his two terms, Romantic Organicism, no longer sit as happily together as they once did, when each helped to validate the other.[2] Romantic studies have become uneasy about continuing to be identified too closely with a body of theory that seems to sanction transcendence, idealism, totalisation, and formal unity, and Armstrong is keenly aware of this. While voicing a Wordsworthian lament for 'the glory and the dream', his study succeeds in keeping in play a term with an honourable history, which for many writers and readers remains at the core of a theorised romanticism; but it does not achieve this without a degree of ingenuity. Organicism has an impeccable pedigree in German idealist philosophy, and Armstrong respects this by locating his own book 'at the intersection between German idealism and English romanticism' (6). This busy junction continues to be the site of challenging theoretic criticism;[3] but, as Armstrong himself appreciates, to speak of German idealism as the 'origin' of British romanticism's conception of organicism (183) is to risk some potential embarrassments, particularly in relation to what Armstrong sees as the twin dangers of *vitalism* and *formalism*—of using organicism to validate analogies of 'natural' growth on the one hand, and to sanction a notion of ideal form on the other.[4] It is odd that these two defining facets of

---

[1] Charles I. Armstrong, *Romantic Organicism: From Idealist Origins to Ambivalent Afterlife* (Houndmills: Palgrave Macmillan, 2003), 1.

[2] Susan Wolfson discusses how the aesthetic of 'organic' form 'became a synecdoche for Romanticism'. See her *Formal Charges: The Shaping of Poetry in British Romanticism* (Stanford: Stanford University Press, 1997), 5.

[3] Significant recent volumes include Paul Hamilton, *Metaromanticism: Aesthetics, Literature, Theory* (Chicago: University of Chicago Press, 2003); *Idealism without Absolutes: Philosophy and Romantic Culture*, ed. Tilottama Rajan and Arkady Plotnitsky (Albany: SUNY Press, 2004); Thomas Pfau, *Romantic Moods: Paranoia, Trauma, and Melancholy, 1790–1840* (Baltimore: Johns Hopkins University Press, 2005); and Simon Swift, *Romanticism, Literature and Philosophy: Expressive Rationality in Rousseau, Kant, Wollstonecraft and Contemporary Theory* (London and New York: Continuum, 2006). See also Mark Kipperman, *Beyond Enchantment: German Idealism and English Romantic Poetry* (Philadelphia: University of Pennsylvania Press, 1986).

[4] See Armstrong, *Romantic Organicism*, 1–10, 184.

organic theory, present in the earliest German investigations into the topic (they are brought together in Goethe's botanical experiments in the 1780s, for example),[5] are now regarded as the Scylla and Charybdis of organicism—to be skirted with extreme care. It is as if the presence of ideals has become an embarrassment to idealist theory.

My own contrasting pragmatic approach will be evident throughout this book; but in attempting to identify a native eighteenth-century organic that is empirical in character I need to place it alongside the idealist tradition of organicism, which has until now set the agenda for critical debate. The latter has tended to block from view what is a very different concept with different principles. Also, by being closely implicated in the need to identify 'Romanticism', the idealist tradition of organicism has tended to devalue modes of eighteenth-century thought that can be understood as 'organic' in a different sense. It is on this ground that the book takes issue with organicism's tendency to define itself through a set of binaries that demonise empirical thinking. In championing the latter I want to open up an alternative native tradition of organic thought and show how an awareness of this eighteenth-century 'organic' can contribute to a deeper understanding of the 1790s in particular. Before that topic is brought into focus in Chapters 2 and 3, this opening chapter will approach the tradition of idealist organicism through the two overlapping concepts that have been crucial to it: organic form and organic unity.

The concept of 'organic form' contrasted with its opposite, 'mechanic form', was introduced into philosophical literary criticism by A. W. Schlegel and S. T. Coleridge. In Coleridge's eighth Shakespeare lecture (1811), the famous passage translated from Schlegel expresses what is a crucial distinction, not just between images and artistic styles but between two fundamental principles:

The form is mechanic when on any given material we impress a pre-determined form, not necessarily arising out of the properties of the material, as when to a mass of wet clay we give whatever shape we wish it to retain when hardened. The organic form, on the other hand, is innate; it shapes as it develops itself from within, and the fullness of its development is one and the same with the perfection of its outward form. Such is the life, such the form.[6]

The exciting implications of this distinction, extended by Coleridge so as to set mechanical 'fancy' against organic 'imagination', and dualistic 'allegory' against unifying 'symbol', were embraced by many twentieth-century

---

[5] See Philip C. Ritterbush, *The Art of Organic Forms* (Washington, DC: Smithsonian Institute Press, 1968), 3–5. Goethe published his *Metamorphosis of Plants* in 1790. See *Goethe's Botanical Writings*, trans. Bertha Mueller, with an introduction by Charles J. Engard (Woodbridge, CT: Ox Bow Press, 1989), 31–81.

[6] *Coleridge's Shakespearean Criticism*, ed. T. M. Raysor, 2 vols (London: Constable and Co, 1930), i.224. On Coleridge's indebtedness here to Schlegel, see G. N. G. Orsini, 'Coleridge and Schlegel Reconsidered', *CL*, 16 (1964), 97–118. Orsini's parallels are reproduced by Norman Fruman, *Coleridge: The Damaged Archangel* (London: Allen and Unwin, 1972), 159–60.

writers on romantic literature, because they exemplified the notion of a romantic revolution in thought. These uncompromising binaries could easily be mapped, powerpoint-style, onto a historical grid that showed enlightenment mechanism overthrown by romantic organicism, with the static, predictable patterns of Lockean association and Newtonian science giving way to a world of ideas that was dynamic and creative. It is a powerful myth. Gordon McKenzie's *Organic Unity in Coleridge* (1939) was structured around just this move from dead fixities to dynamic vitalities, a paradigm based in addition on the passages in *Biographia Literaria* where Coleridge attacks empirical association as 'the universal law of the *passive* fancy and *mechanical* memory',[7] a concept challenged by the powers of creative imagination. The latter for Coleridge is a living idea rather than a dead thing; and his words, however often they are repeated, still catch fire as we read:

[The secondary imagination] dissolves, diffuses, dissipates, in order to re-create; or where this process is rendered impossible, yet still at all events it struggles to idealize and to unify. It is essentially *vital*, even as all objects (*as* objects) are essentially fixed and dead. / FANCY, on the contrary, has no other counters to play with, but fixities and definites. The Fancy is indeed no other than a mode of Memory emancipated from the order of time and space... it must receive all its materials ready made from the law of association.[8]

In response to the dynamics of Idea, who could possibly choose the eighteenth-century empirically based world: static, predictable, and second-hand, with all its values arbitrarily assigned to 'fixities and definites'? It seems to be a choice between life and death.

It was a simple enough move to interpret this scenario as a dramatic shift in the history of ideas. In *PMLA* 1951, Morse Peckham described how 'this mighty static metaphysic, which had governed perilously the thoughts of men since the time of Plato, collapsed of its own internal inconsistencies in the late eighteenth century', to be replaced by a fresh idea. '[T]he new thought', he declared, 'is organicism... the universe is alive. It is not something made, a perfect machine; it grows.' Answering his own question, 'What then is Romanticism?', Peckham replied: 'it is the revolution in the European mind against thinking in terms of static mechanism and the redirection of the mind to thinking in terms of dynamic organicism'.[9] The most extreme development of Peckham's dualism was offered by Hans Eichner, who interpreted 'the Romantic revolt against mechanism' as effecting a deliberate reversal of all its ideas: 'the major Romantic systems', he writes, 'attempted to escape the dilemmas of the mechanical philosophy by replacing all its basic assumptions by the exact opposites.'[10]

---

[7] *Biog. Lit.*, i.103–4 (Ch. 5).
[8] Ibid. i.304–5 (Ch. 13).
[9] Morse Peckham, 'Toward a Theory of Romanticism', *PMLA*, 66 (1951), 5–23 (10, 14).
[10] Hans Eichner, 'The Rise of Modern Science and the Genesis of Romanticism', *PMLA*, 97 (1982), 8–30 (14). He notes that his paper is 'largely an elaboration of Peckham's theory' (25 n. 2).

   The irony, of course, is how fixed and definite this binary now seems, how
very inorganic is the notion of literary history it assumes. For this picture to
be convincing, and appear less like a child's board-game played with coun-
ters, there had to be a full and scrupulous working through of its implica-
tions, and an awareness of literary developments and influences across a
broader field. This was provided two years later by M. H. Abrams's *The
Mirror and the Lamp*, one of the most influential critical studies of romantic
writing. The book gave a more measured, scholarly, detailed, and substan-
tial account of the literary history that Peckham had scanned with feverish
urgency; but the model was the familiar one. The key assertion remained the
passivity of the Lockean mind: 'John Locke', Abrams writes, 'was able to
levy upon a long tradition of ready-made parallels in giving definition to his
view of the mind in perception as a passive receiver for images presented
ready-formed from without.'[11] This conceptualises and exemplifies an intel-
lectual laziness that is almost shocking: hand-me-down notions are used to
support preconceptions, and a simple 'definition' substitutes for a genuine
inquiry. Locke's empirical perception (with its rejection of innate ideas) is
thus drained of any creative potential. The term 'passive receiver' simply
ignores the vital activity of the Lockean mind in reflection.[12] Looking at this
kind of summary statement today, it is hard to see why a set of innate ideas
should necessarily have a more dynamic impact on the mind than the
infinitely vast and various materials of human experience with all their
possible combinations.
   Abrams nonetheless relishes the critical opportunities given him by his
metaphors, and with Coleridge's sanction he repeatedly sets eighteenth-
century mechanism (constructed and inert) against organic vitality (living
and growing), exploiting what he terms 'the contradistinction between
atomistic and organic, mechanical and vital—ultimately between the root
analogies of machine and growing plant' (171). In place of finer distinctions,
there is one clear *contra*distinction that marks out the opposing sets of
terms. It is surprising that in 1953 the word 'atomistic' could be used so
innocently without any sense of its dynamic potential, but for Abrams it
describes discrete units of empirical perception combined mechanically like
coloured beads on a string. Analogy carries the argument. Abrams's ten-page
section on 'Coleridge's Mechanical Fancy and Organic Imagination' de-
velops this binary through the poet's own words in the passages quoted
above; but there is a hint of embarrassment at the degree to which the
Coleridge being quoted is the post-1811 writer, not the man of the

---

[11] M. H. Abrams, *The Mirror and the Lamp: Romantic Theory and the Critical Tradition*
(New York: Oxford University Press, 1953), 57.
[12] The best concise account of the dynamics of Lockean 'reflection' is Jules David Law, *The
Rhetoric of Empiricism: Language and Perception from Locke to I. A. Richards* (Ithaca/
London: Cornell University Press, 1993), 1–17.

1790s.[13] The latter is explicitly excluded from this section, Abrams points out, 'in order to sharpen the contrast between the categories of mechanical and organic psychology'. He therefore leaps across 'four decades' straight to *Biographia Literaria* (1817), followed by a letter of 1815, *Aids to Reflection* (1825), *Table Talk* (1835), the *Philosophical Lectures* (1818–19), the *Shakespeare Criticism* (1811–19), *The Statesman's Manual* (1816), and the *Treatise on Method* (1818), out of which he constructs a fascinating summary of Coleridge's thought about organicism. To assemble a body of Coleridgean theory on this topic is valuable, but its very cohesiveness raises a difficulty for literary criticism, especially for texts written in some cases twenty years earlier. Besides the obvious problem of anachronism, there is a danger of constituting 'Coleridge's thought' as an explanatory gloss to the poems, and using them for illustrative examples of ideas only crystallised much later.[14]

Near the beginning of the chapter, Abrams describes Coleridge's 'revolt' against the 'uniform tradition' of eighteenth-century theories of mind. The intricate question of potential continuities is brushed aside:

> Scholars have recently emphasized that Coleridge himself was indebted to English precedent for some of his leading ideas, but it is misleading to stress the continuity of Coleridge's mature psychology of art with that which was current in eighteenth-century England. In all essential aspects, Coleridge's theory of mind, like that of contemporary German philosophers, was, as he insisted, revolutionary. (158)

Several questions are begged in this circular argument, which awkwardly shifts its ground from 'leading ideas' to 'mature psychology of art'. The assumption is that Coleridgean maturity can be equated with German ideas and his immaturity with home-grown ones, so that any suggested 'continuity', as a token of immaturity, can be justifiably ignored. The critic decides what is 'mature' and 'essential'. What is so fascinating about Abrams's mechanistic passage (which overleaps Coleridge's mental development) is not its true and obvious point about Coleridge's embracing of German philosophy, but the way it reveals the critic's anxiety to slice away potential continuities with contemporary British thought. There is no footnote to inform the reader who these 'misleading' scholars were.[15]

As a scholarly investigation into the dynamics of romantic organicism, *The Mirror and the Lamp* remains unrivalled; but as literary history the book appears today to be fatally compromised. It works with a unitary

---

[13] *The Mirror and the Lamp*, 167–77. Much of this section is a revised version of Abrams's earlier article, 'Archetypal Analogies in the Language of Criticism', *UTQ*, 18 (1948–9), 313–27.

[14] Kathleen M. Wheeler finds an ingenious way round chronology by arguing that Coleridge's 1790s poems 'seem to be expressive of an idealism and a theory of mind as creative which Coleridge perhaps could not yet fully understand' (*The Creative Mind in Coleridge's Poetry* (London: Heinemann, 1981), 16).

[15] For a discussion of this topic, see Daniel Stempel, 'Coleridge and Organic Form: The English Tradition', *SiR*, 6 (1967), 89–97.

concept of eighteenth-century empirical philosophy ('the tradition of Hobbes and Hume', 159) which is taken to represent a single 'mechanical archetype' (160) against which Coleridge can be defined. At many points therefore the argument is uncomfortably stretched when Abrams's binary disallows what are potentially more organic developments in Coleridge's earlier career. The book cannot do justice to his eighteenth-century roots or to the complexity of his literary relations with his contemporaries and predecessors. Even a potential soulmate like Wordsworth is criticised for somehow failing to grasp the great idea to which Coleridge's study of German philosophy has led him: 'Wordsworth's vocabulary', Abrams notes with regret, 'showed a regressive tendency to conflate the organic imagination with mechanical fancy, by describing it once again in terms of the subtraction, addition, and association of the elements of sensory images' (181). This threatens to undermine the very foundations on which *The Mirror and the Lamp* is built. Abrams is appalled:

> The imagination, Wordsworth says, is creative; yet, he asks, 'is it not the less true that Fancy, as she is an active, is also, under her own laws and in her own spirit, a creative faculty?' Worse still, Wordsworth indicates not only that fancy is creative, but that imagination is *associative*: both powers alike serve 'to modify, to create, and to associate'. (181)

My own book is written from a viewpoint that relishes an embarrassment like this. Wordsworth's failure to grasp what is at stake (for both Coleridge and Abrams) is regrettable, but it can be regarded from another angle as suggesting a more spacious, because less taxonomic, imagination: Wordsworth can, in a positively associative way familiar to eighteenth-century Sensibility, hold two ideas simultaneously in play and appreciate similarity, difference, and variety. He is also not afraid to mix together what Coleridge and his critic want to keep apart. What will come through in this study is Wordsworth's uneasiness with idealism and its implications, his grounding of vision in human experience, and his acute sensitivity to the associative and the temporal. It is easy to say that his quoted remarks, which recall Addison's *Spectator* essays on 'the Pleasures of the Imagination' (1712),[16] demonstrate a 'regressive tendency' back to early eighteenth-century empiricism; but the passage (from Wordsworth's 'Preface to the Edition of 1815') shows that he is thinking outside Coleridge's boxes.[17] This did, as we know, determine his friend to label things more carefully in his *Biographia*. But Wordsworth had his own quiet, subversive point to make: his suggestion that the imagination of a Pope or Swift might surprise us if viewed 'under her own laws and in her own spirit' suggests that the associative power of the early eighteenth-century sympathetic

---

[16] Nos. 411–21 (21 June–3 July 1712). See *The Spectator*, III, 535–82.
[17] *The Prose Works of William Wordsworth*, ed. W. J. B. Owen and Jane Worthington Smyser, 3 vols. (Oxford: Clarendon Press, 1974), iii.36–7.

imagination might usefully set the terms for its own type of creativity. The Coleridge of the 1790s had known this very well. His drift away from this knowledge has for too long been seen as a measure of his maturity as a thinker.

Abrams's evident frustration at this point in his book (directed not only at Wordsworth) is a sobering reminder that the critic of Coleridge's theoretical work is in an especially difficult position as potentially both explicator and collaborator. Paul Hamilton has written refreshingly about this: 'In the gaps and incoherencies of *Biographia Literaria* we find his encouragement to watch the enlargement of our own minds as we piece out, supplement and imaginatively verify the theory of imagination he has promised and then has artfully failed to supply.'[18] Expressed in these terms our activity comes across, we might note, as a distinctly empirical procedure: one of adding, verifying, and modifying in line with our own experience. Such critical practice ought perhaps to be borne in mind when Coleridge's widely dispersed statements on 'organic unity' are being considered. An empiricist mental map can sometimes be a useful supplement to an idealist vision.

Being a value-concept itself, 'unity' is much easier to identify and talk about than it is to evaluate. Like 'sublimity', this term in the critical lexicon seems to possess its own warranty, so that the more unified or the more sublime, the better. 'Organic unity' in particular has tended to carry a substantial premium to the degree that it achieves perfection within itself. We saw how shaping clay was for Coleridge a mere mechanical art: forms moulded by human fingers, however skilful, demand forethought, even planning; whereas a plant or tree can stretch out into full achievement of its inner principles without the need of a guiding hand. It stands perfectly expressing itself. All the dynamics are centrifugal. It grows into form, and its completion (Coleridge's 'fullness') comes with being left alone.

As an image of artistic creation this raises problems. The artist/poet in the process is airbrushed away; or to speak more philosophically, he appears to be essentialised into a kind of guiding intuition active within the idea. The poet is not a man creating but a soul being; he is nothing less than the perfect idea working itself out:

The poet, described in *ideal* perfection, brings the whole soul of man into activity, with the subordination of its faculties to each other, according to their relative worth and dignity. He diffuses a tone, and spirit of unity, that blends, and (as it were) *fuses*, each into each, by that synthetic and magical power, to which we have exclusively appropriated the name of imagination.[19]

---

[18] Paul Hamilton, *Coleridge's Poetics* (Oxford: Basil Blackwell, 1983), 1.
[19] *Biog. Lit.*, ii.15–16 (Ch. 14). In *The Statesman's Manual* (London: Gale and Fenner etc., 1816) Coleridge exhorts the artist to something like a willed naturalness: 'What the plant is by an act not its own and unconsciously, that must thou make thyself to become' (76). This expression of free will, remarks Abrams, 'runs counter to an inherent tendency of the analogy to which he is committed' (*The Mirror and the Lamp*, 324).

There is indeed a magical raptness to this idealism, but also an ontological danger that when projected onto a wider screen, individual artistic purposes will be replaced by more powerful and universal ones. The process will resemble the activity of a world soul, which fulfils a larger necessity and silently sanctions a natural hierarchy ('subordination...according to their relative worth and dignity'). After all, shorn of its mystical dimension, the concept of *unity* can be defined bluntly in terms of what is 'necessary': 'In the unified object,' writes the philosopher John Hospers, 'everything that is necessary is there, and nothing that is not necessary is there.'[20] Expressed in direct, mechanistic terms like these, the coerciveness of the idea is clear, and in reading this sentence we know that the quirky, odd, sportive, or deformed will be dispensed with. When this 'unity' is troped as organism, and thus given a dynamic aspect, it can appear more benign, even providential, with the necessity internalised. It seems now that an inner law or determining principle is literally expressing itself, pushing outwards. What drove Goethe on his long search for the *Urpflanze*, the 'archetypal plant', was the expectation that when he discovered it he would encounter the essential form of Nature itself, and be able to project from the archetype an infinite range of plant types, which, he told Herder, 'will be imbued with inner truth and necessity', and he added confidently: 'And the same law will be applicable to all that lives.'[21]

Given this uncompromising image of a life force or inner necessity, it is easy to see how the concept of organic unity could bring with it an inspirational sense of purpose. Instead of merely exemplifying the mechanisms of the Newtonian system (the argument ran) with its 'blind operation of physical forces' or 'meaningless flux in the realm of matter', the universe could be seen to have a determined life and direction, so that 'to be like the universe and to be like a living tree were essentially the same thing'.[22] The key to the universe was an inner law, not an externally imposed one. But all this might, of course, be mechanism under another name. The vitalist analogy could subsume the organic impulse into a greater System of Nature with aims of its own.

Here we encounter the teleological problem in living systems, which has long been debated by philosophers, botanists, biologists and theologians. Early eighteenth-century physico-theological arguments about design and purpose (the Creator as supreme architect) were an awkward precedent, and potentially embarrassing for any discussion of organic unity that indicated a pre-existing purpose.[23] The ghost of Newton-inspired Deism hovered over

---

[20] John Hospers, 'Problems of Aesthetics', in Paul Edwards (ed.), *Encyclopaedia of Philosophy*, 8 vols. (New York: Macmillan/Free Press, 1967), i.35–56 (43). See also G. N. G. Orsini, 'The Organic Concepts in Aesthetics', *CL*, 21 (1969), 1–30 (1–4).

[21] Goethe to J. G. Herder, May 1787. See Ritterbush, *The Art of Organic Forms*, 4.

[22] James Benziger, 'Organic Unity: Leibnitz to Coleridge', *PMLA*, 66 (1951), 24–48 (33, 34, 40).

[23] See Richard Olson, 'On the Nature of God's Existence, Wisdom and Power: The Interplay between Organic and Mechanistic Imagery in Anglican Natural Theology, 1640–1740', in

the topic. If Goethe in the 1780s was prepared to see nature as fulfilling an ideal design, equivalent to a universal law, Kant introduced into aesthetic judgment the more scrupulous idea of 'an end underlying the internal possibility of the object', and he kept this within the remit of human reason as 'purposiveness without purpose' (*Zweckmässigkeit ohne Zweck*). Rather than being predicated on an end, it was contingent on aesthetic judgment—the beauty being the form of finality within the object.[24] In making this distinction between purpose and purposiveness Kant was anticipating urgent debates in German science during the 1920s and 1930s, when the notion of a supreme 'goal-conscious will' in life forms would develop disturbing wider implications.[25]

In an idealist context it is hard to dissociate organic unity from a sense of power, whether it be located in a divine plan, a law of nature, or a self-driven impulse. In *Aids to Reflection* (1825) Coleridge sees such a power as endogenous, arising from within an organ, so that 'the characteristic shape [of the organ] is evolved from the invisible central power'. Quoting this passage, Abrams remarks that 'by Coleridge's analysis, an organism is inherently teleological', but 'to replace the mental artisan-planner by the concept of organic self-generation makes it difficult, analogically, to justify the participation of consciousness in the creative process'.[26]

The key is in that word 'analogically'. Much discussion of organic unity during the past two hundred years has allowed analogy/metaphor too much authority, and critics since the 1950s have come to acknowledge this.[27] Reified abstractions have continued to move in satisfying arcs, inscribing their own patterns for contemplation, but again one can sense an awkward shifting of critical position away from the full implications of idealist concepts. The key idea of unity has usually been at the centre of this debate. Any

---

Frederick Burwick (ed.), *Approaches to Organic Form: Permutations in Science and Culture* (Dordrecht: D. Reidel, 1987), 1–48. For further background, see Richard S. Westfall, *Science and Religion in Seventeenth-Century England* (New Haven, CT: Yale University Press, 1958), and Thomas McPherson, *The Argument from Design* (London: Macmillan, 1972).

[24] Immanuel Kant, *The Critique of Judgement*, trans. J. C. Meredith (Oxford: Clarendon Press, 1964 edn), 75–80 (§17).

[25] See Moritz Schlick's important essay, 'Philosophy of Organic Life' (1925), reprinted in Herbert Feigl and May Brodbeck (eds), *Readings in the Philosophy of Science* (New York: Appleton-Century-Crofts, 1953), 523–36. Schlick discusses the 'purposiveness' of organic life, while remarking that the term *purpose* 'should really be banished from biology right from the start' (528).

[26] *The Mirror and the Lamp*, 173, quoting *Aids to Reflection*, 267. Here Abrams anticipates Wimsatt's point (see note 30 below).

[27] Maureen McLane has referred to notions of a poem as an organism or 'living totality' as 'the organic fallacy' (*Romanticism and the Human Sciences* (Cambridge: Cambridge University Press, 2000), 23–5). On the role of the biological analogy behind 'organic form' as the organising trope of the critical establishment, see Mary Poovey, 'The Model System of Contemporary Literary Criticism', *Critical Inquiry*, 27 (Spring 2001), 408–38; and Frances Ferguson, 'Organic Form and its Consequences', in Peter de Bolla, Nigel Leask, and David Simpson (eds), *Land, Nation and Culture, 1740–1810: Thinking the Republic of Taste* (Basingstoke: Palgrave Macmillan, 2004), 223–40.

direct appeal to human experience has, as ever, to be kept at bay; but increasingly a nagging question suggests itself: if organicism is rooted in the living organism, why in criticism is it insistently located on an idealist plane rather than at the level of individual perception, sense, and memory? With this question remaining unspoken, from the 1960s much of the writing about 'organic unity' can be seen to push towards the crisis, the critical showdown, that Armstrong's book announces, which is to some extent a loss of faith in the organic metaphor.

Attacks on organic analogies in works of art are easy enough to make, since any image can be literalised to absurdity. In the case of organic unity the original analogy was drawn by Socrates, when he advised Lysias that 'every discourse ought to be a living creature, having a body of its own and a head and feet; there should be a middle, beginning and end, adapted to one another and to the whole'.[28] After quoting this advice on rhetorical structure, Catherine Lord notes the weakness of the parallel: 'a piece of literature does not have a head and feet any more than an animal has a beginning, middle, and end'; and she goes on to argue that 'not all attributes of an organism are a part of its essence, but it is a part of the essence of an organism to have accidents, non-essential features . . . if a poem is to be like a living organism, then padding is inevitable'.[29]

Critics should be careful not to be caught on the same analogical hook they are uncovering; also, this argument plays dangerously with the concept of 'essence' in a way that is finally not helpful. A subtler, though no less combative assault on organic unity was mounted by W. K. Wimsatt at a MLA seminar in 1970. For him, the traditional idealist analogy (for example, Schiller's remark that a poet should *be* a plant) entailed an artistic creativity that was 'as radically spontaneous as possible—that is, indeliberate, unconscious'. This, Wimsatt argues, ignores a crucial element of human creativity, which is 'its capacity for self-revision, rearrangement, mending'. He adds: 'a lobster can lose a claw and regrow it; the human body heals cuts and regrows a finger nail. But there is no action of any physical organism that remotely approaches the power of the human mind to revise and recast *itself*.'[30] This argument gains added force in relation to Coleridge, whose indefatigable revisions and recastings have usually been reconciled to his ideal of organic unity only through a scenario of frustration

[28] Plato, *Phaedrus*, 264C.
[29] Catherine Lord, 'Organic Unity Reconsidered', *JAAC*, 22 (1964), 263–8 (264). Lord's article solicited a response from P. Æ. Hutchings, 'Organic Unity Revindicated?', *JAAC*, 23 (1965), 323–7.
[30] W. K. Wimsatt, 'Organic Form: Some Questions about a Metaphor', in David Thorburn and Geoffrey Hartman (eds), *Romanticism: Vistas, Instances, Continuities* (Ithaca/London: Cornell University Press, 1973), 13–37 (22–3). The essay first appeared in G. S. Rousseau (ed.), *Organic Form: The Life of an Idea* (London/Boston: Routledge and Kegan Paul, 1972), 62–81.

and failure. Wimsatt, however, uses his point to challenge a view of romantic creativity closely associated with the 'New Criticism'.

For the author of *The Verbal Icon* (1954) to shift emphasis in this way from product to process, from the autonomous text to the contingencies of human artistry, and to view the process as one of continual self-revision by the author, must have seemed a bold move from someone closely identified with the principles of the 'New Critics' and who had denounced the 'intentional fallacy'.[31] By 1970 the concept of organic unity had become identified with their formalist values, to the extent that Paul de Man's challenge to organicism was an attack on two fronts simultaneously, along what he termed 'the line that links...the structural formalism of the New Critics to the "organic" imagination so dear to Coleridge'.[32] De Man's insistence on the temporal dimension of literary form allowed him to view organicism's trajectory of 'origin, continuity, growth, and totalization' as running in parallel with a 'level of ironic awareness, where all is discontinuous, alienated, and fragmentary'. The American New Critics, he argues, never fully brought their 'language of irony and ambiguity' to engage with 'their commitment to a Coleridgean notion of organic form'.[33]

Ironic engagement has become the project for those more recent critics of romanticism who have remained committed to working with organicism as a concept. The urge towards unity/totality remains in place, but is countered by an opposing dynamic that questions or undercuts it.[34] For Murray Krieger, this dialectical move offered a means of holding the idealist system together without having to accept its totalising implications, which for him had disturbing political ramifications. He wanted it to subsume an oppositional element that could check its power. In his 1988 Wellek Library Lectures, *A Reopening of Closure: Organicism against Itself*, Krieger made this a key idea: 'As I am describing it,' he says, 'built into the mystical dialectic of organicism, with its magical imposition of unity, is a negative thrust that would explode it.'[35] As in a classic dialectical embrace, the negative and positive thrusts are mutually dependent, but here the terms do not meet each other from opposing directions; rather it is an 'opposition between the would-be autonomous part and the would-be totalizing whole'

---

[31] Introducing the essay in *Organic Form*, his collection of the three MLA seminar papers, Rousseau comments that 'Professor Wimsatt's paper took the chairman and other panellists by surprise' (4).

[32] Paul de Man, 'Form and Intent in American New Criticism', in *Blindness and Insight: Essays in the Rhetoric of Contemporary Criticsm*, 2nd edn (London: Methuen, 1983), 20–35 (27–8).

[33] Paul de Man, 'The Rhetoric of Blindness: Jacques Derrida's Reading of Rousseau', in *Blindness and Insight*, 104.

[34] Cynthia Chase noted in 1993 that it had become almost the norm to place emphasis 'on Romantic texts "questioning" or undercutting the unifying action to which they aspire' (*Romanticism*, ed. Cynthia Chase (London: Longman, 1993), 'Introduction', 13).

[35] Murray Krieger, *A Reopening of Closure: Organicism against Itself* (New York: Columbia University Press, 1989), 40.

(40), a struggle that for Krieger helps to define the aesthetics of organicism. He conceptualises a force field within which organic unity is able conditionally to operate: 'the absorptive power of any would-be unity must at every moment be challenged by that which would break it apart' (41). The pull towards unity and the drive to fragmentation, the centripetal and centrifugal, engage each other. In setting such a universal, virtually interplanetary, context, Krieger might be thought to be evoking a quasi-Newtonian system of opposing forces held in balance. But this organic form begins to look more like a dialectical version of eighteenth-century 'order in variety': 'Organicism's call for *unity*, it should now be clear, occurs only in the company of its opposite, the call for a *variety* that gives to any attempted unity a dynamics that threatens its stability' (41). To make 'variety' one of the terms in a dialectic is very strange, given that the concept (by any reasonable definition) is an accommodating one that celebrates the mixed/assorted—it is hardly a 'negative thrust'. Variety is the alternative to unity, not its antithesis. And with the use of the word 'company', what has been a supposed strife of opposites even begins to look potentially companionable. At this moment it is as if behind Krieger's dualism there is the ghost of another idea waiting to take shape, in which variety will be allowed to have its say and become a characteristic of the organic—without needing to be on one side of a binary structure.[36]

Perhaps realising this, Krieger, with admirable critical honesty, begins towards the end of the lecture to wonder if his defence of organicism may have pushed too far into dynamic dualities. He poses the question 'whether it is appropriate still to use the term *organicism* to cover the paradoxical attempt to loose the anti-unifying forces' (52). As a critic he dearly wants, unlike de Man, to see organic unity in anti-totalising terms; but he finds himself having to accept, as he looks back across history, that 'from Aristotle to Kant to Coleridge to the New Critics, this tradition has pursued the integral unity of the work of art as its primary objective' (51). There are grounds for an interpretive dilemma here, given that the organic metaphor, while sanctioning (though not necessarily demanding) this unity, would seem by definition to resist polarities. The different parts of a living organism tend to further life not by being in opposition to each other, but rather by interdependence and symbiosis. The analogy clearly must not control the idea, but neither ought it to be jettisoned entirely, or the word will be severed from the principles that helped it develop as a concept. By the final page of Krieger's fascinating lecture, he literally hardly knows which way to turn. It is a binary nightmare. He watches '[d]istinctions...undo themselves': 'inside can be seen as outside, the closed can be seen as the open, the open

---

[36] Krieger almost suggests this himself: 'far from being an antagonistic intrusion, the *variety* side of the *unity-in-variety* motto is built into organicism's sense of itself and requires a fuller reading of it by us' (50).

as closed. Every direction can be seen as a two-way street' (55). Confronted with this impasse, the reader wonders whether, by being presented through a vision of semiotic antagonism, his argument in defence of organicism hasn't tested it to destruction.

This is the point at which Charles Armstrong, as we saw, opens his important recent study, which traces organicism from its 'idealist origins' to an 'ambivalent afterlife' in modern criticism. Armstrong takes his direction from Krieger's model of a totality riven by internal tension and conflicting drives.[37] In so doing he conceives of a whole that already contains the possibility not merely of Krieger's dialectic, but of its own '*internal* deconstruction'.[38] Given that he is concerned with a specifically 'romantic organicism' originating in German idealism, Armstrong bases his definition of the term on the writings of Coleridge and Schelling: 'organicism is not understood as a fact of nature or as a merely aesthetic phenomenon in their texts, but rather as a *grounding systematics for understanding all holistic structures*. It is, to put matters simply, a way of thinking meaningfully about wholes' (2). In place, therefore, of an organicism based on principles of nature or aesthetics, the concept supersedes those categories (with their implications of vitalism and formalism); but in doing so, within its ambitious 'holistic aspirations' it encounters 'unbridgeable difference'. The result is a universal that overrides specific principles, but is riven by 'underlying aporias', gaps that can never be closed. Armstrong fascinatingly entwines idealism and deconstruction, prising open as he does so the 'inherent problems of organicism'; but the final problem he leaves us with is not contradiction, bad faith, or false confidence, but a complete enigma. As an idealist theory, organicism sought in the tradition of Coleridge and Schelling to reconcile opposites by finding a language of expressive power within the individual organism and a mystical absolute that could embrace it, so that the symbol might function like a human soul subsumed into God the Three-in-One. All potential tensions and contradictions, all strains between mortality and divinity, might disappear in one translucent layering of meaning:

[A] Symbol . . . is characterized by a translucence of the Special in the Individual or of the General in the Especial or of the Universal in the General. Above all by the translucence of the Eternal through and in the Temporal.[39]

No alternatives here. Nothing engages, let alone clashes, with anything else. All occupies the same space at the same eternal moment. It is this Absolute with which Armstrong's idealist concept finally keeps faith; and however much critics may wish to demolish it, it can elude and survive every assault.

---

[37] Armstrong, *Romantic Organicism*, 7. He praises Krieger's 'decisive contribution to modern criticism on this issue' (8).

[38] Ibid. 7.

[39] Samuel Taylor Coleridge, *The Statesman's Manual* (1816). See *Lay Sermons*, ed. R. J. White. *Collected Works*, vi.30.

Armstrong's language catches something of Coleridge's raptness as he evokes the Idea of organicism. No image can represent it; no principle can express it; no theory can interpret it; it is totally comprehensive yet utterly incomprehensible. But it is not a mere mystery either—this idealist organicism can only be spoken about in the language of deity itself:

While the resistance of organicism to theoretical formulation risks rendering it invisible and impossible to locate, it simultaneously tends towards making it omnipotent. Nowhere to be found, and therefore impossible to circumscribe, organicism may be presumed to be everywhere at work. (4)

We have reached a critical vanishing point. There is nothing there, and yet all else is somehow locatable in relation to it.

At the end of his book Armstrong recognises that organicism has been traumatised. It has reached an 'afterlife'; and while some suspect that deconstruction has killed it, he is more hopeful that even if the body cannot be 'fully resuscitated' the surprisingly resilient Idea can live on. He is left not with organicism, but with the miasma of the organism itself, in whose presence he finally believes he can talk openly:

Let me put an end to such pretences and admit it: the organism is a wandering spectre. From one definition to the other, it submits itself to metamorphosis, to a profound conceptual instability, displaying itself as a necessarily virtual phenomenon in the process. (184)

By dissolving into the ghost of an organism, a 'necessarily virtual phenomenon', the concept ceases to have a function or a meaning. Any reference point is lost; and even the word 'profound', working to ward off any potential playfulness in the thought, cannot locate one. Organicism's usefulness as a term of critical inquiry would seem to have drained away amid self-contradiction, abstraction, and evasiveness. Admirably, Armstrong remains true to his deconstructive approach in acknowledging the critical impasse and refusing an easy playful solution.[40]

Is there any way forwards from here? It is clear that the issue of literary *form*, which had been the foremost concern of the idealist tradition of organicism, has now become a cause of critical uneasiness. If in response Krieger and Armstrong have had recourse respectively to dialectical and deconstructive approaches, others have sought to recover the principle of the living organism and to view organicism in more developmental terms, emphasising exploratory process rather than determining idea. In introducing his collection of essays, *Approaches to Organic Form* (1987), Fred Burwick notes that his choice of title recognises how far 'approaches' fall short of 'attainments', and he adds: 'There is, after all, an inherent difficulty

---

[40] '[I]f organicism's afterlife promises to continue to be an embattled site subject to radical revisions and denunciations, things are as they should be' (Armstrong, *Romantic Organicism*, 186).

in adequately defining "organic form" . . . [b]ecause it emerges through pro-
cess, organic form resists definitions which try to identify form as if it were
fixed and definite. Thus it is more apt to discuss the forming and shaping,
rather than the form or shape.'[41] Burwick finds it appropriate to use the term
'organic' not to describe a completed shape, but to indicate how that form is
achieved (an adverbial emphasis). My own study is in sympathy with this,
but with the caveat of not wishing to identify the organic too closely with
what is merely embryonic, fluid, and undefined. For the sake of my later
argument it is important to make some distinctions here, and not just to
substitute, in place of an achieved unity of form, an 'anything-goes' shape-
lessness or incompletion.

An organic text can have a satisfying sense of completeness, though that is
not what makes it 'organic'. In what follows, readings that 'fix' and 'define'
(to employ Burwick's negative associations here) will usually be avoided, but
only so far as to shift the critical emphasis onto locating a text's 'character',
an idea no less clear and specific, but which combines form and expression in
a sense that includes the human dimension of the word. The adjustment is
crucial, and involves a move from questions of unity to matters of integrity.
My study is committed to viewing the organic as a living principle, and a
notion of organic *process* is a valuable reminder of the contingencies of lived
experience waiting to complicate any theorising about 'organicism'. This
book will keep that idea in mind. But I want to steer away from the
trajectory followed by Kathleen Wheeler, who is prepared to run the vitalist
analogy the full distance and celebrate organicism as a protean concept in
which identities can morph freely. In this more carnivalesque approach,
metamorphosis becomes the leading idea. 'In organic criticism', Wheeler
writes,

All forms are open-ended and in the process of change, growth, and development.
Forms and unities are never static and fixed as in structuralism. New forms, shapes,
parts, wholes, and unities are constantly growing out of the old ones. Hence, a work
of art does not have fixed parts and a static whole or unity. It has the character of
living things, things that are in growth, change, development, evolution without any
final aim.[42]

The passage reads like a translation from Ovid's *Metamorphoses*; and
its insistent plurality links this vision to the world of continuous process

---

[41] Frederick Burwick (ed.), *Approaches to Organic Form*, ix. Burwick defines his own
approach in contrast to that of G. N. G. Orsini, for whom 'organicism refers to the ultimate
result, not to the genesis but to the relation of the parts in the work once the whole process of
composition is finished' ('Organicism', in *Dictionary of the History of Ideas* (New York:
Scribners, 1973), iii.421–7, quoted by Burwick, x).
[42] Kathleen M. Wheeler, *Romanticism, Pragmatism and Deconstruction* (Oxford: Blackwell,
1993), 199. Wheeler is at this point describing 'the organic theory of art as expressed by
Coleridge and Dewey'. See also her earlier study, *The Creative Mind in Coleridge's Poetry*
(London: Heinemann, 1981).

envisaged in Pope's *Dunciad* where embryonic ideas never reach wholeness
and fulfilment. The restless freedom of Wheeler's concept, verging on an-
archy, pushes the organism metaphor to its limit, and we seem to be watch-
ing lots of wriggling things under a microscope. Having reached a crisis,
organicism has here retreated to its primal stage where it can claim the
infinite power of potential without any risk of achievement. Teleology has
become aimless play. All forms betoken incompletion. Simultaneously the
critical act is in danger of becoming little more than excited observation.

In face of this, it is necessary to suggest that some concern with 'process' as
well as product does not preclude critical stringency, and indeed ought to
make analytical attention to formal matters a more complex business—an
issue brought into focus by the genre of the 'romantic fragment'. Here
another distinction becomes important. Incompletion, which for Pope was
a sign of cultural breakdown, could later in the century become a guarantor
of authenticity. In this regard it is useful to remember Friedrich Schlegel's
declaration that 'the romantic kind of poetry is still in the state of becoming;
that, in fact, is its real essence: that it should forever be becoming and never
perfected'.[43] According to this famous formulation, value is transferred
from the completed whole to the fragment, something that is, in the entirety
of its fragmentariness, a token of the ideal, a process that has captured the
'essence' through an eternal striving. To think about textual 'becoming' in
this way is fully compatible with the idealist tradition of organicism, to the
extent that for the theorists of the Jena circle the 'fragment' was (in the
words of Sophie Thomas) 'an ideal form for the Ideal, so to speak, the elusive
"literary absolute"'.[44] My own interest in process, however, is not of this
kind.

Moving outside the idealist tradition, and the aesthetic and critical im-
passe it appears to have reached, it will be possible to open up a different,
empirical 'organic' that is rooted in eighteenth-century Sensibility. Under the
aegis of Sensibility (as a mode of intellect as well as feeling) writers and
philosophers found fascination in the intricate mechanisms of sensation,
perception, and understanding.[45] I realise that to associate process with
'mechanism' appears, in light of the earlier discussion, to sanction the very
binary of organicism/mechanism that I want to deny. The term is being used

[43] *Athenaeum* Fragment 116. Friedrich Schlegel, *Philosophical Fragments*, trans. Peter
Firchow (Minneapolis/Oxford: University of Minnesota Press, 1991), 32.
[44] Sophie Thomas, 'The Fragment', in Nicholas Roe (ed.), *Romanticism: An Oxford Guide*
(Oxford: Oxford University Press, 2005), 502–20 (511). Anne Janowitz similarly remarks that
'the affirmation of the Romantic fragment poem is an affirmation of the ideal' ('The Romantic
Fragment', in Duncan Wu (ed.), *A Companion to Romanticism* (Oxford/Malden, MA: Black-
well, 1999), 442–51 (449)). See also D. F. Rauber, 'The Fragment as Romantic Form', *MLQ*, 30
(1969), 212–21.
[45] When Northrop Frye suggested that the key to texts of 'Sensibility' was to be found in their
interest in *process*, he touched on an idea that links texts of a widely varying character. See
Northrop Frye, 'Towards Defining an Age of Sensibility', *ELH*, 23 (1956), 144–52.

in this book, however, not as the opposite of organicism, but as itself embodying the organic principle. I am arguing that the eighteenth-century organic tradition is rooted in human mechanisms in a positive and dynamic way. In this non-idealist, non-romantic context, rather than signalling an unceasing striving for perfection, 'process' becomes something in itself curious and eloquent. It brings together the formation of a poem and the formation of a thought. With this in mind, my discussion wants to move the 'organic' back into a human world of self-reflective knowledge, one that has an interest not only in the 'why' but also the 'how' behind experience. I want to return the Idea to the individual mind, and the aesthetic to the human organisations that produce it.

In her recent essay on 'Organicism' (part of a project to revisit Raymond Williams's *Keywords* volume), Tilottama Rajan offers a way forward for a term that has increasingly become a 'dead metaphor'. She argues for a return to a concept that 'might actually be used to deconstruct aesthetic ideology variously, through the relation between "life" and "organization," the different kinds of animate organization, and the location of the border between organic and inorganic, human and inhuman'.[46] Her refreshing stress on organic 'life' recognises the degree to which an idealist organicism has suppressed the implications of time. 'Organic form', writes David Simpson, 'has no visible history, but exists wholly in the present.'[47] Under the banner of shunning 'vitalist analogies' theorists of this organicism refused to incorporate the temporal dimension, without which 'life' means absolutely nothing. As we know, the nature of life is to continue within time and eventually to die. To consign this substantial truth to the category of analogy is a critical sleight of hand, which assumes that the organic can somehow exist as pure Idea in a non-temporal domain of *structure* and *unity*. Rajan pointedly concludes: 'in Anglo American thought, the theory of organic form has become associated with complexly unified structures, and because of this curious conflation of organism and "structure," operates in a timeless oblivion to the fact that organisms are generated, born and die' (50).

To separate the organic from life, therefore, is not to remove a constricting metaphor but to shed a critical responsibility. It is to sacrifice, in the cause of 'being', a notion of organic function or organic activity, and to substitute a theoretical reification, Organic*ism*, something with a merely fictional existence. The inescapable paradox of this book is that, like 'organic form' and 'organic unity', 'organicism' is an inorganic concept. It is an idea rather than a phenomenon, a category rather than an activity. When organic things happen, the result is not 'organicism'. That is why it is within the idealists'

---

[46] Tilottama Rajan, 'Organicism', *English Studies in Canada*, 30 (2004), 46–50 (47).
[47] David Simpson, 'Coleridge on Wordsworth and the Form of Poetry', in Christine Gallant (ed.), *Coleridge's Theory of Imagination Today* (New York: AMS Press, 1989), 211–25 (216).

much-despised 'mechanism' that we can find the organic in operation. David Simpson again sums this up well in Coleridgean terms:

It is the mechanic form...that dramatizes the intervention of human agency; the organic form disguises that same agency as a spontaneous evolution...Mechanic or fanciful form displays the joins that have been necessary to shape it; organic or imaginative form effaces the details of its own construction. (215–16)

To reverse these labels, then, can help us locate an eighteenth-century empirical 'organic', which recognises the particular pressures under which things are made and sustained, and how their character is shaped by them. In place of the perfect orchid there stands an old armchair. As I hope we shall see, it is not Keats's well-wrought urn but the broken wooden cup in Wordsworth's 'Ruined Cottage' that is the organic object. Aspects of human effort, need, ingenuity, and endurance are inextricably part of its impure and associative meaning.

Organising poetry in the 1790s entailed, I think, a recognition of these complex facets of living organisations and their varied potential. In these dramatically unsettled years questions of continuity and change were everywhere, and all the old forms and structures were in play. Events moved rapidly across the European stage, and Coleridge's generation was especially conscious of the dramatic clash between universal values and the swift movement of time. Issues of 'human agency' or 'spontaneous evolution' had a trajectory that cut across all aspects of life and art. On what terms might the new be constructed? Could anything—should anything—continue in the old ways? What joined things together? Where was the basis of new values for new times? At the heart of questions like these was the topic of continuity itself and how change could be effected: to what extent should it transform rather than accommodate? This challenge had both private and public manifestations, and the two following chapters will examine a pair of concepts—personal identity and history—in which matters of continuity are an urgent concern. They are of course mixed with each other (as personal history and national identity), and such entanglements will be encountered. My argument is that both notions had taken on an organic character during the eighteenth century, and that in the 1790s this featured significantly in how Coleridge, Wordsworth, and their friends thought about themselves and their work.

2 Organic Constitutions: Identity

> Therefore am I still
> A lover of the meadows and the woods,
> And mountains; and of all that we behold
> From this green earth; of all the mighty world
> Of eye and ear, both what they half-create,
> And what perceive; well pleased to recognize
> In nature and the language of the sense,
> The anchor of my purest thoughts, the nurse,
> The guide, the guardian of my heart, and soul
> Of all my moral being.
>
> —William Wordsworth, 'Lines written
> a few miles above Tintern Abbey', ll. 103–12

As we saw in Chapter 1, it is misleading to use the later Coleridge to fix the Coleridge of the 1790s or to set a trajectory for his and his friends' intellectual 'development'. That untroubled word can hardly do justice to the way many individuals of the time were baffled by the swirl of ideas and events, the collision of hopes and realities. Famously, the changes wrought in the so-called 'Lakers' were a matter of mirth for later writers like Byron; but for the poets themselves during that decade it was difficult, in a context of 'mental fight', to reconcile an alert responsiveness to current events with a principled consistency. For those caught up in the drama of ideas, vitalist analogies of growth/development laid too smooth a path and assumed too steady a notion of human identity.

It is to Locke's *Essay Concerning Human Understanding* that we can turn for a theory that appropriately confronts the problem of how a person survives change. In Locke's vocabulary the phrase can be re-worded as 'how personal identity persists through time'. In examining the question in these terms he is refusing to isolate human 'identity' as a given, but insists that it can only be claimed through activity, through participating in 'Life'. Identity comes into being within a temporal context through an act of comparison, 'when . . . we compare it with it self existing at another time, and thereon form the *Ideas* of *Identity* and *Diversity*'.[1] In this way our personal identity is not an

---

[1] John Locke, *An Essay Concerning Human Understanding*, 2nd edn. (1694), II.xxvii ('Of Identity and Diversity'), para 1. Quotations are taken from the edition by Peter Nidditch

ontological category but a dynamic process, continually being confirmed as we perceive, experience, think, and remember:

This also shews wherein the Identity of the same *Man* consists; *viz.* in nothing but a participation of the same continued Life, by constantly fleeting Particles of Matter, in succession vitally united to the same organized Body. (§6)

Lockean identity resides neither in the material body alone nor in an immortal soul, but in successive confirmations of a persisting life.[2] It is part of the vital processes of the human *organisation*, a term which as early as the fifteenth century could be used to indicate not only the physical functioning of the body as an articulate system of limbs and organs, but also the proper coordinating of its elements, including the relationship between body and soul.[3] In discussing identity, Locke stresses durability, not structure. A living thing like an oak tree differs from a mere 'Mass of Matter' through temporal continuity rather than structural unity. 'The one', he notes, 'is only the Cohesion of Particles of Matter any how united', while the tree 'continues to be the same Plant, as long as it partakes of the same Life, though that Life be communicated to new Particles of Matter vitally united to the living Plant, in a like continued Organization' (§4). In stressing the term 'vitally united', Locke turns the emphasis away from a holistic unity towards a constitutional integration; new things can be added or mixed in, but they become united so long as they 'participate' in, or 'partake' of, the ongoing life, the living continuity. John Yolton's phrase about Lockean identity, 'organised life in matter', usefully draws these aspects together.[4] In this dynamic scenario, what is fixed and permanent might be of less moment than what is temporarily accommodated.

(Oxford: Clarendon Press, 1975). Future quotations from this chapter are identified by paragraph number. Coleridge wrote to his brother George on 6 Nov. 1794 that he had made 'a diligent, I *may* say, an intense study of Locke, Hartley and others who have written most wisely on the Nature of Man' (Griggs, 126). On 18 Feb. 1801, however, he told Josiah Wedgwood that it had recently occurred to him that 'Locke's Essay was a Book which I had really never *read*, but only *looked thro*' (Griggs, 679). His long negative critique of Locke's *Essay* follows in a series of letters (679–703). See Postscript, p. 309 below.

[2] '[G]reat parcels of Matter', Locke says, can be changed, and yet the identity remain: ''Tis not therefore Unity of Substance that comprehends all sorts of *Identity*'; nor does the soul determine identity, since 'there be nothing in the Nature of Matter, why the same individual Spirit may not be united to different bodies' (§6–7). See n. 44 below.

[3] See *OED*, s.v. 'organization', 1a ('Chiefly *Biol*'): 'The development or coordination of parts (of the body, a body system, cell, etc.) in order to carry out vital functions; the condition of being or process of becoming organized. Also: the way in which a living thing is organized; the structure of (any part of) an organism'. A book of surgery (1425) spoke of an 'organizacioun of veynez [veins]'; a translation of Ranulf Higden's *Polychronicon* (BL Harley MS [*c*.1475]) remarks that 'the body of man was so proporcionate to the sawle that equalite of complexion was in hit, conformite of organization'.

[4] John Yolton, *Locke and the Compass of Human Understanding* (Cambridge: Cambridge University Press, 1970), 150. The Earl of Shaftesbury seized on the idea that a tree 'lives, flourishes, and is still one and the same even when by vegetation and change of substance not one particle in it remains the same' (*The Moralists. A Philosophical Rhapsody*, iii.1). For Shaftesbury, however, this expressed a universal, harmonious, purposive Nature. See n. 63 below.

As Locke begins to expound his ideas through this chapter 'Of Identity and Diversity' (added for the second edition of the *Essay*, 1694) it becomes clear that a paradoxical aspect of the topic is developing. Personal identity does not reside in what is tightly cohesive and unified, but in what we might rather think of as being tenuous and liable to interruption. It is in a continuing *consciousness* that human identity resides ('in this alone consists *personal Identity*', §9): this is what transforms us from a *man* (in the anthropological sense) to a *person*, a distinction vital to Locke's argument. To be a 'person' (a being with a personal identity) is to be conscious of a self that persists through any number of temporal and spatial relocations: it 'can consider it self as it self, *the same thinking thing in different times and places*; which it does only by that consciousness, which is inseparable from thinking' (§9: my italics). In this way, personal identity is part of our awareness of location and situation, and represents a connecting up of experience, in which memory plays a vital role: 'as far as this consciousness can be extended backwards to any past Action or Thought, so far reaches the Identity of that *Person*' (§9). Although consciousness will inevitably be interrupted (e.g. through sleep or forgetfulness), this in no way precludes a continuing identity; indeed the activity of the mind is able to bridge not only breaks in time but even changes of body: 'it must be allowed, That if the same consciousness...can be transferr'd from one thinking Substance to another, it will be possible, that two thinking Substances may make but one Person. For the same consciousness being preserv'd, whether in the same or different Substances, the personal Identity is preserv'd' (§13). Locke refuses to see this (as his opponents did) as a *reductio ad absurdum*; instead it becomes a vivid illustration of what might be involved conceptually in two people being of the same mind. It follows, he says, that 'whatever has the consciousness of present and past Actions, is the same Person to whom they both belong' (§16). It is thus possible for two 'men' to be one 'person', and for one 'man' to be two 'persons'. The sceptical Hume would of course later reject the concept of a continuing identity, but Locke is anxious to preserve something that will underpin personal responsibility, and indeed personal salvation.[5] In an earlier manuscript dating from 1683 he can be seen working out the implications of this idea:

Identity of persons lies not in haveing the same numericall body made up of the same particles, not if the minde consists of corporeal spirits in their being the same. But in the memory and knowledge of ones past self and actions ~~with the same concern one had formerly~~ continued on under the consciousness of being the same person ~~under the certain knowledge~~ whereby every man ownes himself.[6]

[5] Defending Locke's distinction in 1769, Edmund Law argued that Locke's term *person* 'denominates [man] a moral agent, or an *accountable* creature' (*A Defence of Mr. Locke's Opinion concerning Personal Identity* (Cambridge: J. Archdeacon, 1769), 2).

[6] Bodleian MS Locke F.7, 107, quoted by Michael Ayers, *Locke. Volume II: Ontology* (London/New York: Routledge, 1991), 255.

Locke pares down the text, realising that degrees of 'concern' or 'certainty' are tangential: the fundamental point is to have ownership of oneself and simultaneously, it is implied, to 'own up' to what one does. 'For it is by the consciousness it has of its present Thoughts and Actions, that it is *self* to it *self* now, and so will be the same *self* as far as the same consciousness can extend to Actions past or to come' (§10).

Locke's word for this complex of ideas in which an acknowledgement of the past might be a pledge for the future is 'self-consciousness', a philosophical term first used in this chapter, which stresses the linking up of one's experience across time.[7] As we have seen, it also draws on the idea of owning a 'self' for which one is accountable: 'I being as much concern'd, and as justly accountable for any Action was done a thousand Years since, *appropriated to me now by this self-consciousness*, as I am, for what I did the last moment' (§16; my italics). Locke's 'self-consciousness' in this way involves an appropriation, or claiming of ownership of one's mind, and it can thus be a guarantor of a personal integrity that binds together any number of different actions and experiences and takes responsibility for them. (In this passage he wittily implies that a person who shares Brutus's consciousness might be held responsible for the death of Caesar.) Through stressing the temporal dimension of identity Locke resists an abstract ontology, shifting the emphasis away from wholeness of being towards integrity of living. The empirical notion of personal identity sustained by this 'self-consciousness' achieves a sense of continuity not through a continuous 'being', but rather by a continual reaffirmation of one's self in the repeated recollection of perceptions and responses. It is interesting to find Coleridge, as late as 1809, picking up Locke's philosophical term in a way that stresses how we link our experiences across time (my italics):

[I]f men laugh at the falsehoods that were imposed on themselves during their childhood, it is because they are not good and wise enough to contemplate the past in the present, and so to produce by a virtuous and thoughtful sensibility that *continuity in their self-consciousness*, which Nature has made the law of their animal life.[8]

Coleridge's thought has distinctively Lockean elements, and not just in terminology. The idea that continuity of self is 'produced' by recollection has an empirical implication, and 'to contemplate the past in the present' implies a superimposition of images rather than an atemporal idealist transparency (a distinction that will become important for some of the poetic

---

[7] The word 'self-conscious' had been first used by Ralph Cudworth in 1688, but in a more limited sense of being reflectively aware of ourselves and without the temporal dimension (*OED* s.v. 'self-conscious', 1a). A striking contrast to this empiricist concept is the idealist 'consciousness' discussed by Marshall Brown, 'The Pre-Romantic Discovery of Consciousness', *SiR*, 17 (Fall 1978), 387–412.

[8] Samuel Taylor Coleridge, *The Friend*, no. 3 (10 Aug. 1809). See *The Friend*, ed. Barbara E. Rooke. *Collected Works*, iv(ii).41. See also iv(i).40.

analysis later in this book). The remark is brought even closer to Locke by Coleridge's footnote, where he quotes some lines from '[a] contemporary poet [who] has exprest and illustrated this sentiment with equal fineness of thought and tenderness of feeling:

> My heart leaps up when I behold
>   A rain-bow in the sky!
> So was it, when my life began;
> So is it now I am a man;
> So let it be, when I grow old,
>   Or let me die.
> *The Child is Father of the Man,*
> *And I would wish my days to be*
> *Bound each to each by natural piety.*[9]

This is not a celebration of continuous being, but of the power that binds past experiences together; it delights in the confirming effect of the revisited moment. The lyric reminds us that alongside the Wordsworth of the 'spots of time' is the poet of the rhythms of time; and it suggests that a visionary 'spot' accrues value because it is a mental location that can be returned to again and again.[10] Coleridge sees this prayer for continuity as the product of 'a virtuous and thoughtful sensibility'.

The notion of continuity without continuousness is a crucial one for this book. The Lockean self has the potential to span discontinuities, and this gives it a diachronic character. Rather than stressing the synchronic 'moment' of self-awareness (with its visionary implications),[11] Locke emphasizes the self as a function of the discursive reason, the consciousness that underpins conscience (Hamlet's 'looking before and after').[12] Jonathan Bennett hits on this point in his discussion of what he terms Locke's 'diachronic identity'; but he treats it in negative terms, as if Locke has somehow been unable to unify his theory. It is a fascinating passage, in which the modern philosopher makes an unnecessary mystery out of what for Locke is clear but disconcerting. Bennett says:

I cannot find in this chapter, or anywhere else in the *Essay*, any working notion of mental continuity that goes beyond the mere possibility of reidentification of a single mind or soul or person at different times. The concept of a person could be such as to permit such a reidentification across an ontological gap; and, while I have no

---

[9] William Wordsworth, *Poems, in Two Volumes* (London: Longman, 1807), ii.44.

[10] On the links between Lockean perception and Wordsworthian subjectivity, see Mahmoud K. Kharbutli, 'Locke and Wordsworth', *Forum for Modern Language Studies*, 25 (1989), 225–37.

[11] Locke does allow for a synchronic individuality: 'this Organization being at any one instant in any one Collection of *Matter*, is in that particular concrete distinguished from all other' (§4). See Ayers, *Locke. Volume II: Ontology*, 220–1.

[12] *Hamlet*, IV.iv.37. The idea goes back to Cicero, *De Officiis*, i.11 (*totius vitae cursum videt*).

evidence that Locke believed that there are such gaps, nothing in his thought seems to reflect a solid conviction that there are not.[13]

We are back with the concept of a potential idealist unity fractured by *aporiai*. But where Bennett's philosophical language assumes an 'ontological gap', Locke celebrates the power of the human mind to bridge discontinuities. Bennett's hesitantly offered term 'reidentification', with its hint of an element of recognition, usefully characterises Locke's concept of personal identity. Locke's theory does not merely concede the idea of interruption, it embraces it ('this consciousness being interrupted always by forgetfulness', §10), and the quirks and depredations of time are part of his mental picture.[14]

The theologians of his day were less accommodating. Bennett's reservations, in fact, echo those of Locke's contemporary critics, for whom such gaps exposed the error of not using the immortal soul to guarantee a continuum.[15] They attempted to expose his argument by showing the dangers of discounting the soul's ultimate sanction on human existence. They wanted something to remain constantly in place that would not only unify individual identity but also preserve it for resurrection. The most formidable opponent of the Lockeans, Samuel Clarke, used this argument to challenge their theory of identity:

[Y]ou make *Individual Personality* to be a mere *external imaginary Denomination*, and nothing at all in reality: Just as a *Ship* is called the *same Ship*, after the Whole Substance is changed by frequent Repairs; or a *River* is called the *same River*, though the Water of it be every day new. The *Name* of the Ship, is the same; but the *Ship it self*, is not at all the same: And the continued *Name* of the River, signifies Water running in the same Channel, but not at all the *same Water*.[16]

The name may be the same but the identity, he declares, is quite different. Clarke will have no truck with paradoxes: he takes his stand on a literal 'reality', which makes his odd slippage from 'the *same River*' to 'the *same Water*' an uncomfortable one—it is either philosophically naïve or tactically

---

[13] Jonathan Bennett, 'Locke's Philosophy of Mind', in Vere Chappell (ed.), *The Cambridge Companion to Locke* (Cambridge: Cambridge University Press, 1994), 89–114 (113).

[14] For a reading of Lockean 'consciousness', which argues that 'for both Locke and Hume ... even the existence of the self is at best an embarrassment', see Stephen Bygrave, *Coleridge and the Self: Romantic Egotism* (Houndmills: Macmillan, 1986), 13–15. Bygrave analyses 'spatial and temporal displacement' in Coleridge's poems, concluding that they 'are not ... a continuing attempt to validate consciousness by reference to memories of the self, as Locke implies, but rather the reverse: forays which validate the existence of self to the consciousness' (131). My reading of Locke understands him, in contrast to Hume, as validating identity by reference to consciousness.

[15] Raymond Martin and John Barresi view Locke's 'apparent tolerance of discontinuity' as a major stumbling block in the eyes of his opponents (*Naturalization of the Soul: Self and Personal Identity in the Eighteenth Century* (London/New York: Routledge, 2000), 32).

[16] Samuel Clarke, *A Third Defense of an Argument Made use of in a Letter to Mr Dodwel, to prove the Immateriality and Natural Immortality of the Soul* (London: James Knapton, 1708), 64–5.

disingenuous. The famous example of Theseus' ship, originally described in Plutarch's *Life of Theseus* and used in philosophy seminars on 'identity' ever since,[17] has for Clarke a self-evident commonsensical answer. But the story suggests a further intriguing hypothetical, which is neatly summarised by Michael Ayers: 'A ship is repaired plank by plank until none of the originals remain. The original planks, which have been preserved, are put together to make a ship. *Which of the later ships is the original ship?*'[18] This certainly poses a nice choice, but is it really the most searching and useful question we can ask? By centring on an ontological category of the 'original ship' established at its moment of construction, this does not take us very far.[19] Perhaps other more productive, and Lockean, questions might shift the focus from the idea onto the experience: 'Which ship has a memory?', 'Which is the ship with more adventures to tell us?', or even 'Which is the more organic ship?' These interrelated questions open up issues more sympathetic to Locke's empirical understanding of identity as something that exists through time, and which allows for adaptation, replacement, and repair.

The dispute for which Locke was responsible raised fundamental questions that had a bearing on many fields, including ethics, theology, politics, and literature. It initiated what Raymond Martin and John Barresi have called 'a revolution in personal identity theory' in which 'the self as immaterial soul was replaced with the self as mind':

This replacement involved movement away from substance accounts of personal identity, according to which the self is a simple persisting thing, toward relational accounts of personal identity, according to which the self consists essentially of physical and/or psychological relations among different temporal stages of an organism or person.[20]

Within these new temporal dynamics Locke opened up areas of the subjective and situational, so that truth itself as well as human identity seemed to be destabilised; but the implications were also creative in direction. The new emphasis on modes of organisation meant that an issue of identity was pushed towards one of meaning, and therefore gained a potential literary significance. A text was free to move from the realm of Idea to the world of Lockean ideas, and thus to open up an experiential and interpretive space. It seemed as if 'truth' and 'meaning' might not after all be occupying quite the same ground. The inherent could expand into the discursive; and associative pathways introduced possibilities for curiosity, suggestion, and play. The text of eighteenth-century Sensibility, paralleling the organic mapping

[17] See *Plutarch's Lives, Translated from the Greek by Several Hands*, 5 vols. (London: J. Tonson, 1683–6), vol. i (Theseus, 22–3).
[18] Ayers, *Locke. Volume II: Ontology*, 247.
[19] It would be unproductive to ask of a football club with a long and distinguished history, 'which is the original club: 1888, or 2008?'
[20] Martin and Barresi, *Naturalization of the Soul*, ix.

of the human body through its lines of communication (vessels, nerves, animal spirits, etc.), set out to explore the implications of this 'revolution'.

In this way Locke helped usher in what Charles Taylor has called modernity's 'new time sense', which he relates to 'the disengaged, particular self, whose identity is constituted in memory'. We have to break the too easy critical association between Lockean memory and mere nostalgia, and understand how 'identity-as-memory' is a more complex modern idea. This time sense, remarks Taylor, 'has also changed our notion of the subject... he can only find an identity in self-narration. Life has to be lived as a story.' Out of this, says Taylor, comes the modern novel.[21]

Sterne's *Tristram Shandy* is an organic work about the intricate machinery of the human mind. From its opening conceptual moment, when the three mechanisms of clock, novel, and life are simultaneously set going, we watch things germinate and grow. Seeds are sown, ideas implanted, impressions received, sensations communicated, and these in turn make links with other experiences, until a full fictional *cerebellum* develops equipped with its intricate network of associations. Through all the confusion and folly of the Shandy household the life force threads its erratic way. It is a novel of prolific seminal energies, in which meaning is tumultuously generated not only from every sentence on every page, but at the infinite points of connection between them. This book of spiders' webs, thread papers, cross-purposes, puzzled skeins, knots, and entangled filaments is acutely aware of how 'texts' are (as etymology tells us) woven together, so that all text becomes context.[22]

The novel traces the activity of a Lockean consciousness, to the extent that the processes of thought and writing become intimately linked. There are many continuities, but there is very little that is continuous: both mind and narrative are working across unavoidable gaps. In repeated acts of retrieval and recollection, the self-conscious narratives move back and forth through time (the book's palpable medium), piecing material together in an attempt to represent coherent meaning:

In good truth, when a man is telling a story in the strange way I do mine, he is obliged continually to be going backwards and forwards to keep all tight together in the reader's fancy... there is so much unfixed and equivocal matter starting up, with so many breaks and gaps in it,—and so little service do the stars afford, which, nevertheless, I hang up in some of the darkest passages. (vi.33)

The asterisks ('stars') sprinkled through the book are visible markers of what is missing, or censored, or suggested. But like the many rhetorical *aporiai*

---

[21] See Charles Taylor, *Sources of the Self: The Making of the Modern Identity* (Cambridge: Cambridge University Press, 1989), 288–9.
[22] Walter Shandy speaks of the human brain as 'this incomprehensible contexture in which wit, memory, fancy, eloquence, and what is usually meant by the name of good natural parts, do consist' (*Tristram Shandy*, ii.19).

('I have dropped the curtain over this scene for a minute,—to remind you of one thing,—and to inform you of another,' ii.19) they function also to draw us imaginatively closer to the text, with its whisperings, nudges, and hints, while we make our way along the track. Rather than being a sign of undecidability, these stars, like the book's black and blank pages, tease and stimulate the reader's sense of participation. To make a fine distinction: they represent not a failure of unity but the difficulty of finding continuity. The book seems to hold in creative balance both a sense of loss and a sense of proliferating possibility.

Tristram's personal identity similarly unfolds by fits and starts. The novel is concerned not with the continuous but with the *successive*, an idea with a different emphasis. Walter Shandy, well versed in theories of all kinds, understands Locke's dynamic notion of identity, and he attempts on one occasion to unravel it for his brother Toby. He explains how succession and duration work in giving us our idea of selfhood; and as he does so he makes a subtle adjustment from 'existence' to 'continuation of the existence', as if the latter idea were needed to ensure our sense of ourselves:

> For if you will turn your eyes inwards upon your mind, continued my father, and observe attentively, you will perceive, brother, that whilst you and I are talking together, and thinking and smoking our pipes: or whilst we receive successively ideas in our minds, we know that we do exist, and so we estimate the existence, or the continuation of the existence of ourselves, or any thing else commensurate to the succession of any ideas in our minds, the duration of ourselves . . . Now, whether we observe it or no, continued my father, in every sound man's head, there is a regular succession of ideas of one sort or other, which follow each other in train just like—A train of artillery? said my uncle Toby.—A train of a fiddle-stick!—quoth my father (iii.18)

Walter's phrase 'the duration of ourselves' renders selfhood precarious at the very moment of confirming it. Throughout the narrative the finely spun thread of ideas is vulnerable to time ('Time wastes too fast: every letter I trace tells me with what rapidity Life follows my pen', ix.8). Unable to claim the certainty of Idea, whatever empirical knowledge can be won from time's flow is liable to be superseded, lost, or forgotten. Much of it becomes 'waste'. In the nature of Lockean empiricism, every immediate experience, so direct and tangible, slips instantaneously into memory, so that all certainties become to some degree recollections.[23] In this world there is no idealist transcendence either of time or of the human medium (the mental vehicle that carries all knowledge). Every truth has to be mediated, conveyed by this vehicle through space and time, much as Susannah hurriedly carries the

---

[23] On Lockean memory and aspects of eighteenth-century poetry, see Steve Clark, ' "Between Self and Self's Book": Locke and the Poetry of the Early Romantics', in Thomas Woodman (ed.), *Early Romantics: Perspectives in British Poetry from Pope to Wordsworth* (Houndmills: Macmillan; New York: St Martin's Press, 1998), 30–54.

name 'Trismegistus' along the corridors of Shandy Hall ('But stay—thou art a leaky vessel, *Susannah*, added my father', iv.14) only to find that half of it has leaked away. Any 'truth' tends to be refracted by the medium through which it passes, placed usually in invisible inverted commas.[24]

Sterne's Lockean landscape is partly an inheritance from Renaissance scepticism (both Erasmus and Montaigne understood the follies of human certainty) but located firmly in the context of a modern analysis of mental processes. It is far from the confident realm of Idealism, where on the plane of eternity Ideas hold their form and fight their conceptual battles. By contrast, Uncle Toby's mental battlefield is a difficult terrain, and his big obsessive idea becomes bogged down in representation, in tracing spatial relations and allowing for angles and trajectories. He struggles in time and space to tie his truth down, but remains forever in the process of its recovery.

One especially organic aspect of the book is the way its various forms of life become part of the Shandean ecosystem, an interactive group of beings whose seemingly wayward thoughts and behaviour weave the fabric of the novel.[25] Elements of randomness, accident, error, interruption, and confusion are drawn unknowingly into a pattern. The innumerable instances of interruption, for example, tend to be at points where another idea is accessed, causing sudden refractions and diversions of the line of thought. It is, after all, a text in which nothing runs straight, where cannonballs take an elliptical path and bowls follow their bias across the bowling green; mental obliquity and the digressive loops of the story turn the arabesque into the book's expressive motif.[26] But divergences tend to make new connections, and cross-purposes form witty interactions. The novel's ubiquitous dashes serve—like physical breaths taken—to pause and then resume, both to separate and to join. Without the innumerable breaks there would be no connecting threads; without the interruptions there would be no continuations (the phrase 'continued my father', and others like it, occurs repeatedly in the book); and without the gaps there would be no moments of delightful human electricity, like that between the adjacent forefingers of Toby and Mrs Wadman in the sentry-box (viii.16), or Tristram's instant of love, when Nannette's hair unravels before him during the dance and 'a transient spark of amity shot across the space betwixt us' (vii.43). Some of the most human moments in the novel are those where gaps are crossed in this way.[27] It is

---

[24] '[T]here is a fatality attends the actions of some men: Order them as they will, they pass thro' a certain medium, which so twists and refracts them from their true directions' (i.10).

[25] Tristram sees his book as a kind of healthy organic exercise: 'True Shandeism, think what you will against it, opens the heart and lungs, and like all those affections which partake of its nature, it forces the blood and other vital fluids of the body to run freely through its channels' (iv.32).

[26] See Peter Conrad, *Shandyism: The Character of Romantic Irony* (New York: Barnes and Noble, 1978).

[27] The book is fascinated by gaps, whether the erotic slit in Nannette's petticoat (vii.44), in Mrs Wadman's apron (ix.25), or the 'hiatus' in Dr Phutatorius's breeches (iv.27). 'Error, Sir, creeps in thro' the minute holes, and small crevices, which human nature leaves unguarded' (ii.19). Tristram repeatedly promises a 'chapter of button-holes'.

useful to remember that in the book's empirical world all ideas must negotiate space and time.

One tantalising discontinuity of which the novel is acutely conscious is that between body and mind/soul. Here *Tristram Shandy* engages with the modern scientific theories of human organisation that underpin Lockean identity. By mid-century the old taxonomies of faculty psychology and the bodily humours had given way to organic accounts featuring the nervous system, the animal spirits, and the fibres and vessels that circulate the life force.[28] Texts of Sensibility explore this dynamic scenario in which *sense*, *thought*, and *emotion* work together and open up lines of communication between the external physical world and the internal world of idea. Taken out of their separate hierarchical compartments into the same field of operation, they are somehow able to cross the divide between matter and spirit. It is no easy elision, however, but a precarious translation that raises the intractable problem of how this organised being is functioning when a mental operation has a physical effect (David Hume considered this 'voluntary motion' the most mysterious principle 'in all nature').[29] In the Lockean world, to move from a thought to a bodily response (from embarrassment to a blush) makes cause and effect operate seemingly across a void, like Newtonian gravity exerting its force at a distance through empty space.[30] Tristram finds a brilliant image to convey the enigma of this mutual responsiveness that yet remains distinct: 'A man's body and his mind', he remarks, 'are exactly like a jerkin, and a jerkin's lining; rumple the one—you rumple the other', iii.4). But as his book has already shown, a whole text can disappear down the fissure.[31]

In contrast to Berkeleyan idealism, Locke's version of reality must negotiate continually between idea and physical matter, the recalcitrant stuff that Berkeley was able to dispense with and thereby circumvent the awkward issue. The problem of working across this mind/matter divide is raised at every turn: eighteenth-century theorists of Sensibility become ingenious at locating some mediating vehicle or medium that explains how the human system is organised. In the late 1740s Professor Robert Whytt of Edinburgh developed his *sentient principle* ('an immaterial, undivided substance that could "feel" stimuli and necessarily directed the appropriate response');[32]

[28] See Michael V. DePorte, *Nightmares and Hobbyhorses: Swift, Sterne, and Augustan Ideas of Madness* (San Marino: Huntington Library, 1974), 3–53.

[29] This is voluntary motion. See David Hume, *An Enquiry Concerning Human Understanding* (1777), Section VII, Part I. For a more detailed account of this aspect of Sensibility, see David Fairer, 'Sentimental Translation in Mackenzie and Sterne', *EC*, 49 (1999), 132–51.

[30] The parallel led to a concept of the 'aether' as a mysterious, extremely fine medium through which such forces could operate. See Ian Wylie, *Young Coleridge and the Philosophers of Nature* (Oxford: Clarendon Press, 1989), 29–31. See n. 34 below.

[31] Yorick's sermon 'dropp'd thro' an unsuspected fissure in thy master's pocket, down into a treacherous and tatter'd lining' (ii.17).

[32] Christopher Lawrence, 'The Nervous System and Society in the Scottish Enlightenment', in Barry Barnes and Steven Shapin (eds), *Natural Order: Historical Studies of Scientific Culture* (Beverly Hills/London: Sage, 1979), 19–40 (25).

William Smith conceived of the *animal aether*, an 'intermediate material' that was the physiological equivalent of Newtonian aether, an 'infinitely fine and elastic fluid' in the nerves, which 'makes the cement between the human soul and body; and is the instrument or medium of all its actions and functions';[33] and David Hartley postulated, though not with much confidence, an 'infinitesimal elementary Body to be intermediate between the Soul and gross Body'.[34]

It was Hartley's ability to negotiate this problem of continuity between thought and matter which seems to have impressed Coleridge when he singled him out in 'Religious Musings' (1796) as 'he of mortal kind | Wisest, he first who mark'd the ideal tribes | Down the fine fibres from the sentient brain | Roll subtly-surging' (391–4). The *ideal* and the *sentient* become continuous, and Coleridge's vocabulary gestures toward the fineness and subtlety of the process involved. The more minute the scale, the less implausible might the crossing of the physical barrier be, so that Hartley's tiny 'vibratiuncles' (little vibrations) seemed almost convincing as a basis for mental association. In his *Observations on Man* (1749) Hartley conjectured that in Locke's sensation–pain continuum he had located what he termed his 'Solution of Continuity', so fine that it could almost count as an idea, causing him to wonder whether 'this minute invisible Solution of Continuity in the infinitesimal medullary Particles of the Brain, is not that common Limit' (i.37). On such fragile hinges could swing the confidence of religious belief, as Jerome Christensen comments: 'Hartley's philosophy quests... for the third term that is not merely the name for continuity but continuity itself, for the bridge between the visible and the invisible—for the God who is, "according to Scriptures, All in All."'[35]

A few years earlier Hartley's friend Dr George Cheyne had faced this same difficulty in describing the way 'Mind or Soul' initiates motions in the body. He knows some kind of continuity must be operating, and in attempting to describe it he finds himself drawing on the language of botany. What he presupposes is a distinctly organic mechanism:

How [Mind or Soul] exerts these Powers on *divinely organiz'd* Matter, I do not here pretend to say; but I conceive it acts on the Organs by means of the *Mechanism* of the Brain and its *Nerves*, which are an Infinity of differently situated, complicated and stretch'd little *Filaments* or *Fibrils*, fill'd with a soft *milky* cellular Substance, (like a *Rush* with its *Pith*) contain'd in small *membranous* extremely *elastic* Sacks or *Tubuli*, all whose *elastic* and *energic* Virtue consists in the proper *Tension* or *Vibrations* of these Sacks or *membranous* Coats, spread over all the *Solids* of the Body, which being

---

[33] William Smith, *A Dissertation upon the Nerves* (London: W. Owen, 1768), 42, 44, 49.

[34] David Hartley, *Observations on Man, his Frame, his Duty, and his Expectations. In Two Parts* (London: S. Richardson, 1749), i.34. Hartley describes his vibrations as being excited and sustained partly by Newtonian 'aether' (i.13–16).

[35] Jerome Christensen, *Coleridge's Blessed Machine of Language* (Ithaca: Cornell University Press, 1981), 41. The quotation is from *Observations on Man* (1749), i.114.

extremely *elastic* and *springy*, convey *harmonious* and divinely proportion'd *Vibra-tions*, *Undulations* and *Tremors*, excited outwardly by Objects to this *sentient* and *intelligent* Principle.[36]

We find ourselves inside a complicated spatially conceived sensorium where relativity, responsiveness, and communication are the theme. Nothing occu-pies its own independent ground but each element is poised like fine gothic tracery about to spring to life (the *Fibrils* are 'differently situated, compli-cated and stretch'd'). Everything in this scene is ready to relate, respond, touch, tremble, and convey; and the doctor emphasizes the elasticity and springiness all around, where the little tubes or sacks ('*membranous* Coats') simultaneously contain and spread sensation. Cheyne finds himself charac-terising an organic sensibility of snail-horn responsiveness, a system on the brink of erotic/hysteric arousal.

To dismiss this description as 'mechanical' would hardly do justice to the way Cheyne imagines the human organism here. Being an example of the eighteenth-century organic, the passage has little investment in structure or unity, but is urgently concerned with processes, conveyances, channels of communication, and mediation, the mechanisms through which life circu-lates and meanings form. And the good doctor ends with a modest gesture of his own that shows another facet of the eighteenth-century organic: 'This is the best Idea I can conceive,' he concludes, 'others may explain the Matter better, if they can.' Organic truths, such as those of georgic husbandry, tend to be advisory ones, based on experience, and they have the potential to be superseded if they prove misleading or impractical. Here Cheyne suggests that others may have things to add. The organic is always ready to be supplemented or redirected: its meanings are workable and tend to be communal—and often provisional. When challenged, an organic idea does not come crashing down, but looks to occupy fresh ground. In summing up this accretive, revisionary aspect of empirical thought, J. D. Law has written that '[e]mpiricist reflection is a self-critical procedure, in which perpetual correction and revision (of impressions, of language, and of judgments) are more important than the establishing of permanent categories or conditions of knowledge.'[37]

This is the challenging context in which a Lockean consciousness must find its way. Lacking metaphysical reach or perpendicularity of principle, and without the inherent force and purity of an epiphany, an organic *thought*, which is consciously mediated through space and time, which

---

[36] George Cheyne, *The Natural Method of Cureing the Diseases of the Body, and the Disorders of the Mind Depending on the Body* (London: Geo. Strahan, and John and Paul Knapton, 1742), 94. On Cheyne's theories and Sensibility, see G. J. Barker-Benfield, *The Culture of Sensibility: Sex and Society in Eighteenth-Century Britain* (Chicago: University of Chicago Press, 1992), 6–15.

[37] Jules David Law, *The Rhetoric of Empiricism: Language and Perception from Locke to I. A. Richards* (Ithaca/London: Cornell University Press, 1993), 14.

encounters doubts and questions, which is checked, tested, and re-thought, and seems finally to emerge rather than announce itself, can hardly be weakened in the process. Thoughts of this kind are infused more deeply into personal experience. An organic context can be a testing ground where complex forces are organised. There they can find strength not in firmness and solidity, but in tensile durability (a term civil engineers are well versed in). To be responsive and flexible is not to lack strength, as any boxing trainer, or ballet dancer, knows. Inside the mobile, less self-assured organic world, positions of power may be outflanked, and certainties can be traced to their very *un*certain source; confidence tends to become a hollow echo; words of judgment take on a mechanical sound; and principles turn out to be soapboxes. In this theatre, Truth must play before a difficult audience.

By mid-century the Lockean view that personal identity resided in human consciousness was well established. The lengthy article on 'Identity' in Ephraim Chambers's *Cyclopaedia* (1728) is a summary, often word-for-word, of Locke's chapter, and David Hume in 1740 acknowledged that '[m]ost philosophers seem inclin'd to think, that personal identity arises from consciousness.'[38] It is possible, as we shall see in the rest of this chapter, to track the continuing influence of Locke's organic concept of identity into the 1790s and beyond, and to recognise its crucial role in Unitarian thought through figures like Priestley, Barbauld, and Hazlitt. The 'Revolutionary Controversy' post-1789, in its pitting of organic and idealist theories against each other, was continuing the arguments about the nature of human identity and consciousness that Locke had set in motion a hundred years earlier.

It was around the burning issue of *continuity* of consciousness/identity and the related problem of bridging the material and ideal that the debate was sustained. For some, the problem of finding a philosophical basis for a self that persisted through the vagaries of time and experience remained intractable, and Locke seemed to have raised a difficulty rather than solved one. Through his concept of *organisation* he had willingly incorporated the discontinuous (a feature of human memory), loss, replacement, addition, and growth, as being modifications (modal developments) of one continuing self-conscious identity. The rigorously sceptical Hume, however, would have no truck with a diachronic self, and he argued that those interruptions in consciousness proved that our continuing identity is a fiction:

For when we attribute identity, in an improper sense, to variable or interrupted objects, our mistake is not confin'd to the expression, but is commonly attended

---

[38] Ephraim Chambers, *Cyclopaedia: or, An Universal Dictionary of Arts and Sciences*, 2 vols (London, 1728), 370; David Hume, *A Treatise of Human Nature*, ed. L.A. Selby-Bigge, rev. P. H. Nidditch, 2nd edn. (Oxford: Clarendon Press, 1978), 635 (I.iv.6, Appendix). On the debates about Lockean identity, 1696–1738, see Christopher Fox, *Locke and the Scriblerians: Identity and Consciousness in Early Eighteenth-Century Britain* (Berkeley etc.: University of California Press, 1988), 38–68.

with a fiction, either of something invariable and uninterrupted, or of something mysterious and inexplicable, or at least with a propensity to such fictions. (I.iv.6)

As a 'variable and interrupted object', a human being cannot be said to have a personal identity at all. By the synchronic logic of this passage, Humean *identity* is not temporal or in any way dynamic; it follows that it can only be a photograph, not a film (the medium that creates an illusion of continuity from successive images). On a similar basis *meaning* could only ever be a word, never a poem. As conceived by Hume, identity can neither be expressed nor developed. Pursuing his argument, it would not be possible to talk of the *identity* of a wave, a flame, or a wind, which exist not as substance (water, fire, air) but as modes/modifications, and thus have no meaning outside time. Some modern philosophers have accommodated this notion of a dynamic identity with the help of a concept of the *continuant*: '[I]t does seem possible', Michael Ayers writes, 'to conceive of processes and activities... as being more substance-like than we have considered: as being, as it is sometimes put, "continuants."' He goes on to discuss the 'blurring' of 'events and things', raising the possibility that, to avoid Hume's synchronic slicing, we might 'think of the entity in question [the wave, for example] as an occurrence taking time, or as a mobile disturbance or activity with a life-history'.[39] It could also help, we might add in our literary and period context, to think of it as a phenomenon of *Nature*. In a climate of Hume's inorganic philosophic scepticism, one feature of this ubiquitous eighteenth-century concept of Nature was to offer discursive support (a 'language') for human identity, a spatiotemporal continuum that could embrace discrete things/events with some kind of meaning.

For Hume, of course, such reliance on a supportive frame of meaning/value was inadmissible. Looking back at his words quoted above, it is clear that his pointed thrust about 'something mysterious and inexplicable' alludes to the argument of those Christian opponents of Locke who needed the soul to underwrite human identity. (Locke's theory found opposition on the same issue from sceptic and believer alike.) Isaac Watts and Samuel Clarke both argued that the soul never intermitted its vigilance, never slept, and was thus the ultimate guarantee that one's identity was not only continuous but would be available for final judgment and salvation. The concept of the immortal soul avoided at one stroke Locke's awkward acceptance of intermittence/interruption: 'if the Soul be, as We believe, a *permanent indivisible Immaterial Substance*, then all these Difficulties vanish of Themselves', Clarke optimistically concluded.[40]

[39] Ayers, *Locke. Volume II: Ontology*, 106–7.
[40] Clarke, *Third Defense*, 91. As Isaac Watts put it, 'there is no such thing as the Sleep of the Soul' (*Reliquiae Juveniles: Miscellaneous Thoughts in Prose and Verse* (London, 1734), 338). The issue of whether personal identity involves 'message continuity' or 'bodily continuity' is at the centre of modern theological debate on the Resurrection. See Frank B. Dilley, 'Resurrection and the "Replica Objection" ', *Religious Studies*, 19 (1983), 459–74 (465).

In this way the continuing eighteenth-century debate over organic con-
tinuity of identity widened to draw in larger issues of belief and meaning. It
gained additional relevance during the 1790s, when the radical re-thinking
of human and political constitutions was taking place. Two friends who
were to play central roles in this, Joseph Priestley and Richard Price, debated
the matter in print during 1777–8 in the wake of Priestley's *Disquisitions on
Matter and Spirit* (1777). The following year in *A Free Discussion of the
Doctrines of Materialism, and Philosophical Necessity* (1778) the pair am-
icably set out their opposing arguments in terms of the Lockean problem, as
summarized by Priestley:

[T]he difference between us [is] chiefly this. He [Price] supposes that the powers of
perception and thought reside in an immaterial substance, but that the exercise of
these powers is made to depend on the organization of the body; whereas I suppose
these powers to reside in the organized body itself, and therefore *must* be suspended
till the time when the organization shall be restored.[41]

The nature of organisation becomes a key issue here. Priestley, the more
Lockean of the two, is able to admit modifications even of an extreme kind:
death, decay, and dispersal 'suspend' our identity until the scattered mater-
ials of the body are eventually reassembled. In arguing that continuity of
identity overrides loss and replacement Priestley runs counter to both Clarke
and Hume. To make his point he draws a Lockean analogy: '*forests*, which
consist of *trees* growing in certain places, preserve their identity, though all
the trees of which they consist decay, and others grow up in their places'.[42]
For all his materialism, Priestley is no literalist: he is clear that the identity of
the forest only makes sense as an idea of continuity through time, and that
although what constitutes it (its constitution, we might say) will inevitably
change as things die, decay, germinate, and grow, the identity survives. In
contrast Richard Price looks to a permanent unchanging ideal element, the
immortal soul, to contain our unique identity; and he cannot accept Priest-
ley's view because it implies, he says, that 'the soul loses its existence at
death'.[43] Price wishes to retain the soul's continuous life as vital to salvation,
our link to divine truth, and he cannot conceive of identity being lost and
reconstituted.[44] He suspects that his fellow clergyman regards the soul
('the being that thinks and acts') as a mere mode of material organisation.

---

[41] Joseph Priestley, *A Free Discussion of the Doctrines of Materialism, and Philosophical
Necessity, in a Correspondence between Dr. Price, and Dr. Priestley* (London: J. Johnson and
T. Cadell, 1778), xvi.

[42] Joseph Priestley, *Disquisitions Relating to Matter and Spirit* (London: J. Johnson, 1777),
158.

[43] Priestley, *Free Discussion*, 78.

[44] Without the individual soul, Price remarks, 'may not I and Dr. Priestley be the same man,
since the organization of our bodies is the same, and only the matter different?' (ibid. 77). Unlike
Price, Priestley follows Locke in distinguishing 'man' from 'person' (*Matter and Spirit*, 157).

Priestley, for whom mind and body are effectually *'one and the same thing'*,[45] has no place for a detachable immaterial soul as a divine identity card. He is indeed happy to allow for natural processes: the power of thought can return, he says, when the physical materials are gathered up and 'revivified' (he avoids the word 'reanimated'):

Thus when the body is dissolved by putrefaction, its power of thinking entirely ceases; but, no particle of the man being lost, as many of them as were essential to him, will, I doubt not, be collected, and revivified, at the resurrection, when the power of thinking will return of course.[46]

As Priestley had remarked the previous year, 'dispersion of parts, is only a *decomposition*; and whatever is *decomposed*, may be *recomposed* by the being who first composed it'.[47]

Priestley's God works within a natural organic cycle incorporating decay and dissolution. His power is manifested not pantheistically *as* nature, but as the organiser *of* nature.[48] It is clear that whereas the more idealist Price is looking to an essence that will persist through every potential modification, something pure outside time and process, Priestley the materialist natural philosopher always remains within both. He cannot countenance an idealist 'immaterial substance' because this assumes 'the notion of there being something in man quite different from his corporeal organized system'.[49] On the other hand Priestley is happy to contemplate decomposition and putrefaction, given that what he terms 'the same *stamina*, or those particles that really belonged to the *germ* of the organical body' (161) will survive.[50] The suggestion here is that each human being will be re-grown from his/her individual constitutional rudiments. For Priestley, resurrection conjures up an image of organic potential rather than ideal perfection. The raising of the dead will be according to nature's own model.

Priestley's Unitarian acceptance of humanity's place within the processes of nature develops the organic implications of Locke's discussion of personal identity. The published debate with Richard Price shows that the arguments

---

[45] See Priestley, *Matter and Spirit*, 28. Coleridge summarised Priestley's view as follows: 'Body and spirit are therefore no longer absolutely heterogeneous, but *may* without any absurdity be supposed to be different modes, or degrees of perfection, of a common substratum' (*Biog. Lit.*, 88, 91).

[46] Priestley, *Free Discussion*, 83.

[47] Priestley, *Matter and Spirit*, 161.

[48] Priestley distanced himself from pantheism, asserting that in his scheme, 'every thing is the *divine power*; but still, strictly speaking, every thing is not *the Deity himself*' (*Matter and Spirit*, 41–2). See H. W. Piper, *The Active Universe: Pantheism and the Concept of Imagination in the English Romantic Poets* (London: Athlone Press, 1962), 37.

[49] Priestley, *Matter and Spirit*, 50.

[50] *OED*, s.v. 'stamina', 1: 'The native or original (as opposed to adventitious) elements and constitution of anything; the nature, structure and qualities of an organism, as existing potentially in its nascent state; the rudiments or germs from which living beings or their organs are developed.'

that first broke over Locke's *Essay* were still reverberating eight decades later, and at the heart of them remained the question of continuity. By placing emphasis on self-consciousness, rather than a God-given soul, Locke allowed *experience* (i.e. specific local perception and reflection in time and space) to be both the initiating impulse and the sustaining pulse of our identity—thus constituting a 'person' who is quite unlike any other.[51] From this viewpoint Priestleyan resurrection can be seen as the redeeming of a personhood such as might have developed within a characteristically Unitarian community of growing individuals. In the context of the late 1770s this organic picture is part of a mounting Unitarian challenge to what Priestley labelled 'the immaterial system' centred on the pre-existence of an immortal soul and on Jesus as embodying the divine essence.[52] Rejecting this transcendental dimension, the personal experiential truth that underpins late eighteenth-century Unitarianism is grounded in Lockean perception.[53] A subjective mental space for self-consciousness here becomes a Unitarian 'conscience', a growing knowledge of the world and our place within it, which guides human progress. This principle of growth is the vital element in a philosophy that reaches its truths not by direct vision or spiritual authority, but by a more organic generation of each person's intellectual energies.

Moving into the 1790s, the long-standing arguments about idealist and experiential theories of identity became focused on questions of human potential in relation to an idealism that needed to break free of continuities. The terms of debate were now more sharply defined by revolution. In the wake of 1789 the concept of 'potential' itself could not avoid placing human powers and political power in the same equation and asking how they might be brought into alignment. What principles should come into play? Is the 'real' represented through the refractions of individual perception and reflection, or is there a transparent universal world of Idea that transcends human mediations/prejudices and can directly invoke the Absolute as ultimate 'reality'? It was a time of binaries, and this either/or (nominalist/realist, materialist/idealist) question with its strong political inflection was a fundamental one capable of being re-phrased in many ways. In a revolutionary context the Lockean model of continuing identity did not obviously lend

---

[51] Locke accepts the existence of the soul, but denies it any innate powers or thoughts: 'I see no Reason therefore to believe, that the *Soul thinks before the Senses have furnish'd it with Ideas* to think on' (*Essay*, II.i.20).

[52] Priestley praises Locke for 'contending, that whatever exists must exist *somewhere*, or in *some place*, and by shewing that, for any thing that we know to the contrary, the power of thought may be superadded by the Divine Being to an organized system of mere matter' (*Matter and Spirit*, 270).

[53] On Locke's influence on eighteenth-century Unitarianism, see Earl Morse Wilbur, *A History of Unitarianism: In Transylvania, England, and America* (Cambridge, MA: Harvard University Press, 1952), 232–4; on Locke's strong interest in Unitarian ideas, see John Marshall, 'Locke, Socinianism, "Socinianism," and Unitarianism', in M. A. Stewart (ed.), *English Philosophy in the Age of Locke* (Oxford: Clarendon Press, 2000), 111–82.

itself to being born again—its basis was recollection rather than inauguration. Also, the empiricist's rejection of innate ideas could be seen as a denial of a language of 'rights' sanctioned by an innate birthright. These rights might be claimed more urgently by a person whose identity, rather than being shaped by experience and memory, had been repressed by them. They could speak of potentially infinite powers now lost.

On the other hand, a language of 'rights' is the very foundation of Locke's *Two Treatises of Government* (1690) and *A Letter Concerning Toleration* (1689), texts that established modern thinking about natural rights (freedom within natural law) possessed equally by every human being.[54] From an empiricist viewpoint a new-born child, free of any preconceptions, has the vast potential of the world awaiting it, and waiting to be questioned too. In Locke's view a person has the natural right to pursue his/her own individual path, to place their own 'innocent delights' even before a wider 'duty': 'I have', says Locke, 'under government...a liberty to follow my own will in all things, where the rule prescribes not.'[55] Here there is no mental template, no programmed imagination, no source of knowledge with a prior claim on personal experience. The excitement lies all in the future. At the moment of birth there is no glance backwards at trailing clouds of glory, wispy traces of an eternally illuminated hierarchy in a dimension beyond your reach where Idea is enthroned. No, the discovery is all yours to make:

> Haste, little captive, burst thy prison doors!
> Launch on the living world, and spring to light!
> Nature for thee displays her various stores,
> Opens her thousand inlets of delight.[56]

Anna Barbauld's 'To a little invisible Being who is expected soon to become visible' (?1795) pictures a newly liberated consciousness bursting into the world. The poem generates its excitements by anticipating what this 'germ of new life' (l. 1) will inherit when it leaves the womb. The Unitarian Barbauld, protégée and friend of Priestley, recognises the 'lofty claim' the newly born has, but it is within the created world that its full potential will be graspable, its identity formed:

---

[54] See A. John Simmons, *The Lockean Theory of Rights* (Princeton: Princeton University Press, 1992), 68–120.

[55] John Locke, *Second Treatise*, in *Two Treatises of Government*, ed. Peter Laslett (Cambridge: Cambridge University Press, 1988), §128, §22. On Locke's influence among radical circles in the 1790s, see John Dunn, 'The Politics of Locke in England and America in the Eighteenth Century', in John Yolton (ed.), *John Locke: Problems and Perspectives* (London: Cambridge University Press, 1969), 45–80 (67–9).

[56] Anna Letitia Barbauld, 'To a little invisible Being who is expected soon to become visible', ll. 29–32. The poem was first printed in Barbauld's *Works* (1825), i.199–201. Given its placing, William McCarthy and Elizabeth Kraft (*The Poems of Anna Letitia Barbauld* (Athens/London: Georgia University Press, 1994), 296) suggest a date *c.*1795.

> What powers lie folded in thy curious frame,—
> Senses from objects locked, and mind from thought!
> How little canst thou guess the lofty claim
> To grasp at all the worlds the Almighty wrought!   (5–8)

The poem gains an empirical charge by anticipating the instant when the baby's senses will be unlocked and experiences will begin. Until then, the scene is one of a limited life form awaiting the moment its potential is revealed. This is close to how Locke describes it:

> [A] *Foetus in the Mother's Womb, differs not much from the State of a Vegetable*; but passes the greatest part of its time without Perception or Thought, doing very little, but sleep in a Place ... where the Eyes have no Light, and the Ears, so shut up, are not very susceptible of Sounds.[57]

Independent identity has not yet been formed. The expectation of what awaits this living creature throws full emphasis on what Wordsworth in 1798 will call 'the mighty world of eye and ear'.[58]

This anchoring 'language of the sense' opens up everything for the infant, who begins to access ideas at the precise moment its own sensations begin. It is even the gateway to the sublimest thoughts.[59] Experiential personhood begins to be formed at birth, until which time the foetus and the mother share a symbiotic identity. In her poem Barbauld focuses on the separating out of one individual from another, understanding it not as a severance but as the beginning of an intimate attachment. It will be an expansion of the mother's interest into what becomes an object of love, a new being that is an extension of her self: 'She longs to fold to her maternal breast | Part of herself, yet to herself unknown' (21–2). It is separation that initiates love and connection. Like Priestley the experimental scientist, Barbauld recognises that the smallest new unit within nature can become a vital part of the greater scheme, its value emerging only when its individual powers encounter others. Priestley wrote: 'Every new fact should be carefully examined, as a treasure of unknown value, the real worth of which time, and the discovery of other kindred powers in nature, may bring to light.'[60] Nothing is so

---

[57] Locke, *Essay*, II.i.21.

[58] William Wordsworth, 'Lines written a few miles above Tintern Abbey', 106–7. See the epigraph to this chapter.

[59] Ibid. 109. Locke grounds even sublime experience in early sensation and reflection: 'This is ... the Groundwork, whereon to build all those Notions, which ever he shall have naturally in this world. All those sublime Thoughts, which towre above the Clouds, and reach as high as Heaven it self, take their Rise and Footing here' (*Essay*, II.i.24).

[60] Joseph Priestley, *The History and Present State of Discoveries relating to Vision, Light, and Colours*, 2 vols (London, 1772), i.56. This is quoted by Jane Stabler in her valuable article exploring links between Barbauld, Priestley, and Coleridge: 'Space for Speculation: Coleridge, Barbauld, and the Poetics of Priestley', in Nicholas Roe (ed.), *Samuel Taylor Coleridge and the Sciences of Life* (Oxford: Oxford University Press, 2001), 175–204 (184).

insignificant that it cannot have meaning and therefore value, since both concepts develop together.

The crucial dimension here is time, which works, not as an arbiter, but as the unfolder of potential. Priestley's modest statement brings us to the heart of the organic matter of this book: in place of a framing truth or directing purpose there are discovered values and emerging meanings. Things that might appear small, discrete, and isolated can find, and help to make, a context for themselves. Meanings are in that way discursive, working across connections and associations. The aim is not to be unified and complete, but to be more integrated and thus more articulate.

One writer who took the logic of this organic integration to an extreme was John 'Walking' Stewart, a friend of Wordsworth,[61] whose ideas combine an empirical grounding in the senses with a universal system that is close to a materialist pantheism. Stewart, who had gained his name by walking in five continents (he seems to have traversed by foot more of the earth than anyone before him), believed he had inaugurated a new age in 1790 with *The Apocalypse of Nature; wherein the Source of Moral Motion is Discovered, And a Moral System established, through the Evidence and Conviction of the Senses*. In that final phrase he deliberately distances himself from the spiritual or visionary. For him, human beings are nothing else but temporary 'modes of organization' consisting of physical material that comes together for a time and finds an identity, before disintegrating and returning to the pool of indestructible matter in the universe. This latter is 'the great integer, nature' of which every living thing is a 'fraction'. In *The Revolution of Reason: or the Establishment of the Constitution of Things in Nature* (1794),[62] Stewart expounds what might be described as a panbiomorphic universe (it deserves an entirely new term just for itself), in which human identity is no different in category from a wave, flame, or wind, having an entirely modal existence. All 'modes' emerge through the continual alternation of incremental and excremental dynamics within nature (like the ebb and flow of the tide), and human modes have their material repeatedly replaced: 'the human body', Stewart says, 'renovates the whole of its matter in the course of eighteen days'.[63] There is therefore no such thing as a 'positive or absolute identity':

[61] On Stewart's influence on Wordsworth, see Kelly Grovier, ' "Shades of the Prison-House": "Walking" Stewart, Michel Foucault and the Making of Wordsworth's "Two Consciousnesses" ', *SiR*, 44 (Fall 2005), 341–66; and 'Dream Walker: A Wordsworth Mystery Solved', *Romanticism*, 13 (2007), 156–63.

[62] Dr Grovier (private communication) convincingly dates *The Revolution of Reason* to 1794 from Stewart's eccentric calendar inaugurated by his own *Apocalypse of Nature* ('From the aera of intellectual existence, or the publication of the apocalypse of nature, an. 4').

[63] John Stewart, *The Revolution of Reason: or the Establishment of the Constitution of Things in Nature* (London: J. Ridgway, [1794]), 15. Stewart's cycle considerably accelerates Lord Shaftesbury's calculation of 7 to 14 years. See *The Moralists. A Philosophical Rhapsody*, iii.1 (*Characteristicks* (1711), ii.101).

Identity of mode is nothing but apparent sameness, caused by a fluxion of matter or particles in contiguity or juxtaposition, so organized as to transmit the effects of passing or arriving atoms, and constitute thereby individuality, in order to mechanize energy, or give it that unitary form or figure, which, like the units of number in the powers of numeration, may systematize the aggregate energy of the whole of existence. (13)

Stewart has therefore no room for any structural concept of 'unity': his living organisations are aggregates formed by 'contiguity or juxtaposition'.[64] They each take a temporary 'unitary form or figure' just as arithmetical figures represent merely sum totals: 57, say, or 507, or even 42.

   Stewart's organic world is entirely a material, spatiotemporal one, and his picture of a cycle of decomposition and recomposition recalls Priestley's materialist acceptance of human decay. But in place of Priestley's eventual resurrection, here nature is all in all; it reconstitutes its universal energies, so that death for Stewart is simply 'the dissolution of organized matter' (233): '[w]hen any mode is acted upon by a cause which procures its organization to cease, the equilibrium of its incremental and excremental motion is lost: the latter obtains a preponderance, and brings on a slow but total decay' (18). This is a universe without spirit and without immortal souls; but it is full of endlessly varied living melodies: '[t]he word soul', he comments, 'implies the continuation of associated accidents, when the substance which creates them is dissolved. What! When the violin is burned, does it's tune dance about in aerial existence?' (107). In this world it is human beings who make the music.

   'Walking' Stewart's organic system of mechanized energy is an extreme example of how 'mechanic' and 'organic' can be brought together rather than left in traditional opposition, and his ideas have many modern resonances. The notion of an organic mechanism is one that has now returned to prominence through developments in cyberscience, with biological systems forming the organisational model, and in turn this new thinking about the organic has returned to influence biology.[65] In their ground-breaking *Autopoiesis and Cognition: The Realization of the Living*, Humberto Maturana and Francisco Varela set out to show 'that there is an organization that is common to all living systems, whichever the nature of their components', and 'that living systems are machines' (76). In doing so, their arguments continue to explore the implications of identity that Locke had highlighted:

----

[64] Throughout *The Revolution of Reason* Stewart uses the phrase 'unity of self and nature' to indicate that we are composed of nature's materials. He sees the universe as one thing (nature), but all organisations within it are aggregates: for anything in existence to have its own unity would be meaningless.

[65] See Evelyn Fox Keller, *Refiguring Life: Metaphors of Twentieth-Century Biology* (New York: Columbia University Press, 1995), 79–118. A discussion of Locke opens Jack Wilson's *Biological Individuality: The Identity and Persistence of Living Entities* (Cambridge: Cambridge University Press, 1999).

Autonomy and diversity, the maintenance of identity, and the origin of variation in the mode in which this identity is maintained, are the basic challenges presented by the phenomenology of living systems to which men have for centuries addressed their curiosity about life...we are emphasizing that a living system is defined by its organization and, hence, that it can be explained as any organization is explained, that is, in terms of relations, not of component properties.[66]

Their relational concept of 'autopoietic machines' ('unities whose organization is defined by a particular network of processes (relations) of production of components...not by the components themselves or their static relations') is almost recognisable as a description of the dynamics of *Tristram Shandy*. Their mechanisms are akin to those of Sensibility, being based on 'the nervous system as a network of lateral, parallel, sequential and recursive inhibitory and excitatory interactions' (79, 127). Although they repeatedly use the term 'unity', it soon becomes clear that it is being defined in terms of temporal continuity and process, and thus comes very close to Locke's concept of identity as 'a participation of the same continued Life':

Accordingly, any structural transformation that a living system may undergo maintaining its identity must take place in a manner determined by and subordinated to its defining autopoiesis; hence, in a living system loss of autopoiesis is disintegration as a unity and loss of identity, that is, death. (112)[67]

The Earth currently has two universal living systems, one in the physical world and the other in the virtual world, and they both 'live' by being empirical, dynamic, and organised. To understand them, and learn from them, it would be wise not to treat them as a binary of the organic and the mechanistic. We now realise that we must understand the intricate interlocking mechanisms of the natural world, just as we need to recognise the organic opportunities of the World Wide Web.[68] Modern communication has evolved a virtual universal sensorium, an infinitely expanding nervous system of prompts and responses, representing nothing less than a vast empirical memory that constitutes the most capacious brain ever conceived.

An age ago in 1977, as part of his attack on eighteenth-century empiricism for being passive, static, uncreative, and predictable, Robert Langbaum argued that 'Lockean man is like a computer' because he can only give back 'what has been "programmed" into him'. In those times the computer analogy seemed like a limitation, but now we can understand the infinitely

[66] Humberto R. Maturana and Francisco J. Varela, *Autopoiesis and Cognition: The Realization of the Living*. Boston Studies in the Philosophy of Science no. 42 (Dordrecht/Boston/London: D. Reidel, 1980), 73, 76.
[67] Marjorie Levinson uses the idea of *autopoiesis* interestingly in relation to Wordsworth. See her 'Romantic Criticism: The State of the Art', in Mary A. Favret and Nicola J. Watson (eds), *At the Limits of Romanticism: Essays in Cultural, Feminist, and Materialist Criticism* (Bloomington/Indianapolis: Indiana University Press, 1994), 269–81.
[68] See John Battelle, *The Search: How Google and Its Rivals Rewrote the Rules of Business and Transformed Our Culture* (London: Nicholas Brealey, 2005).

creative potential of empirical mechanisms, clickstream 'identities', and digital memories. Langbaum nonetheless argued that in reaction against a restricted system with 'a fixed number of sensations', Wordsworth had helped to introduce 'the new romantic concept of the self'. In this dynamic self, says Langbaum, personal identity evolves 'through experience'; and he conjectures how the poet would have answered Locke the mechanistic Philosopher:

[Wordsworth's] answer would be that computers will never be human—will never have continuity or identity—until they are born and grow up and can therefore have the changing memory of change that constitutes awareness of one's own identity.[69]

It is a remarkable scenario, given that this concept of human identity is in every respect Lockean.

As was argued in the previous chapter, the old binary of mechanistic empiricism against a dynamic 'romanticism' should now be laid to rest.[70] The latter term does not need to define itself in opposition to a labelled block of ideas, and this particular package oversimplifies the 'romantic' as much as it does empiricism. Without a closer understanding of the many varied strands in eighteenth-century empiricist thought (of which this Lockean chapter has isolated just one) then the intellectual and poetic landscape of the 1790s risks being oversimplified. The eighteenth-century debates about personal identity that have been sketched here persisted through the 1790s and beyond, and the implications of Locke's experiential approach to 'identity and diversity' were if anything sharpened by the sociopolitical pressures of the revolutionary decade. These ideas were in the air. One day in 1794, according to his own account, the young William Hazlitt was stirred into thought about the question of his own identity, and about 'the conscious principle which alone connects the successive moments of our being together'.[71] He voiced his theory to Coleridge in 1798 and later expounded it in his earliest published work, *An Essay on the Principles of Human Action* (1805), which is a recognisably Lockean document.[72] In familiar terms Hazlitt describes how personal identity, as a mode of continuity, overrides interruptions:

[The child's] interests as an individual as well as his being must therefore be the same ... as long as he retains the consciousness of his past impressions connecting

[69] Robert Langbaum, *The Mysteries of Identity: A Theme in Modern Literature* (New York: Oxford University Press, 1977), 30.
[70] For a clear discussion of Romantic dynamics set against a 'mechanistic' Enlightenment paradigm, see Mark S. Lussier, *Romantic Dynamics: The Poetics of Physicality* (Houndmills: Macmillan; New York: St Martin's Press, 2000), 13–46.
[71] William Hazlitt, *An Essay on the Principles of Human Action* (London: J. Johnson, 1805). *The Complete Works of William Hazlitt*, ed. P. P. Howe, 21 vols (1930), i.29.
[72] See William Hazlitt, 'My First Acquaintance with Poets', in *Complete Works*, xvii.106–22. For an analysis of the *Essay*'s theorising on the imagination, see David Bromwich, *Hazlitt: The Mind of a Critic* (New York/Oxford: Oxford University Press, 1983), 46–57.

them together in one uniform or regular train of feeling: for the interruption of this sense of continued identity by sleep, inattention or otherwise seems from it's being afterwards renewed to prove the point more clearly. (i.29)

Building on this Lockean basis, and incorporating the concept of the sympathetic imagination that had developed since the 1720s,[73] Hazlitt came to the conclusion that while personal identity is indeed formed by the connected threads of our past experiences, any identification with our future selves, however forceful, can only be imagined; an active self-interest can therefore be no different in principle from an empathy for others. His essay moves from the connectedness of memory and sensation to the projections of a lively imagination. For Martin and Barresi, Hazlitt's 1805 essay represents 'the culmination of a kind of perspective on personal identity that began with Locke', while moving it towards fresh psychological insights 'that would not again be considered seriously until our own times'.[74]

To sum up my argument in this chapter: concepts of 'the romantic self' defined in opposition to 'empiricism' or 'the Enlightenment', or even 'the Eighteenth Century', have a tendency to overlook the organic features of Lockean identity and their persistence through the 1790s. Critical interest in the idealist theory of 'organic form' developed by Schlegel and Coleridge after 1800 has drawn attention away from an earlier empirical 'organic' that was interested in modes of organisation, and in how meanings and values are generated through individual experience. By tracing some of the implications of Locke's account of personal identity, I have simultaneously tried to develop a reading of this organic that might constitute a native tradition running through the eighteenth century, and to set it alongside those dominant readings of a 'Romantic Organicism' concerned with teleological dynamics and issues of form and unity. In looking at an alternative scene I have wished to notice how within the constraining human dimensions of space and time small things relate and combine with each other, and how elements of association, aggregation, juxtaposition, mixture, and superimposition work to keep living systems alive. At a time when all foundational principles were being questioned and structures of every kind were being challenged, the nature of 'organisation' was at the forefront of people's minds, not least for Coleridge, Wordsworth, and their friends. At a time of widespread constitutional reorganisation, they were aware as individuals and citizens of the debates about continuity, identity, meaning, and value. The nature of history was at the centre of these, and on that topic also it is possible to identify an eighteenth-century organic tradition that helped shape the arguments of the decade. The question of what might constitute 'organic history' is the subject of the following chapter.

---

[73] See Walter Jackson Bate, 'The Sympathetic Imagination in Eighteenth-Century English Criticism', *ELH*, 12 (1945), 144–64.

[74] Martin and Barresi, *Naturalization of the Soul*, 139–48.

3   Organic Constitutions: History

Subsequent additions to historic buildings, including minor accretions such as conservatories, porches, balconies, verandas, door dressings, bargeboards or chimneys, do not necessarily detract from the quality of a building. They are often of interest in their own right as part of the building's organic history. Generally, later features of interest should not be removed merely to restore a building to an earlier form.

—*Planning Policy Guidance 15: Planning and the historic environment* (HMSO, 1994), Annex C5

As if in reaction to the complexities of dating something called 'the Romantic period', a concept of 'the *moment* of Romanticism' has become popular. Whether it is the *pristine* moment, the *iconic* moment, the *oneiric* moment, or simply 'the *defining* moment' of Romanticism, the need for a transformative 'moment' is evident in some critical writing. At one stroke the *Idea* of Romanticism can be declared without having to identify, characterise, and track any complex *phenomena* we might call 'Romantic'. The Idea is freed from history, while simultaneously intervening decisively in it. In their influential study, *The Literary Absolute*, Philippe Lacoue-Labarthe and Jean-Luc Nancy raise the stakes by making it also the quantum moment of 'the literary', the invention of literature. With absolute precision they pronounce that Romanticism 'constitutes the inaugural moment of literature as *production of its own theory*'.[1] Of course, this statement also realises the moment of their own theoretic inauguration. It is the performative language of the critic as *Logos*.

We are once again encountering the phenomenon of the Absolute, which has nowhere to go and nothing to say, because its unconditional condition is simply to be. It is its own category, relationless, without discursive meaning. Taking issue with their claim for literature as absolute knowledge, Jan Plug catches nicely the invertebrate quality of an absolute idealism that can be all over the place because it doesn't occupy time or space:

The literary *absolute* recuperates difference for identity, establishing itself as the ultimate identity of being and thinking, reality and ideality. As such, it ultimately

---

[1] Philippe Lacoue-Labarthe and Jean-Luc Nancy, *The Literary Absolute: The Theory of Literature in German Romanticism* (Albany: SUNY Press, 1988), xxii. In their preface the authors specifically abjure a historical approach to Romanticism ('we are not engaging in an archival enterprise . . . a monumental or antiquarian history'), though they offer a useful brief sketch of 'the massive equivocity that underlies the term "romanticism."' (3).

maintains the structure of absolute idealism with the 'difference' that the absolute now finds its ultimate fulfilment in the literary.[2]

There are no coordinates here, no penultimate to make the *ultimate* mean something. The more that word is used (here three times) the more enigmatic the notion becomes: there is seemingly a 'structure' with no space to occupy, a 'fulfilment' with no process behind it. It would appear that in this unarticulated (and inarticulate) form, all truth is absolute, all value intrinsic, and all meaning evidently tautological, since there is no room to extend or develop it.

The notional pinhead becomes even more crowded when idealist organicism and 'modernity' are reintroduced into this synchronic frame. The result is Donald Wesling's insight that 'Modernity and organic form are born at the same time ... their origin, at the moment of Romanticism and Coleridgean poetics and methodology, is our moment too.'[3] This is the cultural equivalent of the Big Bang—we are all of us simultaneously caught up along with Coleridge in the very moment of modernity-as-now, a situation that unerringly recalls the fervid presentness of Swift's 'ultimate' modern, who writes his *Tale of a Tub* shortly after his release from Bedlam. He is living the actual *now* of his text and thus claims, he declares, 'an absolute Authority in Right, as the *freshest Modern*', so that, as he remarks in his preface, 'what I am going to say is literally true this Minute I am writing'.[4]

The contrasting organic history I want to characterise in this chapter is one that is discounted by idealist theory as being empirical, archival, antiquarian. It must be admitted that instead of the Absolute, organic history tends to give us the multifarious, even the muddled; in place of the Idea is the awkward fact; instead of the defining moment there is an uncertain tradition. This organic history exists within time and is filtered through experience and contingency. It thus becomes difficult to exploit it as a tool for some end, since it has none—hence its irrelevance not merely for idealist philosophers, but for anyone who would view history teleologically as having a purposive direction. From the viewpoint of Marxist materialism, for example, mere 'historicism' is nostalgic self-indulgence, the province of the garrulous storyteller of romance. In the words of Walter Benjamin in the 1930s:

The historical materialist leaves it to others to be drained by the whore called 'Once upon a time' in historicism's bordello. He remains in control of his powers, man enough to blast open the continuum of history.[5]

[2] Jan Plug, 'Romanticism and the Invention of Literature', in Tilottama Rajan and Arkady Plotnitsky (eds), *Idealism without Absolutes: Philosophy and Romantic Culture* (Albany: SUNY Press, 2004), 15–37 (15).

[3] Donald Wesling, *The Chances of Rhyme: Device and Modernity* (Berkeley: University of California Press, 1980), 2.

[4] Jonathan Swift, *A Tale of a Tub, etc.*, ed. Frank Ellis (Frankfurt: Peter Lang, 2006), 56 (Section V), 10 (Dedication).

[5] Walter Benjamin, *Theses on the Philosophy of History*, 16, in *Illuminations*, ed. Hannah Arendt (London: Fontana/Collins, 1973), 264. More recently, Jerome Christensen has spoken of

The enemy of both idealism and materialism, the so-called 'historicist' luxuriates in the story of the past, so that the potentially decisive 'now' is rendered impotent. In contrast, Benjamin's 'historical materialist' intervenes dramatically to destabilise the status quo.

This is revolutionary language. It was the talk of late summer 1789, when during the constitutional debates in the French Assembly 'the continuum of history' confronted the philosophical Idea, and lost. Since then, there has been a tendency to align 1790s 'Romanticism' with the latter, and to view the former as the equivalent of a reactionary *ancien régime*, rather than as what it in fact was: a 'reformist' position that took the American and British constitutions as models. The revolutionary Idea, however, won the day decisively. The defeated 'Américanistes' who looked back to historical precedent were practical-minded reformers, and they were not fired by nostalgia but by pragmatism. Attempting to make sense of the past and find continuities with it is not, I hope to show, a nostalgic recoil from new challenges, but something more dynamic and committed. By making what I term this 'organic' sense of history the focus of discussion, I want to trace the eighteenth-century roots of an idea that could be both thought-provoking and imaginatively attractive to intelligent young reform-minded individuals in the 1790s. Closely linked to the notions of organic identity discussed in Chapter 2, this history offered not conservative nostalgia, but more subtle and challenging ideas about the self and the world. It becomes clear how organic modes of thought might refuse a revolutionary confrontation: their mixed and adaptive character resisted polarities, and thus served to complicate any line of thought that appeared clear-cut or decisive. Organic history encouraged the kind of thoughtfulness which revisited, measured, and re-aligned ideas, and as such was deliberative, open to amendment, collaboration, and negotiation. It was therefore alien to the political labelling that the language of dispute often reaches for. Whatever terminology we use to represent the full spectrum of opinion at this period (revolutionary–radical–reformist–conservative–reactionary) these limited categories will inevitably oversimplify what from an organic viewpoint is more relational and developmental.[6] Positions changed during the 1790s, but so did the local and national context; and the importance of 'context' is, as I hope we shall continue to see, at the heart of organic meaning.

Eighteenth-century organic history, like Lockean personal identity, is neither continuous nor unified, but takes its character from elements of mixture, accretion, and association. In many ways it represents a broader projection of those processes of organising experience discussed in the

'the historicist, dead set on decoding the iron logic of past events' (*Romanticism at the End of History* (Baltimore: Johns Hopkins University Press, 2004), 2).

[6] For a considered analysis of the range of 'reformist' and 'radical' positions in the 1790s, see Pamela Edwards, *The Statesman's Science: History, Nature, and Law in the Political Thought of Samuel Taylor Coleridge* (New York: Columbia University Press, 2004), 11–28.

previous chapter. With an openness to the impure and untidy, it resists being directed by a metaphysical Idea, an absolute reality or universal truth, or teleologies of any kind. The emphasis is not on making history but on understanding it. It does not offer an agenda, but is attentive to the minuted records, trying to make sense of the materials of the past while remaining itself firmly in the present. But the 'now' of this history, like an organic identity pieced together from memory, is to some extent a survivor, a sum of the past (with a wise knowledge, one would hope). It is not a confident inaugurating 'moment', but something closer to a layered awareness of the present; it aspires to be a rich narrative rather than a vivid drama. Organic history offers no vantage point for declaring the truth, but works to retrieve meanings from what may be faded or fragmentary, so that its characteristic image is the uncertain, exploratory, even disappearing line.

Perhaps the eighteenth century's greatest linear visualiser of history was Giovanni Battista Piranesi, whose engravings explore a series of mighty edifices caught in its gaze. They offer a range of historical scenarios, from fantasies of structural power to scenes of melancholy decay; from the bold defiance of time to plates in which the artist traces its depredations with an almost palpable awareness of its processes, felt along the tendons of his own hand. Through his eighteenth-century eyes we can gain a sharper awareness of three distinct modes of history, which came into conflict during the 1790s when the nature of history itself was at the centre of debate.

In the title page to his earliest work, the *Prima Parte di Architetture* (1743), Piranesi gives us an eloquent image of history as destruction and loss (Figure 1). At the bottom of the picture are jumbled architectural fragments, but towards the centre, defiantly legible, is the title of his work, which seems freshly cut into the marble. Alongside, the urn and bust still stand miraculously clear and sharply defined, and the title slab leans back, simultaneously facing them and the light. In the foreground a sinister funerary pyramid encroaches from the left but only with the effect of brightening everything else. The threat hovers there, but this remains a scene over which an ancient temple presides, and where classic lines hold their ground despite the work of time and the barbarian hordes. The eternal forms still shine through.

But the image was later reworked by Piranesi, and here I think we're drawn into a different world (Figure 2). The stark juxtapositions of the earlier plate have now become more integrated in mood and texture. What we see is no longer a gothic threat to the classical, but an organic convergence of the forces of growth and decay—a scene of evolving history. In this second picture, Time is at work and new forms are taking shape before our eyes. Here the urn moves from being a product of art to a process of nature; or more precisely it elicits from the engraver a different technique where lines cease to contain and define but become wandering, excrescent, and suggestive, simultaneously mouldering but also moulding new shapes from

1. Giovanni Battista Piranesi, *Prima Parte di Architetture* (1743). Frontispiece: first version.
Reproduced by permission of the Ashmolean Museum, University of Oxford.

2. Giovanni Battista Piranesi, *Prima Parte di Architetture* (1743). Frontispiece: later version.
Reproduced by permission of the Ashmolean Museum, University of Oxford.

the material. In a visual joke Piranesi now makes the tree behind appear to grow out of the urn itself, hinting at continuities between art and nature. A gap between the dead and the living has been bridged, and the urn seems to be ageing, absorbed into the ongoing life around it. The carved inscription is less incisive; it is fading and cracking, but now clambering figures greet it with a sense of excited discovery. The old is somehow the new, something remarkable and intriguing. In this scene the emphasis has shifted from a text as objective statement to a text in process of being read, mediated to us through the responses of the human figures—and their sensibilities, knowledge, and curiosity are now part of the meaning of the plate. But the finger is pointing, not to the words, but the space beneath them where a cloudy miasma hints at shapes beginning to emerge. In Piranesi's equivalent of the blank page in *Tristram Shandy*, our eyes are directed to a gap, but one that imagination is invited to fill—'Please but your own fancy in it', Tristram says to his readers (vi.38). In this scene crammed with *memorabilia* there remains an inviting space for a text not yet written. The negative image of destruction has been reworked to express the continuities—and possibilities—of history, but also to suggest what a precarious enterprise this is likely to be, conducted not as a reassuring narrative of completion but as a more exploratory exercise of curiosity that attempts to piece together meaning from something jumbled and decaying.

When Edmund Burke spoke of the British constitution as a historical inheritance he did so in mixed terms like these, which acknowledge the degree to which continuities are compromised by decay and fragmentation. Whereas Tom Paine in *Rights of Man* (1791) looked optimistically for a freshly carved, pristine constitutional text, and poured scorn on history's 'musty records and mouldy parchments',[7] Burke celebrated historical processes and local accretions as something that guaranteed the nation's continuing organic life: 'The parts of our constitution', he remarked, 'have gradually, in a long course of time, accommodated themselves to each other, and to their common, as well as to their separate purposes.'[8] Articulated through such images, the 'Revolutionary Controversy' of the early 1790s was in some respects a debate about the validity of history. One of its prime questions focused on the matter of continuity: must we repeatedly dust off and piece together meanings from the past, or should mankind be free to start again, to announce the birth of a New Adam and discard the accumulated chronology, the unreconstructed back-story? Precedent, it was argued, led to prejudice; and the sheer weight of historical evidence and authority compromised the clarity of thought needed to see directly into the

---

[7] Thomas Paine, *Rights of Man*, ed. Henry Collins (Harmondsworth: Penguin Books, 1976), 67. All future references will be to this edition.

[8] Edmund Burke, *A Letter from Mr Burke, to a Member of the National Assembly* (London: J. Dodsley, 1791), reprinted in *The Writings and Speeches of Edmund Burke*, ed. Paul Langford, 12 vols (Oxford: Clarendon Press, 1981–), viii.331.

truth of things. 'We have no occasion to roam for information into the obscure field of antiquity,' said Paine, 'The real volume, not of history, but of facts, is directly before us.'[9] It is a text, he implies, that is clear and simple, and above all unmediated. For Burke, however, it was the complicated intertexture of history that made it so precious: it meant that we had to recognise that truth and value are not abstractions, but are embedded in human experience and need to be viewed from multiple perspectives in time and space. Once again, the empirical claim is made in denying the self-sufficiency of Idea. In Burke's thought, 'meaning' is not inherent, but is discovered and expressed through discourse. He therefore has an argumentative investment in the habitual, connected, and associative. Principles of retrospection and incorporation are integral to the nature of Burke's organic constitution, which sees the past as expressing a national inheritance. What Burke valued was not an incisive, unambiguous constitutional declaration, but a cumulative historical tradition, its line scarcely decipherable in places, but organically embodying what he called 'the great mysterious incorporation of the human race ... [which] moves on through the varied tenour of perpetual decay, fall, renovation, and progression'.[10]

What Burke's detractors saw, of course, was futile nostalgia for an old gothic structure that had outlived its usefulness. 'Why was it a duty', responded Mary Wollstonecraft in her *Vindication of the Rights of Men*, 'to repair an ancient castle, built in barbarous ages, of Gothic materials?'[11] This alludes to earlier eighteenth-century celebrations of the nation's historically 'mixed' constitution grounded in the body of English law, an institution which Lord Lyttelton had characterised in 1735 as resembling an 'old *Gothick* Pile':

The Foundations of it are deep and very lasting; it has stood many Ages, and with good Repairs may stand many more; But the Architecture is loaded with a multiplicity of idle and useless Parts; when you examine it critically, many Faults and Imperfections will appear; yet upon the whole it has a mighty awful Air, and strikes you with Reverence and Respect.[12]

It was this ramshackle edifice of historic common law that William Blackstone similarly described as 'a huge irregular pile'. It had become, he wrote in 1746,

[9] Paine, *Rights of Man*, 207. John Whale remarks that Paine 'short-circuits the whole of history by making it look like a rather inadequate and forlorn product of human invention' (*Imagination under Pressure, 1789–1832: Aesthetics, Politics and Utility* (Cambridge: Cambridge University Press, 2000), 56).
[10] Edmund Burke, *Reflections on the Revolution in France*, ed. Conor Cruise O'Brien (Harmondsworth: Penguin, 1986), 120. All future references will be to this edition.
[11] Mary Wollstonecraft, *Vindication of the Rights of Men* (London: J. Johnson, 1790), 100 (reprinted in *The Works of Mary Wollstonecraft*, ed. Janet Todd and Marilyn Butler, 7 vols (London: Pickering and Chatto, 1989), v.41).
[12] George Lyttelton, *Letters from a Persian in England, to his Friend at Ispahan* (London: J. Millan, 2nd edn., 1735), 71. The Persian traveller is being guided round Westminster Hall. The book was reprinted in 1793.

swollen, shrunk, curtailed, enlarged, altered and mangled...with many of its most useful parts pulled down, with preposterous additions in other places of different materials and coarse workmanship, according to the whim or prejudice or private convenience of the builders. By which means the communication of the parts is destroyed, and their harmony quite annihilated.[13]

But as a legal reformer he saw his project to be not the building's demolition but its repair. As a haphazard growth it had accrued so many documents, musty rolls, charters, and evidences—a wealth of human experience, judgment, and folly—that it was hard to discern any controlling shape.

Burke's opponents recognised exactly the same thing, but to them this constitutional gothic grotesque was less an intertext of oddly connected parts than one huge, oppressive edifice.[14] When they looked at it they saw something closer to Piranesi's *Carceri d'Invenzione*, his engravings of imaginary prisons. Here the engraver explores a markedly different line, and I think conveys a less benign sense of history. In *Carceri* Plate VII, for example (Figure 3), the lines do not play or wander but seem to be obeying some impersonal force. Connections between the various planes of walkways and bridges are misaligned, or even absent. The tiny figures only add to the sense that this is not a scene that invites a human response. It has been designed by a single mind-as-system, determined and implacable. The brutal, jagged lines seem part of a plan that is withheld from us: seen from a wider angle the design might make sense, but we are caught in one perspective. Rather than being invited to explore, these figures are trapped within the unsettling space. Nothing grows or develops, just endlessly reproduces,[15] and the accumulated masonry shows no signs of decay; the massed lines build up as appositions rather than interconnections. There is no playful movement: they abut each other without engagement or continuity. Rather than suggesting a connected narrative, this scene offers a disturbing enigma, and our curiosity is tinged by fear. It speaks of oppression and tyranny. Everything is old and set in stone; supporting structures underpin other supporting structures, as if to shore up a massive project beyond our reach or influence. There appears no way out, and the only escape might be with the help of gunpowder.

---

[13] William Blackstone to Seymour Richmond, 28 Jan. 1746 (MS Harvard Law School Library; quoted by Ian Doolittle, *William Blackstone: A Biography* (Haslemere: I. Doolittle, 2001), 44).

[14] Helen Maria Williams remarked: 'the old constitution is connected in my mind with the image of a friend confined in the gloomy recesses of a dungeon, and pining in hopeless captivity' (*Letters Written in France in the Summer 1790, to a Friend in England* (London: T. Cadell, 1790), 71–2).

[15] Thomas De Quincey's *Carceri*-inspired dream captures the potential of its architecture for endless frustrating self-reproduction, organic yet disturbingly disconnected. See *Confessions of an English Opium-Eater*, in *The Works of Thomas De Quincey*, ed. Grevel Lindop et al., 21 vols (London: Pickering and Chatto, 2000–3), ii.68.

3. Giovanni Battista Piranesi, *Carceri d'Invenzione* (*c*.1745), Plate 7 (second state). Reproduced by permission of the Ashmolean Museum, University of Oxford.

These three Piranesi plates suggest different readings of history. In the first an ideal, classical past is recoverable from the depredations of time; in the second, history is a continuing organic process of decay and growth, loss and potential; while in the third, history has become an imprisoning fatalistic structure. To say that these might represent history as seen respectively by Edward Gibbon, by Thomas Warton, and by Tom Paine (classical history, antiquarian history, and radical history) is probably too neat, but it does help me to convey the distinctive qualities of eighteenth-century 'organic' history (the second of the three) in terms of its mixed aesthetic and its antiquarian character. Where Figures 1 and 3 tend to exploit dramatic contrast, Figure 2 integrates its different parts by mood/tone so that the pieces seem to play and converse with each other. Rather than rediscovering an ideal form hidden amongst the rubbish, it suggests that meaning can be found in the fragments and confused lines themselves. The engraving challenges notions of hierarchy and inherent value by bringing substance and decoration, figure and symbol, stone and leaf, dead and living, into the same visual discourse, making us notice textures and discover new modes of attention. In this organic world, we have moved from beautiful forms to interesting shapes.

What I am characterising as 'organic history' emerged into prominence in Britain during the eighteenth century, a period when historicist scholarship, antiquarianism, archaeology, and local history began to flourish.[16] Being led by practical research (artefact and record) rather than theory, it had to accommodate discontinuities and decay, and involved a fascinating struggle not only to trace meanings across time but to discover new meanings in the temporal process itself. These tend to have 'gothic' elements to the degree that they are uncertain, labyrinthine, ambivalent, provisional—rather than clear and prescriptive. The truths of this history tend to be circumstantial ones, dependent on context. From the writer's viewpoint, instead of a confident assertion of one's own power to 'perform' meaning through the Adamic 'now' of the text, to declare truth and intervene in history, organic history has tended to reward a more circumspect empirical curiosity, in which a capacity to notice things goes along with a recognition of the often haphazard way meanings and values evolve. In this scenario, loss can be registered as gain, as the poet and painter John Dyer found in the 1720s while sketching ruins on the Sacred Way in Rome:

---

[16] Eighteenth-century literary historicism is a large topic. See René Wellek, *The Rise of English Literary History* (Chapel Hill: University of North Carolina Press, 1941); Arthur Johnston, *Enchanted Ground: The Study of Medieval Romance in the Eighteenth Century* (London: Athlone Press, 1964); Lawrence Lipking, *The Ordering of the Arts in Eighteenth-Century England* (Princeton: Princeton University Press, 1970); Trevor Ross, *The Making of the English Literary Canon: From the Middle Ages to the Late Eighteenth Century* (Montreal/Kingston: McGill-Queen's University Press, 1998).

I can't help thinking the triumphal arches more beautiful now than ever they were, there is a certain greenness, with many other colours, and a certain disjointedness and moulder among the stones, something so pleasing in their weeds and tufts of myrtle, and something in the altogether so greatly wild, that mingling with art, and blotting out the traces of disagreeable squares and angles, adds certain beauties that could not be before imagined.[17]

It is in the 'disjointedness and moulder' that he discovers the lineaments of a new, non-classical aesthetic. This is not something asserted by the structure of the masonry, but is traced intriguingly *among* the stones, in the decaying materiality itself, in the stones' subtle articulation of a meaning between, rather than in, or beyond, themselves. It is a creative moment when Dyer recognises that he is looking less at things than at random dispositions and relationships, mere weeds and outgrowths, sketching what is superimposed and accretive, working with gaps and organic malformations, with decay and growth together. The artist's tracings move towards potential narrative, and indeed years later they underpinned his melancholy poetic recollection of his Italian journey, *The Ruins of Rome* (1740).

What Dyer and Piranesi are seeing is really history as evolution, but not in terms of a smooth progress. Clearly, dramatic event and sudden loss are being subsumed into growth and change of a more comprehensive kind. They leave their mark, but the effect registered is a more mixed one, neither smooth nor dramatic. What we are given is neither a teleological history (looking to some end or completion) nor a deconstructive history (working synchronically as events of disruption), but something closer to a discursive history that attempts a connective reading of its scattered materials. As a mode of narrative this is no easy continuity—quite the opposite—since the connections are made with recalcitrant materials across the fissures of time. Such gaps are important (as we saw in the previous chapter in terms of Lockean identity) because in defiance of the logic of scepticism they confirm the presence of a persisting consciousness, through which growth and continuity are perceptible (Chapter 4 will find the process at work in Wordsworth's 'Lines written a few miles above Tintern Abbey'). Organic history has its own version in the way the author's personal tastes and insights can seem to be guiding the reader through the story.

One writer who found a living text in the 'mouldering roll' of the past and attempted to represent it as narrative was Thomas Warton, the pioneer literary historian whose influence on the work of the Coleridge circle during the 1790s was considerable. He began his lifelong archival researches in 1750 at a time when the materials of literary history were largely unexplored

---

[17] John Dyer to ?, *c.*1724–5. See *John Dyer: Selected Poetry and Prose*, ed. John Goodridge (Nottingham: Trent Editions, 2000), 22. The letter was first printed by William Hilton Long-staffe, 'Notes respecting the life and family of John Dyer the Poet', *The Patrician*, 4 (1847), 7–12, 264–8, 420–6, and 5 (1848), 75–81, 218–35. The quotation occurs at 4, 266.

and the few written accounts took the form of biographical dictionaries, bibliographies, catalogues, editions, commentaries, anthologies, and diagrams of literary 'schools'.[18] Warton's choice of a narrative format was by no means obvious, but he determined to move away from existing schematic models towards a more organic and developmental approach.[19] Through the recovery of poetic texts and his tracing lines of connection between them, Warton enabled readers and writers to appreciate the richness of Britain's literary past and to view it as an uneven story, producing the first connected account of literary history from the Conquest to the beginning of the seventeenth century.[20]

As the first narrative of English literature, Warton's lines are forever wandering, disappearing and being retraced, and he frustrated his more polite readers by his failure to offer a smooth and tasteful progress through the centuries. Warton knew that his materials were diverse and vast (the *History* mentions some seven hundred manuscripts and twice as many printed books), and he was unwilling to systematise what was an extraordinarily varied and wide-ranging field. Whereas both Pope and Gray had projected a history of poetry on a scheme that divided poets tidily into separate 'Schools',[21] Warton resisted the taxonomic approach because, 'like other ingenious systems, [it] sacrificed much useful intelligence to the observation of arrangement'. He explains in his Preface that '[t]he constraint imposed by a mechanical attention to this distribution, appeared to me to destroy that free exertion of research with which such a history ought to be executed, and not easily reconcileable with that complication, variety, and extent of materials, which it ought to comprehend.'[22] Warton presents his own history to the reader as having a more capacious and flexible character.

He set out with the aim of showing the improvement of English poetry from barbarity to refinement; but as his project developed he came to see that a smooth line of progressive history was not going to be true to his subject. 'I have often deviated', he writes, 'into incidental digressions; and

---

[18] See Wellek, *Rise of English Literary History*, 131–65.

[19] On Warton's earlier attempts to organise his materials, see David Fairer, 'The Origins of Warton's *History of English Poetry*', *RES*, 32 (1981), 37–63. On the 'romantic' character of narrative literary history, see Clifford Siskin, *The Historicity of Romantic Discourse* (New York: Oxford University Press, 1988). See also David Perkins, *Is Literary History Possible?* (Baltimore: Johns Hopkins University Press, 1992), 86–7.

[20] For a full account of Warton's work on the *History*, see *Thomas Warton's History of English Poetry* (facsimile edition), intro. David Fairer, 4 vols (London: Routledge/Thoemmes Press, 1998), i.1–70.

[21] See below, pp. 122–3. On the diagrammatic sketches of the history of English poetry drawn up by Pope and Gray, see Wellek, *Rise of English Literary History*, 162–5. Gray's plan includes the First, Second, and Third 'Italian Schools' and splits Milton, Cowley, and Waller into separate groupings. For Gray's letter and Warton's reply, see *The Correspondence of Thomas Warton*, ed. David Fairer (Athens/London: University of Georgia Press, 1995), 280–5.

[22] Thomas Warton, *The History of English Poetry, from the Close of the Eleventh to the Commencement of the Eighteenth Century*, 3 vols (London: J. Dodsley, etc., 1774–81), i.v.

have sometimes stopped in the course of my career... for the purpose of collecting scattered notices.' In Warton's heavily footnoted volumes, continuities are won from a struggle with uncooperative sources, in face of a digressive impulse and a delight in details gathered from obscure records. He becomes aware that an attempt to chart the 'progress' of poetry is being countered by repeated relapses and setbacks (the whole of the fifteenth century is for Warton one great setback), with loss and renewal of inspiration, followed by recovery and re-connection to the tradition. It is clear that had he continued his history through the seventeenth century, the story would have become one of partial decline and would not have climaxed in an 'Augustan' achievement post-1660 (he speaks of 'the national taste... corrupted by the false and capricious refinements of the court of Charles the Second', iii.440). 'Refinement' was not a positive word for Warton because it suggested filtering out the boldness and variety of the native tradition. He wanted things to exhibit a strong individual character and not be compromised by codes of politeness, regularity, or morality (Calvinism was the enemy here). In the *History* he admires both gothic extravagance and classical simplicity; but he dislikes imitation ('that bane of invention') especially when it tries to refine its cruder original.[23] He is no generic purist, and is genuinely delighted by cultural mixtures. In Elizabethan times, he recalls, '[e]ven the pastry-cooks were expert mythologists. At dinner, select transformations of Ovid's metamorphoses were exhibited in confectionary: and the splendid iceing of an immense historic plumb-cake, was embossed with a delicious basso-relievo of the destruction of Troy' (iii.492). Organic history indeed.

Warton devotes the final chapter of volume iii to a celebration of Elizabeth's reign, when romance was imbued with the classical spirit, and reason and imagination engaged creatively with each other. Variety and ambivalence provide the keys to what is for him 'the most POETICAL age of these annals':

[T]he reformation had not yet destroyed every delusion, nor disinchanted all the strong holds of superstition. *A few dim characters were yet legible in the mouldering creed of tradition.* Every goblin of ignorance did not vanish at the first glimmerings of the morning of science. Reason suffered a few demons still to linger, which she chose to retain in her service under the guidance of poetry. (iii.496; my italics)

Warton continues in this vein, conjuring the excitements of an uncertain history pieced together from the fading past. A sense of incongruity, which in other hands might have been satiric, here creates a richly ambivalent experience, the dawning light of reason without the full glare of enlightenment. Warton understood the spell of dark corners. Not only were cupboards and

---

[23] Warton, *History of English Poetry*, ii.463. Discussing Pope's Chaucerian imitation, *The Temple of Fame* (1715), Warton comments: 'I think I am walking among the modern monuments unsuitably placed in Westminster-abbey' (i.396).

dusty corners a speciality, but he packed into his footnotes material from
monastic records, wardrobe lists, legal documents, letters, charters, and
inventories. Lines of thought were often diverted down inviting narrow
passageways. His curious extended footnote on the history of medieval
beards would not seem out of place in *Tristram Shandy*.[24]

What Laurence Sterne's hero says of his life story ('In a word, my work is
digressive, and it is progressive too,—and at the same time')[25] could be the
epigraph of Warton's *History*; and the erratic wavy lines of Tristram's
narrative catch the spirit of Warton's book also, quirky arabesques that
track the shifting character of the material. Both these texts, the fictional
and the historical, progress by confronting a disordered mixture; they re-
peatedly turn aside to notice things, then return and recall themselves to the
job in hand ('I ought to have mentioned this before', Warton adds disarm-
ingly at the end of one footnote).[26] And where Sterne's narrative lines turn,
twist, and entangle, while also manifesting disconcerting holes and fissures,
Warton also works his materials with an awareness that for every traced
connection there is a gap. Both these large eighteenth-century books give us
history-as-process: where Tristram is assembling his selfhood from the odd
experiences of his life, so Warton is trying to find a way through the untidy
miscellaneousness of the literary past. In their attempts to write their re-
spective histories these books share an empirical sensibility in which know-
ledge is always a kind of reconstruction from the scattered materials of
perception.

An historical sense thus emerged during the eighteenth century in which
ideas of growth and mixture combine, in which discontinuities (Dyer's
disjointedness) are subsumed into larger continuities, disparate details are
embraced by intangible associations, digressions turned into repeated recon-
nections. By acknowledging time-as-process, what I understand as 'organic'
history tends to be linear rather than hierarchical, and associative rather
than taxonomic. It is untidy, antiquarian, localised history, the kind in which
the youthful Thomas Chatterton took delight as he set out to recreate
around his invented Rowley poems a whole panoply of fictional pedigrees,
inventories, deeds, coins, heraldries, maps, and inscriptions, but out of
which grew a complete imagined world and a lost tradition of poetry.[27] In
the *Reflections* Burke invokes Britain's inherited liberties in terms that
exactly describe Chatterton's Rowleian world: 'it has a pedigree and illus-
trating ancestors. It has its bearings and its ensigns armorial. It has its gallery
of portraits; its monumental inscriptions; its records, evidences, and titles'

---

[24] Warton, *History of English Poetry*, ii.362–3.
[25] Laurence Sterne, *Tristram Shandy*, ed. Melvyn New et al., 3 vols (Gainesville, Fl: Univer-
sity Presses of Florida, 1978–84), i.22.
[26] Warton, *History of English Poetry*, iii.450, note z.
[27] For the fullest account, see Donald S. Taylor, *Thomas Chatterton's Art: Experiments in
Imagined History* (Princeton: Princeton University Press, 1978).

(121). What Tom Paine saw as mouldy lumber was for Burke, Warton, and Chatterton the very fabric of the past (in Chatterton's case fabricated) which sanctioned their own writing. From a radical viewpoint, Chatterton's project would seem to exemplify a model of 'conservative' Burkean history, characterised by mementoes, genealogies, and an idealised patriotism. But this is to ignore how the youth used his Rowley archive to indict contemporary culture and align himself with the radical Wilkes and against 'Bristol's current clerical intelligentsia . . . the corrupt agents of a false political and cultural establishment'.[28] He aimed to create a multilayered regional culture, with the fifteenth-century Bristol of Rowley and Canynge at its centre, where local charities and honest virtues might operate. A compound phrase like 'satiric nostalgia' is needed to catch the way Chatterton finds in the old feudal relationships something more genuine and sustaining than impersonal modern systems can offer. His medievalist texts, we should remember, were supplemented by verse satires exposing court corruptions and the national power structure they sustained.

An organic language can make the language of power uneasy. Like Dyer's crumbling triumphal arch it is made to speak differently. The smooth confidence of the powerful may easily be disconcerted by an unfamiliar voice, an awkward detail, a rough surface, or unpredictable movement. Adaptive texts that are elusive, quirky, and hard to categorise are able to short-circuit centres of power—political, social, or critical. They refuse to be drawn into dialectic, to play by the rules. As we know, power systems need to be self-contained for maximum efficiency; upon entering loose, untidy organic territory, however, their effect is localised and dispersed. The charge, almost literally, is earthed. The power game is refused. This is an odd metaphor, but is no less appropriate for that, and it hopes to carry the point that a binary politics, which sounds so combative and strong, has the weakness of rigidity, a failure to adapt and move into a new area.

Such thoughts have a particular bearing on another poetic text that has the character of organic history and which is hard to categorise both politically and generically. Entering Mary Leapor's 'Crumble-Hall' (1751), the reader moves through a labyrinthine old manor house in which the history of many generations is embedded.[29] But the building is not read for us in any clear and coherent way: meanings of all kinds are jumbled together, the symbolic with the anecdotal, and hierarchies and order go for nothing. There are emblems and remnants at every level from the armorial achievements of its former Plantagenet owners to the rusting bric-a-brac in the attic. The heroic tapestries are awkward and baffling, but we admire the polished brass nails on the back of an armchair. In the banqueting hall, where knights

---

[28] Jonathan Barry, 'Chatterton in Bristol', *Angelaki*, 1:2 (1993–4), 55–81 (74). Barry characterises Chatterton's work in terms of 'patriotic radicalism'.

[29] Mary Leapor, *Poems upon Several Occasions* (London: J. Roberts, 1751), 111–22.

and rustics once mingled, our attention switches between the spider's web in the roof and the family coat of arms that must be dusted once a year. Our guide, the chattering maidservant, takes us on a winding route through a place where she, for all her humble station, feels at home. She directs us round the house's twists and turns like an expert, leading us along the mouse-infested passageways, up to the roof and down again to the kitchen, where the smells of well-hung game, boiled cabbage, and foaming bran compete with the sounds of clattering, barking, and snoring. This is no even progress, but like the history of the building, our route is a twisting and uncertain one that doubles back upon itself:

> Would you go farther?—Stay a little then:
> Back thro' the Passage—down the Steps again;
> Thro' yon dark Room—Be careful how you tread
> Up these steep Stairs—or you may break your Head (ll.94–7)

The history too seems a tale of reversal and decline rather than of progress. But as Leapor continues to describe it we realise the place is animated and full of life—thanks not to its owners, who are either absent or asleep, but to the servants who keep the place going. It is with a cry of pain that Leapor signals the house's approaching destruction. Already the old oak trees are being felled and carted off like aged retainers no longer of use:

> Shall these ignobly from their Roots be torn,
> And perish shameful, as the abject Thorn;
> While the slow Carr bears off their aged Limbs,
> To clear the Way for Slopes, and modern Whims (ll.173–6)

The scene is being levelled, and the house will follow, its gothic incongruities swept away, to be replaced (as it indeed was) by an elegant Palladian mansion, in which a maidservant will know her place.

Perhaps because of its mixture of tones, a lively delight alternating with sharp judgment, 'Crumble-Hall' has been hard to place poetically and politically. It has been interpreted as a servant's satiric resistance to the feudal values of the gentry, and conversely as a conservative text that looks back nostalgically to the old order.[30] Each reading finds quotations to support it. But a radical/conservative binary oversimplifies Leapor's shrewd intelligence, which recognises how ambivalent history can be, and how puzzling its messages are. From the outset we see that it is an inconvenient, gothic structure. Bits have obviously been added on here and there;

---

[30] The former line is taken by Donna Landry, *The Muses of Resistance: Labouring-Class Women's Poetry in Britain, 1739–1796* (Cambridge: Cambridge University Press, 1990); the latter by Richard Greene, *Mary Leapor: A Study in Eighteenth-Century Women's Poetry* (Oxford: Clarendon Press, 1993).

the rooms are a jumble with no sign of planning. Form, unity, and symbol count for nothing, and there is no shaping ideal. But this need not be regarded as satiric criticism. Like a historical archive, the house and its contents have somehow accumulated over time, and it has become a mixed economy, largely independent of its negligent owners, and capacious enough to accommodate many forms of life, including Leapor herself. The organic quality lies here, in the way her practical, empirical perception guides us through the poem. This directing spirit is no abstraction, but something almost integral to the physical fabric of the place.

In the world of Warton, Tristram, Chatterton, and Leapor, the text of history is a weave of heterogeneous detail and imaginative projection, which has 'gothic' potential. A classical edifice would show the joins, but gothic, as its eighteenth-century aficionados understood, can accommodate a diversity of styles and add-ons. This kind of archival history tends to be provisional, and continuities are not necessarily conservative. As every politician knows, to make the voice of the past articulate to the present can be disconcerting and raise unsettling questions. The eighteenth-century antiquary was a figure who often shocked his politer contemporaries.[31] Ease and authority were hard to achieve, while doubts, loss, fragmentation, difficulty, and frustration were forever breaking through. In the world of antiquities (what Francis Bacon called 'Historie defaced') the impetus was more likely to be active curiosity rather than nostalgia.[32] The intriguing puzzles of antiquarian history typified by the textual lacuna ' ... [*hic multa desiderantur*] ...' became a staple topic of satire.[33]

Joseph Warton caught this well in a humorous epistle to his brother Thomas, contributed to the latter's verse collection, *The Oxford Sausage* (1764). It climaxes with a curse in which the historian is made to confront his nightmare scenario:

> But now may Curses every Search attend
> That seems inviting! May'st thou pore in vain
> For dubious Door-ways! May revengeful Moths
> Thy Ledgers eat! ...[34]

[31] See the classic study by D. C. Douglas, *English Scholars, 1660–1730* (2nd rev. edn; London: Eyre and Spottiswoode, 1951). As an unconventional Oxford professor, Thomas Warton was famously idiosyncratic and indecorous (see *The Poetical Works of the Late Thomas Warton, B.D.*, ed. Richard Mant (Oxford, 1802), i.ciii–cvi).

[32] 'Historie defaced, or some remnants of History, which have casually escaped the shipwreck of time' (Francis Bacon, *The Advancement of Learning*, ed. Michael Kiernan (Oxford: Clarendon Press, 2000), 65).

[33] Swift, *A Tale of a Tub*, 76 (Section IX: 'On Madness').

[34] 'Epistle, From Thomas Hearn, Antiquary, To the Author of The Companion to the Oxford Guide', in *The Oxford Sausage* [ed. Thomas Warton] (Oxford, 1764), 28; see Warton's *Poetical Works*, ii.189–91.

This gothic scene is one of gaps and frustrations, with lines often leading nowhere; but it suggests the potential excitements as well. What might, we wonder, be revealed in the moth-eaten ledgers or through a dubious doorway? The historian is placed in a situation akin to that of an Ann Radcliffe heroine a generation later, such as Adeline in *The Romance of the Forest* (1791), who finds a door hidden behind an arras, leading to long-abandoned apartments. Within one closet she makes the kind of discovery that would have thrilled Warton:

It was a small roll of paper, tied with a string, and covered with dust. Adeline took it up, and on opening it perceived an handwriting. She attempted to read it, but the part of the manuscript she looked at was so much obliterated, that she found this difficult, though what few words were legible impressed her with curiosity and terror... Adeline's light was now expiring in the socket, and the paleness of the ink, so feebly shone upon, baffled her efforts to discriminate the letters.[35]

The manuscript is of course the diary of a murdered prisoner who turns out to be her father, through whom Adeline is eventually able to claim her name and her inheritance. Thanks to a piece of fragmentary history she becomes integrated with her own history. It is easy to detect a conservative strand here; but woven into this 'patrimony' plot is a more radical scenario in which the manuscript allows her to expose a story of tyranny and cruelty—much as a modern war-crimes tribunal might piece together its documentation. Both Warton and Adeline are tracing the faint lines of history, but in Adeline's romance the fictional materials cooperate. The materials of the historian were more recalcitrant, and the acts of recovery more problematic.

For Paine, Burke's story of patrimony and inheritance turned the British Constitution into the text of gothic romance. Paine refused to think of the nation's history in these sentimental terms, and he wanted to break the familial link by insisting that each generation is an independent unit possessing the right to decide separately for itself: 'Every age and generation must be as free to act for itself, *in all cases*, as the ages and generations which preceded it' (63). In place of this language of discrete generations, Burke talks of a benign bequest, 'the patrimony of knowledge which was left us by our forefathers' (199), of 'a *stock* and root of *inheritance*' (109), an image of vital sustenance being drawn from the past.[36] One of the duties of the present, he maintains, is sustaining the organism's continued life.

The past for Burke is not detachable, and this has implications for written tradition. The nation's store of records and documents is its connective

[35] Ann Radcliffe, *The Romance of the Forest*, ed. Chloe Chard (Oxford: Oxford University Press, 1986), 116, 128 (chs. 8 and 9).
[36] 'We wished at the period of the Revolution, and do now wish, to derive all we possess as an inheritance from our forefathers. Upon that body and stock of inheritance we have taken care not to inoculate any cyon alien to the nature of the original plant' (Burke, *Reflections*, 117).

tissue, those 'vast libraries, which are the history of the force and weakness of the human mind; through great collections of antient records...which attest and explain laws and customs and continue the regards and connexions of life beyond the grave' (272). Paine in contrast denies any communication between past and future ('two non-entities, the one out of existence, and the other not in, and who never can meet in this world', 64–5). His project of discontinuity and discreteness, with only the 'now' having existence, is the opposite of Burke's concept of a contractual relationship 'between those who are living, those who are dead, and those who are to be born' (194–5), which he sets against the French Revolution's 'unsocial, uncivil, unconnected chaos of elementary principles' (195).

Reading the situation retrospectively, Burke saw such a return to first principles as a mode of *disorganisation*. The *OED*'s first recorded use of the verb is Burke's in 1793, in reference to the French Convention's decree 'for disorganizing every country in Europe, into which they should on any occasion set their foot'.[37] The identity of France was in Burke's terms being disorganised by its division and subdivision on a 'geometrical basis' into departments, communes, and cantons, an arrangement imposed by 'square measurement' (286). It was thus, by ignoring traditional local ties, losing its old *organised* nature. This was destroying Burke's concept of the organic nation, which he had articulated eight years earlier: 'a nation is not an idea only of local extent, and individual momentary aggregation; but it is an idea of continuity, which extends in time as well as in numbers and in space'.[38] In this constitutional dispute, Burke's historical archive encounters Paine's pristine text. A single document, which is the Painite constitution, is written, and by that inscription the new age is declared, while the body of the Burkean constitution labours through time, accommodating itself to change like the Lockean oak, adding and subtracting: '[It] moves on through the varied tenour of perpetual decay, fall, renovation, and progression. Thus, by preserving the method of nature in the conduct of the state, in what we improve we are never wholly new; in what we retain we are never wholly obsolete' (120).

This concept of a history that might act as the national equivalent of an organic personal identity was directly challenged by revolutionary thought, which wanted to structure the nation afresh. The new Adam needed no

---

[37] Edmund Burke, *Observations on the Conduct of the Minority* (1793). Reprinted in *The Writings and Speeches of Edmund Burke* (gen. ed. Paul Langford), vol. viii: *The French Revolution 1790–1794*, ed. L. G. Mitchell (Oxford: Clarendon Press, 1989), 424–5. In fact Burke had first used the word in *Reflections*, 302.

[38] Burke's speech 'On a Motion Made in the House of Commons...for a Committee to Enquire into the State of the Representation of the Commons in Parliament' (1782, not delivered), quoted in J. G. A. Pocock, 'Burke and the Ancient Constitution—A Problem in the History of Ideas', *The Historical Journal*, 3 (1960), 125–43 (140). See also Steven Blakemore, *Burke and the Fall of Language: The French Revolution as Linguistic Event* (Hanover, NH/ London: University Press of New England, 1988), 7.

family album. An uncoupling of past from present was absolutely necessary. The return to 'elementary principles' meant stripping away all associative context so as to locate intrinsic value, and also discounting all personal prejudices by removing anything subjective that might filter and refract—and thus distort—the truth. John Whale has spoken of 'the transparency of Paine's revolutionary literalism',[39] and this insight offers a helpful contrast with Burke's commitment to what is refracted. Burke writes:

These metaphysic rights, entering into common life, like rays of light which pierce into a dense medium, are, by the laws of nature, refracted from their straight line. Indeed in the gross and complicated mass of human passions and concerns, the primitive rights of men undergo such a variety of refractions and reflections, that it becomes absurd to talk of them as if they continued in the simplicity of their original direction.[40]

In Burke's organic constitution the primitive and originary have been mediated by time and experience in ways that reflect the complex stresses of the nation's history. For Paine, however, this Shandean deviation by particular circumstance meant that truth and justice were being compromised. The original idea had become so overlaid by accumulated organic rubbish that it no longer represented the thing itself.

A text in which this revolutionary logic is laid bare is William Godwin's *Political Justice* (1793), a book which in effect offered the supportive philosophical framework for a new ideal constitution. With occasionally shocking clarity, the book's argument is constructed rigorously *a priori* on the grounds of what Godwin terms 'the nature of things and the system of the universe'.[41] Although Godwin revised this uncompromising document for later editions in 1796 and 1798 so as to bring human experience and emotions into the picture, it was the first edition, intended 'to place the principles of politics on an unmoveable basis',[42] which had the greatest impact. Although not intended as a 'system', the 1793 text builds up an entirely consistent rational structure, which it is possible to reconstruct from the individual components. It is evident that Godwin's standard throughout is one of perfection: any degree of constitutional imperfection is 'injurious' (iii.106), and even preferring 'a less good to a greater' can result in 'absolute

---

[39] John Whale, 'Literal and Symbolic Representations: Burke, Paine and the French Revolution', *History of European Ideas*, 16 (1993), 343–9.

[40] Burke, *Reflections*, 152.

[41] William Godwin, *An Enquiry Concerning Political Justice* (London: G. G. J. and J. Robinson, 1793). Reprinted in *Political and Philosophical Writings of William Godwin*, ed. Mark Philp, 7 vols (London: William Pickering, 1993), iii.138. Future page references to this latter volume will be given in the body of the text. There are many echoes of Shaftesbury's *Characteristicks* (1711), as in 'No man can love virtue sufficiently, who has not an acute and lively perception of its beauty, and its tendency to produce the only solid and permanent happiness' (iii.132).

[42] William Godwin, *Collected Novels and Memoirs of William Godwin*, ed. Mark Philp, 8 vols (London: Pickering and Chatto, 1992), i.49.

evil' (88). In Godwin's model there are no relative values. Justice ('moral duty') is a transparent universal idea, 'pure' and 'unadulterated' (i.e. unrefracted and unmediated), and this concept is intrinsic to the system of 'just' reasoning his work sets out. 'Truth', he says, 'is in reality single and uniform' (104); it is 'everlasting' (50) and thus 'at all times and in all places the same' (104). It is therefore axiomatic that things are inherently good and evil in themselves. This means that in deciding questions of moral duty (the book's core idea) all context and contingency can be discounted. The moral unit is not the Lockean 'person', but the individual 'man' stripped of character, preferences, tastes, emotions, and anything we tend to call 'human' qualities. All social relationships are consequently irrelevant ('Society is nothing more than an aggregation of individuals', 54).[43] 'Man', in Godwin's system, is a logical unit defined as 'the subject of legislation' (104).

In contrast, organic meanings lie not in 'the thing itself', but in the relations between things, and they acknowledge aspects of character and circumstance; they are filtered through experience and coloured by impurities. They therefore can have no place in Godwin's model, which specifically counters eighteenth-century organic thinking at every point. It is fascinating to see how clearly he understands the organic, and how directly and consistently he attacks all its features. Because his truth is single and his justice undeviating ('if truth be one, there must be one code of truths', 135), he sets himself against mixture and variety. He attacks any concession to situation (truth is independent of all 'particular existences', 132). It follows that those people who take specific circumstances into account become what Godwin terms 'accommodating moralists' (135). Any form of retrospect or recollection is irrelevant (172), since truth is unaffected by time or place (103–4). There is no valid appeal to be made with regard to personal feelings or commitments, to national 'habits' or 'character' (103).[44] There are consequently in Godwin's 'justice' no individual facets, no personal angles, no unique discoveries, no truths of experience, no acts of judicial interpretation. There is no room at all for sentiment, so that any notion of 'gratitude', a personal 'favour', or a 'promise' must not be permitted to over-ride what is the inherent 'right' of 'intrinsic merit' (51, 53, 87). In this Houyhnhnm world,[45] all elements of relation and mediation must be discounted, since they will cause diversions. The direction in which Godwin is steering (or rather *heading*, since his line never deviates) becomes clear when he describes the logical ideal of his model whereby the truths would be those of geometry (173), and the minds of human individuals as sure as billiard balls (168–9).

[43] For Godwin this 'aggregation' is a sum total, not a consolidation through time.

[44] For Wordsworth's reaction against this, see p. 268 below.

[45] The Swiftian parallel has been drawn by Mark Philp, *Godwin's Political Justice* (London: Duckworth, 1986), 95.

Godwin's is no platonic system, but a logical construction built on the empirical premise that there are no innate ideas, and that all our knowledge comes through the senses subject to principles of association.[46] This makes his rigorous exclusion of any subjective and experiential factors (memories, emotions, personality) all the more bold and striking, and noticeably un-Lockean. He allows for a stream of human consciousness, but it is 'the unity of uninterrupted succession' that he stresses, not the variety (180–1). The key to Godwin's system is mental convergence: 'every idea, however complex, offers itself to the mind under the conception of unity. The blending of numerous impressions into one perception is a law of our nature' (183). The necessarian Godwin is driven by a zeal for pure, undeviating rectitude, in which things will always run straight ('a single deviation, infects the whole', 139). The world of *Tristram Shandy* would be anathema to him.

It is fascinating, therefore, to find that his words echo Sterne's text at several points. They do so, however, as an attack on those organic aspects of the novel's mechanisms discussed in the previous chapter, with their subjective, individualist, and erratic implications. Tristram's idiosyncrasies, his cluttered and feverish mind, and his wayward personal history are the antithesis of Godwin's commitment to geometrical rectitude based on 'a principle of unity in men's tempers, propensities and transactions' (160). There are several intriguing moments in Godwin's text when he seems to be echoing Sterne's Walter Shandy, the theorist and systematiser who is repeatedly frustrated by the way actual life refuses to conform. At the point where Godwin dismisses 'accident and chance' as humanity's failure to understand that 'every thing takes place according to necessary and universal laws' (162), he argues that even the most committed proponent of free will,

> if an incident turn out otherwise than they expected [will] take it for granted, that there was some unobserved *bias*, some habit of thinking, some prejudice of educa-tion, some singular *association of ideas*, that disappointed their prediction . . . [and] they return, like the natural philosopher, to search out the *secret spring* of this unlooked for event. (162, my italics)

We recall Walter Shandy's trust in 'the secret spring' that will counterbalance the evil of Tristram's squashed nose (iv.8) and set things straight again. In Sterne's novel the theories of Tristram's exasperated father repeatedly fail to straighten Tristram's wayward path; indeed (as with the naming) they end up distorting it even further. Walter's ambitious scheme for directing his son's education, the *Tristrapaedia*, never catches up with the life it is meant

---

[46] 'We bring into the world with us no innate principles . . . [our notions] are regularly generated in the mind by a series of impressions, and digested and arranged by association and reflexion' (10–11). Godwin's text closely recalls at different points Hobbes, Shaftesbury, Locke, and Hartley. See n. 41 above.

to be shaping; it can only trail in the wake of Tristram's accident-prone journey through time and space.[47]

Linear history is after all a limited concept, and organic history recognises how such lines might be erratic, elliptical, interrupted, interwoven, or cross-hatched. Tim Ingold, in his recent history of the line, characterises *life* in Sternean fashion as 'a manifold woven from the countless threads spun by beings of all sorts...as they find their ways through the tangle of relationships in which they are enmeshed'.[48] It was important, however, for revolutionary argument in the 1790s to differentiate the uncertain, tangled, and interrupted lines of history (anathema to Paine) from the ideal straight line of reason and justice (as advocated by Godwin);[49] but it could also be polemically useful to project the latter onto an historical plane as showing us the way into the future. This entailed dismissing any history that was not philosophically determined. History could simultaneously be shaped into an idea that might be projected into, and underpin the logic of, an idealised future.

Facts, however, might not be cooperative, and this was a recognised danger. In his history lectures delivered in the École Normale, Paris, 'in the third year of the Republic' (i.e. 1794–5), C. F. Volney argued that philosophy could give history the direction it needed, whereas a plethora of facts could not:

Historical facts...floating like phantoms in the irregular mirror of the human understanding, where they connect themselves with the most extravagant fancies, can only reach *likelihood* and *probability*.

In Volney's inorganic reading, the distorting human medium will always tend to complicate and refract what should be clear and direct. But he goes on to argue that if history were given 'an analytic or philosophical arrangement', then human 'prejudices' would be tracked down and 'destroyed'.[50] Philosophy, then, is a surer guide to the future than human experience.

To see history as a linear narrative was one thing, but to accept its trajectory was another. In the minds of some revolutionary thinkers of 1789 it was a continuum simply waiting to be blasted open (to recall Benjamin's phrase). Perhaps in their mind's eye they held before them Joseph Priestley's popular *New Chart of History* (first issued in 1769 and later updated), in which he set out to visualise the shape of the past and draw lessons from it (see Figure 4). With the chart spread out before him, an

[47] Sterne playfully mocks the notion of geometrical necessity when Corporal Trim's posture exemplifies 'the necessity of this precise angle of 85 degrees and a half to a mathematical exactness' (ii.17).
[48] Tim Ingold, *Lines: A Brief History* (London/New York: Routledge, 2007), 3.
[49] Paine mocked the uncertain 'line' of Burke's monarchical genealogy (*Rights of Man*, 100). Godwin talks of 'the exact line that duty prescribes' (*Enquiry*, ii.v), 'the line of rectitude' (v.viii), and 'the precise line of unalterable justice' (v.xvi).
[50] C. F. Volney, *Lectures on History, delivered in The Normal School of Paris, by C. F. Volney...Translated from the French* (London: J. Ridgway, 1800), 2, xviii.

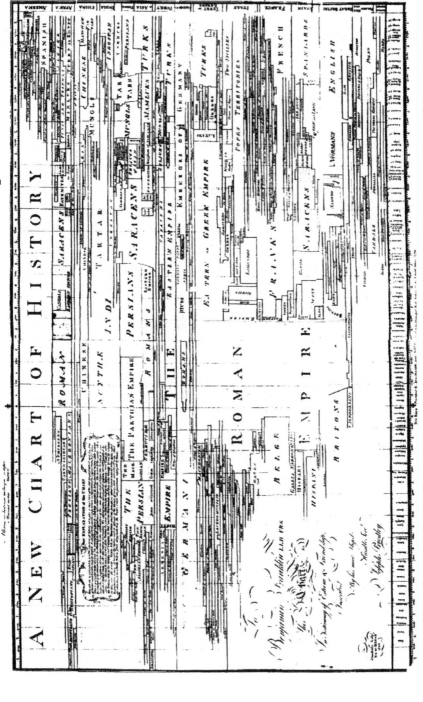

4. Chart from Joseph Priestley, *A Description of a New Chart of History, Containing a View of the principal Revolutions of Empire, That have taken Place in the World*, 2nd edn (London: J. Johnson, 1770). Reproduced by permission of the Bodleian Library, University of Oxford. Shelf mark G. Pamph 1185 (5).

ambitious young man might be tempted to make his mark upon it. Across this single plane, history, it seems, could be turned by a mere stroke of the pen. And the blank spaces look inviting. We notice at once the large empty area represented by the Roman Empire near the centre of the picture—registering like a focus for meditation—only to be followed by frantic layers of jagged complexity. In the accompanying text Priestley meditates on the message of the scene, as if scanning a vast battlefield:

They are rather melancholy reflections, which the view of such a chart of history as this is apt to excite in the minds of persons of feeling and humanity. What a number of revolutions are marked upon it! What broken appearance, in particular do the finest, and most cultivated parts of the earth exhibit, as Greece, Italy, Persia, and Egypt! What torrents of human blood has the restless ambition of mortals shed . . . may the contemplation of their fatal effects be a motive with us to keep a strict watch over our own; but let not the dark strokes which disfigure the fair face of an historical chart affect our faith in the great and comfortable doctrine of an over-ruling Providence.[51]

He expresses the hope 'that the chart of history some centuries hence will not be intersected and disfigured, in so shocking a manner' (21). Priestley's reformist Unitarianism in 1769, however, was different from revolutionary thought twenty years later.[52] Leaving things to evolve under the guidance of a benign providential God was not something that appealed to the revolutionaries of France. Impatient with notions of growth and development, they wanted in effect to incise a bold vertical line on Priestley's chart of history—declare the revolutionary moment. As it happens, Priestley, in a strangely prescient passage, had invited his readers to do just that:

The French chart, though drawn several years ago, supposes every thing to remain as they then were till the year 1800 . . . as I do not have the gift of prophecy, I have left that space a blank, to be filled up by those who purchase the chart, as the changes shall take place.[53]

With increasing irony, this passage remained unchanged through the 'corrected' editions of 1789, 1793, and 1797. Priestley the theologian and

---

[51] Joseph Priestley, *A Description of a New Chart of History, Containing a View of the principal Revolutions of Empire, That have taken Place in the World*, 2nd edn (London: J. Johnson, 1770), 18. See Arthur Sheps, 'Joseph Priestley's Time Charts: The Use and Teaching of History by Rational Dissent in late Eighteenth-Century England', *Lumen*, 18 (1999), 135–54; and Daniel Rosenberg, 'Joseph Priestley and the Graphic Invention of Modern Time', *Studies in Eighteenth-Century Culture*, 36 (2007), 55–103.

[52] By 1794 Priestley believed the Second Coming was imminent, but he advised 'patience' in face of 'the great scene, that seems now to be opening upon us', given that 'it is evident that it is wholly out of our power to alter' (*The present State of Europe compared with Antient Prophecies; A Sermon* (London: J. Johnson, 1794), 32). In his appendix he quotes with approval the words of David Hartley: 'Our duty is . . . to preserve the government, under whose protection we live, from dissolution, seeking the peace of it, and submitting to every ordinance of man for the Lord's sake' (35–6).

[53] Priestley, *New Chart*, 9–10.

experimental scientist recognised a tension between the organic unfolding of created life and the dramatic 'disfiguring' strokes of human intervention. Though his own optimism remained undaunted, he could not allow an optimistic idea to discount the complications of past experience.

French thinkers in the 1780s, taking their lead from Rousseau, were much bolder. The crucial debates over the proposed new constitution, which reached their climax in the French Assembly during the late Summer of 1789, offer a fascinating scenario of history and experience confronting philosophy and reason; and they anticipate the terms of the controversy that Burke would stir up in 1790. The actors in the drama understood that at the heart of their struggle was the question of history, in particular whether historical precedent and past experience should play a role in shaping the constitution, or whether it should be created *de novo*. Of strategic importance, and cited by both sides, was the dispute during 1787–8 between the American constitutionalist John Adams and the Marquis de Condorcet.[54] These two men had set out the grounds of their opposition clearly, with Condorcet denouncing Adams as an 'empirical' thinker (373), which he was, while Adams regarded Condorcet as 'a Man of Science, but little acquainted with History'.[55] 'The science of government', Adams declared, 'can be learned only from experience, [which is] the only Source of human knowledge'.[56] In his *Defence of the Constitutions of Government of the United States of America*, he uses a language of organic political economy in which the various forces in the state are effectively managed. Writing as America's first Ambassador to Britain, Adams celebrated 'mixed' government, stressing the balancing of constitutional powers in Britain and the United States through their bicameral legislatures. For Condorcet, the approach of Adams and the constitutional 'empiricists' served merely to endorse the status quo ('they… justify what is the case, but have never tried to discover what could or should be done').[57] To be truly effective and obtain 'more certain results', Condorcet urged that a constitution needed to be 'in conformity with reason'; otherwise it might be compromised by unpredictable circumstances. Because 'the ordinary method is really an empirical one', Condorcet regretted, 'we can neither accurately predict its results nor calculate them'.[58] There was a real danger, he thought, that the proposed constitution would be

---

[54] The Adams–Condorcet dispute is traced by C. Bradley Thompson, 'John Adams and the Coming of the French Revolution', *Journal of the Early Republic*, 16 (1996), 361–87. Unless otherwise noted, material in this paragraph is taken from Thompson's article.

[55] Written by Adams on the flyleaf of his copy of Antoine-Nicolas de Condorcet's 'Quatre lettres d'un bourgeois de New-Heaven sur l'unité de la legislation', printed as an appendix to Filippo Mazzei, *Recherches historiques et politiques sur les États-Unis* (Paris: Froullé, 1788). The note is quoted in full by Thompson, 'John Adams', 374.

[56] John Adams, *Defence of the Constitutions of Government of the United States of America* (London, 1787), 375.

[57] Condorcet, [?Letter 4], quoted by Thompson, 'John Adams', 372.

[58] Condorcet, [72, 30] [?Letter 4], quoted ibid. 374.

hamstrung by precedents, compromise, and adaptation. Too much would be left to chance.

The Adams–Condorcet arguments were continued in the French Assembly during the months following the storming of the Bastille. The report of the Constitutional Committee recommended a 'mixed' constitution based on the British and American models, the products of history and experience, which would reflect the existing social structure and balance its powers. Opposed to this were the Rousseauistes, led by men like the Abbé Sieyès and the Abbé Grégoire, for whom the constitution ought to be an act of the sovereign General Will, periodically declared. In Rousseau's *Du contrat social* (1762) the language of the political *moment* had come into its own: 'the moment the people is legitimately assembled as a sovereign body,' Rousseau writes, 'all jurisdiction of the government ceases.'[59] At this *moment*, writes Keith Baker, the constitution can be declared 'as a direct emanation of the general will'.[60] Rousseau's 'Sovereign' is thus deemed to be an entirely present-tense concept, not being bound by history or existing laws (even its own) but embodying the national will at that moment by its coming together. It is a unitary embodiment, not a representative body. It evinces the supreme power of 'now'. Its declarations are therefore infallible: 'the Sovereign, merely by virtue of what it is, is always what it should be' (i.7). For the revolutionary thinkers it is a realised Idea: 'Its will is always legal, it is the law itself,' said the Abbé Sieyès.[61] History had no contribution to make. As Baker puts it, 'Philosophical principles were to be their touchstone, not historical experience.'

Jean-Joseph Mounier, however, as Chair of the Constitutional Committee, tactically advocated a middle ground between reason and experience, and he urged the Assembly to 'consult the lessons of experience and not disdain the examples of history'.[62] He deplored what he called 'arbitrary and philosophical ideas' (261) and urged that a constitution should be a balance of powers. It was the British constitution that became the focus of argument. In pressing his points Mounier cited Blackstone alongside Montesquieu and John Adams. 'Faithful to their historical and experiential way of thinking', Baker writes, the committee 'offered a view of a constitution as a building to be maintained and perfected by constant minor repairs' (282).

Where the reformists appealed to empirical experience, for the revolutionaries such messages were too mixed and complicated. For Sieyès the

---

[59] Jean-Jacques Rousseau, *The Social Contract*, trans. Maurice Cranston (London: Penguin Books, 1968), 139 (iii.14).

[60] Keith Michael Baker, *Inventing the French Revolution: Essays on French Political Culture in the Eighteenth Century* (Cambridge: Cambridge University Press, 1990), 257.

[61] Emmanuel Joseph Sieyès, *Qu'est-ce que le Tiers État?* (1789), ed. R. Zapperi (Geneva, 1970), 180. Quoted by Baker, *Inventing the French Revolution*, 257.

[62] Baker, *Inventing the French Revolution*, 277. Quotations from the *Archives parlementaires* are referenced to Baker's chapter 11 ('Fixing the French Constitution'), 252–305.

voice of the nation must be single; otherwise, France would become 'a realm bristling with barriers of all kinds, a chaos of customs, regulations, and prohibitions particular to each locality' (300). An appeal to the experience of history was just what the Abbé Grégoire wanted to avoid. The nation had to seize control over history, which was giving confusing signals. History, he said, was in danger of offering too many contradictory examples, so that no clear message could be extracted:

The history that is too often invoked is an arsenal where everyone finds all kinds of weapons, because it offers examples of all kinds . . . instead of supporting a principle, the multiplicity of facts often demonstrates the violation of principles. (279)

Clear principles were in danger of being overwritten by conflicting empirical evidence.

Recognising the dangers for the Revolution of becoming mired in the complexities of history, Condorcet urged simplicity. In his *Sketch for a Historical Picture of the Progress of the Human Mind* (posthumously published in Year 3) he set out a plan to retrieve from history a clear sense of direction, an interpretable pattern that could, in a simple universal language, show humanity's progress and point it the way to perfection. Impatient with uncertainties and confusions, he sought 'simple, precise propositions'.[63] Condorcet's optimistic history would have

a precision and a rigour that would make knowledge of the truth easy and error almost impossible. Then the progress of every science would be as sure as that of mathematics, and the propositions that compose it would acquire a geometrical certainty. (199)

The history of mankind, he writes in his Introduction,

is linked by an uninterrupted chain of facts and observations; and so at this point the picture of the march and progress of the human mind becomes truly historical . . . it is enough to assemble and order the facts and to show the useful truths that can be derived from their connections and from their totality. (9)

Condorcet pictures an orderly march to perfection—taxonomic and progressive.

An optimistic totalised history of a very different kind (not surprisingly) is offered by John 'Walking' Stewart, whose manifesto, *The Revolution of Reason* (1794), we encountered in the previous chapter. Stewart's organic universe also embodies the idea of progress as the evolution of history itself, but for him its lines were far from direct and needed very careful and patient negotiation. Given his underlying principle that we are all temporary modes of matter infinitely recyclable within 'the great Integer, Nature', it follows that history is nothing less than a form of extended mass identity, something

[63] Antoine-Nicolas de Condorcet, *Sketch for a Historical Picture of the Progress of the Human Mind*, trans. June Barraclough (London: Weidenfeld and Nicolson, 1955), 198.

The base, or first circle, represents despotism,

The second, limited monarchy,

The third, aristocracy,

The fourth, mix'd government,

The fifth, representative government,

The sixth, democracy,

The seventh, state of enlightened nature.

5. John Stewart, *The Revolution of Reason: or the Establishment of the Constitution of Things in Nature* (London: J. Ridgway, [1794]), p. xxiii.
Because of copyright problems this is a computerised version made by the author.

of which we are literally a part. The human body is absorbed into history itself:

History furnishes it with all the advantage of extended identity to obtain the experience of past epochas, and atoms of matter become the reader of what they probably were formerly the writers or agents.[64]

Human identity is history. In this ultimate organic context, improvement will come only slowly by a circuitous process (see Figure 5). In Shandean fashion Stewart announces that 'the line of progress which connects predicament and perfectability, resembles the parabola' (225).[65] Thanks to 'the identity or unity of self and nature in the indestructibility of matter', human organisations can gradually improve through what he calls the 'graduated spiral line of improvement':

> The base, or first circle, represents despotism,
> The second, limited monarchy,
> The third, aristocracy,
> The fourth, mix'd government,
> The fifth, representative government,
> The sixth, democracy,
> The seventh, state of enlightened nature.

His illustration is a version of the Shandean arabesque (Figure 6). Stewart issues a warning against cutting through these lines and attempting to bypass the unfolding narrative of history. He sees the snail-like meandering as a providential process, dependent on individual amelioration rather than any direct intervention in the process:

---

[64] John Stewart, *The Revolution of Reason: or the Establishment of the Constitution of Things in Nature* (London: J. Ridgway, [1794]), 23.
[65] In *Tristram Shandy* Uncle Toby's researches lead him to the discovery that cannon balls do not travel in a straight line: 'he found the precise path to be a PARABOLA' (ii.3).

[17]

Nothing, Trim——said my uncle
Toby, mufing——

Whilft a man is free—cried the Cor-
poral, giving a flourifh with his ftick
thus——

Vol. IX.   C

6. Laurence Sterne, *Tristram Shandy*, vol. 9 (London: T. Becket and P. A. Dehondt, 1767), p. 17.
Reproduced by permission of the Brotherton Collection, Leeds University Library.

All attempts of reform in nations to pass by any one degree is highly dangerous, but to pass over two, as from despotism to mixed government, would be impossible; the civic temperament of the people, not having power to invert the line of improvement towards the vertex, it must fly off in the tangent of anarchy, and recoil back into a more profound despotism; this was the attempt and error of France, whose horrors of anarchy, when they shall have reached their climax, must exemplify the truth of this moral diagram. (xxiv)

The revolutionaries, he implies, attempted to leave the path, impatient with its uncertain direction.

In Stewart's model, the link between organic history and Lockean identity is taken further as the two merge into one. If individual beings (modes) are absorbed into history, then history is literally composed of the experience of millions. It is in that sense an organised body with an inherent potential memory, and an ability to develop organically through its members. Any impatient attempt to leap at perfection will be destructive because it will short-circuit the vermicular course of historical change. History, Stewart argues, will then show the symptoms of a psychological disturbance on the model of sentimental hysteria. His picture is an allegory of what amounts to a national nervous breakdown:

Perfectability, in attempting to pass over the gradations of improvement (as above noticed) outruns intellect, and increases so powerfully the momentum of passion, that as it must necessarily retrograde to meet intellect, it forces it lower upon the scale by the weight of its returning and sudden fall; in other words, the coercive force of law and despotism must be increased by all retrograde motions of policy. The French nation, who have attempted to arrive at perfectability, without the gradation of system, will no doubt, eventually form a dreadful example of the above problem. (227)

This organism is clearly not something to be played around with. Organic history and human identity here come together, and in Stewart's theory they begin to take on a layered character, with history being a sedimentation of human experience, visualised almost like a stratigraphic record.[66]

The possibility of something of value emerging from this cumulative process is recognised in the UK government's planning guidelines that provide the epigraph to this chapter. In that 1994 document, the phrase 'organic history' reads as a synonym for 'character', an acknowledgment that a historic fabric can accrue interest and value from what is mixed, quirky, or even incongruous. It warns against the notion of returning to a pure original, appreciating how later additional features may supersede any primary intention or design and become integrated into the building. Indeed it makes specific allowance for the traces, through time, of diverse needs, tastes, and experiences. This kind of history hints at a variety of lost stories and episodes, which if recovered, through documents or archaeology, will not deliver a universal truth, but are more likely to offer mixed messages about difference, relationship, and process. Small details have a place in the story, and are eloquent in themselves. This homely parable works as a philosophical example not unlike Theseus's ship, which in the previous chapter showed how eighteenth-century arguments over identity overlapped those about history. In both scenarios the issue is how a living continuity can accommodate interruption, addition, and alteration.

Drawing back from Stewart's extraordinary vision of recursive progress, I want to end this chapter closer to home with a picture that captures well the complex and muddled lines of organic history that this chapter has been trying to characterise. The eloquent drawing (Figure 7), made in about 1804, shows 'Judith', otherwise known as Cowper's Oak, the venerable tree on Yardley Chase near William Cowper's home, and the subject of his unfinished late poem 'Yardley Oak' of 1792. The image seems to capture in one powerful aesthetic statement the difficult intertexture of organic history. The

---

[66] In the 1790s William Smith (1769–1839) was preparing his first map of geological strata. See Simon Winchester, *The Map that Changed the World* (London: Viking, 2001).

C.Library
HALIFAX

7. Judith, or Cowper's Oak. Frontispiece to William Hayley, *Supplementary Pages to the Life of Cowper* (Chichester: J. Seagrave for J. Johnson, 1806). Reproduced by permission of Leeds University Library.

shape is grotesque and deformed, with a dark fissure at its centre and strange growths obtruding from its sides. It seems a thing of terror and alienation. Yet the more we look, we notice the fine tracings of branches, twigs, and leaves, which work outwards from the rotten misshapen core. For Cowper it represents an image of a Britain still clinging on to its gothic constitution:

> Embowell'd now, and of thy antient self
> Possessing nought but the scoop'd rind that seems
> An huge throat calling to the clouds for drink
> Which it would give in riv'lets to thy root,
>
> .   .   .   .
>
> Yet is thy root sincere,[67] sound as the rock,
> A quarry of stout spurs and knotted fangs
> Which crook'd into a thousand whimsies, clasp
> The stubborn soil, and hold thee still erect.
> So stands a Kingdom whose foundations yet
> Fail not, in virtue and in wisdom lay'd,
> Though all the superstructure by the tooth
> Pulverized of venality, a shell
> Stands now, and semblance only of itself.[68]

Looking at Cowper's oak, we can recognise his mixed feelings about the paradoxical object before him. Around the yawning rotten gap are the delicate traceries of new life. To debate the nature of history in the 1790s was to engage with an image like this, in whose mixture of decay and growth, deformity and whimsicality ('crook'd into a thousand whimsies') there is also considerable tensile strength, and endless potential for exploration. Guided by this organic spirit, the remainder of the book will trace some of the lines of identity and history that run through the poetry of Coleridge, Wordsworth, and their intimate circle during the 1790s.

---

[67] From the Latin *sincerus* ('sound, uncorrupted').

[68] William Cowper, 'Yardley Oak', ll. 110–24, in *The Poems of William Cowper*, ed. John D. Baird and Charles Ryskamp, 3 vols (Oxford: Clarendon Press, 1980–95), iii.81.

II

4 'Sweet native stream!': Approaching Tintern Abbey

WORDSWORTH'S POEM POPULARLY known as 'Tintern Abbey', first pub-
lished in *Lyrical Ballads* (1798), opens with two slight dislocations, respect-
ively of space and time. The scene, the full title tells us, is 'a few miles above'
the abbey, and it opens with the phrase: 'Five years have passed'. Although
the poem insists on its precise date ('July 13, 1798') and on the details of the
present scene ('these…these…these…'), it takes its dynamics as a text
from the awareness of distance, from the sense of there being other times and
places in the poem's presence which are not merely 'now' and 'here' but are
part of a continuing and extending identity. Empirical distance, of time and
space, is here not an estranging factor but the prerequisite for intimacy, as
with the pregnant mother in Anna Barbauld's 'To a little invisible Being',
where separation brings both responsibility and love for 'Part of herself, yet
to herself unknown'.[1] Identity is extended and a new connection made.
Similarly, the hints of disjunction and absence in Wordsworth's poem can
be reassuringly healed by recompense and recognition, as part of the poem's
pattern of renewals and revivings. In this text about revisiting, the distance
between things functions not to separate but to offer points of articulation.
Its positives tend to be connectives. The poem works its way (creates its
history) through alternating temporal locations, which stretch back to, and
across, absence; and it finds its own identity through companionship. A
poem in which one in seven lines begins with the word 'Of' clearly has an
investment in reaching for continuities.[2]

This chapter, however, has its own disjunction in that it is not about the
poem itself (which will be returned to in Chapter 11) but about various lines
of connection that link Wordsworth's poem to other companion texts and to
other poetic identities. I want to use its organic character to explore poetic
texts that have a bearing on, or more precisely can offer their bearings to, a
critical understanding of the poem. Ostensibly about the poet's own history
and identity, Wordsworth's lines can also be a vehicle for tracing poetic

---

[1] Anna Letitia Barbauld, 'To a little invisible Being who is expected soon to become visible',
in *The Poems of Anna Letitia Barbauld*, ed. William McCarthy and Elizabeth Kraft (Athens/
London: Georgia University Press, 1994), 296. See pp. 51–2 above.
[2] Twenty-three of the poem's 160 lines begin with 'Of'.

continuities in literary history during the 1790s.[3] This can be appreciated
through looking at the work of another collection of young poets from the
1780s, whose influence helped to shape the poetry of the Coleridge circle in
the next decade.

In the previous chapter Thomas Warton's *History of English Poetry*
(1774–81) offered an example of organic history, and I remarked that
such history 'tends to be linear rather than hierarchical, and associative
rather than taxonomic'.[4] Wordsworth's poem is of course a core text in the
hierarchical 'canon' of English literature, and as such it has been cele-
brated for its intrinsic power. But it is also possible to view it more
democratically as a text that is in friendly converse with others. Its great-
ness as a poem might lie extrinsically in the degree to which it helps us to
hear other voices. One of the problems raised by the concept of a literary
canon is its tendency to encourage static and compartmentalized thinking,
either by invoking a 'classic' timelessness and universality or by forming
artistic hierarchies and orders. In this scheme, 'minor' texts play the
subordinate role of providing analogue material that is then left behind
by the 'major' text, within which all the interesting critical activity is
located. But a poem can be great not by transcendence over other minor
or subordinate poems, but by recognisably sharing a language and con-
ducting a dialogue with them.

The power of a poem (Gray's *Elegy* or Milton's *Lycidas*) can depend on
how it makes its sources articulate by absorbing and developing a tradition.
Here the relationship with the antecedents is a more organic one: questions
of subordination or transcendence are replaced by heredity and kinship—
strength is drawn from connection and inherited powers. A 'canon' in these
terms becomes a familial relationship between texts, and issues of 'major'
or 'minor' have less significance. The text itself may even over-run individ-
ual authors, so that the critical emphasis shifts from addressing discrete
poems to exploring wider poetic identities. A Bloomian scenario in which
works assert their independence as they write off their debts and make their
'great' statements can be replaced by one in which poems proclaim their
intertextual nature and accept responsibility for a shared and developing
language.

The later eighteenth century was a period when such issues came to the
fore with the growing interest in the writing of literary history. As we saw in
Thomas Warton's rejection of Gray's 'mechanical' scheme for a history of
poetry, a static and taxonomic model was being replaced by a more organic

---

[3] Mary Jacobus has examined the development of eighteenth-century landscape poetry in
'Tintern Abbey', including the 'revisit' poem of Warton and Bowles which was useful in 'providing
Wordsworth with a means of asserting continuity as well as change' (*Tradition and Experiment in
Wordsworth's Lyrical Ballads* (Oxford: Clarendon Press, 1976), 104–30).

[4] See p. 72 above.

and developmental one, in a move toward what some theorists have represented as a 'romantic discourse'.[5] One of its defining characteristics, Clifford Siskin and others have shown, is a conviction that literary history is best understood in terms of growth and development. A narrative history, one that traces continuities rather than disjunctions, is for David Perkins (following Siskin's analysis) a 'romantic project'.[6] Whether the term 'romantic' is helpful here depends on the degree to which Wordsworth (rather than, for example, Blake) is used to characterise it. As Siskin has recognised, such a history sits uneasily alongside a revolutionary, rather than a more evolutionary, reading of romanticism. Whatever the case, it is certainly a manifestation of the eighteenth-century organic impulse. As we saw in the previous chapter, the voice is that of Burke's *Reflections* rather than Paine's *Rights of Man*; but Burke's image of the nation as an imaginatively living organism with a network of inherited commitments, values, and affections, has closer affinities to the Wordsworth of *The Prelude* and 'Tintern Abbey', than does Paine's desire to break those threads and 'begin the world over again' on virtuous principles.

The aim of this chapter is to attempt a narrative history of a poem that provides an intriguing case-study of textual interplay. Wordsworth's 'Lines written a few miles above Tintern Abbey, on revisiting the banks of the Wye during a tour, July 13, 1798' has traditionally been seen as encouraging notions of transcendence, particularly in its sublime passages. But something has been lost of the way its power as a poem lies not in how it works at a different level from other texts, but in how it is rooted in them and grows from them. Keats's remark about 'the wordsworthian or egotistical sublime' is such a wonderful idea that the phrase has been allowed to define the poem unhelpfully.[7] In some ways it is a profoundly unegotistical document. This chapter will argue that the 'I' of the poem is a voice that echoes and mirrors many other voices, and the self that it seeks is valued for the relation it bears to earlier selves, not for its un-dependence. Even its moments of sublimation discover what is 'interfused' at a deep level. Alongside the individual recollected history (so easily mistaken for egotism) there is what might be termed a bio-history in its literary relations, and this is what specifically concerns me in this chapter.

---

[5] Robert J. Griffin argues that 'the Wartonian narrative' initiated a 'Romantic literary history', which persisted through the nineteenth and twentieth centuries. See *Wordsworth's Pope: A Study in Literary Historiography* (Cambridge: Cambridge University Press, 1995), 18–21.

[6] Clifford Siskin, *The Historicity of Romantic Discourse* (New York/Oxford: Oxford University Press, 1988); David Perkins, *Is Literary History Possible?* (Baltimore/London: Johns Hopkins University Press, 1992), 86–7.

[7] John Keats to Richard Woodhouse, 27 Oct. 1818. *The Letters of John Keats 1814–1821*, ed. Hyder Edward Rollins, 2 vols (Cambridge MA: Harvard University Press, 1958), i.387.

The full title of Wordsworth's 'Lines' is important: it declares itself to be a poem of the margins, of the 'marge' or river bank, a riparian revisiting that locates itself upstream from the abbey, at the same time beyond the tidal inflow and nearer to the source. As Wordsworth's own note to line 4 makes explicit, 'the river is not affected by the tide a few miles above Tintern'. My discussion will attempt to recover the 'inland murmur' of the poem, so to speak. I want to suggest something of its literary topography, working between the ruined abbey and the source or vital spring, following the stream and its margin to the sacred place, and recovering the echoes that sound in muted tones there. Wordsworth's 'Lines' (such must be the appropriate short title) enact a recovery of a sense of connectedness, of belonging to a stream that is in part an interiorised presence, a life-giving transfusion 'felt in the blood, and felt along the heart' (29), but also a wider relationship to a source that has given him a language and made him articulate as a poet. In the poem itself these rhizomic lines of connection are gathered up into the figure of the sister/friend, the climactic sublimation of 'something far more deeply interfused', whose presence throughout is not acknowledged until line 115. In a similar way Wordsworth's poem, though intimated throughout this chapter, will be addressed overtly only at the end. The 'Lines' written along the river bank between the abbey and the springs provide the model for this exercise in organic literary history.

I want, therefore, to attempt a very different approach from that of Marjorie Levinson, whose influential study of the poem made it an important document in 'new historicism'.[8] In some ways mine is a supplement to hers by being an inversion of her method and conclusions. Where she offers an account of the poem itself by focusing on what it leaves out, this chapter aims, equally paradoxically, to delineate what is present in the poem by an account that leaves the poem itself out. It is literally an *approach to* Wordsworth's 'Lines', and one that, unlike her 'enabling alienated purchase' on the poem, consciously works along its grain, using its motifs and metaphors in order to trace certain lines of inheritance that issue in the poem and give it a 'common life' with others.

In doing so, the discussion resists the kind of universalised history assumed in some 'new-historicist' writing, whereby structures are established within which attitudes become generalised, prescribed, or even predetermined. The materials of such history tend, however detailed, to be static ones—they harden into a 'view of' or 'attitude towards' a situation or event[9]—and the

---

[8] Marjorie Levinson, *Wordsworth's Great Period Poems: Four Essays* (Cambridge: Cambridge University Press, 1986), 14–57. For Levinson, what is excluded from the poem is the social reality of the abbey site, a haunt of beggars bounded by a polluted tidal river busy with traffic.

[9] See especially Alan Liu, *Wordsworth: The Sense of History* (Stanford: Stanford University Press, 1989). Liu, for example, contrasts the 'French view' of Federation Day (14 July) 1790 with Wordsworth's aestheticised view of it in *The Prelude*. David Perkins challenges the basis of Liu's contextual procedure in *Is Literary History Possible?*, 144–8.

details themselves become 'paradigmatic'. According to this method, any individual view in the text will predictably be a divergent one that suppresses or denies history-as-reality, and it will therefore be characterised in terms of silences and omissions, which it is the critic's task to detect by superimposing the chosen paradigm. In face of this judgmental technique, where each writer is implicated in a presumed 'social reality', I want to employ a history that is narrative rather than descriptive, personal rather than universal, organic rather than taxonomic, and one that never rigidifies into a paradigm. I therefore prefer the term 'motif', whose musical associations will allow for continual change and development, individually nuanced and given a particular accent or charge. In the specific case of Wordsworth's 'Lines', for example, to say that the poet does not describe the abbey is not to say, as Levinson does, that it is suppressed or denied,[10] but that, like other subliminal 'presences' in the poem, it makes itself felt without being inscribed through description or direct allusion. In this way I want to raise problems about the issue of 'presence' in the poetry of this period, and to suggest some ways in which a poem 'lives along the line' of its own narrative history.

Thomas Warton's work as the first narrator of English literary history was discussed in the previous chapter. But as a poet too he was an influence on the next generation, not least in the way he drew on the materials of history for inspiration. From the early meditative poem *The Pleasures of Melancholy* (1747) to his public odes as Poet Laureate from 1785 till his death in 1790, Warton's verse is interested in texts from the past, in authentic lost voices, however 'minor'; but they are revived not as something dead, but as a resource that can feed into the work of the modern poet. If his *History* gave the British reading public of the 1780s and 1790s a sense of the capaciousness of the literary past, his *Poems* (1777) offered a model for its infusion into the poetry of the present. To young poets coming to maturity he offered something paradoxically old and fresh, and as a teacher with a wide circle of poetical friends and pupils, he was well placed to be a literary mentor to some of them.

In a *Quarterly Review* article of 1824, Robert Southey singled out Warton as a decisive influence on the poetry of the current generation, and he spoke of Warton's 'school' of poets as 'the true English school'.[11] In the review and elsewhere he mentions four poets as members of this 'school': William Lisle

---

[10] Levinson refers to the 'logical contradiction between title ["Tintern Abbey"] and text' (*Wordsworth's Great Period Poems*, 2).

[11] Robert Southey, review of William Hayley's *Memoirs*, ed. John Johnson, in *Quarterly Review*, 31 (1824–5), 289. See p. 131 below.

Bowles,[12] Henry Headley,[13] Thomas Russell,[14] and John Bampfylde;[15] and to these I would add a further three, Henry Kett,[16] George Richards,[17] and Thomas Park.[18] Beyond this immediate group, Edward Gardner

[12] William Lisle Bowles (1762–1850) came up to Trinity College, Oxford, from Winchester in 1781, and remained there until 1787. His *Fourteen Sonnets* (Bath, 1789) was an immediate success, and its enthusiastic reception by Coleridge and Wordsworth has been frequently noted. See J. B. Bamborough, 'William Lisle Bowles and the Riparian Muse', in W. W. Robson (ed.), *Essays and Poems Presented to Lord David Cecil* (London: Constable, 1970), 93–108. My chapter is indebted to Bamborough's groundbreaking work.

[13] Henry Headley (1765–88), a close friend of Bowles, entered Trinity College, Oxford, in 1781 and was author of *An Invocation to Melancholy* (Oxford, 1785) and *Poems and Other Pieces* (London J. Robson, 1786). In 1787 he published *Select Beauties of Ancient English Poetry*. William Beloe recalled that 'the bias which he took towards ancient English poetry, and the perseverance and zeal with which he pursued and cultivated a knowledge of the earliest English poets, probably arose from his introduction to Thomas Warton, whose History of English Poetry, and other productions in illustration of our ancient bards, were his great and constant favourites' (*The Sexagenarian: or, the Recollections of a Literary Life*, 2 vols (London, 1817), i.174). Headley was described by Henry Kett as being devoted to Warton, whom he 'beheld with admiration, and followed with enthusiasm' (Kett's memoir of Headley prefixed to 1810 edn of *Select Beauties*, iv). Looking back in 1829, Wordsworth recalled Headley as 'a most extraordinary young man—more remarkable for precocity of judgement than any one I ever read or heard of: in his Poems also are beautiful passages, especially in the "Invocation to Melancholy," that I think is the title, but I have not seen the Poems for thirty years' (William Wordsworth to E. H. Barker, 24 July 1824, *The Letters of William and Dorothy Wordsworth*, ed. Alan G. Hill, 2nd edn (Oxford, 1979), v.95). Headley was mourned by Bowles in 'On the Death of Henry Headley', and by Kett in 'Verses on the Death of Mr. Headley'. Kett included both poems in his 1810 edn of *Select Beauties*, xix–xxii.

[14] Thomas Russell (1761–88) moved from Winchester to New College, Oxford, in 1780, and he continued to be an admirer of the two Warton brothers. In 1782–3 he defended Warton's *History* in the *Gentleman's Magazine* (52 (1782), 574; 53 (1783), 124). Russell's posthumous *Sonnets and Miscellaneous Poems* (Oxford, 1789) were dedicated to Joseph Warton. Wordsworth, an admirer of Russell's sonnets, transferred the final quatrain of one of them to his own sonnet 'Iona (upon landing)' as expressing the feeling better than he himself could. See also William Wordsworth to Alexander Dyce, [*c.*22 Apr. 1833] (*Letters*, v.604). Russell died at Bristol Hotwells in 1788, the same year as Headley. He is featured in Bowles's *Elegy Written at the Hot-Wells, Bristol* (Bath, 1791).

[15] John Bampfylde (1754–97), as Roger Lonsdale has shown, was also schooled at Winchester. Although he studied at Cambridge, he had friends in Oxford, particularly George Huddesford of Trinity, and his sonnet 'On having dined at Trinity College Oxford' was included in his *Sixteen Sonnets* (London, 1778), along with 'To Mr. Warton, on reading his History of English Poetry'. In later life he was confined in a madhouse. Coleridge and Southey were stirred by his poetry and life story, and Southey in particular was instrumental in rescuing a significant amount of both. See *The Poems of John Bampfylde*, ed. Roger Lonsdale (Oxford: Perpetua Press, 1988).

[16] Henry Kett (1761–1825), like Headley from Norwich Grammar School, entered Trinity College in 1777 and became a fellow 1784. He lived to disown his youthful verse which he collected as *Juvenile Poems* (Oxford: J. Fletcher, 1793) in a failed bid to become Oxford's poetry professor. He wrote 'A Tour to the Lakes of Cumberland and Westmoreland in August 1798', and interested himself in the reform of the University's syllabus. In 1810 he published a two-volume revised edition of Headley's *Select Beauties* with a sympathetic memoir of his friend and an appendix of Headley's collected poems. Kett drowned himself in 1825. The three 'Headley' poems included by Southey in his *Specimens of the Later English Poets*, 3 vols (London, 1807), are in fact by Kett.

[17] George Richards (1767–1837) entered Trinity College, Oxford, from Christ's Hospital in 1785, and became a fellow of Oriel College 1790–6. Warton was assessor when Richards won the Chancellor's Prize in 1789 for an essay on 'The Characteristic Differences between Ancient and Modern Poetry, and the several Causes from which they result'. He published *The Aboriginal Britons, A Poem* (Oxford, 1791) and *Songs of the Aboriginal Bards of Britain* (Oxford, 1792). His two-volume *Poems* (Oxford: Oxford University Press, 1804) gathered his earlier verse together, much dating from the 1790s. Eventually Richards became Vicar of St Martin's-in-the-Fields, London, 1824–37.

[18] Thomas Park (1759–1834) published his massive *Works of the British Poets* (London, 1805–8), in which Bampfylde and other Wartonians are well represented. Although he

(whose *Miscellanies* was published at Bristol in 1798) has a noticeable Wartonian accent,[19] as does the meditative poetry of Charlotte Smith.[20] The 1795 volume of *Poems* by Bion and Moschus (Southey and his friend Robert Lovell) contains material rooted in the Warton school,[21] and during the 1790s the work of Coleridge and Wordsworth draws from the same 'native stream'.

The first seven names in the above list form a group of younger writers whose work in various ways stood in close relationship to Warton's own; most were bound together by friendship and literary intimacies, and in different ways all can be said to have regarded Warton as a father-figure. Four of them (Bowles, Headley, Kett, and Richards) were at Trinity College, Oxford, where Warton was Senior Fellow, and Bowles, along with Russell and Bampfylde, could boast a twin parentage in being educated at Winchester School, where Thomas's brother, Joseph Warton, presided as Headmaster. This was Thomas's second home during the Oxford vacations, and here the 'Adelphi of poetry' together nurtured the boys' literary talents.[22] At Oxford the Poet Laureate drew around him a noticeable group of poetical young men, as Sir Herbert Croft remarked in 1786: 'the magnetism of Tom Warton draws many a youth into rhymes and loose stockings, who had better be thinking of prose and propriety.'[23] Headley, for example, 'poetical from top to toe' and devoted to Warton, was at the age of 22 clearly following in his master's footsteps, already author of a published volume of poems and of *Select Beauties of Ancient English Poetry*, an anthology of sixteenth- and early-seventeenth-century poetry with scholarly notes and biographies.

---

attended neither Winchester nor either university, he can claim to be part of any 'School of Warton'. His modestly titled *Sonnets and Other Small Poems* (London: G. Sael, 1797) contains unmistakable Wartonian motifs. Park studied antiquities and was deeply read in older English poetry. He projected a completion of Warton's *History of English Poetry*.

[19] Little is known of Edward Gardner (?1752–1823), a school friend of Chatterton, later a wine merchant at Frampton-on-Severn, Gloucestershire. His *Miscellanies, in Prose and Verse*, 2 vols (Bristol, 1798), were published by Biggs and Cottle in the same year as *Lyrical Ballads*. The volumes also contained original poems of Chatterton. Gardner was probably also the author of *Liberty: A Poem* (Bristol, 1776), of which only one copy, at Harvard, has been traced. The library of the Wellcome Institute for the History of Medicine, London, has Gardner's own transcript (MS 2471), dated 1818, of eighteen unpublished sonnets; they include twelve blank-verse sonnets chiefly on religious subjects (three dated 1809–12). His death is recorded in *GM*, 93 (1823), 93.

[20] Charlotte Smith (1749–1806) contributed sonnets to the *European Magazine* (1782). The Warton brothers both subscribed to the enlarged fifth edition of her *Elegiac Sonnets* (1789).

[21] Robert Lovell and Robert Southey, *Poems: Containing the Retrospect, Odes, Elegies, Sonnets, &c* (Bath: R. Cruttwell, 1795).

[22] 'At school I remember we thought we must necessarily be fine fellows if we were but as absent and as dirty as the Adelphi of poetry' (Sir Herbert Croft to John Nichols, 15 May 1786, in John Nichols, *Literary Anecdotes of the Eighteenth Century* (London, 1812–15), v.210). For Southey's high critical estimate of the Warton brothers, see below, p. 131, n. 38.

[23] Croft to Nichols, 15 May 1786.

Besides making a young poet feel in touch with the mainstream of contemporary poetry, Warton showed how that current flowed from long hidden sources. His characteristic impulse to recover and reanimate the past in a way that traced connecting threads with the present (in contrast to Gray's tragic disjunctions) exemplified how that past could be rediscovered as personal history. Along these threads, in a series of 'holy' landscapes, the poet might meditate on relationships, maturity, growth, and change. For this Warton offered a fluid emotional syntax to articulate the characteristic dilemma of continuity facing any organic consciousness. The historian lived within the poet in a symbiotic way.

This interrelationship forms the basis for Southey's characterisation of Warton's poems in his *Quarterly Review* article:

they are ... strongly tinctured by his romantic and chivalrous reading, and by the spirit of our elder poets.

> Nor rough nor barren are the winding ways
> Of hoar antiquity, but strewn with flowers.

Thus he expressed himself, and the truth of this was exemplified in all his writings. No man could at that time have written such poems, unless his studies had qualified him to become the historian of English poetry; nor could any one have composed that history who had not been born a poet.

Southey is quoting the final two lines of Warton's sonnet, 'Written in a blank leaf of Dugdale's Monasticon', a typically Wartonian meditation on the location and recovery of texts. The previous lines are these:

> While cloyster'd Piety displays
> Her mouldering roll, the piercing eye explores
> New manners, and the pomp of elder days,
> Whence culls the pensive bard his pictur'd stores.[24]

'New manners' suddenly retrieves something from the 'mouldering roll'. Where we might expect the word 'old', Warton's 'new' inverts the antiquarian impulse and draws a precariously decaying text into the present, turning what is enclosed and static ('cloyster'd Piety displays') into what is penetrative and dynamic ('piercing eye explores'). In a gesture of connectedness Warton sets the retrospective alongside an awareness of future imaginative possibilities. This is how history works for Warton, as a mediation between a living consciousness and its inherited knowledge.

Again and again in Warton's poetry we encounter a lost text worn away by time, covered in mould, dimly discernible, and usually housed in a remote, concealed place. In the 'Ode Written at Vale-Royal Abbey' he goes into the 'inmost cell ... | ... To pluck the grey moss from the mantled stone, |

---

[24] Thomas Warton, *Poems: A New Edition, with Additions* (London: T. Becket, 1777), 77.

Some holy founder's mouldering name to spell' (74–6),[25] and in 'Ode on the Approach of Summer' he enters a more mystical space with similar intent: 'As thro' the caverns dim I wind, | Might I that holy legend find, | By fairies spelt in mystic rhymes | To teach enquiring later times'.[26] These texts are 'holy' because they are original and revelatory, drawn from innermost places where legend and history meet. The difficulty of access to their language is somehow a guarantee of the value of discarded truth, of a founding or primal tradition awaiting discovery.

The fact that this is a native tradition is emphasised by his sonnet 'On King Arthur's Round-table at Winchester', where again a text is waiting to be recovered:

> on the capacious round
> Some British pen has sketch'd the names renown'd,
> In marks obscure, of his immortal peers.
> Though join'd by magic skill, with many a rime,
> The Druid-frame, unhonour'd, falls a prey
> To the slow vengeance of the wisard Time,
> And fade the British characters away[27]   (6–12)

The table carries a text that is receding from view. It is literally a poetic language that is fading and taking with it the 'British characters'—both the words themselves and the people who had once sat around the table. But the poem ends by asserting that the knights live on, 'unconscious of decay', in the pages of Spenser's *Faerie Queene*. That final remark from Warton the literary historian gains resonance from the fact that it was his *Observations on the Faerie Queene* (1754) that had first shown the presence of Arthurian 'history' in Spenser's poem.[28] Warton's innovative literary source-study functions silently as his own contribution to the recovery of a narrative history.

In tracing links with the past (and *trace*, as verb or noun, is a crucial word in his poetry) Warton becomes an investigator of spaces. His search for hidden writing is associated with a quest for concealed places where such texts might be preserved. The previous chapter quoted from his brother Joseph's humorous poem which pictures him discovering 'dubious door-ways'.[29] In Warton's poems the hidden entries into the past regularly open, as ruined and empty places are peopled and filled with light and music. In his

[25] Ibid. 34.
[26] First published in *The Union* (1753). Text from Richard Mant (ed.), *The Poetical Works of the Late Thomas Warton, B.D.*, 2 vols (Oxford, 1802), ii.27.
[27] Warton, *Poems*, 82.
[28] '[I]t is in Warton's *Observations*...that Malory makes his entrance into literary criticism' (D. Nichol Smith, 'Warton's *History of English Poetry*', *Proceedings of the British Academy*, 15 (1929), 73–99 (76)). See also Arthur Johnston, *Enchanted Ground: The Study of Medieval Romance in the Eighteenth Century* (London: Athlone Press, 1964), 103–4, 115–16.
[29] See above, p. 75.

poem 'The Grave of King Arthur', for example, the ruins of Cilgerran Castle
in Wales come to life. The vaulted roof is lit by a thousand torches, the
tapestries speak, and the minstrels sing. Inside, Henry II listens to the story of
the death of Arthur sung by the bard, who reveals that the King still lies
buried in an unmarked grave before the high altar at Glastonbury: 'Away the
ruthless Dane has torn | Each trace that Time's slow touch had worn; | And
long, o'er the neglected stone, | Oblivion's veil its shade has thrown' (127–
30). On hearing this, Henry vows to recover the body from its obscure
resting-place: 'Ev'n now he seems, with eager pace, | The consecrated floor
to trace; | And ope, from its tremendous gloom | The treasures of the
wonderous tomb' (165–8).[30] Warton's own acts of recovery find a suitable
image in this kind of imaginative archaeology.

The archetype for so many Wartonian encounters with ruined or neglected
places is his 'Ode Written at Vale-Royal Abbey', which moves between the
present and the past until, almost surreptitiously, a technique of ironic
disconnection becomes one of superimposition, and the scene begins to
live as it once did:

> The golden fans, that o'er the turrets strown,
> Quick-glancing to the sun, quaint music made,
> Are reft, and every battlement o'ergrown
> With knotted thorns, and the tall sapling's shade.
>
> The prickly thistle sheds its plumy crest,
> And matted nettles shade the crumbling mass,
> Where shone the pavement's surface smooth, imprest
> With rich reflection of the storied glass.
>
> Here hardy chieftains slept in proud repose,
> Sublimely shrin'd in gorgeous imagery;
> And through the lessening iles, in radiant rows,
> Their consecrated banners hung on high.[31]   (9–20)

Imaginatively, the thistles hint at knightly plumage, and the tall saplings
recall the lofty banners. There is still 'rich reflection' here: even the ivy
seems to enhance the tracery of the windows ('where the tall shaft and
fretted nook between | Thick ivy twines'). This is not emptiness or dilapi-
dation, but reanimation. Warton's ruins are spaces waiting to be brought
back to life by imagination. They contain ancient native writing faded by
time, and records of legends and histories. The texts are veiled, worn, or
buried, but they speak on behalf of a tradition which has been lost and may
be revived.

Linked to these ruins are the many Wartonian secret places, some contain-
ing sacred springs, which become literally sources from which the poet can

---

[30] Warton, *Poems*, 68–71.
[31] Ibid. 30–1.

draw. In 'Invocation to a Water-Nymph',[32] the poet summons the nymph 'in secret Solitude' where she presides over a spring. In seeking her permission to drink from the 'silver Lake', he not only invokes Milton's Sabrina, but absorbs the language of the young Milton himself. Significantly, Warton's final poem, the 'Birthday Ode for 1790',[33] also concerns itself with springs, celebrating a series of health-giving waters: the 'mystic spring' of Bath, the 'dim retreat' in the cliffs at Matlock, the cavernous rocks at Hotwells, Clifton, and the 'rich veins' within the mountains at Malvern. Wartonian ancient spaces are filled with music, echoes, dim or reflected lights, the sounds of water, whispers, murmurs, or chanting choirs.[34]

If it is not the poet himself who inhabits these special removed places, then it is a child—more specifically a foster-child. In a motif of significance for the concept of the 'School of Warton', and for our meandering approach to a Wordsworthian special place, these children have various benign foster-parents who carry the babe off and nurture it in a secret dwelling. It can be the infant Poetry, nurtured by King Alfred in his Saxon cell, or Edward the Black Prince, the 'royal nursling' reared by his foster-mother, the University of Oxford.[35] The model, from Warton's *Pleasures of Melancholy*, is the infant Contemplation,

> whom, as tradition tells,
> Once in his evening walk a Druid found,
> Far in a hollow glade of Mona's woods;
> And piteous bore with hospitable hand
> To the close shelter of his oaken bow'r.
> There soon the sage admiring mark'd the dawn
> Of solemn musing in your pensive thought;
> For when a smiling babe, you lov'd to lie
> Oft deeply list'ning to the rapid roar
> Of wood-hung Meinai, stream of Druids old.[36]

The baby listens to the voice of nature in the sound of an ancient stream, and the sacred presence fosters the first stirrings of consciousness and the 'musing' imagination.

---

[32] Included anonymously in the posthumous volume of his father's poems edited by Joseph Warton, *Poems on Several Occasions. By the Reverend Mr. Thomas Warton* (London, 1748), 21–2.

[33] Warton, *Poetical Works*, ii.135–42.

[34] See, for example, *The Triumph of Isis*, lines 153–6; *The Pleasures of Melancholy*, 201–10; 'Inscription in a Hermitage', 25–30; 'Ode Written at Vale-Royal Abbey', 33–6; and 'Solitude, at an Inn' (Warton, *Poetical Works*, i.15, 86–7, 101, 134, 140–1).

[35] See *The Triumph of Isis*, 216–22 (Warton, *Poetical Works*, i.21–2), and 'On the Birth of the Prince of Wales', 45–8 (Warton, *Poems*, 21).

[36] Warton, *Poetical Works*, i.95. Bowles's verse tribute to his former headmaster is specific about the fostering he had received: 'The first inciting sounds of human praise, | A parent's love excepted, came from THEE' ('Monody on the Death of Dr. Warton' (1800), in *Poems, by the Reverend Wm. Lisle Bowles*, vol. ii (London, 1801), 137–8).

For his young admirers of the 1770s and 1780s Warton himself functioned as a kind of foster-parent and nurturer of literary talent. In Warton's company a young poet could feel he was revisiting the ancient sites, hearing previously lost voices, brushing the moss from the carved stone, reanimating scenes of ruin and desolation, and locating waters from a pure source. These Wartonian motifs offered an emotional landscape that encouraged gestures of reassessment or rededication. As a father-figure, he was not a repressively looming authority but a nurturing parent encouraging articulateness. Warton, the historian of poetry and the poet of history, became a channel of communication between young poets and their literary past.

Henry Headley and Thomas Russell were the two protégés most involved in the study of literary history. Russell wrote two scholarly papers for the *Gentleman's Magazine* (1782–3) defending Warton's *History* against Ritson's attack,[37] and Headley's *Select Beauties* (1787) was a work of scholarship prompted by the material in Warton's third volume. Thomas Park was deeply read in older English poetry, and he felt closely enough attuned to Warton's work to project his own completion of the *History* (his notes were eventually incorporated into nineteenth-century editions of the work). It is no surprise to find, therefore, that in their poetry these three exploited in a distinctly Wartonian manner the reawakening of gothic buildings to the songs of old. Headley, in his *Invocation to Melancholy* (the poem admired by Wordsworth), comes upon a moated hall in a 'lonely dell' obscured by trees, and proceeds to animate it with the sound of the old bards singing their tales of chivalry; lively harping fills the place, and the 'rafter'd roofs' ring to 'the tunes of Chevy Chace and Hardiknute'.[38] Russell's 'Sonnet I' ('In days of old') does something very similar with the 'proud castle', mixing the minstrel's music with the sound of clashing armour;[39] and Thomas Park, in his sonnet 'Written at Windsor-Castle', goes so far as to end the poem with a quotation from Warton's 'Birthday Ode for 1787', celebrating those poets 'That round these banner'd walls, and crested bowers, | Have harp'd the "noblest Bards of Britain's quire!"'[40] Southey's early sonnet 'Dunnington-Castle' is shaped out of this Wartonian material. Here the fate of the 'ruin'd relique' is linked to that of its occupant, Chaucer ('envious age', which has eaten away the building, has also 'sapp'd the fabric of his lofty rhyme'), and imagination's reanimation of the building finds a parallel in the activity of Southey's reader or literary historian, who

---

[37] *Observations on the Three First Volumes of the History of English Poetry* (London, 1782) by Joseph Ritson (1752–1803). See n. 14 above.

[38] Headley, *Poems and Other Pieces*, 12–13.

[39] Russell, *Sonnets and Miscellaneous Poems*, 1.

[40] Park, *Sonnets and Other Small Poems*, 8.

> still shall ponder o'er the page,
> And piercing through the shadowy mist of time,
> The festive Bard of EDWARD's court recall,
> As fancy paints the pomp that once adorn'd thy wall.[41]

The clearest example of a Wartonian 'ruin' poem, and one directly indebted to the much-imitated Vale-Royal ode, is Headley's 'Written amidst the ruins of Broomholm Priory, in Norfolk', in which the poet contemplates a scene that is becoming effaced:

> in vain with curious eye we trace
> The tarnish'd semblance of the sacred place,
> With eye profane its fading tints explore
> That mark the features of the days of yore,
> And fain would eager snatch from ruffian Time
> The moss-grown fragment of a monkish rhyme.[42] (13–18)

As in other Wartonian poems of this type, however, the scene comes to life, as his imagination brings the coloured glass back to the windows and rebuilds the tombs.

Henry Kett's sonnet 'To Time' gives an individual twist to these lines from the past. Here there is an effective contrast between the confident youthful sapling (echoes of the Vale-Royal ode are again clear) and the deep wrinkles scarring the walls of the tower, which become the ancient disintegrating face of Time himself:

> yon moss-mantled tower,
> Whose head sublime derided once thy power,
> Now silent crumbling sinks beneath thy sway.
> The sapling, thy tall streamer, waves on high,
> Whilst thy deep wounds each mazy fissure shows,
> Like wrinkles, furrowing deep thy own grey brows.[43]

In these Wartonian contexts, the tracings of time can link the idea of a personal memory with the quest for a self that has been lost. The text can be a subjective one, like that found by Southey in his 1792 verses 'To Contemplation':

> The scatter'd Abbey's hallowed rounds I trace,
> And listen to the echoings of my feet.
> Or on the half demolished tomb,
> Whose warning texts anticipate my doom:
> Mark the clear orb of night...[44]

---

[41] Southey and Lovell, *Poems* (1795), 61.

[42] Headley, *Poems and Other Pieces*, 37. In 'Verses on the Death of Mr. Headley', Kett revisits Broomholm's 'holy walls' and recalls an earlier visit there with his friend (*Juvenile Poems*, 12–15).

[43] Kett, *Juvenile Poems*, 18.

[44] Printed in Robert Southey, *Poems* (Bristol/London, 1797), 137.

In several poems in their jointly published volume of 1795 Southey and his friend Robert Lovell pursue the Wartonian tracings into the area of personal integrity. In 'The Miser's Mansion' Southey begins by pondering on its 'time-trac'd walls', in a poem which moves Warton's Vale-Royal ode firmly towards the moral issues of wealth and selfishness, as the soul-less building takes on the lineaments of the miser who inhabited it. In a similar way, Lovell's elegy 'The Decayed Monastery' echoes the phrases of Warton's ode and mimics its structure, but ends by investigating the personal human imperatives that lead an individual towards social action. The ruin's 'time-defac'd...inscription' is set aside for a more instructive and pressing exhortation.[45]

Underlying these various motifs is a sense of the connecting stream of human experience. The images of fostering, of recovering distant voices and lost texts, locating springs and 'holy' places, reaching into the past for meanings to illuminate the present, all these are bound up with a concept of an organic history. Such a history seems in interpretive terms to bind together Wartonian texts themselves, and nowhere is this more evident than in relation to Warton's most personal poem about retrieving a connection with the past. His sonnet 'To the River Lodon' is his most influential poem in the sense that its mood, phrases, even syntax, flowed into the work of many 1790s poets. It has reverberations throughout the Warton school and beyond, acting itself as an original authentic text, a native stream from which succeeding poets could, directly or indirectly, draw:

> Ah! what a weary race my feet have run,
>   Since first I trod thy banks with alders crown'd,
>   And thought my way was all through fairy ground,
>   Beneath thy azure sky, and golden sun:
> Where first my muse to lisp her notes begun!
>   While pensive memory traces back the round,
>   Which fills the varied interval between;
>   Much pleasure, more of sorrow, marks the scene.
> Sweet native stream! those skies and suns so pure
>   No more return, to chear my evening road!
>   Yet still one joy remains, that not obscure,
> Nor useless, all my vacant days have flow'd,
>   From youth's gay dawn to manhood's prime mature;
>   Nor with the Muse's laurel unbestow'd.[46]

In this meditation on loss, continuity, and gain, the crucial concept is the return to the source, the re-establishing of contact with the 'native stream'.

---

[45] Southey and Lovell, *Poems*, 31–4, 41–5. In the same volume (51–4) Southey's poem 'Hospitality', ll. 15–46, strongly recalls Warton's Vale-Royal ode.

[46] Warton, *Poems*, 83. In Southey's *Specimens of the Later English Poets* the Loddon sonnet appears twice—once under Thomas Warton, and later also under Joseph Warton. See p. 121 below (and n. 12).

The gap between past and present selves does not close, but each is thrown into relief by the experience. The 'sweet native stream' here is not a Painite originating moment when his identity was inaugurated, but a Burkean recovery of history. 'Tracing back' the interval between, Warton recognises 'marks' both of pleasure and of sorrow, but thanks to the river he remains in touch with a sense of his developing life and what it owes to the past.

In some ways this sonnet can be seen as Warton's reclaiming of his own childhood river from Pope. Warton's birthplace was Basingstoke, on the upper Loddon, which flows into the Thames near Pope's childhood home at Binfield. Significantly, in *Windsor-Forest* (ll. 171–218) the River Loddon, mythologised as the nymph Lodona, rushes into the mighty Thames, whose 'offspring' she is (an odd reversal of their true relationship). Pope and Warton may have shared the same native river, but Pope's eyes were turned downstream, away from the source and towards the current flowing confidently out to the tidal ocean beyond.

For the Wartonians Pope was a commanding figure who, although he had changed the poetic landscape, was inadequate as a creative source for other writers.[47] In much of his work he represented the interruption of the native poetic tradition of Chaucer–Spenser–Milton, which the Wartons had helped restore. He was someone against whom they needed to define their own literary principles—they wished to reach back beyond him to neglected places upstream that were still there but ignored. To one Wartonian, Pope the translator of Homer represented a mighty flood that should not be mistaken for an authentic spring:

[Pope's] translation of Homer, timed as it was, operated like an inundation in the English Republic of letters, and has left to this day indelible marks on more than the surface of our poetry. Co-operating with the popular stream of his other works, it has formed a sort of modern Helicon, on whose banks infant poets are allowed to wander and to dream; from whose streams they are content to drink inspiration, without searching for remoter sources. Whether its waters are equally pure, salutary, and deep, with the more ancient wells of English undefiled, admits of a doubt.

The voice is that of Headley in 1787, measuring his own allegiance to his mentor Warton against the classic text which in the Johnsonian pantheon had marked the pinnacle of poetic achievement. This topographical passage from the preface to his *Select Beauties of Ancient English Poetry* links the putatively personal Loddon sonnet to the broader Wartonian project in

---

[47] Joseph Warton's *Essay on the Writings and Genius of Pope* (1756; 2nd vol 1782) controversially demoted him to the second rank of poets, and Bowles inherited the mantle of his teacher and denigrated Pope in his 1806 edition, becoming entangled in the well-known controversy with Byron. See James Chandler, 'The Pope Controversy: Romantic Politics and the English Canon', *Critical Inquiry*, 10 (1984), 481–509. Robert J. Griffin explores the dynamics of romanticism in terms of the displacing of Pope. See *Wordsworth's Pope: A Study in Literary Historiography* (Cambridge: Cambridge University Press, 1995).

literary history—the fostering of a sense of continuity with those 'remoter sources'. In contrast to the Wartonian stream, the banks of Pope's river were impure and overcrowded.

Warton's Loddon sonnet had many imitators, and during the two decades after its publication in 1777 it established the revisiting of a river bank as the locus for a meditative self-assessment in terms of past and present. The return to the special place allowed the past to be recovered and continuity established. Underneath the sheddings and accretions, the tragedy of loss weighed against the solace of gain, there could be asserted a sense of the self as a developing organism. Revisiting a river bank, albeit in only fourteen lines, implied a personal history in these terms. Bowles's twin sonnets to the rivers Cherwell and Itchin,[48] for example, revisit the banks, respectively, of his days at Oxford and at Winchester. In the former he begins by juxtaposing the optimistic past ('Cherwell, how pleas'd along thy willow'd edge | Ere-while I stray'd') with the rueful present ('And now reposing on thy banks once more'), and, after reference to his 'melancholy way' through life, he ends by taking stock of the gains to be set against what he has lost ('yet something have I won | Of solace'). The Itchin sonnet plays out a similar temporal arrangement:

> Itchin, when I behold thy banks again,
>   Thy crumbling margin, and thy silver breast,
>   On which the self-same tints still seem to rest,
> Why feels my heart the shiv'ring sense of pain?
>   Is it—that many a summer's day has past
> Since, in life's morn, I carol'd on thy side?
> Is it—that oft, since then, my heart has sigh'd,
>   As Youth, and Hope's delusive gleams, flew fast?
> Is it—that those, who circled on thy shore,
> Companions of my youth, now meet no more?
>   Whate'er the cause, upon thy banks I bend
> Sorrowing, yet feel such solace at my heart,
>   As at the meeting of some long-lost friend,
>   From whom, in happier hours, we wept to part.

Warton's strategic 'Since' and 'Yet' had marked syntactically the structure of his poem; they reappear similarly here as the pivotal moments, temporally between the visiting and revisiting, and evaluatively between the loss and gain. A 'since' and 'yet' structure is evident in several Wartonian riverbank sonnets: Coleridge's 'To the River Otter', his tribute to his own native stream, sets the 'Visions of Childhood' alongside 'lone Manhood's cares', and opens with the characteristic exclamation:

[48] The Itchin sonnet was included in Bowles, *Fourteen Sonnets*; the Cherwell sonnet first appeared in the second edition. The texts given here are from the third edition, *Sonnets, with Other Poems* (Bath, 1794), 20, 10.

> Dear native Brook! wild Streamlet of the West!
> How many various-fated Years have past,
> What blissful and what anguish'd hours, since last...[49]

An interesting variation is played by Thomas Park's sonnet 'To the River Witham', which actually uses Warton and his Loddon sonnet as a connective figure. It proceeds with the recollection motif: 'How oft, erewhile, in child-hood's happy hour, | Have I the angler's patient labour plied | Along thy banks' (5–7). The 'yet' section introduces 'memory' to release the temporal interplay, but where we would expect a weighing of loss and gain, the gain is never registered; instead, Warton himself enters the poem:

> Yet memory now,
> E'en o'er these scenes of former joys can pine,
> Care with his rugged furrows marks my brow,
> And past delights, like spectres, grimly shine:
> So did they erst round pensive Warton gleam,
> Warton, the laureate boast of Britain's Academe![50]   (9–14)

A footnote here recalls the reader's attention to the Loddon sonnet. In a significant gesture Warton himself is introduced to the remembered scene, suggesting that the gain for Park is having his mentor as a companion-figure for the revisiting of his own native stream.

In Edward Gardner's sonnet 'On Revisiting the Banks of the Avon near Bristol Hotwells' the banks reconnect the poet to his childhood innocence:

> Ah me! how oft with slow and ling'ring feet,
> Avon I've trod thy grass-grown sedgy side,
> And here once more thy verdant shore I greet
>   .   .   .   .   .   .
> Here innocent I pass'd the listless day...
> O now again I hear thy murmurs slow,
> I see the alders o'er the low waves bend,
> And sure these scenes must sweetest peace bestow,
> They seem the soothings of a much lov'd friend.   (1–12)

In this context any loss is not in a present set against the past, but is evoked as a future possibility ('Farewell dear stream, ah far from thee I go, | Perhaps from paths of peace to those of tearful woe' (13–14)).[51]

The temporal permutations of the Wartonian riverbank sonnet can, there-fore, vary, and indeed such variations are a feature of this minor genre. In Southey's sonnet 'To a Brook near the Village of Corston', as in Gardner's poem, past and present are not juxtaposed and weighed against each other.

---

[49] Text from 1797 *Poems*, 78.
[50] Park, *Sonnets and Other Small Poems*, 25.
[51] Gardner, *Miscellanies*, ii.127–8.

Here instead the current of memory revives the past as a pale but beautiful picture:

> As thus I bend me o'er thy babbling stream
> And watch thy current, Memory's hand pourtrays
> The faint form'd scenes of the departed days,
> Like the far forest by the moon's pale beam
> Dimly descried yet lovely. I have worn
> Upon thy banks the live-long hour away   (1–6)

with the result that when the 'yet' finally arrives it does so to reaffirm continuity; however 'faint' or 'dim', the scene is visually and emotionally present:

> Dim are the long past days, yet still they please
> As thy soft sounds half heard, borne on the inconstant breeze.[52]

These 'recognitions dim and faint' with which 'the picture of the mind revives again' move us a little closer to the Wye.

It is perhaps no surprise that the line of Warton's sonnet which encapsulates the organic connectedness of life ('From youth's gay dawn to manhood's prime mature') is repeatedly reworked in later sonnets and elegies. Charlotte Smith's sonnet 'To Mrs. G.' looks back to 'when life's gay dawn was opening to my view',[53] and Edward Gardner's sonnet 'Written under a Lofty Cliff on the Banks of the Severn on a Summer's Evening' ends with the less than resolute remark, 'On this shore...|...O let me waste what yet remains of manhood's prime'.[54] Bowles's poem on the death of Thomas Russell, 'Elegy Written at the Hot-Wells, Bristol', suitably collapses Warton's line, mourning his friend as 'the lost companion of my youth's gay prime',[55] and when Coleridge penned his sonnet 'to the Rev. W. L. Bowles' in 1794 he tapped into the addressee's own elegiac language: 'Thro Youth's gay prime and thornless paths I went'.[56]

In a similar way, the exclamation 'Sweet native stream!', which ushers in the sestet of Warton's Loddon sonnet, provides riparian poets with a refrain. Charlotte Smith's sonnet 'To Melancholy. Written on the Banks of the Arun, October, 1785' records the sounds along Otway's 'native stream'.[57] The

---

[52] Southey, *Poems*, 112.
[53] Smith, *Elegiac Sonnets*, 10.
[54] Gardner, *Miscellanies*, ii.133–4.
[55] Bowles, *Elegy Written at the Hot-Wells, Bristol*, 7. Bowles consciously echoes Thomas Warton, recollecting the times when he and Russell 'heard the merry bells by *Isis*' stream, | And thought our way was strew'd with fairy flow'rs' (combining the last line of the Dugdale's Monasticon sonnet with line 3 of the Loddon sonnet), and describing the intervening years: 'Thinking how days and hours have pass'd along, | Mark'd by much pleasure some, and some by tears!' (reworking line 8 of the Loddon sonnet).
[56] Samuel Taylor Coleridge, 'To the Rev. W. L. Bowles', *Morning Chronicle*, 26 Dec. 1794. The poem was printed in Coleridge's 1796 *Poems* as 'Effusion I'.
[57] Smith, *Elegiac Sonnets*, 32.

invocation 'Dear native Brook!' that opens Coleridge's Otter sonnet echoes throughout his 'Effusion . . . Written in Early Youth':

> So tost by storms along Life's wild'ring way
> Mine eye reverted views that cloudless day,
> When by my native brook I wont to rove
> While hope with kisses nurs'd the Infant Love.
>
> Dear native brook! like PEACE, so placidly
> Smoothing thro' fertile fields thy current meek!
> Dear native brook! . . . [58]   (79–85)

Coleridge's projected long poem, *The Brook*, was to have been a study in connectedness ('I sought for a subject, that should . . . supply in itself a natural connection to the parts, and unity to the whole. Such a subject I conceived myself to have found in a stream, traced from its source in the hills');[59] and Wordsworth's *The River Duddon, A Series of Sonnets*, written over many years, was eventually to trace a river from spring to estuary. Perhaps in acknowledgement of the Loddon sonnet, what became the first poem of Wordsworth's sequence has for the opening line of its sestet, 'I seek the birth-place of a native Stream'.[60]

When Wordsworth composed his 'Lines written a few miles above Tintern Abbey, on revisiting the banks of the Wye during a tour, July 13, 1798', he was choosing a location for his thoughts which invited a reading in terms of the riverbank-revisited poem popularised by Warton and his school. But he was also drawing upon a wider inheritance available to him through its motifs, locations, and temporal manoeuvres. Underlying Wordsworth's per-sonalised history of revisiting and recovery there is the concept of an organic narrative history such as Warton and his followers had articulated. It is as though the minor genre itself invited contributors to participate in some more communal revisiting that struck the note, even in the supposedly most private moments, of a shared identity. But the configurations are not that simple. In the *poetic* act the self is temporalised, and the individual history, with its unique memories and particular determinations, encounters a more precarious and multiple set of potentialities. Rather than settling into a single universal pattern, the history becomes, through syntactical variation, a series of possible narratives. In this way its organic character is more complex and contingent than the idealist concept discussed in Chapter 1.

It is appropriate, therefore, to continue this narrative by entering the Wye Valley itself in the company, not of Wordsworth, but of three Wartonians

---

[58] *1796 Poems*, 106–7.

[59] *Biog. Lit.*, i.195–6 (ch. 10). Jonathan Wordsworth links Coleridge's scheme for *The Brook* with 'Tintern Abbey' and earlier 'nostalgic revisited rivers'. See *William Wordsworth: The Borders of Vision* (Oxford: Clarendon Press, 1982), 333–4.

[60] William Wordsworth, *The River Duddon, A Series of Sonnets* (London, 1820), 3.

who offer distinct though related voices beside which Wordsworth's may be heard more clearly.

The first text, Edward Gardner's 'Sonnet Written in Tintern Abbey' (1798), locates the speaking voice within the ruined abbey itself. In this poem, typical of Gardner's simple moralized landscapes, the ruin is the temple of man's body victimised by time; but it still contains religious feelings that can be reawakened through contemplation:

> Admiring stranger, that with ling'ring feet,
>> Enchain'd by wonder, pauses on this green;
> Where thy enraptur'd sight the dark woods meet,
>> Ah! rest awhile, and contemplate the scene.
> These hoary pillars clasp'd by ivy round,
>> This hallow'd floor by holy footsteps trod,
> The mould'ring choir by spreading moss embrown'd,
>> Where fasting saints devoutly hymn'd their God.
> Unpitying Time, with slow but certain sweep,
>> Has laid, alas! their ancient splendor low:
> Yet here let Pilgrims, while they muse and weep,
>> Think on the lesson that from hence may flow.
> Like their's, how soon may be the tott'ring state
> Of man,—the temple of a shorter date.[61]

Gardner sustains continuity within the ruinous state: the 'hymn' has merely been succeeded by the 'lesson', and this remains a place in which the tourist is transposed into the pilgrim. The flow of the river has been replaced by the sententious 'flow' of the *memento mori* moral from the abbey, a sentimental equivalent of its ancient dole of charity and hospitality to the poor traveller.

Henry Kett's sonnet 'To the River Wye' (published 1793) omits the abbey, but creates imaginatively out of the natural scene a comparable retreat from the violent world beyond:

> O Wye, romantic stream! thy winding way
>> Invites my lonely steps, what time the night
>> Smiles with the radiance of the moon's pale light,
>> That loves upon the quivering flood to play.
> O'er thy steep banks the rocks fantastic tower,
>> And fling their deepening shadow cross the stream,
>> To fancy's eye worn battlements they seem,
>> Which on some beetling cliff tremendous lower.
> Hark! Echo speaks, and from her mazy cave
>> Sportive returns the sailor's frequent cry,
>> Ah! how unlike thy old bards minstrelsy
> Warbled in wild notes to the haunted wave!

---

[61] The sonnet first appeared in *European Magazine*, 30 (Aug. 1796), and this text is printed by Roger Lonsdale in *The New Oxford Book of Eighteenth-Century Verse* (Oxford, 1984), 819. I give the text as revised for Gardner's *Miscellanies*, ii.97–8.

> Unlike as seems the hurricane's rude sweep,
> To the light breeze that lulls thy placid deep.[62]

In this poem of visual and verbal playfulness (the tone, in more ways than one, is set by the moonlight), Wordsworth's 'steep and lofty cliffs' take on the lineaments of an ancient building as the metaphorical verb 'tower' is literalized in the battlements. At one level of reading the valley is a calm retreat from the storms blowing across the sea, and the exclusions are explicit ones in this poem of supposed absences: the building is absent, the bards are absent, the hurricane is absent. And yet each registers its presence with a fluidity that has an almost uncanny effect. What is supposedly present is the sailor's cry, but this is less substantial than echo's mimicry of it, and it is overtaken by the wild notes of the absent bards, which are evoked in terms of the sublime power of the hurricane (another absentee). The final lulling of the present breeze cannot pacify a poem in which it is the absence that disturbs.

Finally, George Richards's ode 'Tintern Abbey; or, the Wandering Minstrel' brings the ruins to life by filling them with light and sound in a very Wartonian manner:

> Still is the air, and hush'd the wood;
> In soothing silence creeps the flood:
> And evening calms with golden gleam
> The hoary rocks and glittering stream.
> Dark shadowy elms beneath embower
> The cloisters and high-fretted tower
> Of lonely Tintern: tapers bright
> Through lofty windows pour their light;
> And, rais'd by chaunting quires, a sound
> Celestial spreads a charm around.   (5–14)

The place is animated further when a minstrel begins to sing, celebrating the holy building as a place of loving nurture, of grace and healing, of the 'wild' being calmed to stillness:

> Religion, shrin'd in holy walls,
> And watching every bead that falls,
> Shall wean the beating heart from pain,
> Shall still the wild tumultuous vein,
> Shall spread around the faded face
> Her holy calm, her solemn grace.   (75–80)

The holiness in Richards's poem is a function of the exclusion and calmness, yet what is excluded registers itself in softened tones, like the echoes and breezes in Kett's Wye Valley. For Richards the abbey is a sanctuary that will remain accessible long after he has left:

---

[62] Kett, *Juvenile Poems*, 16.

> Adieu, ye holy men:—I go
> To guilty crowds, and scenes of woe.
> Yet oft, to silent virtue true,
> These warbling strings shall sound of you.[63]   (111–14)

We shall be returning to the Wye valley in Chapter 11 to consider the links (more ironic ones) that Wordsworth's poem has with another tradition of eighteenth-century poetry. As a text which longs to forge and sustain connections, it makes the reader sense the precariousness of these tenuous continuities that stretch through space and time, linking the dead with (for the moment) the living. In the ritual reanimation of reading a poem, and returning to re-read it, something of this is reenacted. Recognition and loss, as the classical poets of the underworld knew, are closely related. But the sociable side of Wordsworth's Wye Valley 'Lines' is also powerful. An awareness of Wartonian poetry, as I have tried to show, can allow it to be more effectually heard. What seems a sublime egotistical voice is in fact more socially nuanced, and the poem can be understood as recovering not just a private history, but also a shared literary history for itself in which its language acknowledges the revisitings and recoveries of other poets.

Wordsworth's poem written along the banks of the Wye locates a lost voice among the echoes of the past. As in Warton's Loddon sonnet, a poet revisits an important source and is conscious of what he owes and what he has left behind. The sounds to which Wordsworth is attuned (and we as readers only barely overhear) are elusive ones, but I hope this chapter has captured something of them. In Wordsworth's poem there is no bard, no minstrel-song to echo through the valley; there is no abbey, no holy ground being trodden by spirits from the past, no physical text to be recovered; and yet each of these Wartonian motifs exerts a subtle influence in the poem.

Near the beginning of his final paragraph Wordsworth turns to acknowledge for the first time his sister Dorothy's presence, and he does so with the phrase 'for thou art with me'. In those words we hear an echo of that other valley of the Twenty-Third Psalm, the 'valley of the shadow of death', which for Wordsworth can be faced thanks to the reassurance of a sacred presence, a 'holier love'. In the company of his 'dear, dear Friend' he has no need of the abbey to focus his contemplation; it is her mind that

> Shall be a mansion for all lovely forms,
> Thy memory be as a dwelling-place
> For all sweet sounds and harmonies.   (141–3)

The Psalm ends with the words: 'I will dwell in the house of the LORD for ever'. Far from being excluded from Wordsworth's 'Lines', the building is

---

[63] Richards, *Poems*, ii.16–23.

present throughout in the contemplative procedure of the poem, and in the way in which a human focus is found for the Wartonian special place. As Wordsworth recovers the holy text from his meditation, he reanimates the indwelling spirit as a companion, as a pledge for the future won from his recovery of his own narrative history.

5   Southey's Literary History: Poetry in Retrospect

AGAIN AND AGAIN Robert Southey felt compelled to return to the same story. Over a span of thirty years at each telling it retained the same narrative line of achievement, decline, triumph, corruption, tyranny, and eventual re-emergence and recovery. It was a version of his nation's literary history, but also, given Southey's lifelong pull towards retrospect, was a favourite personal tale. It seems that the story remained lodged in his mind during most of his writing life, and whenever he sensed an opportunity he was happy to revisit it, with minor variations, for another set of readers. Southey evidently planned, but never wrote, a book-length history of English poetry, and Coleridge urged him in that direction.[1] There was certainly one inside him, and he had the breadth of reading to carry it out, along with a detailed knowledge of the obscure literary byways, and an alertness to questions of metre, creative influence, and critical context. Above all, Southey retained in his mind a comprehensive narrative of poetry's development, and it is his repeated articulation of it that forms the core of this chapter. I want first to characterise and assess Southey's account of literary history, and see what it can tell us about his tastes and judgments; but beyond that the discussion will then attempt to address the implications of the revisiting itself, and to link it to that 'quest for home' which Christopher Smith has identified as a recurrent concern of Southey's poetry of the 1790s.[2] As Southey repeatedly returns to his story it becomes a familiar landscape from which he has drawn sustenance. It confirms an association between the development of the national character and the personal values he inscribes on it. The story allows him to attack fashion, slavishness, corruption, mechanism, and materialism, and to locate a restorative tradition that blends understanding and

---

[1] 'Phillips would be very glad to engage you to write a School book for him, the History of Poetry in all nations—about 400 pages...He would give 60£' (Coleridge to Southey, 12 Feb. 1800; Griggs, 570). Coleridge continued urging Southey towards the project in a letter of 28 Feb. (Griggs, 575). On 23 Feb. 1830 Southey wrote to [John Murray]: 'I had long been looking to & preparing for a History of English Literature, beginning where Wartons Hist. of Poetry ends & bringing the subject down to Cowper & Darwin,—that is, stopping just when my own age begins' (Huntington Library, HM 2729). I am grateful to Lynda Pratt for this reference. Southey's *Commonplace Book*, ed. John Wood Warter, 4 vols (Longman, 1849–51), iv.279–351 is devoted to 'collections for history of English literature and poetry'.

[2] Christopher J. P. Smith, *A Quest for Home: Reading Robert Southey* (Liverpool: Liverpool University Press, 1997).

feeling into an organic expression of human nature. Southey's literary history is a means of forging continuities to resist the disruptive pressures that threatened the nation and himself.

As early as 1796 Southey was conscious of a compulsion to narrate his own story. At an age when we might expect youthful self-dramatisation, it seems narrative was the favoured mode for this 22-year-old to assert his identity. He writes to Grosvenor Bedford with the self-awareness and assurance of someone already living his life between hard covers: 'no man ever retained a more perfect knowledge of the history of his own mind than I have done. I can trace the *development* of my character from infancy—for *developed* it has been, not chang'd',[3] and the following year he enlisted Bedford as his 'confessor' to whom he could send biographical instalments that would chart the course of his life so far.[4] Yet hard on the heels of this composed and self-composing young man was the Southey who announced to Tom Lamb in 1798: 'since last I saw you all my views in life, and many of my opinions, have been changed more than once'.[5] It was not narrative continuity but extreme dramatic tension that Thomas Carlyle saw embodied in the old poet of the 1830s:

I said to myself, 'How has this man contrived, with such a nervous system, to keep alive for near sixty years? Now blushing under his grey hairs, rosy like a maiden of fifteen; now slaty almost, like a rattle-snake or fiery serpent? How has he not been torn to pieces long since, under such furious pulling this way and that? He must have somewhere a great deal of methodic virtue in him.[6]

In *The Spirit of the Age* (1825) William Hazlitt located Southey's enigmatic character in a radical whimsicality that was 'wild, irregular, singular, extreme ... With him every thing is projecting, starting from its place, an episode, a digression, a poetic license ... He is pragmatical, restless, unfixed.'[7] And yet Hazlitt recognised that these fits and starts were somehow accommodated to (even subsumed into) a sense of benign temporal continuity, one that mingled the sanguine and melancholy humours: 'Mr Southey's mind is essentially sanguine ... ', he noted, 'It is prophetic of good; it cordially embraces it; it casts a longing, lingering look after it, even when it is gone for ever' (79). The allusion to Gray's *Elegy* hints at how poetic

---

[3] Southey to G. C. Bedford, 31 July 1796 (*Life and Correspondence of Robert Southey*, ed. Charles Cuthbert Southey, 6 vols (London: Longman, 1849–50), i.298).

[4] See Mark Storey, *Robert Southey: A Life* (Oxford/New York: Oxford University Press, 1997), 107. The first letter of the planned series was written on 30 Sept. 1797 (*New Letters of Robert Southey*, ed. Kenneth Curry, 2 vols (New York/London: Columbia University Press, 1965), i.149–51).

[5] Southey to Thomas Lamb, 13 June 1798 (*Selections from the Letters of Robert Southey*, ed. John Wood Warter, 4 vols (London: Longman, 1856), i.56).

[6] Thomas Carlyle, *Reminiscences*, ed. J. A. Froude, 2 vols (London: Longman, 1881), ii.317. Quoted by Smith, *A Quest for Home*, 7.

[7] William Hazlitt, *The Complete Works of William Hazlitt*, ed. P. P. Howe (London and Toronto: J. M. Dent, 1930–4), xi.81. Future references are given in the text.

retrospect offered Southey a means of holding on mentally to fleeting values, unwilling to let go what his heart had embraced.[8]

The subtlety of Hazlitt's chiaroscuro portrait lies in its recognition that inside the man who had notoriously 'defaulted' (to use E. P. Thompson's word[9]) on his youthful radicalism was a tenacious consistency, a repeated need to return, rather than to move on. 'The elasticity of his spirit is unbroken,' Hazlitt comments, 'the bow recoils to its old position' (83). In this image the spirit stretches itself, but the moment of relaxation is a kind of homecoming. This concept of what might be seen (ironically in this context) as a 'default-position' in Southey's nature makes him puzzling but perhaps ultimately consistent.

A similar idea lies behind Hazlitt's judgment of the poetry, where once again the image forms of a conscientious reflection on experience:

Perhaps the most pleasing and striking of all Mr Southey's poems are not his triumphant taunts hurled against oppression, are not his glowing effusions to Liberty, but those in which, with a mild melancholy, he seems conscious of his own infirmities of temper, and to feel a wish to correct by thought and time the precocity and sharpness of his disposition. (83)

Melancholy is again the keynote. Thought is not revelation, but meditation, a continual testing out through time that shows the conscience of the careful reviser. The centripetal movement interests Hazlitt, and has its negative side in what he sees as Southey's quality of stubborn insistence (the opposite of Coleridge's genius for expansive, impetuous speculation). He contrasts Coleridge's orality with Southey's literariness, his need for a reference library. When Southey does reach out it is for a past record, a note he had made earlier: 'Mr Southey evidently considers writing as his stronghold, and if gravelled in an argument, or at a loss for an explanation, refers to something he has written on the subject, or brings out his port-folio, doubled down in dog-ears' (85).

One man's dog-eared portfolio is another man's file of cherished notes, and Southey's sketch of English literary history falls into that ambivalence. Five times between 1807 and 1835 he published a concise narrative of the course of English poetry, in which the same episodes and themes (often the same details) recur. On the public level it represents Southey's attempt to locate the national genius and to follow its erratic course through periods of lost faith, corruption, and false fashion until its re-emergence in the generation prior to his own. There is certainly an insistent character to this, but its very doggedness also reveals a fascinating mix of conservative and radical impulses. We see something that resembles a Burkean system of historical continuities in which tradition is vital; but at critical moments this tradition challenges the status quo. As in Burke, the 'conservatism' has a resistant,

---

[8] Thomas Gray, *Elegy Written in a Country Churchyard* (1751), l. 88.
[9] E. P. Thompson, 'Disenchantment or Default? A Lay Sermon', in C. C. O'Brien and W. D. Vanech (eds), *Power and Consciousness* (London: University of London Press, 1969), 149–81.

stubborn quality. We encounter a national character that has been shaped by recalcitrant human experience rather than by the legislation of the powerful. It is embedded in a tradition of common law, not set in a framework of rules. In this organic constitution Truth is accrued, not declared, and is identified with Memory, the keeper of records who shuns Fashion and declines to adopt hegemonic values. A dog-eared portfolio can survive to embarrass the present. The literary history that Southey celebrates therefore resists regulation and rewriting by an elite—cultural or political—and his favourite critics are those who do not rule or judge. In his 1814 *Quarterly Review* essay, for example, he explicitly detaches the native English tradition from that of the Nordic scalds and Welsh bards.[10] Whereas those 'privileged professors' safeguarded their authority by 'capricious rules', the un-priest-like minstrels represented the genuinely 'popular' origins of English poetry: 'Happily for us our verse, beginning among the people, necessarily assumed from its birth a popular character; and when the English minstrel was admitted into castles and courts, the language of life and passion was the language of English poetry' (1814:62). When vernacular English came to displace the Norman French of the ruling class, the demotic character of the national poetry was set.

In the account of Southey's literary history that follows, these complicating questions about the nature of his conservatism can help to highlight certain facets of Southey's character—moral, political, poetical—in which a continuity of values is paramount.[11] The obvious binary of young radical and ageing conservative does not fit the picture that emerges of a writer concerned with locating the tradition from which his own early poetry grew. I want therefore at the end of the chapter to link Southey's literary history back to that youthful verse of retrospect and 'mild melancholy' which Hazlitt found so 'striking', and which was manifested in his poem 'The Retrospect' (1794). It means inverting chronology and reading back from Southey's later prose into the lyrical verse of the 1790s; but it is my contention that his repeated revisiting of that narrative is in part a reconnection of himself to his own poetic root-system.

Southey's earliest account of the development of English poetry is his preface to the ill-starred *Specimens of the Later English Poets* (1807).[12]

---

[10] *Quarterly Review*, 12 (Oct. 1814), 60–90. Future references are given in the text in the form of (1814:60).

[11] For a close political analysis of Southey's track through the 1790s, see David M. Craig, *Robert Southey and Romantic Apostasy: Political Argument in Britain, 1780–1840* (Woodbridge: Royal Historical Society and Boydell Press, 2007), 13–42.

[12] Robert Southey (ed.), *Specimens of the Later English Poets*, 3 vols. (London: Longman, 1807), vol. i, pp. vi–xxxii. Future references are given in the text in the form of (1807:vi). The writing of the prefatory essay proved a struggle, and Southey was displeased with it when finished: 'I wrote that preface *doggedly* and without liking to do it, or liking it when done' (Southey to G. C. Bedford, 2 Feb. 1807; Southey, *Selections*, i.412). The story of the project is told, and Southey's contributions identified, by Raymond D. Havens, 'Southey's *Specimens of the Later English Poets*', *PMLA*, 60 (1945), 1066–79.

Drawing a vast amount of material into a brief summary was evidently a challenge, and perhaps it was a feeling that he hadn't done justice to the subject that made him repeat the attempt seven years later in a thirty-page article for the *Quarterly Review* (1814) prompted by his reviewing of Alexander Chalmers's *Works of the English Poets* in the previous issue.[13] In two further reviews in the *Quarterly* (of William Hayley's *Memoirs*, 1824,[14] and Frank Sayers's *Works*, 1827[15]) Southey took the opportunity to trace once again the later part of the story, and in 1835 he devoted Chapter 12 of his 'Life of Cowper' to a fifty-page essay entitled 'Sketches of the Progress of English Poetry from Chaucer to Cowper'.[16] In each of these accounts it is during the eighteenth century that English poetry rediscovers its true path and delivers an inheritance to the 1790s generation. This idea of reconnecting poetry to its living past helps to shape Southey's history, and in identifying a tradition sympathetic to his own work he clearly feels that he understands, and speaks for, the national character. He is interested in locating the point at which a personal retrospect becomes emblematic of larger continuities. When Hazlitt talks of Southey's mind as 'rather the recipient and transmitter of knowledge, than the originator of it' (86) he is emphasising the mediating role that Southey himself valued in poets of the past.

What Southey thought they were transmitting is suggested by the introductory words of his 1814 essay. Perhaps conscious of his recent appointment as the country's Poet Laureate, he likens the story of poetry's development to the legal constitution of the nation: 'In this ['the history of English poetry'], *as in our laws and institutions*, however it may have been occasionally modified by the effect of foreign models, a distinct national character has predominated' (1814:60—my italics). Southey's underplaying of 'foreign models' in favour of a more nationally constituted poetry is evident in his rejection of a formal scheme of poetic 'schools' like those Pope and Gray had outlined in their plans for a history of poetry.[17] Gray, for example, had grouped his poets under the 'School of Provence', the first, second, and third 'Italian Schools', and the 'School of France'. In his preface to the *Specimens* Southey rejects this in favour of a home-grown narrative:

---

[13] On Southey's anonymous reviewing for the *Quarterly*, see Kenneth Curry and Robert Dedmon, 'Southey's Contributions to *The Quarterly Review*', *WC*, 6 (1975), 261–72.

[14] *Quarterly Review*, 31 (July 1824), 265–311. Future references are given in the text in the form of (1824:265).

[15] *Quarterly Review*, 35 (Jan. 1827), 175–220. Future references are given in the text in the form of (1827:175).

[16] *The Life and Works of William Cowper…with a Life of the Author*, 15 vols (London: Baldwin and Cradock, 1835–7), i.291–343. Future references are given in the text in the form of (1835:291).

[17] Pope's sketch plan was first printed by Owen Ruffhead, *The Life of Alexander Pope* (London, 1769), 425. This, along with Gray's sketch posted to Thomas Warton in 1770, were both easily available to Southey in *The Poetical Works of the Late Thomas Warton, B.D.*, 2 vols, ed. Richard Mant (Oxford, 1802), vol. i, pp. liii–lxii.

'The classification of our Poets into schools is to be objected to, because it implies that we have no school of our own' (1807:xiii). He does not want to make structural categories out of what he thinks are only shifting fashions: 'We have had foreign fashions in literature, as well as in dress, but have at all times preserved in both, a costume and character of our own' (1807:xiii). The concept of a national 'character' offers him the idea of continuity he needs, and could not have been achieved through the taxonomic structures of Pope and Gray.

In refusing their well-known schemes Southey can be seen to be adopting the organic view of literary history pioneered by Thomas Warton in his *History of English Poetry* (1774–81), whose preface, as we saw in Chapter 3, explicitly rejects the models of Pope and Gray because of their 'mechanical' nature.[18] Warton's monumental work, which Southey admired, offers instead a narrative of potential continuities and retrospects that bears a family resemblance to Southey's own. The latter at times reads like a summary of how Warton might have completed his history had he progressed beyond 1600. It is evident, therefore, that Southey's projected continuation (see n. 1) would have been a Wartonian one.

At the heart of Southey's sense of national character, and something he particularly emphasises in his 1814 essay, is the raw material of the English language, the 'ore' out of which poetry is made. It is clear that his ideal, lying between crudeness and over-refinement, is a practical working of the materials that doesn't sacrifice strength to ornateness: 'the mere ore of speech', he notes, 'must be refined before it can be ductile enough for verse. On the other hand, the process of refining may be carried too far' (1814:61). It is a metaphor that recalls an image used in his 1807 preface where he characterizes the Restoration wits as 'the Birmingham trade of verse', alluding to the town's mass production of metal buttons and buckles. He recognises its equivalent in the manufacturing of fashionable poetic accessories, 'turning a song...complimenting a lady...pointing an epigram' (1807:xxix). In all five accounts Southey sets himself against those poets who pander to the luxury market. He repeatedly associates stylistic fashions with the ornate, the mechanical, and the temporary. Against this he sets his 'core' values of independence, strength, and nature.

Given this conviction of the dangers of over-refinement, it is no surprise that Southey consistently challenges the eighteenth-century 'Progress of Refinement' narrative of literary history. This received its classic statement in Samuel Johnson's *Lives of the English Poets* (1779–81), in which Waller and Denham play the crucial role of 'refining' the poetic language and thus pave the way for the crowning achievement of Dryden and Pope.[19]

---

[18] See above, p. 70.
[19] Samuel Johnson, *Lives of the English Poets*, ed. Roger Lonsdale, 4 vols (Oxford: Clarendon Press, 2006), ii.123–4 ('Life of Dryden').

Johnson's trajectory of poetry's rise to perfection in Pope's *Homer* is repeatedly and indignantly contradicted by Southey: 'Never indeed did ignorance more impudently expose itself than when it awarded to Waller the praise of having first refined our verse, and to Pope that of having perfected it! Spenser is the great master of English versification' (1814:72).[20] With that final sentence it becomes clear that Southey belongs to the first of the opposing critical 'parties' identified by Vicesimus Knox in 1782:

> I think it is not difficult to perceive, that the admirers of English poetry are divided into two parties. The objects of their love are, perhaps, of equal beauty, though they greatly differ in their air, their dress, the turn of their features, and their complexion. On one side, are the lovers and imitators of Spenser and Milton; and on the other, those of Dryden, Boileau, and Pope.[21]

Johnson's 'Progress of Refinement' narrative made it difficult to conceive how poetry might develop beyond Pope's perfection of the heroic couplet: 'New sentiments and new images others may produce', he concluded, 'but to attempt any further improvement of versification will be dangerous.'[22] Southey overturns this declaration by maintaining that the heroic couplet, in comparison with the Spenserian stanza and the blank verse of Shakespeare and Milton, is inimical to the strength of the British character ('a fashion imported from France, with the French accompaniments of frippery, tinsel, and false ornament'; 1835:293).[23] For him, the whole period from 1660 to 1740, which for Johnson is the peak of English poetry, represents an aberration, a 'pinchbeck age' (1835:313) during which the native ore was forgotten. 'The time which elapsed from the days of Dryden to those of Pope, is the dark age of English poetry' (1807:xxix).[24]

For Southey, one virtue of the English language (in contrast to the Italian) is its inherent lack of grace and sweetness, which makes poets strive for 'something more'. This has led to problems when '[f]eeble wits have attempted to supply what was wanting by finical ornaments, and affectations of various kinds' (1814:64); but through skill, experience, and their honest struggle with the language, English poets have become expert at harnessing its power. 'Thus', concludes Southey, 'the very defects of that

---

[20] 'Johnson gave it the sanction of his great authority, that Waller and Denham began to refine our versification...But there was no subject of which Johnson, if he knew any thing, knew so little as of our early poetry' (1835:294). Southey repeats the point on 306.

[21] Vicesimus Knox, *Essays Moral and Literary* (London, 1782), ii.186 (no. CXXIX, 'On the Prevailing Taste in Poetry').

[22] Johnson, *Lives of the English Poets*, iv.79 ('Life of Pope').

[23] Southey adds that blank verse 'is so perfectly in accord with the genius of our language, and so excellently adapted to its purpose' (1835:293). On the association of blank verse with British liberty during the eighteenth century, see David Fairer, 'Creating a National Poetry: The Tradition of Spenser and Milton', in John Sitter (ed.), *The Cambridge Companion to Eighteenth-Century Poetry* (Cambridge: Cambridge University Press, 2001), 177–201 (187–9).

[24] Southey repeats this thirty years later: 'The age from Dryden to Pope is the worst age of English poetry' (1835:311).

language have been made advantageous to our literature, as long winter nights and stormy seas have given us our maritime skill' (1814:65).[25] It is no coincidence that for Southey the period of the Armada represented, as it had done for Warton, 'our golden age' of English poetry (1807:xxiii).

In Southey's history it was Chaucer who first imprinted a specific English character on the generic materials that formed the staple of medieval literature throughout Europe.[26] His distinctive founding achievement was *The Canterbury Tales*, in which the poet 'had an eye and an ear, for all the sights and sounds of nature; humour to display human follies, and feeling to understand, and to delineate human passions' (1807:xvii). Southey acknowledges Chaucer's debts to the French and Italian poets, but he brushes them aside by emphasising the observed human truth in Chaucer's work: 'Strong English sense, and strong English humour characterize his original works. He caught with a painter's hand the manners and features of the age, and he penetrated with a poet's intuition into the recesses of the human heart' (1814:65). Underlying each of Southey's accounts of the history of English poetry, explicitly or implicitly, is this Chaucerian combination of observation, insight, intelligence, and feeling. For Southey these are virtues in any age: 'As a painter of manners, [Chaucer] is accurate as Richardson; as a painter of character, true to the life and spirit, as Hogarth' (1807:xvii).

The century that followed Chaucer is for Southey, as for Warton, an age of relapse.[27] What marks his account is an emphasis on the disruptive 'political convulsions' of the period, when patronage and the encouragement of the arts broke down and a true sense of the national character was lost. In its place came a fashion for ornateness and pedantic Latinism, attempts at artificial elevation and ornament that substituted polysyllabic grandiloquence for 'the firm and manly step of natural strength' (1814:61). '[V]apid imitations' of Chaucer's more ornate experiments were produced by his 'idolatrous admirers', and like all idolaters they showed 'a singular ingenuity in selecting defects for the object of their worship' (1814:65). Forgetting the genius of their native language, they sacrificed the natural strength of English:

The southern nations of Europe dilute their sounds into polysyllables; we, contrariwise, at some occasional expense of euphony, purchase condensation and strength; in this respect our national character and our language have acted upon each other, and the fashion of the style ornate was an attempt in direct contradiction of both. (1814:66)

[25] Southey repeats this point about the 'difficulty' of English in his 1835 essay: 'More difficulty requires more care, and where that difficulty arises not from any preposterous fashion, or unreasonable rules, but from the character of the language, it tends to improve the artist' (1835:302–3).
[26] 'The poems anterior to Chaucer, are, without exception all, of those kinds which are indigenous everywhere; legends, hymns, verse-chronicles and romances' (1807:xiii–xiv).
[27] Warton characterised the fifteenth century as a period when, after Chaucer's 'genial day in an English spring... winter returns with redoubled horrors' (*History of English Poetry, from the Close of the Eleventh to the Commencement of the Eighteenth Century*, 3 vols (London: J. Dodsley, etc., 1774–81), ii.51).

For Southey, strength is associated with 'condensation'. It is an idea that has its equivalent in a notion of 'character' where virtue means recognising what is essential and keeping faith with it, even at a cost. The ideal is an integrity tested through time. This passage, like many others in these essays, is weighted with the ethical implications of concentration and self-consistency.

In his characterisation of fifteenth-century poetry Southey identifies an associated cluster of dislikes: pedantry, ornateness, fashion, elitism, false elevation, imitation, and idolatry. They reappear generally in his retellings of the history of poetry as symptoms of bad faith and neglected values. What links them is a lack of inherence or groundedness. Each concept is in some way partial, localised, or distorted. It is clear that Southey is convinced of the enduring strength of English, and that he takes this to be an organic quality that binds elements together. Features that are detachable, incidental, or temporary tend towards dispersal and therefore weakness.

The distinction is evident in his comparison of the Italian ottava rima with the Spenserian stanza of *The Faerie Queene*. The former has 'two defects': it 'pauses too regularly at the end of the first quatrain', and 'the concluding couplet is merely placed at the end of the stanza, not growing out of it' (1814:72). Together these features tend to disconnect parts from the whole. In contrast Spenser offers a more organised and tightly knit arrangement:

> But the stanza of the Faery Queen is framed with such consummate skill that all its parts are indivisibly interlaced, and the rhythm proceeds with increasing strength and fulness through the whole till it is wound up in a harmonious, rich and perfect close. (1814:72)

Rather than seeing the Spenserian stanza as diffuse and over-intricate, as some critics of the 1660–1740 period had done,[28] Southey appreciates its combination of capaciousness and tightness. Integrity is the unspoken value-word in Southey's literary history.

After the Elizabethan golden age, when 'more poems that are worthy of preservation were produced, in the course of half a century, than in any former or any subsequent age of English literature' (1835:301), integrity, both national and personal, was lost. As Southey reaches the period of 'the decline and fall of poetry' (1814:74) initiated in the reign of James I, he is in no doubt that it is part of a wider national malaise, but one in which writers played an influential part. In his 1814 essay he even seems to give shameful priority to a loss of poetic responsibility, which opened the way to national disaster: 'The causes of that decline are to be found in the misdirected talents of the best writers, and the cause of the fall in the moral corruption and intellectual degradation which succeeded an era of civil strife, of fanaticism

---

[28] The anonymous author of *Spencer Redivivus* (London, 1687), a heroic couplet version of Book I of *The Faerie Queene*, boasted that (s)he had removed the obstacle of Spenser's 'tedious Stanza'. See R. M. Cummings (ed.), *Spenser: The Critical Heritage* (London: Routledge, 1971), 216.

and hypocrisy' (1814:74). A key figure in this decline is Joshua Sylvester, whose translation of the works of Du Bartas had considerable vogue in the early Stuart period. For Southey he was an 'Icarus' who 'mount[ed] upon waxen wings' (1814:75) and was cherished by the court and worshipped by the many ('for children will always be attracted by trinkets and tinsel'; 1814:74). Rather than work *with* the English language, Sylvester asserted his power *over* it ('No writer ever ventured more freely to mould the language to his will'), and the consequences were malign: 'he was a won-derful rhyming machine... [f]rom his time, and probably in consequence of his success, the heroic couplet generally superseded every other metre for works of length' (1814:76–7). Sylvester's Du Bartas becomes emblematic for Southey of the nation's collapse into faction and idolatry, and his barely concealed emotion in the following passage suggests echoes nearer home:

Such bloated reputations usually end in blotches, for there is always a reaction in these things: one generation seems to pride itself upon defacing the idols of the last; not infrequently they destroy to-day the golden calf which yesterday they set up, and when idolaters turn iconoclasts, they act as if the outrageousness of the one excess were to efface or atone for the folly of the other. (1814:74)

In place of consistency and continuity, there is violent reaction and counter-reaction. Polarised energies have replaced organic integrity.

At a time when the whole country worships a golden calf, there is virtue in isolation, and it is possible for the national character to be sustained by a single individual. Southey finds in Milton's bitter divorce from his age the guarantee of his cultural value:

Milton, like Alfred and Roger Bacon, was so much beyond his age, that he produced scarcely any effect upon it. During the civil wars intolerance had produced cant and hypocrisy; a total depravity succeeded the Restoration; and poetry shared in the degradation of thought, feeling, manners, and principle; for its wares were of course adapted to the market. (1814:81–2)

In the equivalent passage in Southey's review of Sayers's *Works* Milton's writing of *Paradise Lost* is offered as evidence that 'minds of the highest order belong to other ages, and not to their own' (1827:186). They may be isolated from the fashionable present, but they form more extensive and enduring connections. With the strength of his blank verse linking him back to Shakespeare, but severing him from his contemporaries, Milton is seen by Southey as an Abdiel-figure of solitary resistance at a time when everything around him is being devalued: 'In the moral and intellectual debasement of Charles the Second's court, the language itself was debased' (1827:187). To underline his point Southey takes out his dog-eared portfolio and quotes again his own passage of twenty years earlier about 'the Birmingham trade of verse' (1827:189).

If Milton was honourably lonely, Pope enters the scene as the sociable *milord* dressed in the latest Parisian style. Southey even adopts a French accent to accommodate him: 'He imported *l'art de parler toujours convenablement*, the *etiquette* and *bienséance*, the court language and full-dress costume of verse' (1807:xxx). In Southey's review of Hayley's *Memoirs* Pope's Homer is a mannequin parody of its translator: 'Pope had sent the English Homer into the world, laced, ruffled, periwigged, and powdered, in a full dress court suit of embroidery' (1824:286). What for Johnson was the greatest poem of the age is for Southey 'a corruption...which will long continue to taint the public taste' (1827:191). '[N]o other work in the language so greatly vitiated the diction of English poetry' (1835:313).[29] An earlier pattern of literary history repeats itself: just as Chaucer had his superficial imitators, so Pope trailed in his wake a host of followers, who 'culled every thing that was vicious in his style for imitation, and what was good they spoilt by misapplying it' (1814:88). Southey's laughter at their expense is easily won, but the humour is not incidental. He sees in their fondness for antithesis, caesura, transposition, zeugma, etc. a blinkered concern for individual effects at the expense of the poetic whole. It fits his wider characterisation of Pope himself as an emblem of tyrannic disconnection, a poet ironically isolated by his very pre-eminence: 'Pope was our first and only dictator' (1835:292). Southey awards him the dubious honour of bringing to fulfilment a poetic school, and then closing it down: 'The Anglo-Gallican School which Pope had perfected died with him...not one writer since his days, who has acquired the slightest popularity, has been formed upon this school' (1807:xxxi). There is a contradiction here, given Southey's dismissal in the same essay of the classification of literary history into continentally derived schools; but over the years he continued to relish the aberrant concept of 'a French school introduced in the country of Shakespeare' (1835:293).[30]

True to the logic of these judgments, in his 1814 essay Southey turns to two of Pope's most eminent 'dunces' to suggest that during the poet's lifetime the critical climate was beginning to change and rebellion was at hand. Aaron Hill and John Dennis (both of whom feature in *The Dunciad*) are praised for their commitment to poetic liberty and power. Southey delights in quoting a passage from Hill that expresses exactly his own view of the centrifugal tendency of the 'French heroic' couplet, its inability to cohere: ''tis like the flowing of soft sand in hour-glasses', Hill says, 'seeming liquid while confined to its close currency, but flies dispersed, and opens its loose quality as soon as shaken out, and trusted to hard weather' (1814:83). The imagery is close to Southey's own. A few pages later Dennis is praised for his

---

[29] Southey's judgment echoes that of the Wartonian Henry Headley. See p. 109 above.

[30] Cf. '[I]t is a noticeable fact, that of all the poets in the intermediate half-century, not one who attained to any distinction which he has since held, or is likely to hold, was of the school of Pope. That school has produced versifiers in abundance, but no poet' (1835:314).

attempt to resurrect a poetry of passion that will 'delight and reform the mind, and so . . . make mankind happier and better'. The two men's criticism was prophetic—Dennis, however, 'did not live to see the dawn of the Reformation which he desired; but it was not long delayed' (1814:89).

Southey's 'Reformation', when it did come, was not a revolution, but a reconnection to poetry's sources. The main current was released again, and Pope and his school could be left behind like an ox-bow lake cut off from a river. At this point all five essays convey a renewed sense of progress and a gathering of pace as Southey moves to images of rediscovery and collaboration. With relief he turns from a static language of 'imitation' to the dynamics of 'influence', a concept that he mentally differentiates. Unlike the 'servile and mechanical' copying of fashionable effects,[31] 'influence' is the spirit of life in Southey's organic system, a natural transfusion from poet to poet.[32] It is notable that Southey avoids celebrating individual 'genius' as a unique phenomenon.[33] The poets he values, great and small, are those whose work is developmental, in which he can 'trace' (another of Southey's favourite dynamic, connective words) the lines of transmission between past and future: 'A discriminating reader', he says, 'may trace in the productions of every poet the influence of his predecessors in the art' (1827:197). Southey's greatest condemnation, therefore, is of those poets of temporary fashion who have proved sterile rather than generative, like Erasmus Darwin and Robert Merry ('Della Crusca') in the 1790s:

Such of our readers as recollect what the state of our literature was five-and-thirty years ago, will not be surprised at seeing the names of Cowper, Darwin, and Merry, classed together, as having been then each in full sail upon the stream of celebrity, which very soon floated two of them, by a short cut, into the dead sea (1827:197).

Darwin, who sought a heartless mechanical perfection (1827:198–9), is paired with the leader of the 'Della Cruscan swarm' that flourished in its brief 'summer's day' (1814:90). Both have been judged by time, cut off from the current of poetic development. For Southey, however, 'Time, like an ever rolling stream' (to quote Isaac Watts's celebrated hymn[34]) does not bear 'all its sons away' to oblivion. For him, time is an organising principle, the

---

[31] Southey quotes approvingly Cowper's comment: 'Imitation, even of the best models, is my aversion; it is servile and mechanical' (1827:201).

[32] In his early sonnet 'To the Fire', Southey celebrates it as an emblem of a friendly 'influence' connecting generations: 'I would wish, like thee, to shine serene, | Like thee, within mine influence, all to cheer... | ... So might my children ponder o'er my shrine, | And o'er my ashes muse, as I will muse o'er thine' (Robert Southey (and Robert Lovell), *Poems: Containing the Retrospect, Odes, Elegies, Sonnets, &c* (Bath: R. Cruttwell, 1795), 67).

[33] The nearest Southey comes is in the preface to *Specimens* when he notes that 'Young's manner was unique; it is a compound of wit and religious madness; but that madness was the madness of a man of genius' (1807:xxxii). In his *Conjectures on Original Composition* (London, 1759) Young celebrated the originality of natural genius, something that Southey notably refrains from doing.

[34] 'Our God, our help in ages past', in Isaac Watts, *The Psalms of David* (London, 1719).

ultimate guarantor of continuity and value: 'Erroneous judgments in the court of criticism are always, sooner or later, reversed by time' (1824:287). In this essay, as elsewhere, Southey's instance is the rediscovery, after decades of neglect, of William Collins's odes, which exemplify how poetry recovered its impetus in the second half of the eighteenth century.[35]

Time's benign connectedness takes its place among the other organic images that shape Southey's narrative, and nowhere is this more evident than in William Cowper's *The Task* (1785). This poem (which in Southey's story marks the final reconnection between nature, the national character, and the human heart) is seen as emerging naturally out of a fertile soil, and at the opportune moment: 'At any time the Task must have been successful', he notes, 'but at no time could the circumstances have been more favourable for its reception. For the revival of that true English taste, which this poem mainly contributed to promote, had already been begun' (1835:292).[36] It was Cowper's achievement to be the counter to Pope's: his blank verse translation of Homer (1791) compensated for the deleterious effects of his predecessor's, and his example opened up the possibilities for poetry again: 'if Pope shut the door, Cowper opened it' (1835:314).

As each essay moves towards its close, the revivalist roll call of poets evokes new aspirations and responsive sympathies:

Thomson recalled the aspirant to the love of natural scenery, and the feelings connected with it, for which the school of Pope had neither eyes nor hearts. Young struck a chord (and with a powerful hand) which vibrated in every mind that was either under the influence of sorrow, or constitutional melancholy, or religious enthusiasm. (1824:286)

In all the essays Thomson and Young are paired in just this way: 'We were brought back by Thomson . . . to the love of natural objects. Young taught us with what success a true poet might appeal to the religious feelings of the human heart' (1827:192).[37]

The most important pairing in Southey's narrative, however, is that of the two men who did most in his eyes to revive the pre-1660 tradition of English poetry and enable the full story to be told: Thomas Warton's *History of English Poetry* and Thomas Percy's *Reliques* (1765) together 'promoted, beyond any others, this growth of a better taste than had prevailed for the hundred years preceding' (1835:338). Through them 'the rising generation' was reawakened to the glories of the Elizabethan age (1827:193). Percy 'led the way' in what Southey sees as the literary equivalent of Methodism: 'To borrow a phrase from the Methodists, there has been *a great revival* in our days—a poetry out of the spirit' (1814:90).

---

[35] 1814:89–90; 1824:287; 1835:321.

[36] Cf. 'the poem appeared . . . just at the fulness of time, when the way had been prepared for it' (1835:336).

[37] Cf. '[Thomson] brought with him stores of observation from the country, [Young] a strong devotional passion' (1814:89).

In Warton in particular Southey recognised someone who combined several aspects of himself: a poet, scholar, biographer, and editor, whose graph of the peaks and troughs of literary history virtually tallied with his own, and who had been a distinguished Poet Laureate ('the only poet since Ben Jonson who ha[s] done honour to the office', 1824:289). Warton plays a vital structural role in Southey's narrative of national and poetic continuities as a figure who mediated between history and poetry: 'No man could at that time have written such poems, unless his studies had qualified him to become the historian of English poetry; nor could any one have composed that history who had not been born a poet' (1824:289). Through his own poetry Warton infused 'the spirit of our elder poets' into a fresh generation of young writers in the 1780s (1824:289). In bringing his historical narrative up to the present, Southey is able finally to identify what he terms 'the true English school' (now used positively for the restored native tradition) as 'Warton's school', concluding that '[i]f any man may be called the father of the present race, it is Thomas Warton' (1824:289).[38] In several of the essays he discusses the work of the group of Warton's poetic children, which was discussed in the previous chapter: Thomas Russell, John Bampfylde, Henry Headley, and William Lisle Bowles,[39] and it is to the latter, the sole survivor, to whom Southey voices his personal gratitude directly: 'Bowles, who yet lives, and to whom we gladly offer our thanks for the pleasure which we derived from his poems in our younger days' (1814:89). With those words Southey consciously inserts his youthful self into his narrative of literary history. In a letter to Bowles the following year he makes explicit what amounts to a poetical kinship:

I am indebted to you for many hours of deep enjoyment, and for great improvement in our common art,—for your poems came into my hands when I was nineteen and I *fed* upon them. Our booby critics talk of *schools*, and if they had had common discernment they might have perceived that I was of your school.[40]

In quoting this passage, Christopher Smith calls these remarks 'rather disingenuous';[41] but they explicitly confirm how Bowles helped Southey to

---

[38] Southey also recognised the important contribution of Thomas Warton's brother Joseph (1722–1800), Headmaster of Winchester, 1766–93: 'The Wartons were far from writing purely; but no men contributed so much to the reformation of English poetry. They brought us back to the study of the Elizabethan writers; and under the elder brother, Winchester may almost be said to have become a school of poets' (1814:89). The review continued with a discussion of Headley, Russell, Bowles, and Bampfylde as working under the Wartons' influence (*Quarterly Review*, 11 (1814), 89). See above, pp. 99–101.

[39] On 20 Dec. 1793 Southey borrowed from the Bristol Library Headley's Wartonian anthology, *Select Beauties of Ancient English Poetry*, 2 vols (London, 1787), exchanging it on 23 Dec. for Cowper's Homer. See George Whalley, 'The Bristol Library Borrowings of Southey and Coleridge, 1793–8', *The Library*, 5th ser., 4 (1950), 114–32.

[40] Southey to Bowles, 21 Feb. 1815 (reprinted in *A Wiltshire Parson and his Friends: The Correspondence of William Lisle Bowles*, ed. Garland Greever (London, 1926), 150).

[41] Smith, *A Quest for Home*, 341.

integrate himself into a continuing history of poetry. Smith's comment echoes the established critical view that the so-called 'first-generation Romantics' outgrew their early infatuation with Bowles. But if we place Southey's 1815 letter alongside another text written in that same year—the moving tribute to Bowles in the opening chapter of Coleridge's *Biographia Literaria*—we get some sense of how these poets continued to value him as a keepsake of their earlier selves. For Coleridge he was 'heart-honour'd', and represented, especially through his sonnets, the binding together of nature, friendship, and personal retrospect.[42] To 'outgrow' Bowles was a contradiction if your link with him was an organic one bound up with the continuity of your own history. You did not outgrow Bowles, you grew out of him—a very different idea.

It is something close to this cluster of principles that shapes Southey's narrative of the English poetic tradition, and shapes his important early poem 'The Retrospect' too. What he perpetually revisits is a dynamic story of loss and recovery, in which retrospect functions not as nostalgia but as a mode of reconnection, a reconfirming of faith. This is the insistent theme of Bowles's sonnets, and the Southey in his early forties who tells him 'I was of your school' is not only gratefully claiming kinship, but is also acknowledging influence as a mode of integrity. Through the figure of Bowles, Southey was able to tap into Wartonian history and its model of friendly continuity, in which Spenser in particular exemplified (to use Greg Kucich's words) 'the spirit of generous and enabling transmission'.[43] For the young Southey this was what Bowles also represented at a crucial juncture in his life: 'My favourite poet was Spenser,' he recalled, 'but at the age of what might be termed poetical puberty when the voice of song began to be fixed, I had Bowles by heart.'[44] The Spenserian inheritance that Bowles embodied made the difficult moment when Southey's poetic voice broke one of 'enabling transmission'.

Much like his friend Coleridge, Southey associated Bowles with the heart (for both of them it was the primary organ of memory) and with the revisiting of childhood scenes.[45] When on 11 April 1794 Southey found himself at the spot near the village of Corston, near Bath, where as a schoolboy he had washed every day in the stream, it was Bowles's sonnet 'To the River Itchin' that came to mind and spoke for him.[46] Out of the unexpected moment of return, over which Bowles's spirit presided, emerged both Southey's 'Corston' sonnet and 'The Retrospect'. This particular convergence of the

---

[42] See Chapter 8 below.

[43] Greg Kucich, *Keats, Shelley, and Romantic Spenserianism* (University Park: Pennsylvania State University Press, 1991), 46.

[44] Southey to G. C. Bedford, 7 Aug. 1814 (*New Letters*, ii.105).

[45] See Chapter 8, n. 6.

[46] 'There is something in the recollection of scenes of child hood that give a pleasing melancholy to the mind . . . on this subject Bowles has written so very beautiful a sonnet that I am sure the inserting it will delight you' (Southey to G. C. Bedford, 13 April 1794 (*New Letters*, i.52)).

place, the spirit, and the two poems is occupying Southey's mind when he writes to H. W. Bedford later that year:

Have you read Bowles's sonnets? They are most beautiful. I know no poems that ever went so much to my heart. Dilly sells them.

'The Retrospect' is my best piece. I have mentioned the murmuring brook there. Take this sonnet conceived upon its bank . . .[47]

There follows a transcript of the sonnet he later entitled 'To a Brook near the Village of Corston', in which the young poet watches the current while memory sketches 'the faint-form'd scenes of the departed days'.[48] As was seen in the previous chapter, 'To a Brook', modelled on Bowles's sonnets to the Itchin and the Cherwell, belongs to the genre of riverbank poetry through which a number of poets of the 1780s and 1790s were able to draw together ideas of personal retrospect, temporal continuity, and poetic inheritance.

All these are strategically combined in 'The Retrospect', which opens Southey's *Poems: Containing the Retrospect, Odes, Elegies, Sonnets, &c*, the debut volume produced jointly with his friend Robert Lovell under the signatures of Bion and Moschus.[49] For a young man to launch his poetic career with a thirteen-page retrospect may have seemed odd, but it sets a pattern for those later revisitings of his own literary history which have been the subject of this chapter. Both are part of Southey's autobiographical narrative, his need repeatedly to confirm the importance of the source from which his poetic current flowed.

'The Retrospect' enacts this impulse by interweaving a series of textual recollections around the incident of his return to the brook at Corston.[50] If the sonnet gives us the sentimental cameo, the larger poem becomes a strategically literary revisiting too. The intensely personal moment is opened out into a shared space and an ampler span of time—much longer than the twelve years of his own intervening life. The phrase 'Of long-past days I sing' (l. 27) is one of several in the poem that suggest a more distant reach into history. This is also evident in the Spenserian alexandrines interspersed through the text, which introduce echoes from the Spenser–Milton tradition of the eighteenth century. Southey's specific memories of his schooldays are

---

[47] Southey to H. W. Bedford, 12 Nov. 1794 (*New Letters*, i.87). Southey is reiterating what he had urged Bedford on 22 Aug.: 'Buy Bowles poems, and study them well. They will teach you to write better, and give you infinite pleasure' (*New Letters*, i.72).

[48] The text transcribed for Bedford, entitled 'To a Brooklet near Alston', is printed in Smith, *A Quest for Home*, 27. It was published under the revised title as 'Sonnet VI' in Southey's *Poems* (1797). See pp. 111–12 above.

[49] In his memoirs Bowles writes: 'Mr. Cruttwell, the printer, wrote a letter saying that two young gentlemen, strangers, one a particularly handsome and pleasing youth, lately from Westminster School, and both literary and intelligent, spoke in high commendation of my volume, and if I recollect right, expressed a desire to have some poems printed in the same type and form' (*Scenes and Shadows of Days Departed* (London: W. Pickering, 1837), xlv).

[50] See Smith's discussion of the poem in *A Quest for Home*, 13–39, which also explores the psychological aspects of Southey's retrospection.

coloured by poetic recollections of Gray's *Eton College Ode*, Goldsmith's *The Deserted Village*, Shenstone's *The Schoolmistress*, and Beattie's *The Minstrel*, all poems in which youthful education of various kinds is remembered. One instance is Southey's ambivalent memory of his schoolmaster ('Severe his voice, severely grave his mien, | And wond'rous strict he was, and wond'rous wise, I ween', 69–70), which evokes not just the village schoolmaster in *The Deserted Village* but also Shenstone's fondly recalled schoolmistress, with her 'forth-coming rod, unpleasing sight, I ween!'[51] Southey's text shares Shenstone's foreboding about what is 'forth-coming', and it echoes Gray's sense of how vulnerable childhood innocence is: 'Ere future prospects could the soul distress, | When even ignorance was happiness' (123–4).[52]

But Southey's 'Retrospect' expands this private experience by tracing, as Gray's *Eton College Ode* could not, a connective thread with the past, and by giving his poet the company of older sympathetic voices. In what is more than just a quaint gesture, Southey adopts the role of the 'minstrel', his inaugurator of the authentic tradition of English poetry: 'Accept thy minstrel's retrospective lays' (22), he invites, making his 'lyre' not only an expressive medium but also an accompaniment to other earlier voices. The poem is retrospective in this more extended sense, conscious of generational layers of experience. In a similar way, the space of the text extends from 'the sacred spot' (165) to 'the well-trod way' (193) of pilgrimage. Moments of focused detail are widened out to busy scenes, and the dynamics of variety and interest help to turn 'The Retrospect' into a less self-absorbed poem. But although the scene may move around, the effect is not superficial: the 'deep remembrance' (76) remains and is insisted on.

The phrase is used in the poem's most private scene, the first day at school, when the speaker leaves his mother's embrace for the 'despotic rule' of the master. Embarrassment is often a feature of such life-changing moments, and the text risks embarrassing us and himself at the direct way he brings love and fear up against each other in a gesture of sensibility. The effect is cloying ('As loath as even I myself'), but tactically so, given that here his identity binds with his mother's. Then, beginning a fresh paragraph Southey pulls back from his close-up and begins a new more expansive trajectory. The final effect is subtler than we might at first think:

> Years intervening have not worn away
> The deep remembrance of that distant day;
> Effac'd the vestige of my earliest fears,
> A mother's fondness, and a mother's tears;

---

[51] William Shenstone, 'The School-Mistress, A Poem', in Robert Dodsley, *A Collection of Poems*, 3 vols, 2nd edn (London, 1748), i.247–61 (254).

[52] Cf. 'where ignorance is bliss, | 'Tis folly to be wise' (Thomas Gray, *An Ode on a Distant Prospect of Eton College* (London: R. Dodsley, 1747), p. 8).

> When close she prest me to her sorrowing heart,
> As loath as even I myself to part.
>   But time to youthful sorrow yields relief,
> Each various object weans the child from grief ...   (75–82)

Southey doesn't dwell. He is always conscious of the need to move on. He knows his bearings, where his home is, but his attention turns, and ours with it. He is intrigued by the workings of memory, and asks pointed questions about why it tends to transform 'sour' to 'sweet' (115–18). However, in contrast to another of the poem's predecessors, Samuel Rogers' diffuse philosophical poem, *The Pleasures of Memory* (1792),[53] Southey avoids re-living the scene in soft focus. 'The Retrospect', for all its recollective character, is set in the 'now' of the revisiting, whereas Rogers tends to project himself into the remembered scene through the lens of the fancy, as the ghosts of the past appear: 'What soften'd views thy magic glass reveals, | When o'er the landscape Time's meek twilight steals!'[54]

Like Rogers, Southey is interested in the process of mental re-collection, the way certain details gather associatively in the mind.[55] The procedure recalls how in Goldsmith's 1770 poem the village scene begins to function as the reader's own retrospect, with clusters of words at the poem's opening (*sweet, lovely, smiling, charm, bowers*) being gathered up and repeated (in what amounts to a rhetorical *collectio*) as if taking possession of our consciousness too. With a very similar effect, Southey's 'Retrospect' collects in a brief passage (218–30) images that have registered earlier (the brook, the schoolmaster, the face-washing, the orchard fruit, the Lord of the Manor, the 'chace').

But at this point (ll. 225–49) Southey reveals how radically different is his poem from Goldsmith's. Where *The Deserted Village* represents a tragic break with the past, a loss of all the old landmarks and the social cohesion they brought, Southey now uses Goldsmith's elegiac language to make the opposite point. Three exclamatory phrases—'How thou art chang'd!' (225), 'Past is thy day of glory' (233), and 'thou art fallen: thy day of glory past' (241)—punctuate the passage, but this is no mere tug of nostalgia: the phrases effectively mark out the history of the school building through its three successive identities, as manor-house, then school, and finally as farm. They are varied scenes, but we notice how the sociability persists: first, as the manor house, where the 'jovial squire | Call'd all his tenants round the

---

[53] *The English Review* (May 1795), 389, saw Samuel Rogers' *The Pleasures of Memory, a poem in two parts* (London: T. Cadell, 1792) as Southey's chief model (quoted by Smith, *A Quest for Home*, 18); but I would argue that the most important analogue for 'The Retrospect' is *The Deserted Village*.

[54] Rogers, *Pleasures of Memory*, i.91–2.

[55] In his own explanatory notes to the poem ('Analysis of the First Part', vi) Rogers refers to Lockean association of ideas: 'When ideas have any relation whatever, they are attractive of each other in the mind; and the conception of any object naturally leads to the idea of another which was connected with it either in time or place.'

crackling fire'; then as the school echoing to 'the mirthful sound' of children's play; and finally as a family home where in its latest stage the house has found new occupants:

> True, thou art fallen: thy day of glory past,
> Long may thy day of honest comfort last!
> Long may the farmer from his toil retire
> To joys domestic round the evening fire;
> Where boisterous riot once supreme has reign'd,
> Where discipline his sway severe maintain'd;
> May heaven the industrious farmer's labour bless,
> And crown his honest toil with happiness.   (241–9)

The poem, we discover, is finally not about private memory, but about common ground. This passage concerns the nature of superimposed experience, the adaptability of place, and the continuity of the sociable impulse—just the things Goldsmith could not find.

It was in his early 'Botany Bay Eclogues'[56] that Southey followed through to the bleak ending of Goldsmith's poem, in which the dispossessed 'leave the land' to begin life again in the New World.[57] But Southey's Australia, a pastoral landscape 'unbroken by the plough', is also a scene of repeated retrospect. Some of his speakers regret the homes left behind: 'even now I see | The lowly lovely dwelling! Even now | Behold the woodbine clasping its white walls' ('Elinor', 27–9). But balancing these sentimental cameos and the persistence of their former identities is the knowledge that they all have an opportunity to start afresh. Each speaker re-lives their individual history, but only to mark their disconnection from it. In this new world they are 'snug and settled' under their 'humble roof' and find peace from the hardships of their earlier lives: 'we live wonderous well when transported', remarks one of them ('John, Samuel, and Richard', 3). As she pauses from her routine labours a female convict recognises that she has somehow gained a respite from fear and guilt: 'Elinor has nothing new to fear', says the transported former prostitute who spends her days gathering seashells along the shore. In this context, the change of place can be seen as a relief from their individual tragic histories: 'I am haven'd in peace in this corner at last', remarks John, a former sailor. There certainly appears fresh possibility here in the alternative landscape of Paine and Godwin, a levelled scene with all its historical superstructures removed, where the New Adam will step forward to claim his 'rights of nature'. But in Southey's imagination, though the landscape has no history, the individual convicts do. They will continue, like the shepherds of Theocritus and Virgil, to re-enact the same scenes and

---

[56] Written in 1794, and first published as a group in Southey's *Poems* (1797), 75–104.
[57] Oliver Goldsmith, *The Deserted Village, A Poem*, 2nd edn (London: W. Griffin, 1770), pp. 19–23, ll. 343–432.

tell the old stories. Their identities are too ingrained to forget the past entirely.

Nor would Southey wish them to: 'I have been guilty', says one, 'yet my mind can bear | The retrospect of guilt, yet in the hour | Of deep contrition to THE ETERNAL look | For mercy!' ('Frederic', 43–6). The young radical held to the idea that personal integrity is bound up with individual memory and a durable personal identity, which it is not in our hands to discard. In 'The Retrospect' he writes a poem that exemplifies that conviction, and he strengthens it by integrating other poets' personal texts into his own. The history of poetry could in this way be conceived of as a continuing story for others to draw from. Throughout his later life Southey would remain acutely conscious of the tracings and retracings of history, and would continue to associate the formation of his own identity with the character of the nation's poetry. For Southey, a text will survive the rigours of time if it is ingrained deeply enough:

> So when, with unskill'd hand, the rustic hind
> Carves the rude legend on the growing rind,
> In after years the peasant lives to see
> The expanded legend grow as grows the tree.
> Though every winter's desolating sway
> Shake the hoarse grove, and sweep the leaves away;
> Deep in its trunk the legend still will last,
> Defy the storm, and brave the wintry blast.[58]

[58] Southey, 'The Retrospect', ll. 137–44.

6 Between Youth and Age: Coleridge's 'Monody on the Death of Chatterton', 1790–6

> And we, at sober eve, would round thee throng,
> Hanging, enraptur'd, on thy stately song!
> And greet with smiles the young-eyed POESY
> All deftly mask'd, as hoar ANTIQUITY.
>
> —S. T. Coleridge, 'Monody on the Death of
> Chatterton', ll. 130–3, 1796 *Poems*

THE PREVIOUS CHAPTERS have seen two young poets strengthening their sense of individual identity through an act of poetic retrospection. In each case a personal revisiting has been coupled to a wider awareness of literary history. What could have been an entirely private memory attracts the company of other voices and draws on more communal human experience. Both Wordsworth and Southey find value in the kind of spatiotemporal process through which an idea is turned into rich meaning by being layered or faceted, shared and tested. So far the organising of the poetic text has been fairly straightforward; but with Coleridge's 'headlong arrival' on the scene (the phrase is Tom Mayberry's describing the way he entered the Wordsworths' lives at Racedown in June 1797[1]) more complex considerations arise, which are both personal and literary. We can see Coleridge wrestling not just with his own identity but with poetry's various negotiations between idea and embodiment. This unsettling encounter, which informed the critical issues raised in Chapter 1, will be his accompanying theme throughout the book.

In the early 1790s Coleridge's poetic character was intriguingly bound up with that of Thomas Chatterton, the tragic Bristol charity boy whose mythic role as the neglected genius of English poetry was already established. The young Coleridge found in Chatterton not merely a figure with whom he could identify, but one that posed problems for his own art and raised questions about the kind of writer he himself would be. During this decade Chatterton's place in literary history was a contested one, and this gave the young Coleridge a choice of models that he found difficult to resolve, not least because the nature of his own poetic identity was at stake. The fact that

---

[1] Tom Mayberry, *Coleridge and Wordsworth in the West Country* (Stroud: Alan Sutton, 1992), 85.

Chatterton was not just an isolated 'genius' but also a connecting figure whose work linked past, present, and future made him if anything more imaginatively accommodating to other writers. Intent on forging continuities and bridging gaps, the youth caught the spirit of old poetry more convincingly than he replicated it physically, and this made his influence an especially infusive one.

Perhaps no other poet offers such a contrast between a brief and obscure life and a vast and powerful posthumous existence as the figure of Chatterton. When he died in his Holborn garret in 1770 at the age of 17, all he could claim were a scattering of anonymous poems and letters in the newspapers, squibs, imitations, satires, and love verses, and a bundle of documents rather amateurishly forged or 'transcribed', many purporting to be the writings of a fifteenth-century priest and poet, Thomas Rowley. In the years after Chatterton's death, curiosity became intense about this odd conjunction of youth and age, the charity boy who had recovered the voice of a fifteenth-century priest—a language whose words were ancient yet seemed newly minted for an age tiring of politeness and wit. Chatterton fast became an object of wonder to those who, like Dr Johnson, made their way to the muniment room of St Mary Redcliffe, and the young man's writings began to take their ambiguous place in the literary canon. By 1777 Rowley's poems had been given a scholarly edition by Thomas Tyrwhitt, and in the following year the fifteenth-century writer was awarded a chapter in Thomas Warton's *History* of *English Poetry*.[2]

This was less Rowley's triumph than that of his youthful creator. Warton declared that he considered the poems spurious but their teenage originator an undoubted genius. The historian of poetry, however, could not bear to leave them out of his account, knowing that single-handedly they would, if genuine, redeem the fifteenth century from tedium. Rowley looked like the vital missing link that would continue the Chaucerian tradition through to Spenser. Somehow, as with the *History of Bristol* which William Barrett printed in 1789 with many of Chatterton's concocted documents, the youth had the knack of finding exactly what ought to have been there, but wasn't. He supplied connections, completed fragmented stories, compiled family trees, provided origins (the first English pastoral, the first native classical epic, the earliest verse tragedy), and brought alive many scenes and voices from oblivion. Whether Rowley had been rediscovered or simply invented was equally a matter for wonder, and Chatterton's twin selves entered a world where the borderline between fact and fiction had become blurred. Indeed in Herbert Croft's sensational docu-novel, *Love and Madness* (1780), the tragic young poet found a context of emotional frustration, sentimental gesture, and flawed genius that would never be disentangled from him.

---

[2] Thomas Warton, *The History of English Poetry* (London, 1774–81), ii.139–64.

In the Rowley controversy of 1782 the battlelines were drawn up between the scholarly establishment, represented by Edmond Malone, Thomas Warton, Thomas Tyrwhitt, and George Steevens, and the antiquarian believers, Milles, Barrett, Catcott, and Jacob Bryant. At the centre of the debate was the dead Chatterton, with the anti-Rowleyans tending to assert his wonderful genius, and the pro-Rowleyans characterizing him as an ill-educated apprentice quite unequipped to write such accomplished poetry.[3] Thus Chatterton was caught between being a fraudulent genius or an honest ignoramus. It began to seem that this young lad could be anything you wanted him to be. Fact and fiction, life and art, creator and created, had become so intertwined. He was not the most stable model for a budding young poet to adopt. But in 1790, the 17-year-old Samuel Taylor Coleridge copied out his 'Monody on the Death of Chatterton' into the headmaster's Golden Book of his pupils' literary productions,[4] and it was as the author of this poem that he first made his mark as a poet.

Coleridge, in his final year at Christ's Hospital, found much to recognise in the figure of Chatterton: youthful poetic aspirations, high hopes for changing the world, a feeling of estrangement from family and home—and Chatterton's garret was only a short walk from the school. Most strikingly, both were blue-coat charity boys: Colston's School in Bristol, where Chatterton was educated, was founded as a charitable institution by Edward Colston, a Christ's Hospital boy himself. The connections would if anything grow closer during the 1790s with Coleridge's move to Bristol, his intimacy with Southey, Cottle, and the Frickers, and his own marriage on 4 October 1795 in the church of St Mary Redcliffe ('poor Chatterton's Church... The thought gave me a tinge of melancholy to the solemn Joy, which I felt').[5] By 1796 Coleridge, now known as 'the author of the Monody on Chatterton', found he could use the image of the suicidal young poet to his advantage. Writing to Tom Poole in December 1796, he invoked the ghost of Chatterton to impress on his friend an image of his own frantic state:

the Ghosts of Otway & Chatterton, & the phantasms of a Wife broken-hearted, & a hunger-bitten Baby! O Thomas Poole! Thomas Poole! if you did but know what a Father & Husband must feel, who toils with his brain for uncertain bread! I dare not think of it—The evil Face of Frenzy looks at me!

After receiving this letter Poole invited Coleridge to live at Nether Stowey.[6]

[3] Jeremiah Milles, Dean of Exeter and President of the Society of Antiquaries, compared Rowley favourably with Homer, describing Chatterton as merely an 'illiterate charity-boy' (*Poems, Supposed to have been written at Bristol in the Fifteenth Century by Thomas Rowley, Priest, &c.*, ed. Jeremiah Milles (London: T. Payne, 1782), 3, 23).
[4] Christ's Hospital *Liber Aureus*, BL, MS Ashley 3506, vol. i, fols. 44^r–46^v.
[5] Coleridge to Thomas Poole, 7 Oct. 1795 (Griggs, 160).
[6] Coleridge to Poole, 3 Dec. 1796 (Griggs, 275).

Conversely, his friends employed the identification to warn or admonish him.[7] Wordsworth's 'Resolution and Independence' (composed 1802) is only the most famous example of how the figure of Chatterton could be used for this purpose. In a poem that moves from joyous energy to static endurance, from the hare 'running races in her mirth' to the old man beside the pond, it is that latter figure of 'dire constraint' who carries the message, and Coleridge who should be listening to it:

> I thought of Chatterton, the marvellous Boy,
> The sleepless Soul that perish'd in its pride;
> Of Him who walk'd in glory and in joy
> Behind his Plough, upon the mountain-side:
> By our own spirits are we deified;
> We Poets in our youth begin in gladness;
> But thereof comes in the end despondency and madness.   (43–9)[8]

In *Coleridge and the Literature of Sensibility* (1978) George Dekker sees the identification with Chatterton as 'Coleridge's problem'. Indeed it is tempting to turn the Chattertonian Coleridge into a psychological case history, and the poet's use of Chatterton can be overplayed in terms of a personal fixation. There is a danger of letting notions of psychological development shape Coleridge's career too neatly:

At Nether Stowey, I think, Coleridge simply outgrew the identification with Chatterton: the *Monody* became a literary embarrassment, and as a husband and father in his middle twenties he could no longer picture himself as a 'wond'rous boy'.[9]

Dekker has dealt interestingly with the way the tragic figures of Chatterton, Burns, and Werther recur in Coleridge, and in his biographical reading of the early career the 'Dejection Ode' takes its place as the pivotal text. But his view of Sensibility as a morbid and self-indulgent mode means that Chatterton comes to be associated with suicidal tendencies and depressive illness—the 'despondency and madness' of Wordsworth's warning. He is made to represent an unstable adolescence that Coleridge fruitfully outgrew.

But I want in this chapter to steer the discussion away from the pathology and back to the poetry, thinking less about Coleridge's psychological progress than about the artistic influences and choices that characterised his poetic use of Chatterton in the 'Monody'. I have already stressed how unstable the figure of Chatterton was during the two decades after his

---

[7] See Charles Lamb's poem 'To Sara and Her Samuel', sent to Coleridge 7 July 1796 (Marrs, 39), and Poole's comparison of Coleridge and Chatterton as wayward geniuses (Poole to Henrietta Warwick, 6 Feb. 1796: Elizabeth Sandford, *Thomas Poole and His Friends*, introd. Reginald Watters (Over Stowey: Friarn Press, 1996), 84). See also George Dekker, *Coleridge and the Literature of Sensibility* (London: Vision Press, 1978), 64–5.

[8] William Wordsworth, *Poems, in Two Volumes, and Other Poems, 1800–1807*, ed. Jared Curtis (Ithaca: Cornell University Press, 1983), 125.

[9] Dekker, *Coleridge*, 60, 62–3.

death, and this is reflected in the poem itself. The teenage Coleridge was faced with a wide range of possibilities. What he made of these in 1790, and what he then proceeded to do when he rewrote the poem for its first publication in 1794 and the extended version in his *Poems* (1796),[10] together suggest that Coleridge's early poetic styles were attuned to the modulations in Chatterton's posthumous image. What we now call the Romantic myth of Chatterton involved a narrowing down and weakening of a figure who had earlier offered writers much more.

The chapter will concern itself with the earliest three versions of the poem completed in 1790, 1794, and 1796. The 'Monody on the Death of Chatterton' is remarkable in that it spans Coleridge's full poetic career from about 1785 (if we accept that some lines of the first version were written as a school exercise in his 13th year[11]) up to the final text published in 1834, the year of his death—a range of almost fifty years. He continually rewrote and revised it. The 90 lines of 1790 became 107 lines in 1794, 143 lines for his 1796 *Poems*, 135 in 1797, 119 in 1803, 143 again in 1828, 154 in 1829, and swelled to 165 lines in 1834. It is unhelpful, however, to see this as a single work in course of development as I. A. Gordon does ('the *Monody* took him no less than forty-four years to beat into its final form').[12] We begin with irregular Pindarics and end with pentameter couplets, and the texts of 1790 and 1794 are so distinct as to amount in effect to separate poems. In terms of the two earliest versions, of the 90 lines of the 1790 text, only 17 reappear in 1794. I shall therefore be treating them separately as embodying different influences and opportunities, not as part of a single developmental process by which Coleridge is trying to work a poem into unity. The poem is not 'organic' in that traditional teleological sense of growing into form. Its organic qualities, in the sense used in this book, are to be sought in its adaptiveness, how the writing adjusts its emphases in response to a variety of factors, emotional, artistic, and practical. The 'Monody' remains in 'process' in a more Shandean way by reacting to a succession of stimuli and associative encounters. With these in mind the chapter seeks to trace the poem's altering character, and by charting Coleridge's attempts to accommodate the complex phenomenon of Chatterton, to discover what the texts

---

[10] Coleridge's rewritten 'Monody' was prefixed to the 1794 Cambridge edition of the Rowley poems, ed. Lancelot Sharpe, xxv–xxviii ('The Editor thinks himself happy in the permission of an ingenious Friend, to insert the following Monody'). Originally, a 72-line abridgement of the 1790 text was going to be printed and was set in type, only to be cancelled at the last minute and replaced by the rewritten poem. See Arthur Freeman and Theodore Hofmann, 'The Ghost of Coleridge's First Effort: "A Monody on the Death of Chatterton"', *The Library*, 11 (1989), 328–35. They suggest that the additional 36 lines which conclude the 1796 text may have been part of the 1794 rewrite but not printed there because of space.
[11] As Coleridge told William Worship on 22 April 1819. See Mays, ii.170.
[12] I. A. Gordon, 'The Case-History of Coleridge's *Monody on the Death of Chatterton*', *RES*, 18 (1942), 49–71 (49).

can tell us about the shifting coordinates of his own poetic identity during these years.

First it is necessary to establish a fuller context for assessing what Coleridge does with the figure of Chatterton. As the beginning of this chapter suggested, in the twenty years following his death Chatterton could be manipulated and packaged in different ways. Wordsworth's 'marvellous Boy, | The sleepless Soul that perish'd in its pride' is a disembodied poet (unlike his companion Burns who is holding a plough), and the Chatterton celebrated by the young Keats in 1815 is a voice that 'melted in dying murmurs' and perished like 'a half-blown floweret which cold blasts amate'.[13] But the delicate spirit was only one of several competing Chattertons who could be used to make a range of points about poetry and society. Chatterton/Rowley was an ambivalent phenomenon, not least with regard to the place he might take in the history of poetry. It became an issue that had implications not merely for Chatterton but for how literary history itself was coming to be understood. Some of these wider considerations will be discussed later in relation to the new ending the poem received in Coleridge's 1796 collection.

What immediately confronts us, however, is the persistent image of the boy, which has become inextricably attached to Chatterton. As the material listed in John Goodridge's bibliography makes clear, the 'marvellous Boy' has regularly attached itself to works about or inspired by Chatterton.[14] The popular nineteenth-century representation of the poet pictured at the age of nine with long hair and chubby cheeks (the portrait that gained currency in Dix's *Life* of 1837 and a copy of which was owned by Wordsworth), although spurious, is still current today.[15] The picture's popularity must come from the fact that we need to have an image of Chatterton in which he looks like a boy. And the need has been a long-standing one: the engraved programme for a Chatterton commemorative concert in 1784 showed 'Genius conducting Chatterton in the habit of a Blue-coat boy, to her altar'.[16]

In the early years of his posthumous existence, however, Chatterton was also regularly represented as a manly youth who had grown up quickly and was mature beyond his years. This is, after all, closer to the truth. He had ceased to be a charity boy and had been released from his apprenticeship by the Bristol attorney. By the summer of 1770 he had set himself up in London and had climbed the first rung of a journalistic career, arranging an interview

[13] John Keats, Sonnet 'To Chatterton', in *The Poems of John Keats*, ed. Miriam Allott (London: Longman, 1970), p. 10.

[14] See John Goodridge, 'Rowley's Ghost: A Checklist of Creative Works Inspired by Thomas Chatterton's Life and Writings', in Nick Groom (ed.), *Thomas Chatterton and Romantic Culture* (Houndmills: Macmillan, 1999), 262–92.

[15] See Richard Holmes, 'Forging the Poet: Some Early Pictures of Thomas Chatterton', in Groom (ed.), *Thomas Chatterton*, 253–8 (256).

[16] E. H. W. Meyerstein, *A Life of Thomas Chatterton* (London: Ingpen and Grant, 1930), 476. See Goodridge, 'Rowley's Ghost', items 205 and 234.

with the Lord Mayor and negotiating on his own behalf with publishers.[17]
The earliest of the elegies on Chatterton, written by his friend Thomas Cary
and published in the *Town and Country Magazine* in October 1770 two
months after his death, stresses his 'manly soul', which even in infancy had
evinced 'that heroic mental fire, | Which reign'd supreme within the mighty
whole'. There is nothing diminutive or boyish about Cary's portrait of a
young man who had already made his mark on the public stage:

> The public good was ever in his view,
> His pen his lofty sentiments bespoke,
>   Nor fear'd he virtuous freedom to pursue.
>
> Yes, Liberty! thy fair, thy upright cause,
> He dar'd defend, spite of despotic force,
> To crush his much-lov'd country's wholesome laws,
>   Its noble constitution's only source.[18]

This image of Chatterton as the public defender of liberty became widely
known when the elegy formed the epilogue to the *Miscellanies* (1778).[19] The
'manly soul' of Cary's poem is the Chatterton of the 'Decimus' letters, whose
attacks on the political establishment rivalled those of Junius in their con-
trolled invective on behalf of 'the liberty of the subject'.[20] Horace Walpole
had already revealed Chatterton as 'Decimus' and author of the uncom-
promising political satire 'Kew Gardens'. Furthermore, Walpole's *Letter
to the Editor of the Miscellanies* (1779) repeats Cary's description of the
satiric and political Chatterton as mature and far from boyish. Walpole's
Chatterton is dangerous and aggressive, 'a bold young man', one who 'had
formed disciples—yes, at eighteen'—'he demanded his poems roughly and
added, that I should not have *dared* to use him so ill'.[21]

Walpole's characterisation found support the following year when the
satiric and mature Chatterton was again emphasised in Croft's *Love and
Madness* (1780), which gave for the first time a full picture of Chatterton's
London activities, his projected alliance with John Wilkes, and his ambitions

---

[17] See Michael F. Suarez, SJ, '"This Necessary Knowledge": Thomas Chatterton and the Ways of the London Book Trade', in Groom (ed.), *Thomas Chatterton*, 96–113.

[18] Thomas Cary, 'Elegy to the Memory of Mr. Thomas Chatterton, Late of Bristol', ll. 26–8, 42–8. In a letter printed by Milles (*Poems, Supposed to have been written at Bristol*, 19) Cary remarks that Chatterton's 'natural inclination' was to satire, and he maintains that his friend was not the author of the Rowley poems.

[19] John Broughton (ed.), *Miscellanies in Prose and Verse; by Thomas Chatterton, the supposed author of the poems published under the names of Rowley, Canning, &c* (London: Fielding and Walker, 1778), 241–5. The poem is reprinted in Meyerstein, *A Life of Thomas Chatterton*, 540–2.

[20] Thomas Chatterton, 'To the Duke of G——n', *Middlesex Journal*, 16 Feb. 1770; reprinted in *The Complete Works of Thomas Chatterton*, 2 vols, ed. Donald S. Taylor and Benjamin B. Hoover (Oxford: Clarendon Press, 1971), 451.

[21] Horace Walpole, *Letter to the Editor of the Miscellanies of Thomas Chatterton* (Strawberry-Hill, 1779), 15, 39, 37.

as a political journalist. It also printed the precociously satiric 'Apostate Will' (his earliest known poem) and the satire 'Happiness'. Croft concluded that 'Satire was his sort, if any thing can be called his sort' (148). Once again the emphasis was reinforced by a description of Chatterton as manly: 'with regard to Chatterton's face and person, all agree that he was a manly, good-looking boy' (241). In support Croft presents evidence from the poet's landlord, Mr Walmsley, that 'there was something manly and pleasing about him, and that he did not dislike the wenches' (190), and Walmsley's niece told him that 'but for his face and her knowledge of his age, she should never have thought him a boy, he was so manly' (191). In *Love and Madness* readers also encountered for the first time Chatterton's letters from London, in which he tells his mother about Wilkes's interest in him: 'I shall visit him next week...He affirmed that what Mr. Fell had of mine could not be the writings of a youth: and expressed a desire to know the author'.[22]

The image of a manly young satirist was again to the fore in George Gregory's 'Chatterton' article in *Biographia Britannica* (1789), which was published as an independent *Life of Thomas Chatterton* in the same year.[23] In his *Life* Gregory repeatedly praises the satiric verse and prose and under-plays the Rowley material. He emphasises the satiric side of the poet's work by printing for the first time an extract from 'Kew Gardens' and the whole of 'The Prophecy' as Chatterton's. It should by now give us no surprise to find that Gregory's politically engaged poet is also grown up: 'The person of Chatterton, like his genius, was premature: He had a manliness and dignity beyond his years.'[24]

Cary's poem, Walpole's pamphlet, Croft's *Love and Madness*, and Gregory's *Life* present a satirically inclined and politically aware poet, and each links this to his maturity and manliness. It is important to remember that such an image was widely available by 1790, and that to keep Chatterton a boy was partly to shut off his politico-satirical side and exploit the lyricism and sentiment instead. For a poet writing in 1794 the manly, Wilkesite Chatterton could be a dangerous model. The cry of 'Liberty' was an increasingly incendiary one, and it was possible to look back to Wilkes as having inaugurated English political radicalism. Therefore, what Coleridge did between 1790 and 1794 (the earliest published version), specifically the degree to which he presented Chatterton as the manly satirical figure, is of some significance

---

[22] Chatterton to Sarah Chatterton, 6 May 1770 (*Complete Works*, 560). This letter, along with others of Chatterton, was well known, being reprinted in Gregory's *Life* (1789) (see next note). In the same week as this letter, Isaac Fell, publisher of Chatterton's satires in the *Freeholder's Magazine*, was arrested and imprisoned for his anti-ministerial publications. See Michael F. Suarez, SJ, 'What Thomas Knew: Chatterton and the Business of Getting into Print', *Angelaki*, 1.2 (1993/4), 86.

[23] *Biographia Britannica*, ed. Andrew Kippis, 2nd edn (London, 1789), iv.573–619; George Gregory, *The Life of Thomas Chatterton, with Criticisms on his Genius and Writings, and a Concise View of the Controversy concerning Rowley's Poems* (London: G. Kearsley, 1789).

[24] *Biographia Britannica*, iv.589; Gregory, *Life*, 101–2.

for assessing the earliest texts of the 'Monody'. A brief glance at what other poets made of Chatterton during the 1770–94 period will suggest that there was a range of alternative possibilities.[25]

Some like William Hayley (1782) were ready to exploit the political implications of Chatterton as the victim of society's neglect, and to accuse the nation's rich of failing to value its struggling authors ('Too oft the wealthy, to proud follies born, | Have turn'd from letter'd Poverty with scorn'[26]). Hayley's point about the social conscience of the rich was picked up by Henry James Pye in *The Progress of Refinement* (1783), in which he points out that poverty could be used to force the starving poet into flattering the powerful: 'Too oft has Poesy with servile aim | By tyrants favor'd, sung a tyrant's fame'.[27] In each case, thoughts of Chatterton introduce a political dimension into the poem, which in neither case is followed through. Hayley and Pye were far from radical figures, but it is significant that at the point of Chatterton's appearance their respective poems become momentarily tinged with radical possibilities.

In the 1780s the figure of Chatterton often raised issues of this kind. Ann Yearsley, the Bristol milkmaid, in her 'Elegy, on Mr. Chatterton' (1787),[28] reiterates Pye's point about poverty encouraging servility: 'Scorning to fawn at laughing Insult's knee', her Chatterton declares, 'My woes were doubled, deeper rais'd my groan; | More sharp, more exquisite, came Agony' (29–31). Part of the tragic scenario of Chatterton's suffering could be his refusal to surrender to the establishment. In a poem sent to *The Gentleman's Magazine* in 1788, the author, 'R.F.', supported his picture of Chatterton as the victim of 'Lords selfish views' with a footnote reference to the 'Balade of Charitie' and its statement that 'Lordis and Barons live for pleasure and themselves'.[29] Chatterton's 'Balade', one of his most admired poems, was seen as satirically reworking the Good Samaritan parable into a poem about how a wealthy society should deal with its poor. In this regard the unfortunate Walpole is regularly attacked, and a poetic lament for Chatterton will sometimes pivot round to take a swipe at him.[30]

---

[25] A partial list of poetic references to Chatterton is given by A. D. Harvey, 'The Cult of Chatterton amongst English Poets *c*.1770–*c*.1820', *Zeitschrift für Anglistik und Amerikanistik*, 39 (1991), 124–33. See Goodridge, 'Rowley's Ghost' (n. 14 above), items 1–169.

[26] William Hayley, *Essay on Epic Poetry* (London: J. Dodsley, 1782), iv.333–4.

[27] Henry James Pye, *The Progress of Refinement. A Poem. In Three Parts* (Oxford: Clarendon Press, 1783), p. 364 (ii.591–2).

[28] Ann Yearsley, 'Elegy, on Mr. Chatterton', in *Poems on Various Subjects* (London: Printed for the Author, 1787), 145–9. See Bridget Keegan, 'Nostalgic Chatterton: Fictions of Poetic Identity and the Forging of a Self-Taught Tradition', in Groom (ed.), *Thomas Chatterton*, 210–27.

[29] *GM*, 58 (Dec. 1788), 1106–7.

[30] '[Walpole] was wealthy—wealth engender'd pride; | Pride steels the heart when meanness rules the mind; | With pride the poor petition was denied, | And thence the woes of Chatterton combin'd' (John Rannie, Sonnet XI 'Written on the Blank Leaf of Chatterton's Poems', in *Poems*, 2nd edn (Aberdeen: J. Chalmers, 1791), 13).

In the poems that pre-date Coleridge's 1790 'Monody' there is a notice-able divide in treatment. Those mentioned so far have exploited an element of indignation to make points about social hierarchy, poverty, and charity, with one eye on Chatterton the satirist. If this 'satiric' mode takes its cue from texts like the 'Balade' and the chorus from 'Goddwyn' (which became known as the 'Ode to Freedom'),[31] the lyric-descriptive Chatterton of sweet showers, soft dews, and drooping flowers was easily combined with images of the poet's own 'budding genius' to form what we might term the 'lyric' mode of Chatterton celebration. Here the traditional flower passage of classical elegy is combined with the boy's frail body and blighted hopes. The flower image indeed can sometimes be obsessive. In Yearsley's poem the boy is a delicate harebell, a 'languid flower' whose 'beauties drop ungather'd as I sing, | And o'er the precipice by winds are cast'. Her flower is a pathetic picture of compliance, which 'humbly bends to ev'ry blast'—and this in a poem that speaks a few lines later of Chatterton's refusal to fawn to power.[32] It is a useful example of how the same poem can offer contradictory pictures of the poet, depending on the mode being employed at the time. Where Yearsley gives us a harebell, Mary Robinson falls back on the more conven-tional primrose: 'So the pale primrose, sweetest bud of May, | Scarce wakes to beauty, ere it feels decay'.[33] Robinson's Chatterton has been deluded by the fragile allure of the imagination ('Frail are the charms delusive *Fancy* shows, | And short the bliss her fickle smile bestows', 77). Evidently Robinson saw neither boldness nor substance in Chatterton's imagined Rowleyan world.

This lyric mode of Chatterton celebration often extends into an entirely disembodied strain. Robinson's airy phantom 'glides along the minster's walls' to the sound of a 'mournful echo', and Yearsley's 'sad Ghost sings on the buoyant air' before it merges into the breathings of nature ('Hush'd dies the sound').[34] Elusiveness becomes transcendence when the poet's soul, 'immers'd in purest air',[35] is embraced by higher powers. The most beautiful and effective of these disembodied Chattertons is offered by the Wartonian Henry Headley in his 'Ode to the Memory of Chatterton' from his *Fugitive Pieces* (1785). In this poem William Collins meets Keats as Chatterton's spirit is released into the cycle of the seasons. Headley's ode hovers between Collins's 'Ode to Evening', his 'Ode to the Memory of Mr Thomson', and Keats's 'To Autumn':

---

[31] In Charles Cowden Clarke's commonplace book (Brotherton Library, Leeds University, Novello-Cowden Clarke Collection MS 6) the chorus from 'Goddwyn' is anthologized as 'Ode to Freedom' and takes its place alongside other extracts of a radical tendency. See Nicholas Roe, *John Keats and the Culture of Dissent* (Oxford: Clarendon Press, 1997), 95.

[32] Yearsley, *Poems*, 146.

[33] Mary Robinson, 'Monody to the Memory of Chatterton', in *Poems by Mrs. M. Robinson* (London: J. Bell, 1791), 75–9.

[34] Yearsley, *Poems*, 146, 148.

[35] Robinson, *Poems*, 75.

When jocund Summer with her honied breath
(Sweetening the golden grain and blithsome gale)
   Displays her sun-burnt face
   Beneath the hat of straw,
The lily's hanging head, the pansy pale,
(Poor Fancy's lowly followers) in meek
   Attire, shall deck thy turf,
   And withering lie with thee

   .   .   .   .

Remembrance oft in Pity's pensive ear,
At silent eve shall sorrowing toll thy knell,
   And tell to after days
   Thy tale, thy luckless tale.[36]

The poem fades away in assonance and echoes, haunted by Chatterton's unseen presence.

There could be no greater contrast to the 'disembodied spirit' strain than my final category of the 'dramatic', in which a contemplation of the tragic youth brings a disturbing and disturbed body before us. If Collins often lies behind the lyric response, the dramatic frequently catches the febrile quality of Pope's 'Eloisa to Abelard' or his 'Unfortunate Lady'. In this next example they both meet at Elsinore:

See! see! he comes! shield me ye gracious pow'rs!
   How pale and wan his lifeless cheeks appear;
Those cheeks once blooming as the new-blown flowers,
   Now only boast a deadly sallow there.
By yonder aged beech e'en now he stands,
   He spreads his arms and beckons me, I fly!
Stay, friendly shade, alas! it 'scapes my hands,
   It sinks! it's gone! I come! I rave! I die!

This is James Thistlethwaite, a friend of Chatterton, writing as early as November 1770 in *The Gentleman's Museum*.[37] Other examples of the dramatic mode focus on the visual set-piece of the death scene to draw the reader into active emotional involvement, like Edward Rushton's *Neglected Genius* (1787): 'See, where thy wretched Victim lies, | What frantic Wildness in his Eyes: | Hark! how he groans! see! see! he foams! he gasps! | And his convulsive Hand the pois'nous Phial grasps'.[38] A vivid close-up of the poison

---

[36] Henry Headley, *Fugitive Pieces* (London: C. Dilly, 1785), 76.

[37] *The Gentleman's Museum and Grand Imperial Magazine*, 5 (Nov. 1770). See E. H. W. Meyerstein, 'An Elegy on Chatterton', *TLS*, 8 Feb. 1934, 92.

[38] Edward Rushton, *Neglected Genius: or, Tributary Stanzas to the Memory of the Unfortunate Chatterton* (London: J. Philips, 1787), 11. 'R.F.' gives a similar picture: 'Stretch'd on the floor, aghast, he lies! | Now rises, sinks again!' (*GM*, 58 (Dec. 1788), 1107). See Goodridge, 'Rowley's Ghost', item 145.

also features in William Hayley's scene: 'On the bare floor, with heaven-directed eyes, | The hapless Youth in speechless horror lies! | The pois'nous vial, by distraction drain'd, | Rolls from his hand, in wild contortion strain'd'.[39] In the dramatic mode, instead of stillness and spirit we have the grotesque body, its contorted hands gesturing to us. It was this mode that would so powerfully affect Thomas De Quincey in a dream:

I see Chatterton in the exceeding pain of death! in the exhausted slumber of agony I see his arm weak as a child's—languid and faint in the extreme—stretched out and raised at midnight—calling and pulling (faintly indeed, but yet convulsively) some human breast to console him.[40]

A visual representation of this dramatic mode is John Flaxman's drawing *c.*1775–80, 'Chatterton Taking the Bowl of Poison from the Spirit of Despair' (Figure 8),[41] in which the youth reaches out for the bowl of poison offered to him by a frightful dark figure, while behind him Apollo's airborne chariot waits to carry him away. In Hannah Cowley's well-known 'Monody' (1778) Flaxman's three characters enact a little stage drama:

> And now Despair her sable form extends,
> Creeps to his couch, and o'er his pillow bends.
> Ah see! a deadly bowl the fiend conceal'd,
> Which to his eye with caution is reveal'd—
> Seize it, Apollo!—seize the liquid snare!
> Dash it to earth, or dissipate in air!
> Stay, hapless Youth! Refrain—abhor the draught...
> In vain!—he drinks—and now the searching fires
> Rush through his veins, and writhing he expires![42]

My division of the early poetic responses to Chatterton into the three modes of satiric, lyric, and dramatic is not meant to suggest they are mutually exclusive: several poems move from one mode to another and the strands interweave differently. An awareness of these dynamics should help us to gauge the individual character of Coleridge's early monodies and appreciate the implications of his extensive revisions.

---

[39] Hayley, *Essay on Epic Poetry*, iv.235–42. The full passage was quoted in *Biographia Britannica* as 'uncommonly animated and poetical' (595).

[40] Thomas De Quincey, *A Diary of Thomas De Quincey: 1803*, ed. Horace A. Eaton (London, 1927), 156–7.

[41] Iolo M. Williams, 'An Identification of Some Early Drawings by Flaxman', *Burlington Magazine*, 102 (June 1960), 246–51, dates the drawing 'no later than 1780'. He connects it to Flaxman's lost design for a monument to Chatterton exhibited at the Royal Academy in that year. Flaxman may have been responding to Cowley's poem (see next note).

[42] Hannah Cowley's poem appeared in *The Morning Post*, 24 Oct. 1778, and was reprinted in later editions of *Love and Madness*. Gregory gives the whole of the 'beautiful monody' (*Life*, 124–6).

8. John Flaxman, 'Thomas Chatterton Taking the Bowl of Poison from the Spirit of Despair' (*c.*1775–80).
© The Trustees of the British Museum.

What is immediately noticeable about Coleridge's earliest version of his 'Monody', transcribed into the Christ's Hospital *Liber Aureus* in 1790, is its affinity with the dramatic and satiric modes of Chatterton elegies. The irregular Pindaric form assists Coleridge in charting the shifts of emotion and response that play between the poet and his subject. A conventional opening in the first four lines is pushed aside with the image of Chatterton's corpse 'on the bare ground' (8).[43] The presence of the picture of death generates the ebb and flow of the contemplation that follows. The speaker himself becomes the highly sensitized reader of Chatterton's image, the site for the poem's alternation between pity and anger:

> Thy corpse of many a livid hue
> On the bare ground I view,
> Whilst various passions all my mind engage;
> Now is my breast distended with a sigh,
> And now a flash of Rage
> Darts *through* the tear, that glistens in my eye.
>   (7–12; my italics)

In other Chatterton poems before this date the pity and anger were often present, but never so intertwined, and so absorbed into the poet-voice. Rather than the reader being invited to 'look!' or 'hear!' the voice of the poem is enacting the response for us. The identification is partly conveyed through a syntactic ambiguity that hints at the writer's own suicide: in the phrase 'Athirst for Death I see thee drench the bowl!' (6) the dangling non-finite clause attaches itself to the subject of the sentence, the 'I' of the poem, a formula later repeated to exaggerated effect:

> Fated to heave sad Disappointment's sigh,
> To feel the Hope now rais'd, and now deprest,
> To feel the burnings of an injur'd breast,
> From all thy Fate's deep sorrows keen
> In vain, O youth, I turn th'affrighted eye   (40–4)

By a kind of syntactical sympathy the poem's 'I' gathers up Chatterton's miseries and makes them his own.

By favouring the immediacy of a dramatic rather than lyric approach, Coleridge dispenses with the traditional cycle of nature imagery (growth nipped in the bud, etc.) which is the staple of classical elegy. Instead he draws on some of those elements of what I have called the 'satiric' mode of response to Chatterton, and exploits the radical possibilities that enter with them. On the waves of emotion generated by his dramatic contemplation, Coleridge's indignation and anger give voice to rhetorical questions. With the tear glistening in his eye, he turns to accuse his country: 'Is this the land of liberal Hearts!' (13). Where the poem's first exclamation ('I see thee drench the bowl!') had ushered in the dramatic mode, this second one introduces the satiric. Alongside the tragic figure of Thomas Otway (conventionally linked with Chatterton as another victim of poverty) there enters at line 16

---

[43] All quotations from the 1790 monody are transcribed from the *Liber Aureus* (see n. 4 above). This version survives in another manuscript in Coleridge's hand *c.*1792–3, BL Add MS 47551, fos. 8ᵛ–11ᵛ ('the Ottery Copybook'). See Mays, ii.167.

the more surprising figure of 'Hudibras' Butler, representative of the native
English satiric tradition, who specialised in exposing religious hypocrisy.[44]
This overt reference to a dramatist and a satirist helps establish the terms on
which Coleridge's poem is written. Indignation becomes our appropriate
response:

> ... Yet Butler, 'gainst the bigot foe
> Well-skill'd to aim keen Humour's dart,
> Yet Butler felt Want's poignant sting;
>   And Otway, Master of the Tragic art,
>   Whom Pity's self had bade to sing,
> Sunk beneath a load of Woe.
> This ever can the generous Briton hear,
> And starts not in his eye th'indignant tear?   (16–23)

The final phrase conflates indignation and pity. In the summary of Chatter-
ton's writing career that follows, Coleridge continues to emphasise the
national context. The poet's 'many a vision fair' (30) are not confined to
the imagination but instead issue in active benevolence, a concept to which
Chatterton had given a political meaning:

> He listens to many a Widow's prayers,
> And many an Orphan's thanks he hears;
>   He sooths to peace the careworn breast,
>   He bids the Debtor's eyes know rest,
>   And Liberty and Bliss behold   (33–7)

And the monody moves on to make direct allusion to Chatterton's political
writings:

> And now he punishes the heart of Steel,
> And her own iron rod he makes Oppression feel.   (38–9)

At line 55 the pity and indignation, which had earlier combined within the
speaker, and were then satirically externalised as the nation's response, now
become the terms of a dramatic *psychomachia* enacted in Chatterton him-
self. Pity's vision paints for him a sentimental picture of his 'native cot' with
his lamenting sister and mother; but set against this is a pressing reminder
from Despair and Indignation, who retell his woes and recall the miseries
of 'dread dependance', 'Neglect and grinning Scorn, and Want combin'd'
(75–7). Chatterton, with the bowl poised at his lips, is torn between the two
pictures as Pity and Indignation now compete for him. And in this monody
it is the latter that wins as Chatterton embraces death.

The final paragraph evokes Chatterton's liberated spirit, but avoids ether-
ealising him. Instead Coleridge models his ending on that most famous of
monodies, *Lycidas*. The climax is a vindication of Chatterton's 'fire divine'

---

[44] Samuel Butler (1612–80), author of the satiric poem *Hudibras* (1663–78), died in penury.

as a poet. But where Milton's Lycidas is a passive auditor who 'hears the unexpressive nuptial song, | In the blest kingdoms meek of joy and love', in Coleridge's poem Chatterton soars through 'the vast domain' and is himself the singer who keeps the angelic host entertained. He does not evanesce, but ends the poem as a lesson in the necessity of fortitude:

> Grant me with firmer breast t'oppose their hate,
> And soar beyond the Storm with upright eye elate.   (89–90)

Coleridge's 1790 monody is conscious of the literary tradition to which it contributes, and of the range of Chattertons celebrated in the poetry of his day. What is striking is the teenage Coleridge's integration of pathos and anger, and the poet's staging as drama the contending responses within himself. Particularly noticeable, too, is his avoidance of the lyric mode with its tendency to evanesce, fade, and wither. On the contrary, the 'hateful picture' (46) of the poet's death scene is forced on his sight. Also missing is any sign of the delicate boy. The picture of Chatterton that he sees is not childlike, but actually prematurely aged:

> In vain I seek the charms of youthful grace,
> Thy sunken eye, thy haggard cheeks it shews,
> The quick emotions struggling in thy Face,
> Faint index of thy *mental* throes.   (49–52)

This is a man of passion, whose face is lined by his experiences of life.

It is also the prematurely aged poet figured on the Chatterton handkerchief (Figure 9). This exemplary sentimental text, an example of which survives in the British Library, was designed to stanch the very tears it caused to flow. Its visual representation of the tragic youth, engraved from a painting that was 'the work of a friend',[45] holds the central position on the fabric and is read emblematically in the prose and verse descriptions on either side of it. This triptych of Sensibility offers just such a haggard figure as Coleridge is transfixed by. The prose text on the handkerchief explains Chatterton's far from youthful appearance: 'Anxieties and cares had advanced his life, and given him an older look than was suited to his age.' I think it is possible to go further and to see Coleridge's 1790 monody as partly a response to the emotive verses that occupy the right-hand column of the handkerchief. These 38 lines urge the reader to contemplate the picture in an itemized meditation on its details (the handkerchief is in several ways a sentimental development of the old emblem books):

> Pale and dejected, mark, how genius strives
> With poverty, and mark, how well it thrives.

---

[45] The engraved plate appeared in *Westminster Magazine*, 10 July 1782, facing p. 342, along with a slightly different version of the prose commentary. The handkerchief, which must have been printed shortly afterwards, is BL, C.39.h.20. See Goodridge, 'Rowley's Ghost', item 244; Holmes, 'Forging the Poet', 254–6.

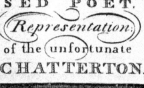

9. The Chatterton Handkerchief (1782).
Reproduced by permission of the British Library. Shelf mark C.39.h.20.

> The shabby cov'ring of the gentle bard,
> Regard it well, tis worthy thy regard;
> The friendly cobweb, serving for a screen,
> The chair, a part of what it once had been.
> The bed, whereon th'unhappy victim slept,
> And oft unseen, in silent anguish, wept   (7–14)

The reader-spectator is not merely prompted, but prodded and cajoled into an emotional reaction. What is more, the handkerchief-poem closes with a remarkable curse on anyone who coldly turns away from the picture:

> Whoe'er thou art, that shalt this face survey,
> And turn, with cold disgust, thy eyes away,

Then bless thyself, that sloth and ign'rance bred
Thee up in safety, and with plenty fed

.   .   .   .

Mayst thou, nor can I wish a greater curse,
Live full despis'd, and die without a nurse.
Or, if some wither'd hag, for sake of hire,
Should wash thy sheets, and cleanse thee from the mire,
Let her, when hunger peevishly demands
The dainty morsel from her barb'rous hands,
Insult, with hellish mirth, thy craving maw,
And snatch it to herself, and call it law.
'Till pinching famine waste thee to the bone,
And break, at last, that solid heart of stone.   (23–38)

These verses set the 'honest warmth' of the sentimental reader against the 'cold disgust' of one who turns his eye away. In its own responsive way Coleridge's monody also begins in coldness ('For cold my Fancy grows... | When Want and cold Neglect had chill'd thy soul', 4–5) and then moves to generate warmth. The enemy in Coleridge's monody, as in the handkerchief, is 'th'unfeeling heart' (74). Coleridge's poem is an exercise in that 'honest warmth' urged by the voice of the linen. Both texts are passionate responses to a man of passion ('his passions were too impetuous', says the handkerchief; 'each strong Passion spurn'd controll', reads line 53 of the monody); both present a prematurely aged face marked by its cares; both also use the satiric mode to accuse their country (Coleridge's 'is this the land of liberal Hearts!' finds its equivalent in the handkerchief's remark that Chatterton's fate was 'a satire upon an age and a nation').

It is impossible to say whether the teenage Coleridge had seen the handkerchief and recalled it when he wrote the first version of the monody, but what is clear is that the two texts belong together in the way they exploit the satiric and dramatic modes of Chatterton celebration. The poet is physically present, mature, marked by his experiences, and he arouses warmth, indignation, and a wider sense of national injustice that is radical in its implications. In other words, both texts resist the lyric mode which eventually won the day and came to preoccupy romantic responses to Chatterton. In that fiction the poet becomes a wondrous spirit rather than a marked body, an evanescent being rather than a standing reproof. It is particularly interesting that when Coleridge revised the monody for publication in 1794 it was chiefly to introduce lyrical passages that quite alter the poem's character. In 1794 it became a very different text, and it was this one that brought Coleridge a degree of public popularity and was influential in establishing the lyric mode's primacy in poetic presentations of Chatterton.

As soon as we encounter the 1794 poem we can see that it features those key elements of the evanescent that his 1790 version had excluded:

> When faint and sad o'er Sorrow's desart wild,
> Slow journeys onward, poor Misfortune's child,
> When fades each lovely form by Fancy drest,
> And inly pines the self-consuming breast;
> No scourge of Scorpions in thy right arm dread,
> No helmed Terrors nodding o'er thy head,
> Assume, O DEATH! the Cherub Wings of PEACE,
> And bid the heart-sick Wanderer's Anguish cease!   (1–8)

This entirely new opening presents a figure that is generalised, diminutive, isolated, childlike, and insubstantial (all those things that the 1790 Chatterton was not) rather than specific, embodied, engaged, communicative, manly. The lost and wandering child of line 2, however, is not even Chatterton himself, but some forlorn, fanciful surrogate, an unspecific symbol of transience.

The poet's tearful reaction to the dead poet is no longer an immediate personal response (the drama is diffused by generalising it as 'Nature's bosom-startling call', 15), and the 'now' of this poem is not the dramatic present, but a term of narrative continuity ('Now...; And now...'). The political exclamation of 1790 ('Is this the land of liberal Hearts!') has in 1794 become a literary question: 'Is this the Land of song-ennobled Line?' (23). Even more pointedly, the figure of the satiric Butler has been replaced by the predictably elegiac Spenser:

> Ah me! yet Spenser, gentlest Bard divine,
> Beneath chill Disappointment's deadly shade
> His weary Limbs in lonely Anguish lay'd!   (26–8)

Samuel Butler's highly relevant battle against 'Want' and 'the bigot foe' have become a vague and world-weary 'Disappointment'.

Some of the urgency of the 1790 version is retained, as in the line 'And her own iron rod he makes Oppression feel' (48). But in the 1794 text the grasping of the 'patriot steel' (47) becomes incongruous three lines later when the lyric mode fully establishes itself (the whole passage is added in 1794):

> Sweet Tree of Hope! thou loveliest Child of Spring!
> How fair didst thou disclose thine early bloom,
>   Loading the west-winds with its soft perfume!
> And Fancy hovering round on shadowy wing,
>   On every blossom hung her fostering dews,
>   That changeful wanton'd to the orient Day!
> Ah! soon upon thy poor unshelter'd Head
> Did Penury her sickly mildew shed: (51–8)

Chatterton is invoked as a marvellous boy, an early bloom nipped in the bud, a delicate, evanescent figure accompanied by a sylph-like Fancy and perfumed breezes. In the passages added for the 1794 version, the monody moves away from Chatterton's discomforting presence. He is not even really dead, but remains as a wistful memory haunting the twilight:

> Ye Woods! that wave o'er Avon's rocky steep,
> To Fancy's ear sweet is your murm'ring deep!
> For *here* she loves the Cypress Wreath to weave,
> Watching with wistful eye the sad'ning tints of Eve.
> Here far from Men amid this pathless grove,
> In solemn thought the Minstrel wont to rove,
> Like Star-beam on the rude sequester'd Tide,
> Lone-glittering, thro' the Forest's murksome pride. (92–9)

The beautiful images cannot conceal the fact that the poet, now suffused by lyric melancholy, has been taken out of society and history. We are furthest of all from fact in the final lines when Chatterton's suicide is Wertherised. The despondent wanderer is closer to the psychic depressive of Thomas Warton's 'Suicide' than to the indignant patriotic bard of Gray:[46]

> With wild unequal steps he pass'd along,
> Oft pouring on the winds a broken song:
> Anon upon some rough Rock's fearful Brow,
> Would pause abrupt—and gaze upon the waves below.[47] (104–7)

It should be pointed out that when Coleridge later turned against the 'Monody on the Death of Chatterton' it was the dematerialising additions that he singled out for the sharpest criticism: '[O]n a life & death so full of heart-giving *realities,* as poor Chatterton's', he wrote to Southey, 'to find such shadowy nobodies, as cherub-winged DEATH, Trees of HOPE, bare-bosom'd AFFECTION, & simpering PEACE—makes one's blood circulate like ipecacacuanha.'[48] Clearly he felt dissatisfied with it, and part of the reason is that the 1794 poem is a mixed and compromised work, which runs through too many moods and makes too many different gestures. It is a more generalised and less focused text than its predecessor. In fact the distinctly characterised 1790 poem deserves to be appreciated in its own right, and the Chatterton that it presents is a more disturbing and radical figure.

Revising the 1794 text for his *Poems on Various Subjects* (1796) Coleridge made a few small verbal changes, but then he printed a further 36 lines to form an entirely new conclusion. As noted earlier, this extension

---

[46] Warton's 'The Suicide', first printed in his *Poems: A New Edition, with Additions* (London: T. Becket, 1777), 42–7, does not name Chatterton, but the suicidal youth was taken by many to refer to him. Coleridge thought Warton's ode 'exquisite' (letter to the editor of *The Monthly Magazine,* Jan. 1798; Griggs, 381–2).

[47] Cf. Warton, 'The Suicide', 28–30: 'Oft was he wont, in hasty fit, | Abrupt the social board to quit, | And gaze with eager glance upon the tumbling flood'.

[48] Coleridge to Southey, *c.*17 July 1797 (Griggs, 333). The references are to the 1794 text, ll. 7, 51, 71–2, and 77 (all were added in 1794 and remained in 1796).

may represent the original 1794 ending, which had to be omitted from the Cambridge volume for reasons of space.[49] At the abrupt end of the 1794 poem Chatterton is poised on the cliff edge and gazes down at the waves; Coleridge's 1796 addition immediately turns this self-destructive image nearer home: '[I] dare no longer on the sad theme muse, | Lest kindred woes persuade a kindred doom'. But, in a move that reflects the emotional counterpoint of the 1796 volume as a whole, the extinction of hope ('the last pale Hope, that shiver'd at my heart') is immediately followed by its resurgence. Coleridge will sail 'o'er the ocean swell | Sublime of Hope' and begin a new life in the Susquehanna valley, where he imagines the figure of Chatterton joining the Pantisocrats in their freedom-loving commune:

> . . . we, at sober eve, would round thee throng,
> Hanging, enraptur'd, on thy stately song!
> And greet with smiles the young-eyed POESY
> All deftly mask'd, as hoar ANTIQUITY.

The emphasis has shifted from an embodied Chatterton suffering at the hands of an unjust society, to Chatterton the liberated spirit who can appear before the Susquehanna campfire to inspire a new generation and another continent. This figure who joins the Pantisocratic circle is the young man who was able through his *alter ego* Rowley to make the poetry of the past sound vividly in the present. It reminds us of the ambivalent double phenomenon of Chatterton–Rowley, while superimposing them as a single composite inspiration—youth and antiquity in collaboration.

The effect of this at the end of Coleridge's 'Monody' is something like that achieved by George Hardinge in his dramatic interlude published at the height of the Chatterton controversy, *Rowley and Chatterton in the Shades* (1782). This amusing 'dialogue of the dead' is premised on the friendly meeting of Rowley and his young creator in the Lucianic underworld. Hardinge's scenario allows the various components of the Chatterton phenomenon to engage with each other. Chatterton greets Rowley ('Who am I, Sir? why, Sir, *I* am YOU, and YOU are *I*'); and together the two new friends encounter a group of men in conversation, who turn out to be Langland, Chaucer, Lydgate, and Spenser.[50] The four of them combine to perform a miniature pageant of the history of poetry—each speaking in his own distinctive poetic style. As they turn and walk off eagerly discussing the new arrival (the 'hendy Boy' who is due to be enrolled 'with poets olde'), Chatterton comments to Rowley: 'Brave poets these: I am always ravished

---

[49] See n. 10 above. The reference to the Pantisocracy project as a current hope supports a dating of 1794 for the 'new' ending, as does the fact that it shares eight lines with the 'Pantisocracy sonnet' ('No more my Visionary Soul'), which Coleridge posted to Southey on 18 Sept. 1794.

[50] George Hardinge, *Rowley and Chatterton in the Shades: Or, Nugæ Antiquæ et Novæ. A New Elysian Interlude, in Prose and Verse* (London: T. Becket, 1782), 6, 34–7.

with their antique melody: but I have given their modes a continued cadence which justly surprizes the world' (37). This expresses nicely Chatterton's role in linking poetry with its past and making connections across literary history.

But Hardinge then goes on to suggest that Chatterton will also inspire the poetry of the future. A 'Troop of Antiquaries' arrives on the scene and, under the guidance of John Leland, proceeds to celebrate the role of historical scholarship in recovering the past and helping it to speak ('Ye, who... | From parchments wip'd th'injurious dust... | Ye, by whose unceasing pains | Old language still fresh lustre gains'). Now in light-hearted mood, as the stage direction indicates, 'the Antiquarians dance in circles', only to be 'interrupted by the shade of a YOUNG POET, who rushes in and sings the following IRREGULAR ODE'. As Rowley, Chatterton, and the antiquarians look on, the young poet performs a sublime ode inspired by Chatterton's spirit.[51] It is a scene that catches the underlying irony of Chatterton's creative relationship with past and future, with Rowley on one side and the young Coleridge on the other.

By dying in his mid-teens Chatterton suddenly became a voice in the past before he was able to register in the present. The wish to keep the young voice alive was understandable, and one way was to make it reverberate in the air, to give it 'a continued cadence'. In doing so, the voice of 'Rowley' too seemed reachable, sustainable. The line separating the poet and the persona grew indistinct. Whether the tones came from the 1460s or the 1760s, they were no longer the province of the antiquarians but were part of a literary story still being written, and with genuine poetic potential. Somehow the coupling of Rowley–Chatterton seemed to have fathered a fresh poetry, which spoke of the past while being freed from it, and which struck its hearers as if caught from the air. The three centuries that stretched back to Rowley only deepened the effect, made it reverberate more. Literary history echoed in the present.

If Hardinge's dramatic interlude enacts how poetry can be transfused from one generation to the next, the 1796 ending to Coleridge's 'Monody' suggests something similar in the way the radical young Pantisocrats 'greet with smiles the young-eyed POESY | All deftly mask'd, as hoar ANTIQUITY'. The figure of Chatterton becomes the soul of Poetry itself, in its essence eternally youthful, ever renewable. And in these lines Coleridge recovers the spirit of Chatterton's verse from its historical embodiment in Rowley. The spirit of poetry finds its way out from beneath the old words, and behind the poet's mask he sees 'young eyed POESY' itself, the potential poetry of the future.

---

[51] Ibid. 38–41.

7 Putting His Poems Together: Coleridge's First Volume (1796)

ON THE OPENING page of *Biographia Literaria* Coleridge looks back at his earliest published collection of poetry: 'In 1794', he writes, 'when I had barely passed the verge of manhood, I published a small volume of juvenile poems.'[1] The first date in Coleridge's literary autobiography is of course wrong; but perhaps there is a touch of wishful thinking too. In April 1794 he was twenty-one, a suitable age for a retrospective volume of 'juvenile poems'. But in April 1796, the correct date, he was twenty-three and a half. Coleridge's insouciance (to put it politely) suggests a lingering embarrassment that it was just a little bit late to be producing juvenilia. Perhaps it crossed his mind that his fellow Christ's Hospitaller, Leigh Hunt, had published his first collection, entitled *Juvenilia*, at the age of sixteen, a warmly received volume that reached a fourth edition by Hunt's nineteenth birthday.[2] In any case, what we have in Coleridge's *Poems on Various Subjects* (1796) is not, strictly speaking, the poet's 'juvenilia' at all. Hunt's volume comprised poems written between the ages of twelve and sixteen. Of the fifty-one poems in Coleridge's first book, one may have been completed by the age of seventeen, a couple more by nineteen, seven of them at twenty, and all the rest completed no earlier than 1794. The great majority are poems of his majority.

At least in the literal sense. But in looking at how Coleridge organised his 1796 volume I want to keep in mind this concept of the immature as something that the book itself exploits. His phrase, 'barely passed the verge of manhood', tiptoes uneasily around the threshold, and can remind us of Chatterton's ambivalent status. The issue of uncertain poetic maturity, I shall argue, is bound up with the character of Coleridge's volume, which I want to read here as a sequence. Reading the contents through from cover to cover is an unsettling experience. A commanding, confident voice is heard, but is interspersed with others that are conventional, naïve, or hesitant. What we might think of as a 'juvenile' note is used self-consciously, even dramatically in places. The poet offers hope of great things but encounters distractions and frustrations. In the *Biographia* passage Coleridge

[1] *Biog. Lit.* i.5 (Ch. 1).
[2] Leigh Hunt, *Juvenilia; or, A Collection of Poems* (London: J. Whiting, 1801). See Nicholas Roe, *Fiery Heart: The First Life of Leigh Hunt* (London: Pimlico, 2005), 49–58.

goes on to talk about the reception of these poems: 'they were received', he says, 'with a degree of favour, which, young as I was, I well knew was bestowed on them not so much for any positive merit, as because they were considered buds of hope, and promises of better works to come'.[3]

Through the course of the volume this dynamic of uncertain hope allows Coleridge a forward-looking idea, but one that is checked, renewed, blasted, revived. It is there to emerge continually at crucial moments. The 'buds' are clearly those of youth, and the reader is frequently reminded of them; but there is a more complex response available. Instead of being simply a volume of 'juvenile poems' the book offers a disconcerting alternation of the distinct phases of a young life—infancy, adolescence, manliness. The 1796 *Poems* moves back and forth through those three registers: innocence, impetuosity, responsibility. There is no easy progress or sense of developing powers through the volume, but an unsettling negotiation with its poetic materials— hesitant steps, daring leaps, purposeful strides (and not necessarily in that order), and they make us continually readjust our view of the poet. The tendency is not to reassure but to arouse concern. It was a subtext to which reviewers responded: John Aikin ended his notice in the *Monthly* with a recommendation that his readers buy the volume and thus help 'to disperse the clouds which have darkened the prospects of a man of distinguished worth as well as of uncommon abilities'.[4] The book was invested in the prospective as much as the achieved.

But given what is known of its production, we might ask, did Coleridge in any sense 'organise' the book at all? Thanks to its publisher, Joseph Cottle, the story of its making has come down to us as a narrative of frustration, crisis, and delay. In his *Early Recollections* forty years later Cottle presents it as a comic plot, with Coleridge as the wayward young hero and Cottle himself functioning as the divine machinery, a providential force who guides, encourages, tempts, cajoles, bribes, tricks, cossets, nags, and gener- ally presides over his protégé's progress—or lack of it.[5] The story of the book's fraught gestation (over ten months rather than the usual nine) and difficult delivery is intercut with Cottle's ministering to the poet at various crucial moments with small items of sustenance for body and spirit: tea, tobacco-pipes, bacon, a pair of slippers, a cheese-toaster, cheerful wallpaper.

Cottle's chronology, however, is hopelessly muddled. Brief notes (what Cottle calls 'Mr. C's little apologies') are interspersed with snatches of reported conversation and letters placed out of sequence, so the reader is given the impression that thanks to Coleridge's dilatoriness the printing, begun in the summer of 1795, was suspended for some six months and not resumed until February 1796. The book was finally published *c.*16 April

---

[3] *Biog. Lit.* i.5–6.

[4] *Monthly Review*, 20 (June 1796), 194–5 (*Coleridge: The Critical Heritage*, ed. J. R. de J. Jackson (London: Routledge and Kegan Paul, 1970), 36–8).

[5] See *Early Recollections*, i.16–17, 51–62, 135–44.

immediately after the printing of Coleridge's preface and his concluding notes (sheets A and N).[6] It is clear the press was held up for several weeks during February–March 1796 while Coleridge still worked on 'Religious Musings', the final poem in the volume, and that he did not deliver his preface until the end of the month. But these printing delays in spring 1796 are in Cottle's account projected back to the previous summer. A letter in which the desperate poet volunteers, in exchange for a dish of tea, to be locked in a room while he writes out 'the whole of the notes & the preface' is placed in summer 1795 instead of late March 1796 where it belongs;[7] and when Cottle announces that with Coleridge's return from Clevedon to Bristol in November 1795 'there was now some prospect that the printer's types would be again set in motion' he quotes a letter of 1797 relating to the second edition.[8] Disentangling this is not made easier by the problem of Griggs's letter 92. In this undated letter written while printing was in progress Coleridge refers to the 'six Sheets already printed' (i.e. B–G, pages 1–96) and he calculates that a further four sheets will be required. He assures Cottle he will have the *notes* by 'Saturday morning by nine o'clock', and that 'On Wednesday Morning by nine o'clock the Preface shall be sent—they cannot want it before,' he adds.[9] Coleridge knows that the copy for sheets A (Preface and Contents) and N (Notes and Errata) will be the final things the printer needs before publication. Griggs dates this letter to October 1795, but as J. C. C. Mays has pointed out, Cottle would surely have complained bitterly at an interruption of six months. 'Week after week' is Cottle's phrase, which seems appropriate for the delays between late February and April.[10] But more than this, it is very difficult to conceive that Coleridge actually felt ready to produce his notes and preface the previous October. All other references to them are in February–March. Certainty is impossible, but Mays's suggestion that the letter could be from late February 1796 is convincing, and this leads to the likelihood that the *Poems* did not go to press until Coleridge had returned from his *Watchman* tour on 13

---

[6] Copies lacking these opening and closing sheets were available on 1 April. See Mays, i.1192.
[7] Coleridge to Cottle, [late March 1796]; *Early Recollections*, i.56; Griggs, 193–4 (to add to the confusion Cottle endorsed this letter 'April 1797'). Cottle similarly associates with summer 1795 Coleridge's letter to Josiah Wade confessing 'my present brain-crazing circumstances' [*c*.14 March 1796]. See Griggs, 190.
[8] Coleridge to Cottle, [early Feb. 1797]; *Early Recollections*, i.137–8; Griggs, 309. Coleridge's reference to his tortuous correction of 'The Destiny of Nations' is glossed by Cottle, 'Religious Musings'.
[9] Griggs, 162–3 (MS Harvard). Griggs notes that 'Cottle took his usual liberties with this manuscript, publishing it only in part and making two separate letters of it.' See *Early Recollections*, i.138–9, 285.
[10] 'This promising commencement was soon interrupted by successive and long-continued delays.... These delays I little heeded, but they were not quite so acceptable to the printer, who grievously complained that his "types, and his leads, and his forms, were locked up," week after week, to his great detriment' (*Early Recollections*, i.52–3).

February.[11] The subsequent hold-up was partly caused by his decision to rework his 'nativity poem' of under 300 lines into the 446-line 'Religious Musings'.

Delay, however, is not the same as confusion. Cottle's mangled story does not mean the volume was unplanned or that Coleridge was not responsible for ordering the contents. The evidence on this is fairly clear. In the Gutch notebook he can be seen working out an arrangement for the 'Effusions' section, so that the Sonnets on Eminent Characters, for example, will be printed in a different order from their first appearance in *The Morning Chronicle*.[12] And from the Rugby Manuscript, which preserves Coleridge's transcribed copy, it is evident that poems were printed in the order in which the poet had transcribed them: when an individual leaf carries two different items on recto and verso they appear in that order in the volume.[13] To consider the 1796 *Poems* sequentially is not only to reproduce its reception by many of its first readers, but to give Coleridge some credit for putting his poems together in a thoughtful way. The result may be disconcerting at times, but it is so in the sense that some poems and groupings of poems function both expressively and critically. Texts not only support and recall each other but also adjust and judge each other. The volume exemplifies how organisation and unity are very different things, and suggests that Coleridge's first book was an organic enterprise because it was not unified.

Reasonably enough, Mays concludes that this first collection is an unsatisfactory and unrepresentative one. He remarks that '[t]he extended, interrupted period of preparation, and its hurried conclusion, make the volume an incomplete statement on Coleridge's behalf'.[14] The characterisation is just; but I want to argue that a sense of incompleteness is strategic, and that rather than failing in an attempt to unify the volume and harmonise its contents Coleridge presents the material so as to highlight its disparateness. Instead of looking for smooth transitions he tends to exploit juxtaposition in ways both self-dramatising and self-critical. The key idea behind this is an awareness that in preparing his first published collection he was both metaphorically and literally bringing himself to book. He was having to acknowledge, and account for, the body of his work. This made the notion of *embodiment* a critical issue, and it is evident he was thinking in that direction. The opening words of the Preface confront the idea head-on: 'POEMS

---

[11] Mays, i.1192.

[12] See *Notebooks*, entry 305; Coleridge's jottings are re-examined by Carl R. Woodring, *Politics in the Poetry of Coleridge* (Madison: University of Wisconsin Press, 1961), 226–7.

[13] See also nn. 39 and 44 below. In assembling the 'Rugby' Manuscript (Harry Ransome Center, University of Texas, Austin) Cottle mounted the individual items himself post-1837 (his confusions are detailed by Mays, i.1176–7); but the order of Coleridge's transcription seems to have been followed by the printer: Mays reports, for example, that the MS of Effusion 15 (Alexander Turnbull Library, Wellington, NZ) 'is almost certainly the top half of a leaf, the bottom half of which contained [Effusion 16]'. The latter is now in the Huntington Library, San Marino, California. See Mays, ii.201, 266.

[14] Mays, i.1192.

ON VARIOUS SUBJECTS written at different times and prompted by very
different feelings; but which will be read at one time and under the influence
of one set of feelings—this is an heavy disadvantage'. (It is, we might say,
simply the definition of a book.) Coleridge appears uneasy about the way
two pluralities (poems and readers) could become an encounter between *the
book* and *the public*: 'We are for ever attributing a personal unity to imagin-
ary aggregates', he goes on to say, 'What is the PUBLIC but a term for a
number of scattered individuals...?'[15] In these words he is unspokenly
raising the same question about his book of 'poems...written at different
times and prompted by very different feelings'. Publication of his poems
raised the difficulty of a diachronic identity acknowledging the defining
moment.

This critical issue of embodiment thus has a bearing on Coleridge's per-
sonal identity. As Locke argued, it involves a negotiation with past experi-
ence, and it is perhaps this that makes Coleridge unsettled. To organise one's
first book of poems is to become acutely aware of a self-projection, which
can tend toward the closely focused and self-expressive like Bowles's slim
volume of sonnets, or which may work in a more objectifying way and have
an element of the self-critical about it; i.e. the book embodies earlier voices
the author finds himself being forced to listen to and acknowledge. The 1796
Poems have something of the former, but I would suggest that in putting
them together Coleridge found himself producing the latter. Viewed in the
light of this potential for self-critique, the prophetic voice with which the
volume ends is not only an ambitious visionary gesture but can be seen as a
move to liberate himself from the retrospective poetic identity that his
collected *Poems* represents.

Finally, the nature of poetic embodiment itself was inevitably implicated
in the project. For Coleridge at this time the question of poetry's negotiation
between spirit and matter was pressing on him: was the poetic, especially in
its lyric tradition, more an animation rather than an embodiment? For a self-
declared Berkeleyan in 1796 this was not a matter of taste but of principle.[16]
Reverberating through the whole volume is Duke Theseus's amused wonder
that 'as imagination bodies forth | The forms of things unknown, the poet's
pen | Turns them to shapes, and gives to aery nothing | A local habitation and
a name'.[17] Does poetry liberate us through its playful elusiveness and
imaginative licence, its 'viewless pinions aery', and is it weighed down by
more substantial, everyday things? Or does poetry have a duty to reach out

---

[15] This can be related to what Lucy Newlyn has analysed as Coleridge's 'lifelong preoccu-
pation with the difficulties of establishing and sustaining a sympathetic readership' ('Coleridge
and the Anxiety of Reception', *Romanticism*, 1 (1995), 206–38 (207).
[16] 'I am a Berkleian', he told Thelwall on 17 Dec. 1796 (Griggs, 278). On 1 Nov. he had
written to Poole: 'Bishop Taylor, Old Baxter, David Hartley & the Bishop of Cloyne are *my men*'
(Griggs, 245). George Berkeley had become Bishop of Cloyne in 1734.
[17] William Shakespeare, *A Midsummer Night's Dream*, V.i.14–17.

to 'heart-giving *realities*'?[18] Not surprisingly, the age-old debate about poetry's relationship to 'the truths of a foolish world' does not seem in the end to be resolved.[19]

In putting together his first volume of poems Coleridge was confronting these various linked problems of embodiment. What did this corpus of work say about himself as a man and a poet? In this chapter I want to look at some of the sequences and juxtapositions in the collection, and to suggest that they are more deliberate and strategic than accidental and inept, and also that they have an organic quality that resists unity in favour of a more varied and unpredictable reading experience.

The trajectory of the volume seems clear enough: from the opening 'Monody on the Death of Chatterton' to the final newly-minted 'Religious Musings' hot off the press. His two most ambitious poems frame the book, suggesting a journey from an image of poetic potential nipped in the bud to a confident, sublime public statement; from the poetry of doomed youth to a voice that might rouse the nation's soul. The volume appears to have what is now termed a good 'exit velocity'. But Coleridge deliberately complicates the close of 'Religious Musings' by breaking off from conjecturing his future role as a member of the angelic choir, with a reminder of his immaturity: 'Till then', he optimistically remarks, 'I discipline my young noviciate thought' (437–8). The image the volume leaves us with is of the novice not yet entered into orders.

Coleridge's phrase is a conventional apology for attempting to evoke the Supreme Being; but within the volume as a whole it is only the final example of what has become a series of withdrawals, steps back to adolescence and to infancy. It is the volume's tactical counter-impulses, as we might call them, which I want to focus on here, its moments of recoil and retreat when, as in Blake's *Book of Thel*, the challenge of realising potential is resisted. The 1796 volume is characterised by its returns to ideas of evanescence, its deployment of retractions, regressions, and dispersals of various kinds, and by the way echoes within the book tend (as actual echoes do) to diminish and grow faint.

A notable example of this is the extraordinary retrogression we make through the first three items of the book, which take us from the Susquehanna to the Pixies' Parlour. In his new ending to the 'Monody on the Death of Chatterton', first printed here, Coleridge imagines Chatterton joining the Pantisocrats in 'peaceful Freedom's UNDIVIDED dale', where they would gather round the youth and listen 'enraptur'd' to his lyric voice: 'And greet

---

[18] Coleridge to Southey, *c*.17 July 1797 (Griggs, 333). The reference is to Chatterton. See Chapter 6.

[19] '[T]he historian, being captived to the truth of a foolish world, is many times a terror from well-doing, and an encouragement to unbridled wickedness' (Sir Philip Sidney, *An Apology for Poetry*, ed. Geoffrey Shepherd (London, etc.: Nelson, 1965), 111).

with smiles the young-eyed POESY | All deftly mask'd, as hoar ANTIQUITY'.[20]
As discussed in the previous chapter, this image conveys the freedom of the
spirit, the sense of new beginnings, which the Pantisocracy project appeared
to offer; and Chatterton finds a place there, representing for them the voice
of the future making itself heard behind the mask of the past. It is as if poetic
inspiration might be liberated from its form, which is seen as a kind of outer
disguise.

It is something of a shock when we turn the page onto the second poem in
the volume, 'To the Rev. W.J.H. while teaching a young lady some song-
tunes on his flute' (a lyric that Coleridge never reprinted), and find ourselves
jolted in the poem's final section away from the music-room with its flautist
and singing maiden back to the Susquehanna and 'Freedom's UNDIVIDED
dale'. The phrase is repeated here, but in its new context the image has a very
different register; it becomes transformed into a space of allegorical
romance:

> In Freedom's UNDIVIDED dell,
> Where *Toil* and *Health* with mellow'd *Love* shall dwell,
>   Far from folly, far from men,
>   In the rude romantic glen,
>   Up the cliff, and thro' the glade,
>   Wand'ring with the dear-lov'd maid,
>   I shall listen to the lay,
>   And ponder on thee far away!

A commitment to Freedom turns into a gesture of pensive recollection;
dwelling becomes remote wandering. What might have been a scene of
physical intimacy dissolves into an aural memory. Immediate sounds escape
into the air and become a distant echo. The power of the music lies in its
ability to elude physical constraint.

The move towards the disembodied is continued in the third poem, 'Songs
of the Pixies', introduced as follows:

[H]alf way up a wood-cover'd hill, is an excavation called the Pixies' Parlour. The
roots of old trees form its ceiling; and on its sides are innumerable cyphers, among
which the Author discovered his own cypher and those of his brothers, cut by the
hand of their childhood. At the foot of the hill flows the river Otter.

To this place the Author conducted a party of young Ladies, during the Summer
months of the year 1793; one of whom, of stature elegantly small, and of complexion
colourless yet clear, was proclaimed the Fairy Queen: On which occasion the follow-
ing Irregular Ode was written.

We step back to the place of childhood innocence only to find a poem of
adolescent sexuality. 'Songs of the Pixies' has an ethereal erotic charge, an
imaginative electricity: 'Fancy's children, here we dwell: | Welcome, LADIES!

---

[20] For a fuller discussion of the 1796 ending to the 'Monody', see pp. 157–9 above.

to our cell' (3–4). The language dissolves the conceptual boundary between matter and spirit, creating an atmosphere in which anything may potentially embrace anything else. The songs evoke scents on the breeze, the play of colour across surfaces, an aural softness that is almost palpable. The 'pixies' caress the young poet in a teasing erotics that hovers at the edge of the tangible:

> Weaving gay dreams of sunny-tinctur'd hue
>   We glance before his view:
> O'er his hush'd soul our soothing witch'ries shed,
> And twine our faery garlands round his head.

With the unsettling word 'witch'ries' the pixies hint at the artful conjuring behind female charm; and the Spenserian enchantment that surrounds this miniaturised fairy queen is something to which the volume will repeatedly return. The songs that emanate from the pixies' parlour recall the world of Pope's sylphs in *The Rape of the Lock* with their 'fluid bodies half dissolv'd in light |... Dipt in the richest tincture of the skies'.[21] Coleridge's version nicely adds a hint of sound to the play of light:

> For mid the quiv'ring light 'tis our's to play,
> Aye-dancing to the cadence of the stream.

'Songs of the Pixies' performs a crucial role in the 1796 *Poems* as an echo chamber for the disembodied ideas that flit through the volume, and reverberations of its faery language will continue to be heard.[22]

'Songs of the Pixies' introduces a succession of poems, in each of which what begins as a sharply defined actuality tends to fade away into a dream. The first of these, 'Lines written at the King's Arms, Ross', opens with the robust gesture of raising a glass in the pub to the memory of the Man of Ross, who embodies the idea of 'VIRTUE'. But the sociable scene dissolves when the poet turns to himself:

> But if, like me, thro' life's distressful scene
> Lonely and sad thy pilgrimage hath been;
> And if, thy breast with heart-sick anguish fraught,
> Thou journeyest onward tempest-tost in thought;
> Here cheat thy cares! In generous visions melt,
> And dream of Goodness, thou hast never felt!   (9–14)

As soon as the poet enters, the realised virtue evanesces into a mere 'dream of Goodness'. In his self-presentation he is unable to embody the ideal, only fantasise about it.

---

[21] Alexander Pope, *The Rape of the Lock* (1714), ii.62–5. In praising 'Songs of the Pixies' in the *Monthly Review* John Aikin commented that 'Ariel, Oberon, and the Sylphs, have contributed to form [its] pleasing imagery' (*Coleridge: The Critical Heritage*, 37).

[22] For a discussion of the poem in relation to Effusion 35 and Coleridge's repeated revisiting of 'Faery' in his poetry, see Jeanie Watson, *Risking Enchantment: Coleridge's Symbolic World of Faery* (Lincoln/London: University of Nebraska Press, 1990), 72–8.

In a similar way, the following poem, 'Lines to a Beautiful Spring in a Village', establishes its location with a series of vivid details (the loitering lovers, the children launching 'paper navies' on the water), but once we turn the page the spring becomes an allegorical river, and a scene of human emotion disperses into one of poetic mood:

> Unboastful Stream! Thy fount with pebbled falls
> The faded form of past delight recalls,
> What time the morning sun of Hope arose,
> And all was joy; save when another's woes
> A transient gloom upon my soul imprest,
> Like passing clouds impictur'd on thy breast.

The poet's thoughts function literally as reflections, and the stream carries them along on its surface. The lines are Thel-like in the way they can only realise self-consciousness in the reflective membrane of simile ('like a parting cloud, | Like a reflection in a glass, like shadows in the water').[23]

The keynote of this opening sequence is what Coleridge calls his 'introverted eye', a turning of the subject round onto the self, rather than reaching out to grasp it. It is symptomatic of a volume in which embodiment is a critical issue that the idea of grasping, or failing to grasp, becomes significant. It is so at the climax of 'Lines on a Friend who died of a Frenzy Fever':

> With introverted eye I contemplate
> Similitude of soul, perhaps of—Fate!
> To me hath Heaven with bounteous hand assign'd
> Energic Reason and a shaping mind
> The daring ken of Truth, the Patriot's part,
> And Pity's sigh, that breathes the gentle heart—
> Sloth-jaundic'd all! And from my graspless hand
> Drop Friendship's precious pearls, like hour glass sand.
> I weep, yet stoop not! the faint anguish flows,
> A dreamy pang in Morning's fev'rish doze.   (37–46)

The movement is from something held and given definition, to a kind of liquefying and loss of identity—from the pearls slipping through the fingers to the sand pouring through an hourglass; 'the faint anguish flows', ending in a feverish, half-waking 'doze' and the final evaporation of something that

---

[23] William Blake, *Thel* (1789), Plate 1. Coleridge's phrase, 'the faded form of past delight', contrasts with his soon-to-be-completed sonnet 'To the River Otter' in which the scene, rather than fading through recollection, comes palpably to life in his imagination ('The crossing plank, and margin's willowy maze, | And bedded sand, that, vein'd with various dyes, | Gleam'd thro' the bright transparence to the gaze'). Here poetic reflection does not merely mirror the surface but breaks through to the river's bed. These lines on the 'Otter' were published in *The Watchman* on 2 April 1796 while the printing of *Poems* was still not complete. Coleridge did not include them in his book. Lines 2–11 of the 'Otter' sonnet formed part of a 28-line poem, 'Recollection'. See *The Watchman*, 167–8. The River Otter sonnet was first published in Coleridge's *Sonnets from Various Authors* (see pp. 198–9 below).

had begun as substantial. The formal implications of this process of dispersal are hinted at in the way Coleridge ironically (almost with a sense of tragedy) juxtaposes his 'shaping mind' and his 'graspless hand'. In doing so he suggests a gap between conception and execution: what is held and shaped within the mind can somehow not be effectually incorporated. This is a language of failure, but not a failure of language: the lines in which it is couched are some of the most powerful in the book.

A sense of slipping out from embodied form lies at the very heart of the 1796 *Poems* thanks to the concept of *effusion*. The central section of the book, and given its own half-title, comprises thirty-six numbered 'Effusions'. None of the poems were composed with that title in mind, and they were never to be grouped in this way again (the concept was dropped from the 1797 *Poems*), but early in 1796 the retrospectively applied term 'effusion' seemed to offer Coleridge a way of indicating how 'thought' in these poems might be treated more flexibly: 'I could recollect no title more descriptive of the manner and matter of the Poems,' he remarks in the Preface, '—I might indeed have called the majority of them Sonnets—but they do not possess that *oneness* of thought which I deem indispensible in a Sonnet'. The emphasis is therefore not on unity, but on more fluid, less contained elements. Coleridge points out that he chose the term 'in defiance of Churchill's line "Effusion on Effusion *pour* away"'.[24] More than two-thirds of the poems in his volume are thus linked to the notion (from the Latin verb *effundere-effusum*) of 'pouring out or forth'. The 'Effusion' is not a containing form.

For Coleridge, bringing himself to book is partly a judgmental process, and he continues to resist a narrative of growing strength and maturity in favour of one that accommodates checks, losses, and failures. The impression is given of a poet putting his poems together in a critical way, with an awareness of the mixed nature of his achievement and the uncertain direction of his career. But he also incorporates the work of his friends into the sequence in a way that makes their voices part of his own scheme (they appear to be adapted to that end). Questions of poetic maturity and embodied form remain linked as the sequence unfolds, and the ordering is such that the manliest, most confidently embodied voice is heard towards the beginning of the sequence, with the effect that once again the reader will become uncertain of the direction in which this young poet is moving.

What is immediately striking is the self-conscious maturity of the retrospective voice that greets us in 'Effusion 1', the sonnet to Bowles, which originally appeared in the *Morning Chronicle* as the seventh of the 'Sonnets on Eminent Characters'. It is made to open the Effusions section on a note of

---

[24] Charles Churchill uses the term satirically: 'Why may not LANGHORNE, simple in his lay, | *Effusion* on *Effusion* pour away, | With *Friendship*, and with *Fancy* trifle here' (*The Candidate* [1764], 41–4). Langhorne published *The Effusions of Friendship and Fancy*, in 1763.

personal gratitude, literally heart-felt, to a writer who has helped him through a difficult poetic adolescence.[25] He recalls the 'thornless paths' of his youth, and 'the *darker* day of life' that followed when he became directionless and 'thought-bewilder'd'. The implication is that Bowles's poetry has helped him grow up and find a direction. Its 'manliest melancholy' provided a bridge from the dreamy personal sorrows of his earlier years to an awakened sense of creative possibility. The pivotal idea is 'Pleasure', which here opens out into something enigmatic and creatively disturbing; it suggests a new world waiting to be given shape:

> Bidding a strange mysterious PLEASURE brood
> Over the wavy and tumultuous mind,
> As the great SPIRIT erst with plastic sweep
> Mov'd on the darkness of the unform'd deep.   (11–14)

The contained energy of this ending strikes a note not heard before in the volume. The Genesis-like brooding portends a realisation of how a disturbed mind ('wavy and tumultuous') could find its chaos moulded into form.

Coleridge now embarks on a succession of poems written in a tone of manly confidence. His addresses to some of the great public figures of the day will not find fading and faintness effective. On the contrary, in the nine further 'Sonnets on Eminent Characters' (though they are not called such here) Coleridge explores, with mixed success, how *eminence* represents an embodying of powers and principles in human form. These poems struggle in their different ways to project an Idea and make it real, or at least *realisable*. For good and ill these people stand forth as actors on a public stage; they articulate the crisis of the time, and help to shape it. Coleridge does not address them so much as effect their presence. The poems, sonnet-odes almost, take on an allegorical character as ideas are given emblematic form in the manner of Collins's *Odes on Several Descriptive and Allegoric Subjects* (1747). In Coleridge the effect can be baroque, as human figures share the canvas with embodied virtues and vices, in a School of Rubens manner. Both human and allegorical are at the same level of reality. The result is occasionally vague and abstract ('Thee stormy Pity and the cherish'd lure | Of Pomp, and proud Precipitance of soul | Wilder'd with meteor fires'),[26] but more often it is uncomfortably clear. Sheridan is a sword-wielding St Michael confronting Satan; Erskine is a priest at Freedom's altar swinging a glowing censer; Pitt is Judas caught in the act of betraying his country with a kiss; Priestley is a radiant figure 'calm in his halls of Brightness', who conjures Religion and Justice to do his bidding. We see Britannia crucified, Religion stripping off her richly decorated garments, a

---

[25] In *Biog. Lit.* Coleridge similarly speaks of Bowles as helping him mature, and he records his gratitude for 'the genial influence of a style of poetry so tender and yet so manly, so natural and real'. Southey recognised Bowles's role in his own poetic coming-of-age (see pp. 131–2 above).

[26] 'Effusion 2' (Burke), 10–12.

smiling Nature lifting her veil, French Liberty leaping 'from the Almighty's bosom... | With whirlwind arm', and Mercy seizing a flaming torch from the hands of a sleeping Justice. In these texts libertarian emotions are distilled to a quintessence in the manner of an old alchemist:

> As if from eldest time some Spirit meek
> Had gather'd in a mystic urn each tear
> That ever furrow'd a sad Patriot's cheek[27]

What an elixir that would be—the essence of patriot liberty! It is as if Coleridge were reaching for a Blakean image of the nation as a renewed youthful body, an active spirit walking abroad.

At significant moments the emphasis shifts to the vocal (many of these figures were famous speakers), and some of the most daring effects occur when Coleridge projects the human voice physically and shows it exerting a liberating force in the world. When Erskine the great advocate begins to speak, British Freedom, which is ready to fly away, flutters her wings as she pauses to hear him. Effusion 10 (Stanhope) mounts to its climax with the voice of Freedom ringing out to the skies and forming a link from Heaven to Earth:

> Angels shall lead thee to the Throne above:
> And thou from forth it's clouds shalt hear the voice,
> Champion of FREEDOM and her God! rejoice!   (12–14)

It is a climactic exclamation, Heaven's voice at full volume. We shall not hear anything like it again until the final poem in the book.

The contrast with the very next lines on the facing page, which form the opening of Effusion 11, could hardly be greater. It is as if Coleridge wished the previous high-decibel imperative to dissolve into the air:

> Was it some sweet device of faery land
> That mock'd my steps with many a lonely glade,
> And fancied wand'rings with a fair-hair'd maid?
> Have these things been?

In a sequential reading of the 1796 *Poems* this has a strong impact. The tentative question hangs in the air, as if a child is pondering the story of the False Florimell in *The Faerie Queene*. The effect is of a sudden troubled return to the Pixies' Parlour. Effusion 11 is of course a re-working of a Charles Lamb sonnet, as the 'C.L.' at its foot indicates, into which Coleridge (much to Lamb's chagrin[28]) has introduced an element of Spenserian deception: the word 'device' is his (Lamb had written 'Delight') and so is the reference in the following lines to 'the wizard wand | Of Merlin'. The three sonnets by Lamb (Effusions 11–13), placed immediately after Coleridge's

---

[27] 'Effusion 8' (Koskiusko), 10–12.
[28] See Lamb to Coleridge, 8–10 June 1796 (Marrs, 20–1). See also pp. 213–16 below.

confident public declarations, move the reader back into a world of romantic
illusion where ghostly presences dissolve and the poet's steps are hesitant
and directionless ('Ah me! the lonely glade | Still courts the footsteps of the
fair-hair'd maid, | Among whose locks the west-winds love to sigh').[29] This
seems to reach backwards, raising the troubling question whether the con-
fident public poems of a few pages earlier are similarly mere sounds in the
air. Lamb was particularly annoyed by the lines his friend introduced as the
sestet of Effusion 12, which successively indulge then dismiss the romantic
dream:

> But ah! sweet scenes of fancied bliss, adieu!
> On rose-leaf beds amid your faery bowers
> I all too long have lost the dreamy hours!
> Beseems it now the sterner Muse to woo,
> If haply she her golden meed impart
> To realize the vision of the heart.   (9–14)

(*Beseems, haply, meed*—even at the moment of waking the language of old
romance lingers on and the image slips into soft focus.) Coleridge's lines turn
on a contrast between dissipation and realisation, the evanescent and the
embodied. Whatever his purposes here, the result is to express the shifting
dynamics of the volume as a whole. The first ten effusions were a bold
attempt to 'realize the vision of the heart', and there is a conscious awareness
here of a desire to recapture that impulse. But there is no easy progress from
one to the other, and as the effusions continue Coleridge seems conscious of
his own unstable, occasionally coquettish, relationship with the 'sterner
Muse'.

On reaching Effusions 17–18 there is no doubt that we have travelled a
long way from the confident poetry of the opening group and have regressed
to what seems like genuine juvenilia. The octosyllabic sonnet 'Maid of my
Love! sweet GENEVIEVE!' and 'To the Autumnal Moon' were written, Cole-
ridge later maintained, at the ages of fourteen and sixteen, respectively.[30]
Both of them hover between innocent boyhood and a sexualised adoles-
cence, with the former recalling Coleridge's feelings for Jenny Edwards, the
daughter of his nurse at Christ's Hospital. This markedly retrospective
interlude continues with another earlier love of his, Mary Evans, being
recalled in Effusion 19 ('Thou bleedest, my poor HEART!'), but here the
innocent scene has turned into one of painful experience. We move from
Effusion 18, which ends with a vision of Hope 'emerging in her radiant
might' out of the clouds of despair and into a clear sky, to a poem in which

---

[29] 'Effusion 11', 10–12.
[30] In the 1828 *Poems* these two pieces were printed first and second in the 'Juvenile Poems'
section, where Coleridge dated them to the ages of 14 and 16, respectively. But Mays (ii.20, 111)
would place them later. 'Maid of my Love!' carries a note recording that 'This little Poem was
written when the Author was a boy.'

Hope is deceptive, both verbally and visually; and in this ordering one text becomes a comment on the other. In Effusion 19 we distinctly hear the voice of someone who has woken up from his optimistic youth and is now questioning himself sternly: 'Reas'ning I ponder with a scornful smile | ... | Why didst thou listen to Hope's whisper bland?' In a scene of adolescent *angst* the poet acknowledges that he had put his trust in an idea that was pleasing but finally illusory:

> Faint was that HOPE, and rayless!—Yet 'twas fair
> And sooth'd with many a dream the hour of rest.

In a self-dramatising move, he pictures himself as a young man caught between the dreams of Hope and the nightmares of Jealousy, whose 'fev'rish fancies... | Jarr'd thy fine fibres with a maniac's hand'. He looks back at what might have been; but the poem's final image of a 'sweet infant... | That wan and sickly droops' on his mother's breast leaves us conscious of little more than the infantilising implications of the scene. In this text images of infancy and adolescence are given a mature reassessment, but only to reach an emotional impasse. Both poems touch on the relationship between Hope and Care, but in Effusion 19 'Care' has moved from the passive idea of *care-worn* to the active idea of car*ing*. At the end of the first poem 'Hope' offers to comfort 'Care', but in the second, 'Care' must tend to 'Hope'.[31]

Following this, Effusion 20, addressed to Schiller, comes as a terrific release into the world of the theatrical imagination. We seem to have jumped from the static *psychomachia* of an old morality play into a *Sturm und Drang* drama, in which fear and horror can be relished through the dynamics of genius ('Ah Bard tremendous in sublimity!'). Coleridge's note describes his delighted reading of Schiller's *The Robbers* one turbulent winter night during his Cambridge days, and this cameo of the impressionable student adds another detail to the unsettled picture the reader is getting of a troubled and wildly various talent. The placing of the sonnet heightens the destabilising effect, and it ends with the poet picturing himself as potentially possessed by Schiller's spirit: 'Awhile with mute awe gazing I would brood: | Then weep aloud in a wild extacy!' The voice breaks off with this phrase hanging in the air. The constraint of the sonnet form imposes itself at the moment of greatest effusiveness; the potential of what Coleridge *would* do is left to reverberate in the silence.

To this point the effusions, with the exception of the octosyllabic seventeenth, have all been regular sonnets under another name, and we have seen in the twentieth (to Schiller) how the containment of the form concentrates the emotional pressure. Now Coleridge finally loosens the sonnet's hold. The move out of the sonnet structure is inaugurated in Effusion 21, 'Composed

---

[31] I owe this point to Jeffrey Hipolito, who suggests that there is here 'an interesting foreshadowing of the paradox that drives the "Dejection" ode'.

while climbing the left ascent of Brockley Coomb, in the County of Somerset, May, 1795', first printed here. The poem is shaped like a sonnet, abab cdcd, efef gg, but then carries an extra couplet, bb, as if the bounds of the form were being consciously exceeded at the moment when the poet's 'introverted eye' comes into play.[32] The last six lines offer a visual 'prospect', only for it to be taken away when the thought turns inward:

> I rest.—And now have gain'd the topmost site.
> Ah! what a luxury of landscape meets
> My gaze! Proud Towers, and Cots more dear to me,
> Elm-shadow'd Fields, and prospect-bounding Sea!
> Deep sighs my lonely heart: I drop the tear:
> Enchanting spot! O were my SARA here!   (11–16)

Here we see an effusion defining itself at a moment of pouring out when the sonnet form is over-run. From the viewpoint of Brockley Combe, the dynamics of Effusion 20 (to Schiller) look like uncomplicated youthful surges of the imagination. Effusion 21 suggests that human energies sometimes involve more careful negotiation. Before the view is gained, the ascent of the combe is not an easy one, and the details of the scene create a sense of uneven movement and varied texture: there is the smooth and level alongside the rough, projecting, and precipitous; there are both blendings and juttings, browsings and burstings, inviting seats and 'forc'd fissures'. The whole effect is of a mixed, discomposed scene, but one in which the processes of organic life are going on:

> Up scour the startling stragglers of the Flock
> That on green plots o'er precipices brouze:
> From the forc'd fissures of the naked rock
> The Yew tree bursts! Beneath it's dark green boughs
> (Mid which the May-thorn blends it's blossoms white)
> Where broad smooth stones jut out in mossy seats,
> I rest...   (5–11)

The structural discipline of the sonnet seems to have relaxed, and around the rhymes the movement of the verse is beginning to shape itself to the sinuous turns and emphases we would find in blank verse.

The move is completed when we turn the page onto Effusion 22 ('To a Friend together with an Unfinished Poem') and encounter the first blank verse in the 1796 volume:

> Thus far my scanty brain hath built the rhyme
> Elaborate and swelling: yet the heart
> Not owns it.

---

[32] See p. 168 above. The sixteen-line poem was categorised as a sonnet in 1797 *Poems*. Graham Davidson describes the final couplet as 'a kind of counterpoint...we can find nothing in the lines that looks forward to that state of mind' (*Coleridge's Career* (Houndmills: Macmillan, 1990), 21).

It reads like a critical auditing of himself. Given their position in the book these opening words appear to signal that 'rhyme' is now being left behind. The context, however, is deceptive. The ambitious unfinished poem ('rhyme') to which Coleridge refers is an early version of 'Religious Musings', sent to Charles Lamb with this epistle in December 1794. In the 1796 volume Coleridge offers no explanatory note, and early readers could not be expected to guess that the poem would, in its completed form, conclude the collection. As it stands, the opening sentence of Effusion 22 suggests a critique on what has gone before, and hints at a more comprehensive self-doubt ('the heart | Not owns it'). The poem is in effect a familiar verse letter, a genre that often exploits generosity, empathy, and personal rapport, and the text makes repeated gestures in that direction; but the sustained tone of manly reasoning distances it from the adolescent sensibility of Effusions 17–21. Rather oddly, this poem is about withholding as well as giving: its outgoing gestures of sympathy are checked by more deliberated considerations.

As soon as the two men's friendship is announced a dissonant note begins to emerge: 'I ask not now, my friend! the aiding verse, | Tedious to thee, and from thy anxious thought | Of dissonant mood'. This jarring element is noticeable when the picture of Lamb's caring for his sick sister (in 'tenderest tones medicinal of love') appears at first to be sympathetically echoed by Coleridge's memories of his own dead sister; but his recollection is given an unsettling edge of self-satire: 'To her I pour'd forth all my puny sorrows, | (As a sick Patient in his Nurse's arms)'. He turns the image against his earlier self. The next line hints that there are things even an intimate epistle cannot share: 'of the heart those hidden maladies | That shrink asham'd from even Friendship's eye'. He expresses hope for Mary Lamb's recovery, but then effectively withdraws it with a comment that God alone will decide, since no human prayer, poetic or otherwise, can have any effect on

> The SPIRIT that in secret sees,
> Of whose omniscient and all-spreading Love
> Aught to *implore* were impotence of mind   (26–8)

The implication is that Lamb's own prayers for his sister might be similarly impotent. It is a stoical sentiment, and one that Coleridge publicly recanted when he republished the poem.[33] Here, however, it works soberly to modify both hope and fear.

This check on the excesses of Sensibility continues in Effusion 23 ('To the Nightingale'), a poem that glances back ironically to the sentimental lyricism of the poet's youthful voice heard most recently in Effusions 17–18. It mocks the tribe of sonneteers who celebrate the moon and the nightingale while they are actually gazing down from their garret at the street-lamp's

[33] In 1797 *Poems* Coleridge added a note: 'I utterly recant the sentiment contained in the Lines... it being written in Scripture, "*Ask*, and it shall be given you"' (67).

reflection in a gutter, or listening to the cry of the night watchman. But this satiric opening clears away the hackneyed images so as to register his own authenticity. He asserts that even the nightingale's 'soft diversities of tone' are not so sweet as the word 'HUSBAND' uttered from the lips of his future wife. Coleridge's concluding reference to his marriage marks a significant stage in his self-presentation in the volume. The poem's odd turns and its touches of parodic humour at the expense of Sensibility ('the delicious airs | That vibrate from a white-arm'd Lady's harp') suggest that a more knowing and sophisticated voice is emerging.

But with the sequence of Effusions 26–31 we unashamedly re-enter the realm of the adolescent erotic imagination, of Cupid's arrows, of lilies and roses, stolen kisses, and various 'shadowy forms of Delight'.[34] To the reader it seems as if we have opened an album of playful love poems. Earlier intimations of poetic maturity and marital stability are delightfully forgotten in this insubstantial world of shifting air and ghosts from the past. A presiding spirit here is Fanny Nesbitt, Coleridge's *inamorata* during the summer of 1793. Wisely, his wife's name, 'Sara', is given in the first two poems, although in manuscript both texts had served to immortalise a variety of girls. In the last line of Effusion 26 'Nesbitt's lovelier lips' became Mary's, then Sara's, though none of them may have been the original inspirer; and 'spotless SARA's breast' in Effusion 27 had been Angelina's, lovely Nesbitt's, and spotless Anna's.[35] In these poems Coleridge shows mastery of the flirtatious tactics he learned from the pixies ('the magic dews, which Evening brings, | Brush'd from the Idalian star by faery wings');[36] and by a kind of metempsychosis a succession of women's bodies act as temporary lodgings for Coleridge's erotic idea. (The final phrase of Effusion 27, 'I'll fix *my* empire here', is less occupying a freehold than deciding on a suitable bed and breakfast.)

Effusions 29–30, two brief lyrics imitated from James Macpherson, are here well placed to reverberate in this excited atmosphere and draw meaning from it. The evanescent Ossian-voice, carried by wind and sea, is a suitable vehicle for a poetry that once again recalls Blake's Thel.[37] Coleridge takes the idea of the weeping lily sighing to the breeze 'in LUMIN's *flowery* vale' and makes it an image of seduction, only with himself as the wind:

---

[34] 'Effusion 30', 14.

[35] Mays, ii.90. He notes of 'Effusion 26': '[Coleridge] was encouraged to make such verses by appreciative local belles like Fanny Nesbitt, Elizabeth Boutflower, and Ann Bacon. The first and third of the mss have the name Nesbitt in the last line, and the second names Miss Boutflower. In subsequent years Coleridge named Mary (Evans) and, in all printed versions, Sara' (i.94).

[36] 'Effusion 26', 5–6.

[37] 'The flower hangs its heavy head, waving, at times, to the gale … The time of my fading is near, and the blast that shall scatter my leaves' (James Macpherson, *The Poems of Ossian and related works*, ed. Howard Gaskill with an introduction by Fiona Stafford (Edinburgh: Edinburgh University Press, 1996), 193). Quoting the passage in his note, Coleridge omits the word 'heavy' (1796 *Poems*, 182).

> But I along the breeze shall roll
>   The voice of feeble power;
> And dwell, the Moon-beam of thy soul,
>   In Slumber's nightly hour.

It is a strange poem that can invoke the idea of 'feeble power' at its climax, but that is what we get. At this point in the 1796 *Poems* Coleridge is conscious of grouping together verses that seem to distil themselves into voice alone, a mere seductive movement of air. The eight-line lyric of Effusion 31 ('Imitated from the Welch') begins by offering physical touch but then suddenly rejects it with a hint of how arousing it would be: 'Ah no!... | That thrilling touch would aid the flame, | It wishes to discover'.

It is at this feverish point that Coleridge places 'The Sigh' as Effusion 32. Here the poem works as a retrospect, bringing to a neat conclusion the series of amorous album verses that have played coyly with the language of seduction. Through the first three of its four stanzas 'The Sigh' charts the sighings, respectively, of childhood, anguished adolescence, and mature reflection. The idea once again recalls a metempsychosis, or progress of the soul, with the breath (*anima*) expressing itself differently as it works through successive bodies. Coleridge is conscious, almost to the point of parody, of poetry's power to transfuse ideas, and arouse unconstraining thoughts. A part of him wanted to achieve a sense of weightlessness, and he considered 'The Sigh' his most successful poem in this line. He wrote to Southey:

> I cannot write without a *body* of *thought*—hence my *Poetry* is crowded and sweats beneath a heavy burthen of Ideas and Imagery! It has seldom Ease—The little Song ending with 'I heav'd the—sigh for thee'! is an exception—and accordingly I like it the best of all, I ever wrote.[38]

The problem Coleridge identifies here has a bearing on the larger question of poetic embodiment, and the timing of his frustrated comment is intriguing. This letter of 11 December 1794 suggests that at the very moment he was writing his 'Sonnets on Eminent Characters' (the series began appearing in *The Morning Chronicle* on 1 December, and the third sonnet, on Priestley, appeared on the 11th) he was looking back on 'The Sigh' as representing a lyric ease he was somehow failing to achieve elsewhere. One implication is that Coleridge felt he was lugging around a '*body* of *thought*' that seemed to be weighing the poems down, and that part of him wanted to give his work a more disembodied quality. An alternative emphasis might imply that he was looking for a way to incorporate thought naturally rather than making it seem an added weight on the verse.

In this context, his remark about sweating under a 'heavy burthen' gives the next poem a satiric edge. Coleridge follows 'The Sigh' disconcertingly with 'To a Young Ass' (Effusion 33). The ordering is deliberate: in the Rugby

---

[38] Coleridge to Southey, 11 Dec. 1794 (Griggs, 137).

Manuscript the text begins on the verso of the same leaf as 'The Sigh'.[39] In
'To a Young Ass' he turns in sympathy to a beast of burden, and he does so
by stressing the animal's awkward tactile reality. On the facing page 'The
Sigh' reaches its end with an image that is left unrealised for the reader: 'Thy
Image may not banish'd be—| Still, MARY! still I SIGH for thee'. This lyrical
weightlessness is also empty. It is with a calculated boldness that Coleridge's
very next words insist on both his and the ass's physical presence in the poem
that follows:

> Poor little Foal of an oppressed Race!
> I love the languid Patience of thy face:
> And oft with gentle hand I give thee bread,
> And clap thy ragged Coat, and pat thy head.

The beast is there, looking at him, and his coat feels rough to the touch.
Coleridge humanizes the creature, but also defiantly makes an ass of himself:
'I hail thee BROTHER', he declares, 'spite of the fool's scorn!'[40] Now for the
third time in the volume the poet's thoughts run to the Susquehanna: 'fain
would [I] take thee with me, in the Dell | Of Peace and mild Equality to
dwell'. This time the young ass would be there to dance for them, but also to
provide their music with its 'dissonant harsh Bray of Joy'. The line stops us
in our tracks with its daring sense of delight. The harsh phrase finds its own
unexpected harmony when 'Bray' is given 'Joy'. This extraordinary poem
announces its dissonance from what has gone before, and its position in the
sequence increases the harshness of the effect. Coleridge uses the tactics of
burlesque. The sound of the braying ass is an authentic one, and it offers a
challenge to the kind of poetry that would refine away physical impurities.

    With the placing of 'To a Young Ass' Coleridge appears to be forcing
towards a crisis the competing claims of body and spirit, and Effusion 34 has
a similar effect. 'To an Infant' is about *grasping* things (its key verbs are
'grasp', 'cling', and 'snatch'), but also about the difficulty of grasping what is
not physical. The ambiguity is an eloquent one at this point in the volume.
The poem begins with a knife being *snatched* from a baby's hand and ends
with the speaker reaching out to grasp at 'FAITH'. The infant's opening
gesture prefigures the 'eager grasp' of 'young desire'. He is a 'breathing
Miniature' of the poet himself, a moody youth who can '[b]reak Friendship's
Mirror with a tetchy blow, | Yet *snatch* what coals of fire on Pleasure's altar
glow!' (my italics). The poet straddles the embarrassments of infancy and
adolescence, and the tactile tension is sustained to the end with the picture of
him clinging to Faith like a small child holding onto its nurse:

---

[39] Rugby MS, fol. 24 (Mays, ii.148, 190).

[40] The scorn was indeed forthcoming. In Gillray's satiric cartoon 'New Morality' (*Anti-
Jacobin Review and Magazine*, 1 Aug. 1798) Coleridge is given an ass's ears. The politics of
the print and George Canning's poem of that name (which it illustrates) and their links to the
Pantisocracy project are explored by David Perkins, 'Compassion for Animals and Radical
Politics: Coleridge's "To a Young Ass"', *ELH*, 65 (1998), 929–44.

> Thrice holy FAITH! whatever thorns I meet
> As on I totter with unpractis'd feet,
> Still let me stretch my arms and cling to thee,
> Meek Nurse of Souls thro' their long Infancy!

The poem ends with that telling word, which appears to sum up human life as something inescapably premature, an extended infancy. The soul seems not to develop but remain attached to the nurse. The passage raises questions about how religious faith sits with ideas of maturity and progress. Is 'Faith' something that must remain innocent and naïvely trusting? Or is clinging to it as if it were something tangible an infantilising idea? In what sense can you grasp and hold onto Faith? Issues of embodiment and maturity are closely linked here in a text conscious of its hesitant steps.[41]

What suddenly greets us as we turn the page is something we have not yet encountered in the volume: a scene of mature, physical human intimacy:

> My pensive SARA! thy soft cheek reclin'd
> Thus on mine arm, most soothing sweet it is
> To sit beside our cot...

Effusion 35 ('Composed August 20th, 1795, at Clevedon, Somersetshire') opens with a picture of domestic peace. It is an image of physical relaxation, an idea sustained through a scene in which nothing is clutched or grasped, or clung to. There is no hand striking the Aeolian harp. In this context, the impetuous word 'snatch'd' is emptied of will and effort: 'How exquisite the scents | Snatch'd from yon bean-field!' There is no childish need for gratification, no adolescent restlessness. The text's mature consciousness celebrates not evanescence, but the wonderfully momentary. The distinction is minute but crucial: we are reminded of what is out there alive in the world, what might be given us at any moment. The lute placed in the cottage window responds to the ebb and flow of air, acting as a sensorium that is able to register the intangible, so that its music bridges idea and sense. The poem can thus organise elements that have to this point in the volume been held in tension with each other:

> The stilly murmur of the distant Sea
> Tells us of Silence. And that simplest Lute
> Plac'd length-ways in the clasping casement, hark!
> How by the desultory breeze caress'd,
> Like some coy Maid half-yielding to her Lover,
> It pours such sweet upbraidings, as must needs
> Tempt to repeat the wrong! And now its strings
> Boldlier swept, the long sequacious notes

---

[41] Kelvin Everest convincingly links this poem to Hartley's description of how a young child learns through 'these mechanical Tendencies, inspired by God' (*Observations on Man* (1749), i.369–70). See Kelvin Everest, *Coleridge's Secret Ministry: The Context of the Conversation Poems 1795–1798* (Hassocks: Harvester Press; New York: Barnes and Noble, 1979), 78–9.

> Over delicious surges sink and rise,
> Such a soft floating witchery of sound
> As twilight Elfins make, when they at eve
> Voyage on gentle gales from Faery Land

It is as if the poetry of the Pixies' Parlour has found an expressive medium
through the music. We meet again here the 'witchery' of Spenserian enchant-
ment, the coy seductiveness of the album verses, but also hints of the bolder
sweep of an ode. But the effects become increasingly elusive until the
paragraph reaches its end in an image of hovering birds of paradise.

   The second paragraph introduces the poet stretched out on the hillside, a
human version of the Aeolian harp, mimicking its effects in his own mind. He
is aware of the tricks of perception ('thro' my half-clos'd eyelids I behold |
The sunbeams dance, like diamonds, on the main') and how he conforms to
the stereotype of passive indolence. His mind is also in a state of surrender to
any idea that might play over it, and the passage becomes a self-conscious
indulgence in Coleridge's disembodied mode:

> Full many a thought uncall'd and undetain'd,
> And many idle flitting phantasies,
> Traverse my indolent and passive brain
> As wild and various, as the random gales
> That swell or flutter on this subject Lute!

However, the poem's indolence and passivity are not lazy, but alert. The blank
verse moves with an ease that is strong and supple, and allows every nuance to
register. The poem's tone is set by the varying dynamics of the Aeolian harp,
but with a quiet pulse lent by the underlying human presence. Hints of erotic
arousal ('swell or flutter') have become subsumed into a universal ebb and
flow: the repeated pairings have the effect of relaxed alternation ('uncall'd and
undetain'd'), quiet as a heartbeat.[42] This is no out-of-body experience, but one
in which the human organism is part of a wider experiential reality, not just a
subjective contraction but an expansion into something larger. At this moment
there comes a sudden surge of thought as this is realised:

> And what if all of animated nature
> Be but organic Harps diversely fram'd,
> That tremble into thought, as o'er them sweeps,
> Plastic and vast, one intellectual Breeze,
> At once the Soul of each, and God of all?

This famous question is introduced by the word 'And': it grows out of what
has gone before. There is no declaratory 'O', or hesitant 'But', or explana-
tory 'For'. With the adjacent words 'sweeps, | Plastic' the idea of a creative
shaping finally returns from Effusion 1 ('As the great SPIRIT erst with plastic

---

[42] On the structural potential of this, see Albert Gérard, 'The Systolic Rhythm: The Structure
of Coleridge's Conversation Poems', *EC*, 10 (1960), 307–19.

sweep | Mov'd on the darkness of the unform'd deep'). Thoughts are conceptually embodied, and the phrase 'tremble into thought' combines the flutter of the breeze with a human sense of awe as God is approached. In the last line the phrase 'At once' combines the immediate and the simultaneous; and the repeated 'of' makes an intellectual point with the ambiguous apposition of individual and universal, in which expressing and containing appear to become the same thing. This is not a 'God o'er all'. The result of these intricacies of suggestion is to make the question of embodiment seem almost irrelevant.

It does not remain so for long, and the paragraph ends with a return to the body beside him, and the eye looking at him. The effect, introduced by an admonitory 'But', is more disconcerting than reassuring:

> But thy more serious eye a mild reproof
> Darts, O beloved Woman! nor such thoughts
> Dim and unhallow'd dost thou not reject,
> And biddest me walk humbly with my God.

To be walking, head bowed, alongside a Being who a moment ago had been so thrillingly interfused with your identity seems like an estrangement. The unspoken implication is that faith has become duty. The reproof of the woman's 'serious eye', however mild, creates a sense of difference, and 'thoughts' become detached from experience. The double negative makes an uneasy negotiation of the whole business. The poem proceeds to realign the mind in a separate dimension, and the disembodied now returns as evanescence: 'shapings' turn into glittering bubbles playing over the surface, mere tricks of the light, and they are seen as immaterial, in all senses of that word:

> Meek Daughter in the Family of Christ,
> Well hast thou said and holily disprais'd
> These shapings of the unregenerate mind,
> Bubbles that glitter as they rise and break
> On vain Philosophy's aye-babbling spring.

'Bubbling', which might have suggested an inexhaustible resource, is rejected in favour of 'babbling'—meaningless chatter. There is no *trembling into thought* here; instead God is announced as something awesomely out there, spoken about, capitalised, while 'Faith' remains feelingly within. Somehow the two can no longer share a space or a language:

> For never guiltless may I speak of Him,
> Th'INCOMPREHENSIBLE! save when with awe
> I praise him, and with Faith that inly *feels;*
> Who with his saving mercies healed me,
> A sinful and most miserable man
> Wilder'd and dark, and gave me to possess
> PEACE, and this COT, and THEE, heart-honor'd Maid!

The poem closes where it began, with domestic peace, and there is reassurance in this, but also a note of retrenchment, a closing down in an act of possession. Coleridge takes refuge in his own. In this ending, embodiment serves as a reassuring repose after the poetic and philosophical risks the poem has taken; its language becomes appropriately settled, but also comparatively inert.

How to follow this poem? In his later 1797 collection it is immediately succeeded by 'Reflections on Having Left a Place of Retirement', a poem that relates to Coleridge's move in November 1795 from the honeymoon cottage at Clevedon to the world of political activity in Bristol. That text would have made a suitable continuation here. In moving from 'Low was our pretty Cot' (1) to 'O FATHER! Let thy Kingdom come!' (72) the 'Reflections' would have been a strong link from the world of the Aeolian harp to that of 'Religious Musings'. Mays suggests that the poem possibly 'was not ready' or that it may have been composed retrospectively in March 1796.[43] Another explanation, which avoids turning the poem into a retrospect (it doesn't read like one), is that the confident trajectory of 'Reflections' was alien to the 1796 volume. It shows a determined adult moving on from what has gone before, and dismissing the 'vision-weaving Tribe... | Nursing in some delicious solitude | Their slothful loves and dainty Sympathies!'

That was not the note on which Coleridge wanted to end his 'Effusions'. Instead we are given, as Effusion 36, 'Written in Early Youth, the Time, An Autumnal Evening'. It is another poem from the summer of 1793 addressed originally to Fanny Nesbitt (with the title, 'Absence: A Poem'), which had appeared in a Dorset newspaper in October of that year. Its placing in the 1796 volume is deliberate: the copy text carries Coleridge's written instruction: 'to be printed the last of the Effusions next to "My pensive Sara."'[44] Coleridge's decision not only to conclude with this poem, but to re-title it 'Written in Early Youth', which it wasn't, looks like a tactical regression, a return to pre-maturity. Mays remarks that 'the poem often gives the impression of echoing Coleridge's own early manner, even in places where it does not'.[45] What is more, as a purportedly juvenile poem it seeks the patronage of two elusive figures who refuse to be confined to a single shape: Fancy ('lovely Sorceress!') and Proteus ('O... were mine the wizard's rod, | Or mine the power of Proteus, changeful God!'). With this unsteady pair presiding, we return to a world of enchanters' spells, moonbeams, and floating whispers ('far-off music, voyaging the breeze!'). In the guise of Proteus, Coleridge takes to an extreme the 'faery' atmosphere of the Pixies'

---

[43] Mays, i.260.

[44] Rugby MS, fol. 31ʳ. The manuscript has the concluding note: 'End of the Effusions'. The poem was first printed in *The Weekly Entertainer* (Sherborne), 28 Oct. 1793. See Mays, ii.101, where it is given its original title, 'Absence: A Poem'.

[45] Mays, i.99.

Parlour, with the poet here picturing himself as Pope's Ariel concealed in the nosegay on Belinda's breast:[46]

> To fan my Love I'd be the EVENING GALE;
> Mourn in the soft folds of her swelling vest,
> And flutter my faint pinions on her breast!
> On Seraph wing I'd float a DREAM, by night,
> To soothe my Love with shadows of delight

It is an exercise in disembodiment. The situation is made even more Protean when we turn to Coleridge's note on this passage, in which there is an extraordinary critical retraction: 'I entreat the Public's pardon', it reads, 'for having carelessly suffered to be printed such intolerable stuff as this'.[47] The annotator gives the impression of being in uncomfortable conversation with the poet, alternately constructing and admonishing his juvenile self.

Coleridge's embarrassed apology has the effect of marking out the passage as a moment of crisis in the volume. His words signal a contemptuous rejection of the eroticised imagination, the alluringly feminine 'wild FANCY' who has to this point been the poem's addressee; and, as if in acknowledgment, the poem itself suddenly shifts viewpoint. The move from the fanciful world of the Pixies' Parlour is marked by a conscious *reversion* of the poet's gaze ('Mine eye reverted views that cloudless day, | When by my native brook I wont to rove'). It is a pivotal gesture, virtually a turning of the head, toward the other local landmark of his Ottery childhood: he looks from the Pixies' Parlour down on the scene a hundred yards away beyond the foot of the hill, where the River Otter flows. From this point Coleridge's retrospect, centred on his 'native brook' (the phrase occurs three times here), opens up an area of spatial memory such as Wordsworth will trace through his Wye Valley 'Lines' of 1798, in the process drawing himself into sympathetic dialogue with Coleridge, Southey, and others.[48]

For Coleridge the Otter represents the site of his earliest poetic ambitions, where 'first young POESY | Star'd wildly-eager'. This phrase recalls the figure of Chatterton as 'young-eyed POESY' at the close of the Monody;[49] but here the scene, rather than opening up the poetic future, is a retrospective one in which possible continuities are closed down. The intermittent glimpses the poem gives us of Coleridge's youthful 'haunts' are elusive, and they lose their features when the scene becomes dark. The poem's final paragraph allows the 'Effusions' section to end on a leave-taking. It suggests a turning aside from the inspirations of youth towards an uncertain and potentially gloomy future. Bringing to a close a poem that is an odd mixture of youthful fantasy and maturer retrospect, the closing lines formally leave Hope behind to fade into night:

---

[46] Cf. Pope, *The Rape of the Lock*, iii.141.   [47] *1796 Poems*, 183.
[48] See Chapter 4 above.   [49] See pp. 158–9 above.

> Scenes of my Hope! the aking eye ye leave
> Like yon bright hues that paint the clouds of eve!
> Tearful and sad'ning with the sadden'd blaze
> Mine eye the gleam pursues with wistful gaze:
> Sees shades on shades with deeper tint impend,
> Till chill and damp the moonless night descend.

The section ends with a spectacular sunset before the last gleam disappears and leaves the poet darkling. The effect is well calculated. It was this promising young man whom the reviewer of the volume wanted his readers to support, so as to help 'disperse the clouds which have darkened [his] prospects'. At this point in the volume the poet does not wish to stride confidently from the stage, but to suggest a melancholy parting.

The penultimate section of the 1796 *Poems*, once more given its own title-page and epigraph, consists of five 'Poetical Epistles'. If the reader has become interested in, even concerned about, the young poet, then in this group of texts he appears to stage a gradual withdrawal from us, so that by the close he has departed the scene altogether. This sense of Coleridge removing himself from the book is strengthened by the way the opening poem struggles toward a spiritual and physical homecoming. 'Written at Shurton Bars, near Bridgewater, September, 1795, in Answer to a Letter from Bristol' is a text that negotiates a way to its destination through an alienating, tempest-beaten landscape. It moves almost allegorically across a panorama that presents a temporal journey in spatial terms, its images re-creating 'the tumultuous evil hour | Ere Peace with SARA came'. Located on the low cliffs overlooking a stormy Bristol Channel, this atmospheric night-piece features derelict dwellings that offer no shelter: a 'reft' house through which 'the sea-breeze moans', and a 'solitary pile | Unslated by the blast', as well as a ship in distress that disappears under the waves. These traditional symbols of the vulnerable human body are supplemented by a series of flickering lights that cannot guide this benighted pilgrim: the 'starry wilder-ness' above, the glow-worm's curious 'green radiance' in the grass beneath, the two flashes of lightning that allow a glimpse of the sinking vessel, and the lighthouse out on Flat Holm in the estuary with its 'storm-vex'd flame'. Into this psycho-dramatic scene the poet projects his former self as a man that would have taken a perverse, self-indulgent delight in it all. He imagines the figure alone on the distant island: 'there in black soul-jaundic'd fit | A sad gloom-pamper'd Man to sit, | And listen to the roar'.[50] But suddenly in stanza eleven, in a move of cinematic daring, the poet's imagination cuts to a sleeping skylark who 'grounds her breast' in a summer cornfield. This

---

[50] Coleridge seems to be recalling the opening scene of Thomas Warton's *The Pleasures of Melancholy* (1747) where the poet offers a picture of gloom-pampered Contemplation seated on a high rock in a stormy night: 'secure, self-blest, | There oft thou listen'st to the wild uproar | Of fleets encount'ring' (12–14).

contrasting image of bodily grounding prepares us for the poem's reassuring arrival when the 'houseless, friendless wretch' is finally taken into Sara's arms. The electrical storm that was earlier raging outside is now transformed to the 'fair electric flame' of sexual excitement, and on this note of physical intimacy the poem finally bursts into illumination, not thanks to a bolt from heaven but with a light from the human eye: 'so shall flash my love-charg'd eye | When all the heart's big ecstacy | Shoots rapid thro' the frame!'.

Had Coleridge wanted to present a more even, progressive, and optimistic trajectory in his 1796 *Poems*, then the epistle 'Written at Shurton Bars' would have made an effective climax to the 'Effusions' section; or it might have led naturally into Effusion 35 and the couple's opening embrace (indeed, with its new title, 'Ode to Sara', it did exactly that in the 1797 *Poems*). Its position in the 1796 volume is an uncomfortable one. As the opening 'Epistle' in a brief section that does little to justify the generic title (as two of the early reviewers pointed out),[51] it is followed by four others in which both the momentum of the volume and the focus on the poet himself are lost. The so-called 'Epistle 2' ('To a Friend, in Answer to a Melancholy Letter'), with its mood of jaunty fatalism, is in fact an imitation of a Latin *ode* by the seventeenth-century 'Polish Horace', Casimir. The whimsical Epistle 3, not least its title, 'Written after a Walk before Supper' (which can have left little time for composition),[52] concerns the Revd Fulwood Smerdon, whose death from a 'frenzy fever' was the subject of an earlier poem; but here we have a verse caricature of the vicar and his wife strolling together, the one virtually bodiless ('So thin, that strip him of his cloathing, | He'd totter on the edge of NOTHING!') alongside a figure who is nothing but body ('SHE large and round beyond belief, | A superfluity of Beef!'). The poet is fascinated by the incongruity, the stuff of nursery-rhyme.

The final two epistles are both addressed to Cottle, the first by Coleridge ('To the Author of Poems Published Anonymously at Bristol, in September, 1795'), and the second ostensibly by Sara. Its title declares that Coleridge himself has now left the scene: 'The Production of a Young Lady, Addressed to the Author of the Poems Alluded to in the Preceeding Epistle', and the poem is subscribed 'Sara', although evidence suggests it is largely her husband's production.[53] This is yet another text about incongruity, in which poetry's airy flights have to negotiate substantial reality. Its Quixotic premise

[51] '[T]heir merit is not, we think, appropriate to epistolary writing' (John Aikin, *Monthly Review*, 20 [June 1796], 194–9); 'We do not think the author very successful in this class of poetry' (*Analytical Review*, 13 [June 1796], 610–12). See *Critical Heritage*, 33, 37.
[52] Coleridge never reprinted the poem. See Coleridge to George Coleridge, 18 Oct. 1796 (*Collected Letters of Samuel Taylor Coleridge*, ed. Earl Leslie Griggs, vol. 6 (Oxford: Clarendon Press, 1971), 1006).
[53] Long afterwards Sara told her daughter that 'she wrote but little' of the poem; the transcript in her handwriting used as copytext for the 1796 *Poems* has corrections that are consistent with her 'copying another person's (Coleridge's) hand' (Mays, ii.337–8).

is drawn from the world of 'old romance' in which a woman's every desire, however fantastic, could be granted. She had only to wish for something, and '[w]afted along on viewless pinions aery | It lay'd itself obsequious at her Feet'. For once, the magic of 'the dear delicious land of Faery' appears to have worked, because Cottle has brought her a replacement thimble. In this courtly mock-romance Cottle plays the role of a drawing-room enchanter ('*Politeness* is a licens'd *spell* | And *you*, dear Sir! the Arch-magician'). In the final scene, Coleridge is reading aloud Cottle's poems to Sara while she sews, and she is so swept up in the thrilling experience that her fingers are in continual danger of pricking; but thanks to Cottle's gift she remains uninjured. The thimble is able to shield her from the physical effects of Cottle's 'thought-bewildering Muse'.

The sequence has ended with a satiric cameo that brings some of the volume's wider divergences into witty conjunction, and certain concealed ironies into play. It places the imaginative world of the Pixies' Parlour back into its original Popean context of mock-heroic. In the final two epistles it has been Cottle's Muse taking centre stage, permitting Coleridge an amused perspective on the uncertainties that have surrounded his own poetical character as projected through the 1796 collection, particularly its ambivalence about poetic embodiment.

While Cottle's Muse takes her bow, Coleridge himself has slipped from the scene. The volume has to this point offered a confusing picture of the young poet, in a collection over which Proteus might be thought to have presided. Coleridge's ordering of the material has avoided the presentation of a consistent character or a developmental narrative. He does not separate off a 'juvenile' voice from a 'mature' one, not because they are not there to be distinguished but because he appears uncertain about viewing his own trajectory in those progressive terms. The collection is not without a degree of strategic disingenuousness. Coleridge does not organise his volume to show a poet who is growing before our eyes, nor does he group his work in a coherent way in terms of genre, subject, or date. Instead there is repeated evidence of a more sceptical self-appraisal, which is not afraid of ironic juxtapositions or sudden changes in tone. I have tried to show that this should not be attributed to hurry, confusion, accident, or lack of thought. Instead the volume can be read as a critical self-presentation in which the poet is both indulging and checking himself.

But like any ambitious performer he knows how to make an effective re-entrance. While the light-hearted satiric laughter is still echoing after Sara's mock-romance, the reader turns the leaf to find a new title page announcing 'Religious Musings'. Beyond a further page-turn, facing the poem's 'Argument' is a quotation that serves as the epigraph. It is subscribed 'Akenside' and is ostensibly an extract from his *Pleasures of the Imagination* (1772):

> What tho' first,
> In years unseason'd, I attun'd the Lay
> To idle Passion and unreal Woe?
> Yet serious Truth her empire o'er my song
> Hath now asserted: Falshood's evil brood,
> Vice and deceitful Pleasure, She at once
> Excluded, and my Fancy's careless toil
> Drew to the better cause!

The second half of the passage (from 'Falshood' onwards) is indeed Akenside; but the opening is Coleridge. The extract is from Akenside's address to his lifelong friend Jeremiah Dyson in which the poet reminisces about his early progress along 'the paths of life'.[54] Coleridge has rewritten eight lines to make his own opening ('What tho' ... asserted'), and in the process he has turned what was in Akenside an unfolding personal retrospect into something dramatic and immediate.[55] The *Pleasures of the Imagination* had described a more gradual development: 'yet serious truth | Her empire o'er the calm, sequester'd theme | Asserted soon' (i.54–6). But that is too leisurely for Coleridge at this moment, and he rewrites the lines in order to declare the 'now' of his poem, and its break with the past: 'yet serious Truth her empire o'er *my song* | Hath *now* asserted'. It is Coleridge officially announcing his maturity.[56] With a fresh commitment to Truth, he has left behind the earlier verse of 'idle Passion and unreal Woe' (this phrase is also Coleridge's), and with it he appears to be dismissing as immature everything that has gone before. It reads as if the poet had departed the scene in order to return in a new character; and the manoeuvre seems to confirm that in organising his volume to this point Coleridge had little investment in presenting his collected poems as a developing achievement, or himself as a continuous poetic identity. A narrative of unsettled impulses, reversals, and frustrations better served his wider purposes. The book's final item is offered not as a culmination but a fresh beginning.

In turning from Sara's thimble to 'Religious Musings', the reader moves from a comic miniature to the apocalyptic sublime—the contrast could hardly be greater. However, when Coleridge spoke about his ambitious poem it was not the poem's lofty flights that he stressed, but rather its foundational quality. He viewed it not in terms of soaring genius but as

---

[54] Mark Akenside, *The Pleasures of the Imagination* (1772), i.48–97. Robin Dix suggests that lines 69–97 were echoed by Coleridge in 'To the Rev. George Coleridge' (1797), lines 9–39. See Robin Dix (ed.), *The Poetical Works of Mark Akenside* (Madison/Teaneck: Fairleigh Dickinson University Press; London: Associated University Presses, 1996), 464.

[55] Akenside had written: 'What, though first | In years unseason'd, haply ere the sports | Of childhood yet were o'er, the adventurous lay | With many splendid prospects, many charms, | Allur'd my heart, nor conscious whence they sprung, | Nor heedful of their end?' (i.49–54).

[56] It becomes Coleridge's equivalent of Pope's famous lines, 'not in Fancy's Maze he wander'd long, | But stoop'd to Truth, and moraliz'd his song' (Alexander Pope, *Epistle to Dr. Arbuthnot* (1734), 340–1).

something substantial. It was a production that carried *weight*: 'I build all my poetic pretentions on the Religious Musings', he told John Thelwall, and he repeated the idea to others.[57] A reader of the reviews might assume that Coleridge would have been most pleased with John Aikin's response in the *Monthly* when he considered the poem's genius as 'on the top of the scale of sublimity' and exhibiting 'that ungoverned career of fancy and feeling'. But given Coleridge's own stress on its substantiality he possibly preferred the judgment of the *Analytical*, that the poem was 'chiefly valuable for the importance of the sentiments which it contains, and the ardour with which they are expressed'.[58] Coleridge felt that the poem built its truths rather than snatched its sublimities, that it *embodied* something important.

'Religious Musings' is, after all, a Christmas poem (the subtitle is 'A Desultory Poem, written on Christmas' Eve, in the Year of our Lord, 1794'),[59] and as such its ostensible subject is embodiment, specifically the incarnation of God as man. But the poem's handling of the concept is compromised by its emphasis on the spirit's liberation from the body, and the power of the divine to transcend the human. From this perspective the poem brings to a climax, though it certainly does not resolve, the issues of poetic and personal embodiment continually raised in the 1796 volume. A reader might expect the poem's theology to rest on the fact of God's becoming Man through the infant Jesus; but from the beginning 'Religious Musings' appears uneasy about expressing the divine in the simply human. The poem's default position is sublimity, and the text's human gestures turn into divine effects. Given that sublimation is the contrary process to embodiment, this has the effect of creating a tension between the human and divine dynamics of the poem.[60]

In Coleridge's poem, the birth of a baby in a stable is lost sight of, and the focus shifts to the glorious birth of light itself, the instant when 'The startling East | Saw from her dark womb leap her flamy Child!' These lines, much to John Thelwall's contempt,[61] have the effect of substituting the mystical birth of the solar system for the scene of a baby in a manger. The result is that the first infant we encounter in Coleridge's text is the Sun, not the Son, and,

---

[57] Coleridge to Thelwall (late April 1796); Griggs, 205. Cf. 'I rest for all my poetical credit on the *Religious Musings*' (to Benjamin Flower, 1 April 1796; Griggs, 197); and 'I pin all my poetical credit on the Religious Musings' (to Poole, 11 April 1796; Griggs, 203).

[58] *Critical Heritage*, 37–8; 33.

[59] The term 'desultory' need not imply laziness or carelessness, but here seems to combine the sense of 'shifting irregularly' (Gilbert White notes: 'I shot at [a bird] but it was so desultory that I missed my aim' (*OED*, s.v. 'desultory', 1) and the sense of 'unmethodical, unsystematic' (Burke speaks of 'writing... not in a desultory and occasional manner, but systematically' (*OED*, s.v. 'desultory', 2)). The 1796 volume as a whole is in this sense a desultory text.

[60] John Axcelson finds a similar tension in the poem's element of human anticipation, which 'works to build a productive tension between the sudden unprecedented work of apocalypse and the temporal experience of human beings' (John Axcelson, 'Timing the Apocalypse: The Career of *Religious Musings*', *European Romantic Review*, 16 (2005), 439–54 (445)).

[61] See Chapter 10 below, pp. 239–40.

unlike the shepherds, the poet never reaches the stable. Throughout the poem, the human body of Jesus is repeatedly subsumed into the aura of the Father:

> Who thee beheld thy imag'd Father saw.
> His Power and Wisdom from thy awful eye
> Blended their beams...   (27–9)

The stakes are also raised for the poet himself. To this point in the volume his progress has been plotted partly in terms of the uncertainties of hope. But in 'Religious Musings' all human hope is transcended, and we move

> From HOPE and stronger FAITH to perfect LOVE
> Attracted and absorb'd: and center'd there
> GOD only to behold, and know, and feel,
> Till by exclusive Consciousness of GOD
> All self-annihilated it shall make
> GOD it's Identity: God all in all!
> We and our Father ONE!   (49–55)

In the 1796 volume to this point, the triad of Hope, Faith, and Love has been dispersed into separate earthly spheres. Hope has appeared as a chimera, an effect of the weather, a rainbow, or a beacon, something that the pilgrim looks to as a guide or finds elusive; Faith has been seen as the nurse's hand that infant man can grasp; and Love has moved between a highly charged erotic atmosphere and a resting human cheek. In lines 49–50 of 'Religious Musings' Coleridge brings them together in a gravitational bond by which their individual dynamics become one: *attracted, absorb'd, center'd*. There is no dispersal now: the movement here is consciously centripetal, drawing the elements towards the core. In the next line this second triad is followed by yet a third: to *behold*, and *know*, and *feel*, where a similar movement is evident. Coleridge is knitting together sense, mind, and emotion, as a progression towards what he terms, a few pages later, a 'common center' (168). But this 'center' is not a confined selfhood. On the contrary, the phrase at this point initiates a counter-movement outwards. The systole–diastole, which we saw lightly figured in Effusion 35, is being acted out in 'Religious Musings' on a universal scale. The individual human being

> [b]y sacred sympathy might make
> The whole ONE SELF! SELF, that no alien knows!
> SELF, far diffus'd as Fancy's wing can travel!
> SELF, spreading still! Oblivious of it's own,
> Yet all of all possessing! This is FAITH!
> This the MESSIAH's destin'd victory!   (173–8)

In these two climactic passages (lines 49–55 and 173–8) the mystical dynamics of the poem are articulated. We move from the centring of God within our 'self-annihilated' identity, to the expansion of the self to encompass everything. The divine is inwardly absorbed and the transformed human projected outwards.

In this poem, therefore, the ultimate emphasis is not on God becoming human, but on humans becoming god-like. It is 'th'Elect, regenerate thro' faith', who are '[e]nrob'd with Light, and naturaliz'd in Heaven' (107). At the heart of the text is not the nativity story of Luke's gospel, but the sixth chapter of the Revelation of St John. The fifth seal, says the poet, has already been opened, and the storm is beginning that will shake the unripe fruit from off the fig-tree (333). For all its title, the poem is set, not on Christmas Eve, but on the eve of the Apocalypse.

'Religious Musings' represents not just a structural break in the 1796 *Poems*, but a break with any notion of an organic history. The poem celebrates the ultimate revolutionary event, the cataclysmic instant when all individual human stories, all personal identities, come to an end as they are swept up in one single phenomenon, when '[t]he Throne of the redeeming God | Forth flashing unimaginable day | Wraps in one blaze earth, heaven, and deepest hell' (426–8). The scale is universal, and all concepts of growth, development, hope, loss, memory, desire, everything through which the human organism expresses itself within time, are absorbed into a single eternal being, the 'ever-living ONE', in whose name it is possible to declare 'TIME IS NO MORE!' (421). An earthly historical revolution has been overwritten by a universal transcendence of all human institutions, categories, identities.

In light of this, the ecstatic close of the poem confidently declares a new totality of form, and in doing so it sets out to transcend all the other materials in the volume. Through the divine vision, everything hitherto seen in human terms is transposed and reshaped:

> Contemplant Spirits! ye that hover o'er
> With untir'd gaze th'immeasurable fount
> Ebullient with creative Deity!
> And ye of plastic power, that interfus'd
> Roll thro' the grosser and material mass
> In organizing surge! Holies of God!
> (And what if Monads of the infinite mind?)
> I haply journeying my immortal course
> Shall sometime join your mystic choir!   (429–37)

The poet declares the ultimate potential of being born again, and of having his mortality redeemed by the divine. As he does so, he glimpses how time and space might translate into the eternal and infinite. Not only the scale of things has changed: the human images with which the earlier poems have worked are swept up into the divine Idea, and the text severs itself from the unsettled personal history that the volume has to this point offered its readers. At the Apocalypse, growth, however precarious, disrupted or compromised, is no longer on the agenda, and living continuities lose their meaning in a language of infinity and eternity.[62] In this way the modest concept of effusion is transfigured into an archetype of unceasing creativity 'ebullient [= boiling over] with creative Deity!' Here any possibility of human organisation is transcended by a universal shaping power 'that interfus'd | Roll[s] thro' the grosser and material mass | In organizing surge'. The echo of the 'delicious surges' of the Aeolian harp only confirms that these are not merely localised currents of air moving through an open casement window, but an irresistible formative power transcending time and space. In place of a human organic that can accommodate failure and loss is a supra-human unifying of all forms under the eye of eternity, with the thought that a single 'infinite mind' is manifesting itself throughout creation.[63] In one of the poem's many exclamatory declarations, the varied truths of experience are short-circuited by a notion of 'SUPREME REALITY!' (148). In concluding with 'Religious Musings' the 1796 volume ends with a text that spurns the rest of the collection, and seems intended to function as a kind of glorious postscript (literally so, an exasperated Cottle probably thought). In Coleridge's struggle to bring himself to book, the need to complete 'Religious Musings' as the final statement of the volume was paramount. It was the poem that would somehow justify, even redeem, all that had gone before. Rising above the problems of embodiment that repeatedly emerge in the collection, this text allowed Coleridge finally to present a confident image of how humanity can become part of the Body of the Elect, embraced by the revelatory Book of God's Word.

[62] Axcelson ('Timing the Apocalypse', 447) points out that at the end of the poem Coleridge envisages the 'Elect' as having a temporal role in shaping the 'perfect forms' of the future (line 266). My own reading emphasises Coleridge's prophetic vision of the apocalyptic moment.

[63] 'There is one Mind, one omnipresent Mind, | Omnific' (119–20). Coleridge had written in *Joan of Arc* (published Dec. 1795) about the theory that '[i]nfinite myriads of self-conscious minds | Form one all-conscious Spirit, who directs | With absolute ubiquity of thought | All his component monads' (ii.44–7).

8   Coleridge's *Sonnets from Various Authors* (1796): A Lost Conversation Poem?

IN AUTUMN 1796, Coleridge put together a modest little pamphlet (so modest it has no title) which offers a case-history of how texts can gather new and even urgent meanings through the circumstances of their transmission. Hitherto largely ignored by Coleridge scholars, and rarely considered as a literary artefact,[1] *Sonnets from Various Authors* (a title of convenience) is, I want to show, an organised collection with both a structured argument and a directed message. It is simultaneously a text and a context; it makes meaning in space and time, through the particular contained circumstances of the sonnet form and of a few weeks during September–November 1796; and under this joint spatial and temporal pressure it creates a Coleridgean text from the individual voices of others. The result is virtually a 'lost' Conversation Poem: a dramatic 'converse' meditating on themes of self and society, friendship and social action, and moving from single lonely thoughts to a more integrated sense of 'one common life'.[2]

Coleridge wrote to Tom Poole on 7 November:

I amused myself the other day (having some *paper* at the Printer's which I could employ no other way) in selecting 28 Sonnets, to bind up with Bowles's—I charge sixpence for them, and have sent you five to dispose of.—I have only printed two hundred, as my paper held out to no more; and dispose of them privately, just enough to pay the printing.[3]

---

[1] A facsimile text of the pamphlet has been edited by Paul M. Zall (Glendale: La Siesta Press, 1968). In the introduction Zall argues that 'the chief motivation for assembling the pamphlet was polemical rather than poetical' (12), and that 'Bowles appeared attractive to [Coleridge] at this time because he provided a model for poetry of revolution aimed at social happiness and moral order' (18). Zall sees the sonnets as organized in five blocks: I–V 'celebrate the pleasures of solitude', VI–IX 'dwell on the pleasures of harmony', X–XIV are 'on the soulful sadness of the lovelorn', XV–XXII are 'concerned with pity and righteous indignation for the plight of the poor', and XXIII–XXVIII are 'on the emotions generated by the fancy, ranging from pity to terror' (12). Zall's is the only consideration of the pamphlet's structure.

[2] Coleridge's pamphlet has been linked by Richard Holmes to the poet's creation of 'an ideal, literary circle' among his friends (*Coleridge: Early Visions* (London: Hodder, 1989), 126). More recently, Gurion Taussig has developed this idea to one of 'a collection in which Coleridge invites the reader to discover unifying points of sympathy between individual poets' (*Coleridge and the Idea of Friendship, 1789–1804* (Newark: University of Delaware Press, 2000), 39).

[3] Griggs, 252.

This little collection of sixteen pages, an octavo printed in half-sheets, consists of a first leaf containing a prefatory essay on the sonnet (signed 'Editor'), followed by fourteen pages of sonnets (printed two to a page). It has no title page, just a short opening paragraph: 'I have selected the following SONNETS from various Authors for the purpose of binding them up with the Sonnets of the Rev. W.L. BOWLES.' This 'sheaf of sonnets', as it is sometimes known, consists of three by William Lisle Bowles, two by Charlotte Smith, one each by John Bampfylde, Thomas Warton, Sir Samuel Egerton Brydges, William Sotheby, Thomas Russell, Thomas Dermody, and Anna Seward, and four each by Coleridge himself, Robert Southey, Charles Lamb, and Charles Lloyd. Not surprisingly, it is a scarce bibliographic item, and of the seven copies known three are indeed bound up with Bowles's sonnets as Coleridge hoped: Stella Thelwall's copy in the Victoria and Albert Museum, and that of Sophia Pemberton (later Mrs Charles Lloyd) at Cornell, are bound with the fourth edition of 1796; and in the Huntington Library Charles Lloyd's own copy accompanies the third edition of 1794.[4]

So, seven years after Coleridge's first ecstatic encounter with Bowles's sonnets as a teenager, memorably described in the opening chapter of *Biographia Literaria*, they are still a touchstone for his own work, a way of reaching out to his friends, and a gauge of his feelings for them. Looking back in 1815, he felt Bowles's influence had been 'for radical good', and remained grateful for 'the genial influence of a style of poetry, so tender, and yet so manly, so natural and real, and yet so dignified, and harmonious, as the sonnets, &c. of Mr. Bowles'. During 1789–90 he had 'made ... more than forty transcriptions, as the best presents I could offer to those, who had in any way won my regard',[5] and now in the Autumn of 1796 he is still wanting Bowles's sonnets to circulate, and is binding up himself and his friends with them. In this little collection of sonnets, Coleridge and they are bound together, *contextus* (from *contexo*, 'to bind or weave together'), like the two pamphlets.

Why at this particular moment think of Bowles and the sonnet? The key is in Coleridge's prefatory essay on the sonnet form, which he defines as 'a small poem, in which some lonely feeling is developed'. He says:

In a Sonnet then we require a development of some lonely feeling, by whatever cause it may have been excited; but those Sonnets appear to me the most exquisite, in which moral Sentiments, Affections, or Feelings, are deduced from, and associated with, the scenery of Nature. Such compositions ... create a sweet and indissoluble union between the intellectual and the material world.

---

[4] V&A: Dyce 8° 1298 (Copy A); Cornell: Wordsworth PR 4161 B4 1796; Huntington: RB123964-5. Also bound up with the Cornell copy is Charles Lloyd's *Poems on Various Subjects* (1795). The other known copies are Princeton: Robert H. Taylor Collection (Mrs Calvert); Dove Cottage: MS 14/2 (?Sarah Hutchinson); Oberlin College: 821.7C67So (Rachel Lloyd); New York Public Library (fragment). Three copies (V&A, Cornell, Huntington) were known to Zall in 1968.

[5] *Biog. Lit.* 15–17.

The sonnet is consequently about finding 'union' from loneliness, and about drawing together the internal and external principles. The very confinement of the form makes it assimilable. For Coleridge a sonnet is companionable in tendency. It can be intimately internalised, and by being lodged in the memory it becomes an organic part of ourselves. Not only that, but in Coleridge's Lockean linking of memory and identity, the sonnet can be jointly appropriated, allowing friends not merely to share the same experience, but to partake in some kind of extended consciousness or persisting identity: 'Easily remembered from their briefness', the preface continues, 'these are the poems which we can "lay up in our heart, and our soul," and repeat them "when we walk by the way, and when we lie down and when we rise up."' In other words, they live with us and become part of our daily routine. In the hands of Bowles, the sonnet becomes for Coleridge the internal equivalent of settled domestic happiness: 'Hence, the Sonnets of BOWLES derive their marked superiority over all other Sonnets...they domesticate with the heart, and become, as it were, a part of our identity'.[6]

The period from late September to early November 1796 was a time when *domestication* was at the forefront of Coleridge's thoughts. Since the collapse of *The Watchman* in May, his prospects had swung giddily around to the dismay of his friends (Lamb called it his 'dancing demon'): to continue journalism in London with the *Morning Chronicle*? To become a dissenting minister? Engage himself as a private tutor? Translate Schiller? Open a day-school in Derby? Lamb wrote on 17 October: 'I grieve from my very soul to observe you in your plans of life, veering about from this hope to the other, & settling no where...lies the fault, as I fear it does, in your *own* mind?'[7] But Coleridge was—at this moment—attempting to settle. His son Hartley had been born on 19 September, and as he assembled his sequence of sonnets he was in Bristol sharing a bed with his new friend Charles Lloyd, now part of the family, all of them intending soon to settle (as he told Lloyd's father on 15 October) to a life of 'rustic' retirement as Tom Poole's neighbours in or near Nether Stowey.[8] Lloyd was ecstatic at his new domesticity with his brilliant tutor and friend, who was addressing poems to him, including 'To C. Lloyd, on His Proposing to Domesticate with the Author'.[9]

In a very different vein, on 22 September, the 'domestic' became the terrifying focus for Charles Lamb's life, on that 'day of horrors' when all his prospects seemed to close down. Breaking the news of his mother's

---

[6] In his letters of Dec. 1796 Coleridge repeatedly associates Bowles's sonnets with the *heart*, and this adds extra point to *circulating* him among friends. He writes of Bowles as 'heart-honour'd Poet', speaks of 'the *heart* and fancy of Bowles', and sends Bowles's sonnets to Stella Thelwall the volume 'which has given me more pleasure, and done my heart more good, than all the other books, I ever read, excepting my Bible' (Griggs, 295, 279, 287). Coleridge's sonnet 'To the Rev. W. L. Bowles' (*Morning Chronicle*, 26 Dec.1794) begins: 'My heart has thank'd thee, BOWLES!'

[7] Marrs, 51.   [8] Griggs, 240–1.   [9] See pp. 230–1 below.

killing by his sister Mary, he wrote to Coleridge: 'You look after your family,—I have my reason and strength left to take care of mine. I charge you don't think of coming to see me. Write. I will not see you if you come.'[10] His letters to Coleridge in the weeks that follow convey a sense of someone managing under terrific spatial and mental pressure ('my mother a dead & murder'd corpse in the next room') as he carefully plans out his family's domestic future and finds ways of 'managing my mind'.[11] As for poetry, he declares, he is finished with it for ever.[12] For Coleridge to turn back to the sonnet at this moment, and draw Lloyd, Lamb, and himself together under the guiding spirit of Bowles, domesticating with the heart, becomes I think an understandable, even significant, gesture.[13]

This pamphlet is indeed a 'turning back' to the sonnet. As we saw in the previous chapter, in his 1796 *Poems* published in April, Coleridge had abjured the form, re-titling all his earlier sonnets 'effusions' and deliberately merging them under that title with the meditative-descriptive poem, the Ossianic ballad, and the ode. The preface to *Poems* had shown a loss of confidence in his ability to write a true sonnet or even compare himself with Bowles:

> Of the following Poems a considerable number are styled 'Effusions'...I might indeed have called the majority of them Sonnets—but they do not posses that *oneness* of thought which I deem indispensible in a Sonnet—and...I was fearful that the title 'Sonnet' might have reminded my reader of the Poems of the Rev. W.L. Bowles—a comparison with whom would have sunk me below that mediocrity, on the surface of which I am at present enabled to float.[14]

By the autumn, with the *Sonnets from Various Authors*, he is able not only to reinstate the sonnet as a form, but interweave his and his friends' sonnets amongst those of Bowles. Coleridge's move from 'effusion' with its Latin sense (from *effundo*) of 'pouring out', but also of immoderate (effusive) squandering and slackening, back to the constraint of the sonnet, is marked in his pamphlet's prefatory essay by a new emphasis on the satisfying completion of an impulse within prescribed bounds: '[The Sonnet] is limited to a *particular* number of lines, in order that the reader's mind having expected the close at the place in which he finds it, may rest satisfied'.

During those weeks when for Coleridge, Lloyd, and Lamb, life was becoming in different ways more localised and contained, and expectations more

---

[10] Marrs, 45.

[11] Ibid. 48.

[12] '[M]ention nothing of poetry. I have destroyed every vestige of past vanities of that kind' (Lamb to Coleridge, 27 Sept. 1796; Marrs, 45). By November, however, Lamb was showing signs of returning to thoughts of poetry.

[13] For Lamb, Bowles was a cherished link between Coleridge and himself. On 10 Dec. 1796 Lamb recalled 'when you were repeating one of Bowles's sweetest sonnets in your sweet manner, while we two were indulging sympathy, a solitary luxury, by the fireside at the Salutation...I have no higher ideas of heaven...Not a soul loves Bowles here' (Marrs, 78–9). The Advertisement to Lloyd's *Poems* (1795) ends with two quotations from Bowles.

[14] 1796 *Poems*, ix–x.

focused, the traditional 'narrow room' of the sonnet offered an appropriate form in which external and internal pressures could find accommodation within prescribed bounds.[15] Through his Bowles-inspired anthology, Coleridge gave himself the opportunity of weaving together—contextualizing—select items of 'lonely feeling' into a more communal mode, so as to bring individual voices into dialogue with each other. It is in this collective and friendly spirit that Coleridge selects and organises the twenty-eight sonnets. Behind the sequential analysis of them that follows is a threefold argument: that *Sonnets from Various Authors* is structured by Coleridge as a composite text; that the individual items work together to create a rich verbal and thematic texture; and that the directing idea of the pamphlet is to provide the voices of Lloyd and Lamb with sympathetic echoes and instructive accompaniments. Coleridge offers understanding and encouragement to his friends, but also (as in life) a degree of frustration, in which the amicably interwoven garland (*antho*-logia) is finally broken, and the poet turns to new horizons.

As editor, Coleridge has also designed his sequence bibliographically. He is conscious of how sonnets are paired on the page, or grouped into four across an opening, and he tries different combinations where appropriate: alternation (*abab*) or enfolding (*abba*), much in the way a sonneteer would be conscious of rhyme pattern. Indeed, the decisive break in Coleridge's sequence comes at the page-turn after Sonnet XIV, suggesting the double-sonnet structure of his collection, in two groups of fourteen.

The first page of text gives the pamphlet an appropriate thematic opening by pairing Bowles's sonnet 'To a Friend' (I)[16] with one by Southey (II).[17] Both poems use the image of life as a journey but offer contrasting perspectives on the road ahead. Bowles, in healing mode, stresses the journey's difficulty ('our Road is lone and long', I.9) and welcomes a consoling respite along the way: 'yet on Life's wide plain | Cast friendless . . . | . . . 'Twere not a crime, should

[15] John Kerrigan has argued that the sonnet offered Wordsworth 'a uniquely comforting abode in which to dwell' ('Wordsworth and the Sonnet: Building, Dwelling, Thinking', *EC*, 35 (1985), 45–75 (57)).

[16] The sonnet 'To a Friend' opened Bowles's extended and revised second edition, *Sonnets, Written Chiefly on Picturesque Spots, During a Tour* (Bath: R. Cruttwell, 1789), which Coleridge copied for his friends. Coleridge was shocked to find the sonnet omitted from the third and fourth editions (1794 and 1796). The other two Bowles sonnets in *Sonnets from Various Authors* had likewise been dropped after the second edition. 'To a Friend' also provided the epigraph to Southey's 'The Retrospect' (see p. 133 above).

[17] All four Southey sonnets in *Sonnets from Various Authors* were first officially published in Southey's *Poems* (1797), printed late Dec. 1796 (see Coleridge's comments on the volume, Griggs, 290). Zall (48) suggests that Coleridge 'could easily have transcribed' Southey's sonnets while the volume was at press; but he is perhaps more likely to have printed them from manuscripts already in his possession. On 11 Dec. 1794 he wrote to Southey about the latter's *Poems* (1795): 'The Sonnets are wonderfully inferior to *those which I possess of yours*' (Griggs, 133; my emphasis)—we know these included 'To the Evening Rainbow' (see n. 35 below). Sonnet II ('With many a weary step') appeared in Southey's volume, p. 114. It is dated '1794' by Southey in his *Works* (10 vols, 1837), ii.93.

we awhile delay | Amid the sunny field' (I.7–11). In his sonnet Southey sees exactly the same terrain, but from a wider and more bracing viewpoint. Poised on a hilltop as 'the cool breeze plays | Gratefully round my brow' (II.2–3), he looks down at the miles already covered ('the journied plain. | 'Twas a long way and tedious!') but then he turns confidently to the way ahead: 'But cease fond heart in such sad thoughts to roam! | For surely thou ere long shalt reach thine home, | And pleasant is the way that lies before' (II.4–5, 12–14). Brought together on the page, these two companions on life's journey offer contrasting qualities: whereas Bowles recognises the difficulties of those who may be walking with him, Southey is impatient to make progress on what is evidently a downward slope. Set in converse, the two voices (comforting and exhorting) offer alternative ways of getting through life, and establish the parameters between which the sequence of sonnets will move: soothing sympathy and admonitory encouragement.

This prepares for the first page-turn, where the reader immediately encounters, not Southey's 'pleasant' prospect, but two of Charles Lloyd's sonnets in which the landscape is uncomfortable, alienating, and full of neurotic suggestion.[18] In the first, Lloyd negotiates a very different hill from Southey's:

> Scotland! when thinking on each heathy hill
>   O'er whose bleak breast the billowy vapours sweep,
>   While sullen winds imprison'd murmur deep
> 'Mid their dim caves...   (III.1–4)

The paired Lloyd sonnets on this page feature disturbing hidden places. The second, 'To Craig-Milton Castle, in which Mary Queen of Scots was confined',[19] describes 'dark damp caverns' which 'breathe mysterious dread, | Haply still foul with tinct of ancient crime', IV.5–6). Both are haunted landscapes ('I've trac'd thy torrents to their haunted source, | Whence down some huge rock with fantastic course, | Their sheeted whiteness pouring, they beguil'd | The meek dishearten'd one', III.6–9). In this context the 'bleak breast' of Sonnet III offers no maternal comfort; and where Southey had welcomed a cool, 'grateful' breeze, Lloyd feels it heavy and menacing:

> the flappings of the heavy bird
> Imagin'd warnings fearfully impart,
> And that dull breeze below that feebly stirr'd,
> Seem'd the deep breathing of an o'ercharg'd heart!   (IV.9–12)

---

[18] Lloyd's two Scottish sonnets were included in Coleridge's 1797 *Poems*, 169–70.

[19] In Charles Lloyd's copy (Huntington) the title is corrected to 'Craig-Miller Castle', and the phrase 'in which Mary Queen of Scots was confined' has been crossed out. This suggests that although Lloyd was living with him at the time, Coleridge did not show him the contents of the pamphlet before printing, and that they may have been intended as a surprise.

The nearest Lloyd comes to a sense of home is merely a distant glimpse of some crofters' cottages ('Thy white cots dimly seen yielding to me | Solace most sweet', III.11–12). In pairing these two Lloyd sonnets Coleridge exploits their gloomy echoes and suggestions of hidden depths, as if to exemplify his own character-sketch of Lloyd which he had sent Tom Poole on 24 September. There he tells Poole of Lloyd's 'having been placed in situations, where for years together he met with no congenial minds, and where the contrariety of his thoughts & notions to the thoughts & notions of those around him induced the necessity of habitually suppressing his Feelings'.[20] To offer Lloyd a congenial context was therefore important for Coleridge, and to bring his friend's personal sonnets into sympathetic converse with others was, I would argue, one of the purposes of *Sonnets from Various Authors*. Writing to Poole, Coleridge stressed the importance for his friend's recovery of the right kind of intimacy: '[Lloyd] is assuredly a man of great Genius; but it must be in tete a tete with one whom he loves & esteems, that his colloquial powers open.'[21]

It is interesting therefore that Coleridge selected for the facing page, to fold down across Lloyd's two poems, the pairing of himself and Bowles. It is a double gesture: to print his own sonnet alongside Bowles's (no longer is Coleridge fearful of mediocrity), and to bring them both tête à tête with Lloyd. With a renewed confidence in himself and the sonnet form, he places his recently completed sonnet 'To the River Otter' (V) beside Bowles's invocation of the soothing powers of Harmony (VI), two healing visions to counterpoise Lloyd's disturbing scenes.

Coleridge's sonnet, perhaps completed with the knowledge of what its honoured place would be, was created out of an unfocused earlier poem in *The Watchman*, entitled 'Recollection',[22] in which lines 2–11 of the sonnet had been embedded. An 'effusion' had now become focused into a sonnet fit to join with Bowles's, the two texts in colloquy with Lloyd's:

> Dear native Brook! wild Streamlet of the West!
>   How many various-fated Years have past,
>   What blissful and what anguish'd hours, since last
> I skimm'd the smooth thin stone along thy breast,
>   Numbering its light leaps! Yet so deep imprest
>   Sink the sweet scenes of Childhood, that mine eyes
> I never shut amid the sunny blaze,
>   But strait with all their tints thy waters rise,
> Thy crossing plank, thy margin's willowy maze,
>   And bedded sand that vein'd with various dies
> Gleam'd thro' thy bright transparence to the gaze.
>   Visions of Childhood! oft have ye beguil'd
> Lone Manhood's cares, yet waking fondest sighs,
>   Ah! that once more I were a careless Child!   (V)

---

[20] Griggs, 237.   [21] Ibid. 236–7.   [22] *The Watchman*, 5 (2 April 1796).

'I skimm'd the smooth thin stone along thy breast'—what a contrast with Lloyd's physically and emotionally resistant landscape of '*huge* rock' and '*bleak* breast' (III.7, 2). Coleridge's maternal image encourages the child's playful energies, his dancing demon. And where Lloyd traced his torrents to their 'haunted source' in the 'sheeted whiteness' of a waterfall, Coleridge finds his native stream a colourful transparency, a bright clear medium. His sonnet's brilliant shift from surface to depth, from the 'light leaps' of his pebble to what is 'so deep imprest', was to leave its mark on Wordsworth's Tintern Abbey 'Lines', but here it offers a reassuring return to the troubling depths of Lloyd's two sonnets with their 'dim caves' of 'mysterious dread'. Placed beneath Coleridge's, the accompanying Bowles sonnet ('O Harmony! thou tenderest Nurse of Pain!') reinforces this assurance with a note of poise and discretion; and as the reader moves from one sonnet to the next, Coleridge's 'Child' meets in the very next line Bowles's 'Nurse'. With its more generalised language Bowles's sonnet acts as a kind of matrix for Coleridge's sharper images: the 'fairest tints' of its 'delightful dream' (VI.5, 7) are waiting for Coleridge to realise them more specifically. But Bowles also amplifies and underscores some of Coleridge's ideas. In his poem the word 'smooth' is linked to 'soothe', and Coleridge's 'light leaps' become 'one suspended transport, sad and sweet' (VI.11)—more rapt and enigmatic. Bowles's calm sonnet is supportive of Coleridge's youthful energies, but in place of Manhood's 'cares' and 'sighs' it sees sorrow itself as part of a healing process, part of a longer span of time: 'Sorrow's softest touch remains | That, when the transitory charm is o'er, | Just wakes a tear, and then is felt no more!' (VI.12–14). Bowles thus acts as a counterpoise to Lloyd's unsettled visions on the facing page. With its emphasis on the healing effect of harmony, Bowles's sonnet reconciles disparities and fuses alternatives, nowhere more subtly than in its third line ('Griefs which the *patient* spirit oft must feel'—my italics), which hovers between offering understanding to the *suffering* soul and exhorting spiritual *patience*. As the sequence proceeds, this almost imperceptible ambivalence will widen out into a more marked duality of sympathy and admonition.

The page turns again, onto two allegorical sonnets by John Codrington Bampfylde and Thomas Warton (VII–VIII) which evoke the delights respectively of Evening and Health. Both of them celebrate purity and innocence, but in different ways, the first through worldly activity, the second in withdrawal to a cave. Bampfylde's sonnet 'To Evening' (VII) overturns the traditional association between evening and melancholy with a scene of active release where the impatient 'youthful Lover', the schoolchildren, and the village labourers are all waiting for Evening as a 'general Friend!' to release their energies in desire, play, and sport.[23] Bampfylde's speaker,

---

[23] Zall (49) suggests the sonnet 'may well have been transcribed from a manuscript owned by Coleridge's friend William Jackson of Exeter'. However, it had in fact been printed as 'To the Evening', in Bampfylde's *Sixteen Sonnets* (1778). The text in *Sonnets from Various Authors* has thirteen lines, owing to Coleridge's conflation of ll. 9–10 ('From Steeple's side to urge the

'mix'd with all', takes on each role himself, without restraint, and concludes: 'So as my Heart be pure, and free my Mind!' (VII.14). His purity is outgoing and his 'wisdom' refuses to be inwardly contemplative—he is able to sustain both through sociable mixing. Warton's sonnet 'On Bathing' (VIII),[24] by contrast, explores the Miltonic combination of chastity and temperance. His figure, Health, is a solitary chaste goddess, glimpsed in line 3 as Diana roaming the windy uplands on an early spring morning ('Watching the hunter's joyous horn', VIII.6), and then contrastingly as a recluse hiding from the oppressive heat of summer within a 'high-arch'd' cave where 'cooling drops distil from arches dim' (VIII.12). The two sonnets by Bampfylde and Warton present two kinds of purity: one an honesty of heart engaged in social activity, and the other a health-giving withdrawal to a benign cave. Juxtaposed on the same page they can make their appeal— L'Allegro and Il Penseroso.

These allegorical dualities continue on the facing page, with a sonnet by Sir Samuel Egerton Brydges (IX),[25] featuring a pair of sleeping nymphs, Silence and Echo. The hunting horn (silent in Warton's poem) now bursts into life and the two figures respond in contrasting ways. Silence is struck with fear and hides in the 'shades'; but her sister Echo is joyously liberated:

> … loud the Horn resounded to the Sky.
>   In shades affrighted SILENCE melts away:
> Not so her Sister—Hark! for onward still
>   With far-heard step she takes her hasty way
> Bounding from Rock to Rock, and Hill to Hill!
>   Oh may the merry Maid in mockful play
> With thousand mimic tones the laughing Forest fill.   (IX.8–14)

These three sonnets, by Bampfylde, Warton, and Brydges, converse with each other and their allegorical figures offer the reader a choice between activity and retreat.

---

bounding ball, | The lusty hinds await thy fragrant call') into a single line ('The lusty Hinds urge the rebounding Ball'). Line 11 of the original ('I, friend to all by turns, am join'd with all') is altered to read: 'I, general Friend! by turns am mix'd with all'. J. C. Bampfylde (1754–97) did not revise the text, so the changes are evidently editorial. On the role of Coleridge and (chiefly) Southey in preserving memorials of the poet, see Roger Londsale (ed.), *The Poems of John Bampfylde* (Oxford: Perpetua Press, 1988), 33–5.

[24] First printed in Dodsley's *Collection of Poems*, vol. 4 (1755). It was included in Warton's *Poems: A New Edition, with Additions* (1777).

[25] Coleridge attributes the sonnet to 'Henry Brooks (*the Author of the Fool of Quality.*)' (i.e. Henry Brooke, *c.*1703–83). The writer was actually Sir Samuel Egerton Brydges (1762–1837), and the sonnet, 'In eddying course when leaves began to fly', was printed in his *Sonnets and Other Poems* (London, 1785) as 'Sonnet V. On Echo and Silence. Oct. 20, 1782'. Coleridge used either the first or second editions (1785, 1789), not the 1795 third edition which revised line 2. Once more Coleridge does some rewriting: Brydges' opening line, for example, has become 'When eddying Leaves begun in whirls to fly'.

Preparation has thus been made for the final sonnet of this opening, another text with an allegorical subject featuring a lost female companion, and a traumatic confrontation between the sociable and solitary impulses. This is Charles Lamb's disturbing sonnet, 'We were two pretty Babes',[26] in which the speaker searches for his twin sister, Innocence:

> My lov'd Companion dropt a tear and fled,
> And hid in deepest shades her AWFUL head!
>   Beloved! who can tell me where thou art,
>   In what delicious Eden to be found,
>   That I may seek thee the wide world around!   (X.10–14)

As in the previous sonnet, a little drama of separation is being acted out; but this echo of the playful allegory of Brydges' Echo and Silence (X.10–11) only serves to raise questions of poetic decorum. As his lost sister, Lamb's personified Innocence touches a different register from Brydges's fanciful wit. The teasing figure of Brydges' poem is delightfully elusive and mocking, and his final note of mimic laughter seems an odd preparation for Lamb's miniature *Paradise Lost*. But the paired sonnets on the facing page (Bampfylde and Warton) also join in the conversation: their contrast of the sociable and solitary impulses helps us register the rather disturbing way Lamb sees adult sociability in terms of violation ('And my first Love for Man's society, | Defiling with the World my Virgin Heart', X.8–9).

But this is only the first of three successive pairings Lamb is given, which will take us up to the mid-point of the twenty-eight sonnets. Sonnet X ends on a note of plaintive frustration ('Beloved! who can tell me where thou art?'), and on turning the page we immediately hear William Sotheby's opening sympathetic echo: 'I knew a gentle maid: I ne'er shall view | Her like again' (XI.1–2).[27] Sotheby's elusive female, however, turns out to be two maids in one, combining the retired graces of Brydges's Silence ('in her silence dwelt | Expression', XI.9–10) with the vivacity of her sister Echo ('oft her mind by youth to rapture wrought | Struck forth wild wit and fancies ever new', XI.11–12). This figure reconciles Il Penseroso with L'Allegro, and as if to mark the new harmony, the presence of Bowles is intimated in the next line, when Bowles's phrase 'Sorrow's softest touch'

---

[26] Lamb had posted the sonnet to Coleridge on 31 May 1796 (Marrs, 8). It was first printed in *Monthly Magazine* (July 1796), 491, and later in Coleridge's 1797 *Poems*, 223.

[27] William Sotheby's 16-line sonnet, 'I knew a gentle maid', was printed in his *Poems: Consisting of a Tour through Parts of North and South Wales, Sonnets, Odes, and an Epistle to a Friend on Physiognomy* (Bath: R. Cruttwell, 1790), 53, and later in the 1794 London edition (*A Tour Through Parts of Wales, Sonnets, Odes, and other Poems*). In both it was entitled 'Sonnet VIII. A Fancy Sketch'. Coleridge has cut it to fourteen lines by omitting lines 14–15 of the original, which lamely read: 'And on her lips, when gleam'd a ling'ring smile, | Pity's warm tear gush'd down her cheek the while'. Sotheby (1757–1833) and Coleridge became friends after their first meeting in 1802.

(Sonnet VI.12) becomes Sotheby's 'Sorrow's lightest touch' (XI.13). Bowles's hand thus rests gently over the ending of Sotheby's sonnet, and helps attune it to Lamb's melancholy.

Sotheby's poem also now acts as prelude to two more of Lamb's sonnets about a lost maid, 'Was it some sweet device' (XII)[28] and 'When last I rov'd' (XIII).[29] If the sonnet is, as Coleridge says, a form 'in which some lonely feeling is developed', then in these two poems Lamb is at his most lonely and lost. There is no escape from the repeated 'lonely glade' (XII.2, 10), just a sigh ('Ah me!') and forlorn aimlessness. Avoiding 'free converse', the speaker turns away from 'the little Cottage which she lov'd' (XIII.9) and is left 'self-wand'ring' through the woods, searching for the real person. In his frustration, idea and reality are split apart ('Her *Image* only in these pleasant ways | Meets me', XIII.6–7). Lamb, in other words, divorces what Coleridge's preface had called the sonnet's 'sweet and indissoluble union between the intellectual and the material world'. For Lamb, mind is cheated, and matter is empty.

On 9 June when Lamb had written in response to Coleridge's 1796 *Poems* he had singled out for praise 'that most exquisite & most Bowles-like of all, the 19th Effusion'.[30] Strikingly, it is this same poem (XIV) that Coleridge now introduces in intimate converse with Lamb's. In this new context, its opening line addressed to the heart appears to be responding naturally to Lamb's line 12: '[It] spake to my Heart, and much my Heart was mov'd' (XIII.12). But within just three lines Coleridge shifts from sympathy to a sterner and more admonishing note:

> Thou bleedest, my poor HEART! and thy distress
> Reas'ning I ponder with a scornful smile
> And probe thy sore wound sternly...   (XIV.1–3)

Coleridge thus gives himself the last word in the first group of fourteen sonnets, and in this internal dialogue he is harsh and demanding of himself. Once more he takes risks with Lamb's sensitivities ('a maniac's hand', XIV.8); but the purpose of his own sonnet is not to soothe, but to show Reason arguing with the emotions. The sestet's message is demanding: why, just when you *need* a vision of Hope, do you discard it? Its bland whispers soothed the good times, so why neglect it at a moment of crisis? You must work hard to keep Hope alive:

---

[28] Published in April as 'Effusion XI' in Coleridge's 1796 *Poems*, 55. Here, given what had happened to Lamb just weeks earlier, it raises a dark vision with its reference to Despair's 'murth'ring knife' (XII.9). Coleridge is not squeamish about the 'day of horrors' and the new resonance these words achieve. The sonnet was revised for Coleridge's 1797 *Poems*, 217.

[29] Lamb had posted Sonnet XIII to Coleridge 31 May 1796 (Marrs, 7). Printed in Coleridge's 1797 *Poems*, 219.

[30] Marrs, 20.

> Thou should'st have lov'd it most, when most opprest,
> And nurs'd it with an agony of Care,
> Ev'n as a Mother her sweet infant heir,
> That wan and sickly droops upon her breast!　　　(XIV.11–14)

The roles ought to be reversed: Hope is not the nurse—*it* must be nursed by *you*. In this favourite sonnet of Lamb's, Coleridge assumes the mantle of Bowles, but in doing so he refocuses the maternal image into a more personally demanding one.

At this mid-point of the sequence the page-turn is suitably dramatic, and we enter the second set of fourteen sonnets. The message is at once a stark one, jolting us out of the introspective mode so as to recognise the misfortunes of others. Confronting the reader across the opening are four vignettes of social injustice: two Southey sonnets, on a pregnant suicide (XV)[31] and a negro slave (XVI),[32] followed by Coleridge's 'Sweet Mercy' (XVII) about a homeless old man,[33] and finally Thomas Russell's sonnet on child beggars (XVIII).[34] In these four sonnets, 'domesticating with the heart' becomes suddenly a more capacious idea.

We first return to Southey, whom we had left on top of a breezy hill optimistically contemplating his path through life. Now it is through him that the sequence widens its horizons, from the private self to another's pain. The road here locates Southey not on a commanding hill, but alongside a 'little mound' containing the grave of one of society's outcasts, a pregnant suicide. In her fate as 'The wretched heir of Poverty and Scorn' (XV.11) the woman (Isabel) is no maternal personification, and though she uncannily resembles the maid of Sotheby's sonnet (XI), the echoes serve only to emphasize the different world we are now in. Sotheby's woman, with her 'mild eye' (XI.5) and pale cheek was an intriguing beauty. Here, however, the 'mild eye' (XV.7) and pale cheek are eloquent because they bring the language of the love sonnet into a poem of social indignation. The recollection of Sotheby's sonnet makes this point uncomfortably.

The message is even starker in Sonnet XVI, Southey's 'The Negro Slave', in which personal emotion and sympathy prompt a political awareness. In this reworking of a sentimental cameo, it is the slave who sheds the tears ('The big drops run | Down his dark cheek', XVI.1–2), leaving the spectator's cheek purposively dry ('I thank thee, Gracious God! | That I do feel upon my cheek the glow | Of indignation', XVI.11–13). The human face is

---

[31] 'Hard by the road', printed in Southey's *Poems* (1797), 111.

[32] 'Oh he is worn with toil!', printed as 'Sonnet III' of 'Poems Concerning the Slave Trade', in Southey's *Poems* (1797), 35.

[33] Printed as 'Effusion XVI' in Coleridge's 1796 *Poems*, 61.

[34] The sonnet, 'Could then the babes', was printed in Russell's posthumous *Sonnets and Miscellaneous Poems* (Oxford, 1789), 10. Lines 11–14 were adopted by Wordsworth as the concluding lines of his own sonnet, 'Iona (upon landing)'.

now registering more complex and urgent responses as the Man of Feeling becomes politicised.

Coleridge continues these images of social injustice on the facing page, with what was 'Effusion XVI' from his own 1796 *Poems*. Here placed after Southey's sonnet, Coleridge's text offers an immediate reaction to his friend's warmth of feeling by moving from emotional response to social intervention, to *active* charity:

> My Father! throw away this tatter'd vest
>   That mocks thy shiv'ring! take my garment—use
>   A young man's arm! I'll melt these frozen dews
> That hang from thy white beard and numb thy breast.
> My SARA too shall tend thee, like a Child:
>   And thou shalt talk, in our fire side's recess   (XVII.5–10)

'Domesticating with the heart' is becoming, in this group of four sonnets, a less inward-looking idea. Coleridge's domestic hearth welcomes a wider human family, as one of Lear's wretches is beckoned from the storm and made part of an intimate circle. For his ending, Coleridge draws on Southey's 'Isabel' sonnet (XV), which had closed with a glimpse of the Good-Samaritan story popular in Charity Sermons ('the proud Levite scowls and passes by', XV.14). Coleridge picks up the word *scowl* and pictures the scene of 'purple Pride, that scowls on Wretchedness' (XVII.11). But then he turns round on it, so as to remind us of the speaker of the parable:

> He did not scowl, the GALILÆAN mild,
>   Who met the Lazar turn'd from rich man's doors,
>   And call'd him Friend, and wept upon his sores!   (XVII.12–14)

And call'd him Friend. In these words Coleridge moves to that more radical idea, for which the Jesus of the Gospels provided the model: the *Friend of Humanity*. The celebration of personal friendship which this garland of sonnets in part represents begins to find a new political dimension.

After Isabel the suicide, the negro slave, and the wretched old man, the fourth sonnet in this opening, by Thomas Russell (XVIII), adds another vignette to the survey of society's outcasts: a group of poverty-stricken babies, who 'from yon unshelter'd cot | Implore thy passing charity in vain' (XVIII.1–2). The rustic 'cot', which has beckoned from several sonnets in the sequence, now takes on a bleaker character. Like Southey's negro slave, a victim of 'the mangling scourge' (XVI.9), this family also suffers 'th'Oppressor's iron scourge' (XVIII.7), an echo that draws colonial exploitation and rural poverty into the same system of oppression. But after these heart-searching images, Russell's poem provides a moving close for the group of four sonnets by pronouncing a Christian benediction on all the oppressed:

> Yet when their last late evening shall decline,
>   Their evening chearful, tho' their day distrest,
> A Hope perhaps more heavenly-bright than thine,
>   A Grace by thee unsought, and unpossest,
> A Faith more fix'd, a Rapture more divine
>   Shall gild their passage to eternal Rest.   (XVIII.9–14)

After this the page turns, and in the very first line, as if to confirm this hope, we meet Southey's reassuring image of the rainbow: 'Mild arch of promise! on the evening sky' (XIX.1).[35] Across the opening are displayed four sonnets grouped *abba*, thus repeating the pattern of the third opening, where Lamb's sonnets on his lost Anna (XII–XIII) were embraced by those of Sotheby and Coleridge (XI, XIV). This time placed at the centre are two feverish sonnets by Lloyd on his grandmother's death (XX–XXI).[36] Both are remarkable for the dramatic immediacy with which they evoke the old woman's ghost ('The passing breeze!—'Twas She!—The friend pass'd by!', XXI.12) and the death-bed scene:

> (O my choak'd breast!) e'en on that shrunk cheek
> I saw one slow tear roll! My hand she took,
>   Placing it on her heart: I heard her sigh,
>   ''Tis too, too much!' 'twas Love's last agony!
> I tore me from her!   (XX.8–12)

Once more, two very fraught poems are sensitively framed by Coleridge. Introducing them (with the rainbow) is Southey's sonnet on Christian hope (XIX). This offers the reader an adjacent death scene of serene leave-taking, one in which the eyes are lifted far beyond Lloyd's suffocating close-up:

> Such is the smile that Piety bestows
>   On the good man's pale cheek, when he in peace
> Departing gently from a world of woes,
>   Looks onward to the realm where sorrows cease.   (XIX.11–14)[37]

After the two Lloyd sonnets, with similar effect, Coleridge places 'To Tranquillity' by Charlotte Smith (XXII),[38] in which the presence of the watchful

---

[35] Printed as 'To the Evening Rainbow' in Southey's *Poems* (1797), 113.

[36] 'Oh, She was almost speechless!' and 'When from my dreary Home' were both printed in Lloyd's *Poems on the Death of Priscilla Farmer, by her Grandson* (Bristol, 1796), 16 and 15. Coleridge reverses the order.

[37] Writing to Southey, 11 Dec. 1794, Coleridge praised this sonnet, 'particularly the four last Lines...divine and fully equal to Bowles' (Griggs, 133).

[38] Printed as 'Sonnet XLI. To Tranquillity' in Smith's *Elegiac Sonnets*, 5th edn (London, 1789), 41. Coleridge reverses lines 11 and 12. On 31 Oct. 1796 Lloyd reported to his mother on his new domesticity with Coleridge: 'The tranquillity of my present situation, & may I add the almost unblemish'd sanctity of manners which I find in Coleridge, are very pleasant to me—I could not be more happily situated' (see Lynda Pratt, '"Perilous Acquaintance"? Lloyd, Coleridge and Southey in the 1790s: Five Unpublished Letters', *Romanticism*, 6 (2000), 98–115 (103)).

and loving mother causes the image of the deathbed (which holds such terrors for Lloyd) to merge into that of an infant's cradle:

> By the low cradles thou delight'st to sit
> Of sleeping infants—watching the soft breath
>   And bidding the sweet slumberers easy lie;
> Or sometimes hanging o'er the bed of death
>   Where the poor languid sufferer—hopes to die!   (XXII.4–8)

Coleridge takes great care in this four-sonnet group to give Lloyd's frantic words a supportive frame, embracing them reassuringly with sonnets on hope and tranquillity, redirecting his disturbing visions in turn towards the rainbow and the cradle. 'Charles Lloyd has been very ill' (he wrote to Tom Poole on 15 November), 'and his distemper... may with equal propriety be named either Somnambulism, or frightful Reverie, or *Epilepsy from accumulated feelings*'.[39] Coleridge brought in Dr Beddoes, and reported to Lloyd's father that 'he *told* me, that your Son's cure must be effected by Sympathy and Calmness'.[40]

The page turns again, and the final opening of four sonnets presents another disturbed text carefully framed by sympathetic voices. Once again the beneficiary is Lamb, who in this sonnet (XXV) stands at midnight on the deck of a ship contemplating suicide.[41] Coleridge prepares judiciously for this disturbing scene with two tranquil sea-pictures by Charlotte Smith (XXIII)[42] and Thomas Dermody (XXIV),[43] both of them lit by a calming moonlight (made calmer in the latter by Coleridge's re-writing). Smith here offers the full strain of the eighteenth-century melancholy sonnet, perfectly exemplifying that union 'in which moral Sentiments, Affections, or Feelings, are deduced from, and associated with, the scenery of Nature' (Preface). A restful note is struck: 'Tho'

---

[39] Griggs, 257.

[40] Ibid. 256.

[41] Lamb's poem was printed under the title 'Effusion XIII. Written at Midnight, by the Sea-Side, after a Voyage' in Coleridge's 1796 *Poems*, 57–8. See n. 44 below.

[42] From Smith's novel, *Emmeline* (1788); printed as 'Sonnet XXXIX. To Night' in her *Elegiac Sonnets* (1789), 39.

[43] Thomas Dermody (1775–1802). As editor, Coleridge takes great liberties with Dermody's text (not all deliberate). The 24-line sonnet, 'Lonely I sit upon the silent shore', was published in *Anthologia Hibernica: or Monthly Collections of Science, Belles-Lettres, and History*, vol. 1 (March 1793), 225, where it is described as 'Written in the 15th Year of his Age'. Coleridge printed lines 1–16 (not noticing lines 17–24 in the next column) in *The Watchman*, 9 (5 May 1796), 328. Preparing the text for *Sonnets from Various Authors*, Coleridge further reduces the lines from sixteen to fourteen (as with Sotheby's sonnet, n. 27 above). He cuts Dermody's opening six lines to four, and in re-writing makes the scene quieter. Dermody's opening is: 'Lonely I sit upon the silent shore, | Silent, save when the dashing surges break | 'Gainst some steep cliff, in low, and sullen roar, | Or the hoarse gulls on night's still slumber shriek. | Soft streams in tremulous vibration o'er | Ocean's broad, frownless front, the lunar ray'. This becomes in *Sonnets from Various Authors*: 'Lonely I sit upon the silent shore, | Silent, save when against the rocky Bay | Breaks the dead Swell: the Moon soft-trembles o'er | Ocean's broad, frownless front, with streamy ray' (XXIV.1–4). By removing Dermody's 'dashing surges', 'roar', 'hoarse', 'shriek', and 'tremulous vibration', Coleridge creates a more calming effect.

no repose on thy dark breast I find, | I still enjoy thee, cheerless as thou art; | For in thy quiet gloom the exhausted heart | Is calm, tho' wretched' (XXIII.9–12). The melancholy mood continues with Dermody's sonnet, in which Tranquillity and Silence manage to keep the ocean's more sublime features under control ('the Moon soft-trembles o'er | Ocean's broad, frownless front, with streamy ray, | Borne in full many a dimpling wave away' (XXIV.3–5).

In the Lamb sonnet that follows, however, the Sublime is released with full force. The storm has now broken, with the midnight wind scattering the ocean waves; and like a good Burkean, Lamb experiences the contradictory *delight* of the sublime mode ('On wings of winds comes wild-ey'd Phantasy, | And her dread visions give a rude delight!', XXV.5–6). Lamb invokes the dark fantasies of a suicide gazing down at the flood:

> When wet and chilly on thy deck I stood
> Unbonnetted, and gaz'd upon the flood,
> And almost wish'd it were no crime to die!
> How Reason reel'd! What gloomy transports rose!
> Till the rude dashings rock'd them to repose.   (XXV.10–14)

Lamb is held on the brink by Coleridge's pivotal word 'rock'd' which in a dizzying way is poised between falling and slumbering.[44] This is the dramatic climax of the whole sequence: Lamb on the edge.

Who better to step forward now at the height of the storm than Bowles? He reaches out to Lamb's reeling visions, and talks him down. To do so, he has to go to the brink himself. But in this dramatic context it is Lamb to whom he is clearly talking:

> Thou whose stern spirit loves the awful storm
>   That borne on Terror's desolating wings
>   Shakes the deep forest, or remorseless flings
> The shiver'd surge, if bitter griefs deform
> Thy patient soul, O hie thee to the steep
>   That beetles o'er the rude and raving tide,
>   And when thou hear'st distress careering wide,
> Think in a world of woe what thousands weep.   (XXVI.1–8)

The place of suicide becomes, for Bowles, a vantage-point from which to contemplate human misery in general. This is not a time to become giddy, but to use Reason. We noticed how Coleridge earlier placed alongside Lamb's Sonnet XIII the sonnet of his own (XIV) that was Lamb's favourite ('most exquisite & most Bowles-like'). Here Coleridge now prints the

---

[44] Coleridge had included his own revision of Lamb's sonnet in his 1796 *Poems*, 57–8. Lamb responded: '"How reason reeld" &.—, are good lines but must spoil the whole *with me*, who know it is only a fiction of yours & that the rude dashings did in fact *not rock* me to *repose*' (Lamb to Coleridge, 8–10 June 1796; Marrs, 20). When Lamb's sonnet later appeared in Coleridge's 1797 *Poems*, 221, the final couplet ('How Reason... repose') was replaced by two rows of asterisks.

original on which his own was based. Bowles's poem carries a message about remembering Hope at the darkest moment:

> if Hope long since forgot
> Be fled like the wild blast that hears thee not,
> Seek not in Nature's fairer scenes a charm;
> But shroud thee in the mantle of distress
> And tell thy poor heart—this is happiness!   (XXVI.10–14).[45]

The page ends. Up to this point, with two sonnets remaining, the reader has followed a sequence which, I have been arguing, creates a conversation out of individual voices. I have suggested that in returning to the sonnet in the autumn of 1796, and confidently measuring himself with Bowles, Coleridge used its ability to 'domesticate with the heart' to engage with, and guide, the voices of his friends Lloyd and Lamb, at a time when domestic intimacies and focused boundaries were offering hope to each of them. Both Lloyd and Lamb used the sonnet as (in Lamb's phrase) 'a personal poem'.[46] Coleridge, however, sees dangers in this and works to steer their texts to a more extensive sympathy within a broader social/political context. Paul Magnuson has stressed the importance of reading poems in their 'precise locations',[47] and I have been trying to do this, both biographically and (perhaps more importantly) bibliographically. As editor, Coleridge is a subtle shaper and dramatiser of these texts; but the drama is happening across and between the pages. Within the frame he has supplied, Coleridge accommodates these units of thought and experience into his more ample scheme. The 'lonely feeling' at the heart of the sonnet form meets the wider embrace of friendship and sociability. And Coleridge is always there drawing out meanings and ironies from individual poems—sympathising, admonishing, encouraging.

There are, however, two sonnets remaining, and with the final page-turn Coleridge springs a surprise. Just when we think he is settling down and drawing his friends into the social circle, we encounter Anna Seward's sonnet to Ingratitude ('Ingratitude, how deadly is thy smart | Proceeding from the form we fondly love!' XXVII.1–2).[48] With this poem Coleridge invokes the betrayal of friendship, and in contrarian mood he chooses to voice it in the words of the very writer whose sonnets he had attacked in the preface as 'laborious trifles'.[49] Through Seward's words we experience the

---

[45] Lloyd used lines 13–14 of Bowles's sonnet 'In a Storm' as the half-title motto for his section of 'Poems', included in Coleridge's 1797 *Poems*.

[46] On 9 June 1796, Lamb had taken Coleridge gently to task for re-wording some of his sonnets in the 1796 *Poems*, telling him: 'I love my own *feelings*. . . . I charge you, Col. *spare my ewe lambs*' (Marrs, 20). See p. 213 below.

[47] Paul Magnuson, *Reading Public Romanticism* (Princeton: Princeton University Press, 1998), 3–10.

[48] Seward's sonnet had just appeared in her *Llangollen Vale, with Other Poems* (London: G. Sael, 1796), 43.

[49] '[T]heir inverted sentences, their quaint phrases, and incongruous mixture of obsolete and spenserian words; and when, at last, the thing is toiled, and hammered into fit shape, it is in

inversion of the sympathetic social converse on which the sequence has been based; and as if to announce this volte-face, Bowles's vision in the previous sonnet of the 'kindred prospect' (XXVI.9) is now transposed to Seward's 'kindred callousness' (XXVII.12).

And the last word, of course, must be Coleridge's. He had opened the pamphlet with Bowles's sonnet 'To a Friend', but he ends the sequence by turning away from Bowles, and his friends, to address the figure of Schiller and celebrate German romantic drama. He evokes the scene in Act IV of *The Robbers*, where a father emerges from an airless dungeon to discover that his son has betrayed him (more ingratitude here). Coleridge's sublime poet, with a Shakespearean 'fine frenzy', almost seems to burst the bounds of the sonnet and reach for the loftier ode:

> Ah! Bard tremendous in sublimity!
>   Could I behold thee in thy loftier mood,
> Wand'ring at eve with finely frenzied eye
>   Beneath some vast old tempest-swinging wood!
>   Awhile with mute awe gazing I would brood,
> Then weep aloud in a wild extacy!   (XXVIII.9–14)[50]

To end his sequence, thus, is in some ways an act of defiance, a turn away from the compact world of the sonnet to a greater challenge beyond— whether his friends liked it or not. Lamb did like it: 'Schiller might have written it', he said.[51] But John Thelwall did not, especially those last six lines. Hence the note Coleridge added after this sonnet in the V&A copy, the one he sent to Mrs Thelwall:

I affirm, John Thelwall! that the six last lines of this Sonnet to Schiller are strong & fiery; and you are the only one who thinks otherwise.—There, a *spurt* of Author-like vanity for you!—[52]

After so amicably guiding the voices of Lamb and Lloyd through the sequence, Coleridge ends almost impatiently with a newly confident aware- ness of his own voice, and with a reminder that the sonnet can burst the bounds of the domestic and express the creative energies of the poet. If *Sonnets from Various Authors* represents Coleridge's least known Con- versation Poem, it ends with an intimation of the world of 'Kubla Khan', opening out the previously contained textual dialogue to project a visionary desiring self. With the final page Coleridge is conscious of turning over a new leaf, and this awareness of his little book as a physical object suggests that he

---

general racked and tortured Prose rather than any thing resembling Poetry. Miss Seward...has perhaps succeeded the best in these laborious trifles' (*Sonnets from Various Authors*, 2).

[50] Printed as 'Effusion XX. To the Author of "The Robbers"', in Coleridge's 1796 *Poems*, 65. For *Sonnets from Various Authors* Coleridge prints lines 1–4 in reverse order.

[51] Marrs, 20.

[52] On Coleridge's poetic debate with Thelwall, see Chapter 10 below.

saw it as something more organic than an appendix. The consideration with which these twenty-eight sonnets have been chosen and ordered is evident in their physical arrangement. Verbal and thematic echoes find palpable expression as the various texts meet, touch, and embrace. Bibliographical coding becomes a mode of communication, and individual 'lonely' meanings become more dynamic as they are released into something greater.

9   Organising Friendship: Coleridge, Lamb, and Lloyd

I HAVE ARGUED that in ordering his *Sonnets from Various Authors*, Coleridge was conscious of organising his friendships too. To be a friend of Coleridge was to enter a powerful force field of someone for whom friendship was 'an idea in process, changing with differing relationships'. In his important study of Coleridge's male friendships during the 1790s, Gurion Taussig finds it useful to distinguish friendship from love in spatial terms: rather than being a yearning for unity, he says, 'friendship constantly negotiates difference, and in respecting another's unique identity concerns itself both with the creation of closeness and the preservation of boundaries between friends'.[1] The organic character of such intimacy comes through in the way that togetherness depends on separateness (as it did for Barbauld's mother and baby). True 'closeness' allows boundaries to touch and engage; creative continuities and interconnections are formed between separate identities.[2] This is where problems can arise.

In the early weeks of their friendship, Southey evidently raised this very topic with Coleridge in a letter that does not survive. Coleridge's reply shows how alert he is to the spatial dynamics of male intimacy, and to its various contingencies (from Lat. *contingo*, 'to touch'). The passage shows him to be conscious of friendship as something that needs to be negotiated with care, particularly in relation to the individual identities of the two parties:

> Warmth of particular Friendship does not imply absorption. The nearer you approach the Sun, the more intense are his Rays—yet what distant corner of the System do they not cheer and vivify? The ardour of private Attachments makes Philanthropy a necessary *habit* of the Soul. I love my *Friend*—such as *he* is, all mankind are or *might be*! The deduction is evident—Philanthropy (and indeed every other Virtue) is a thing of *Concretion*—Some home-born Feeling is the *center* of the Ball, that, rolling on thro' Life collects and assimilates every congenial Affection.[3]

---

[1] Gurion Taussig, *Coleridge and the Idea of Friendship, 1789–1804* (Newark: University of Delaware Press; London: Associated University Presses, 2002), 18, 20. Taussig is developing the distinction pursued by Laurence S. Lockridge, *Coleridge the Moralist* (Ithaca/London: Cornell University Press, 1977), 185–6.

[2] Wordsworth would imagine his potential friendship with Burns in the same organic terms: 'True friends, though diversely inclined; | But heart with heart and mind with mind, | Where the main fibres are entwined, | Through Nature's skill, | May even by contraries be joined | More closely still' ('At the Grave of Burns, 1803', 43–8).

[3] Coleridge to Southey, 13 July 1794 (Griggs, 86).

Coleridge seems aware of how different modes of organisation could come into play, and his vocabulary is suggestive of the pressures that might develop: absorption is at first denied, but then re-emerges at the end as assimilation; there is ardour and intensity, as well as the habitual and congenial; alongside the language of power and distance is that of attachment and affection. He begins with the solar system as his model, but ends with something more localised and homely that is closer to Shandean association ('Life collects and assimilates every congenial Affection'). We move from far-off radiance to the immediate and tactile, from the ardour of the soul to the layerings of experience (*Concretion*), from the majestic sun to the rolling stone. It is within these far-flung coordinates—between 'is' and '*might be*'—that Coleridgean friendship operates.

Organic issues are raised here in terms of individual identity; and the forces being brought into play are potentially creative, supportive, or destructive. At one moment the idea is of sharing and giving; at another it appears to be collecting and assimilating. A radiant illumination promises to find its way into hidden corners, and to burn at close range. The whole passage offers an uneasy scenario, but one that might be borne in mind throughout this chapter, in which poetry not only takes friendship for its subject but provides its medium of expression, almost its contractual terms.

Charles Lamb and Charles Lloyd did not meet till January 1797, but thanks to Coleridge's good offices their poetic association was already in place. As we have seen, the pair had been brought together in *Sonnets from Various Authors*; and Lamb's blank-verse poem 'The Grandam' was printed at the end of Lloyd's 1796 volume, *Poems on the Death of Priscilla Farmer.*[4] (Lamb remarked on 'the odd coincidence of two young men, in one age, carolling their grandmothers'.[5]) Their verses would together occupy a hundred pages of Coleridge's 1797 *Poems*, and their poetic bond would be confirmed in *Blank Verse, by Charles Lloyd and Charles Lamb* (1798). Both men at this time were highly sensitive and emotionally vulnerable, and they came to see Coleridge as their mentor at the deepest level of 'Guide, Philosopher, and Friend'.[6] But within Coleridge's circle, friendship took on different functions. As a pledge of equality it sealed the Pantisocratic brotherhood, the comradeship of the Susquehanna campfire; but for those non-Pantisocrats, Lamb and Lloyd, a friend fulfilled a more protective role, and one that needed to be circumspect and considerate. Friendship was for them inseparable from a process of poetic nurturing, a mixture of encouragement and care that allowed personal meanings to be expressed and

---

[4] Charles Lloyd, *Poems on the Death of Priscilla Farmer* (Bristol: N. Biggs, 1796), 25–7. Lloyd notes: 'I am indebted to a Friend of the Author's for the permission'.

[5] Lamb to Coleridge, 9 Dec. 1796 (Marrs, 74).

[6] Alexander Pope, *Imitations of Horace*, Epistle I.1 ('to Bolingbroke'), l. 177. Sara Coleridge recalled that Lloyd was 'painfully sensitive in all that related to the affections'. See E. V. Lucas, *Charles Lamb and the Lloyds* (London, 1898), 19.

communicated. It helped to give a degree of confidence and self-belief. In this chapter, poetic organisation is therefore not just incidental or illustrative, but is the medium through which friendship operates. It is clear that the finely tuned sensitivities of Lamb and Lloyd required careful handling, and that this consideration had a bearing on the nature of textual meaning as they conceived it. In poetic negotiations their identities and values were at stake.

During this period, friendships among the Coleridge circle were being bonded by poetry, and poetic identities were combined and sometimes blurred. Hardly a letter is without its offerings of intimate verses, its hints and responses, improvements, criticisms, or suggestions. Sonnets are amicably shared ('Of the following Sonnet the four *last* Lines were written by Lamb'[7]) or returned with 'improvements' ('I read with heart and *taste* equally delighted your Prefatory Sonnet. I transcribe not so much to give you my corrections as for the pleasure it gives me'[8]). Coleridge sends the sestet of a sonnet to Southey, begging him 'to weave into it the gorgeous Water Lily from thy stream'—a challenge Southey at once takes up by jotting down a potential octave.[9] Coleridge's collaborator on *The Fall of Robespierre*, and his host on *Joan of Arc*, was happy to go halves with his friend. As Coleridge noted inside Southey's copy of the 1797 *Poems*: 'There were 3 or 4 Sonnets, of which so many lines were written by Southey & so many by me, that we agreed to divide them, in order to avoid the ridiculous anxiety of attributing different lines in the same short poem to two different Authors.'[10]

While writing the phrase 'ridiculous anxiety' Coleridge may have remembered the recent occasion when authorial sensitivities were hurt by the liberties he took in editing Lamb's sonnets for inclusion in his 1796 *Poems*. It became evident that his friend had a deep emotional investment in them. The words had after all been entrusted to a poetic form which, in Coleridge's own words, could 'domesticate with the heart, and become, as it were, a part of our identity'.[11] Lamb sets out as clearly as he can why he feels Coleridge's handling of his sonnets as a kind of violation:

I love my sonnets because they are the reflected images of my own feelings at different times... They are dear to *memory*, tho' they now & then wake a sigh or a tear. 'Thinking on divers things fore done'. I charge you, Col. *spare my ewe lambs* ... I would not wrong your feelings by proposing any improvements (Did I think myself capable of suggesting *em*) in such personal poems as 'Thou bleedest my poor heart' ...Do you *understand me?* ...I say unto you again Col. Spare my *Ewe lambs*.[12]

---

[7] Coleridge to Southey, 11 Dec. 1794 (Griggs, 136).
[8] Coleridge to Southey, 29 Dec. 1794 (Griggs, 146).
[9] Coleridge to Southey, 17 Dec. 1794 (Griggs, 141).
[10] See Mays, i.193.
[11] See p. 194 above.
[12] Lamb to Coleridge, 8–10 June 1796 (Marrs, 20–1). The allusion is to the parable of King David's murder of Uriah (2 Sam. 12), in retribution for which his own child has to die.

This fascinating letter, with its parable of cruelty and sacrifice, suggests that Lamb cherishes his sonnets as representing something innocent and vulnerable that is part of himself. Their words have the power to link him back through memory to what exists no more (Lamb's evidently invented phrase, 'Thinking on divers things fore done', calls to mind the portentous tones of the Anglican prayer book). Rather than working to bring a scene or event into being, or making it live, Lamb's sonnet text represents a memento (linked to a memory) or a token (an authenticating sign) of something no longer present. The poetry is about the sense of loss, not about the original experience, which remains a secret.

This seems to be happening, I think, in the Lamb sonnet Coleridge entitled 'Effusion 11' when he revised it for printing in his 1796 *Poems*.[13] In the opening lines of Lamb's original version, eventually restored in the 1797 *Poems*, we find a moment of human intimacy being re-lived as a motif from romance:

> Was it some sweet Delight of Faery
> That mock'd my steps with many a lonely glade
> And fancied wand'rings with a fair-hair'd maid?
> Have these things been? Or what rare witchery
> (Impregning with delights the charmed air)
> Enlighted up the semblance of a smile
> In those fine eyes? ...　　　　　　　　　　　　(1–7)

The Spenserian language works with real delicacy here, catching the possibly deceptive delight of her response. The phrase 'Enlighted up the semblance' still works in terms of a spell-binding human moment, but adds a hint of falseness, a realisation of the scene as a childish fiction he might have outgrown. The word 'witchery' combines with 'charmed air' to suggest the power of Comus's magic dust, 'of power to cheat the eye with blear illusion'.[14]

Coleridge's changes, beginning with his first-line emendation of 'Delight' to 'device', make the deception explicit; the spell is spelt out:

> Have these things been? Or did the wizard wand
> Of Merlin wave, impregning vacant air,
> And kindle up the vision of a smile
> In those blue eyes ...　　　　　　　　　　　　(4–7)

---

[13] See p. 202 above. Coleridge persisted in printing his revised text when he selected it for *Sonnets from Various Authors* (see p. 000 above).

[14] John Milton, *Ludlow Masque*, 153–6, 164–6 (*The Poetical Works of John Milton*, ed. Helen Darbishire, 2 vols (Oxford: Clarendon Press, 1952–5), ii.190). Cf. 'great *Comus*, | Deep skill'd in all his mothers witcheries' (522–3). Coleridge's 'witchery' in 'Songs of the Pixies' reappears in 'The Eolian Harp' (see pp. 167, 180 above).

Lamb's glimpsed moment is turned into a 'vision', and the intrusive figure of Merlin materialises on the scene (this especially grated with Lamb).[15] Coleridge's air is 'vacant', but in Lamb's text it is 'charmed', atmospherically charged, though by what magic he does not know: the 'witchery' may still be hers. As for the 'blue eyes', Coleridge's phrase puts on record an incidental fact that distracts us from the mystery those eyes possess. We sense how Lamb's poem is about both elusiveness and transience, and the problem of differentiating them; Coleridge's text is, almost sarcastically, wondering what it takes to produce a response (with 'kindle' adding the idea of arousal). His clear division between fact and illusion creates an 'either-or' situation, with 'Or' (line 4) sounding almost like an ultimatum. Lamb's 'Or' simply extends the possibilities. From the moment Coleridge notices the lame repetition of 'Delight' (1) and 'delights' (5) and removes it, it is clear he does not trust Lamb's unresolved wondering—the thread that holds his fragile text together.

The endings of the two versions of the sonnet offer a similar contrast. Lamb continues to wonder quietly, to spin his fine thread:

> And does the lonely glade
> Still court the footsteps of the fair-hair'd maid?
> Still in her locks the gales of summer sigh?
> While I forlorn do wander, heedless where,
> And 'mid my wanderings meet no Anna there!   (10–14)

Coleridge's speaker is realised more dramatically. He gives an audible sigh, and knows she must be somewhere:

> Ah me! The lonely glade
> Still courts the footsteps of the fair-hair'd maid,
> Among whose locks the west-winds love to sigh:
> But I forlorn do wander, reckless where,
> And mid my wand'rings find no ANNA there!

Lamb's aimless wandering becomes Coleridge's frustrated search. Lamb's 'heedless' mood is not 'reckless': it is simply inattentive, oblivious of direction. Lamb's intense memory of her hair is opened out into a full allegorical topos: Coleridge's west winds seem to have taken occupation, and the picture is realised for us like Botticelli's 'Primavera'. Coleridge stages the scene, gives us the rationale, clarifies the picture. We can see what he is doing and why. But somehow, the enigmatic essence of Lamb's sonnet has escaped. We may sense its talismanic meaning for Lamb himself, something we can never fully share but which has power to intrigue us. Coleridge turns a private text into one that is sharper and more immediate for a reader who

---

[15] '[I]t looks so like MR *Merlin* the ingenius successor of the immortal Merlin, now living in good health & spirits, & flourishing in Magical Reputation, in Oxford Street' (Lamb to Coleridge, 10 Jan. 1797; Marrs, 86).

lacks Lamb's unique template of memory. In an uncanny sense Lamb's sonnet really does 'contain' his identity, and it seems as if *meaning* is something he has entrusted to it, rather than expressed by it. Coleridge has developed and embodied it in various ways, but however sympathetically this has been done it has the effect of superimposing his own imagination on that of his friend. It is an entirely amicable gesture, a sharing of identities within the intimacy of a sonnet; but Lamb's text is just too diaphanous not to be overshadowed by the result.

Sympathetic friendship, as we saw in the previous chapter, was something that Coleridge felt able to provide for Lamb and Lloyd. He appreciated Lamb's vulnerability, especially in the wake of the 'day of horrors' (22 September 1796), and wrote in the most graceful and delicate terms to invite him to visit, assuring him that 'no visitants shall blow on the nakedness of your feelings; you shall be quiet, and your spirit may be healed'.[16] He also understood Lloyd's need for 'Sympathy and Calmness', and how an intimate converse could have a positive effect ('it must be in tete a tete with one whom he loves & esteems, that his colloquial powers open').[17] It is almost as if Coleridge had in mind one of Lloyd's own sonnets in which he pictures his soul responding to just such a friend. Before he met either Coleridge or Lamb, Lloyd published his debut collection, *Poems on Various Subjects* (1795), and the volume opens with a 'Dedicatory Sonnet: Ad Amicos', in which he invokes the fostering power of his small band of friends:

> How would the soul unsatisfied, and cold,
>   Pine all unconscious of its secret powers,
> Those powers did fostering Friendship ne'er unfold,
>   Nor ward with fond attempt each storm that lowers.
> To You then, of the firm, tho' little band
>   Of those I love!—who sweetly have endear'd
> Some moments far too fleeting, and have fann'd
>   The trembling flame of virtue, who have rear'd
>   That *secret worth* that heeds nor blame nor praise—
>   To You I consecrate these random lays.[18]   (5–14)

The 'fostering Friendship' Lloyd celebrates here slides uneasily between the parental and the fraternal. What begins as a soul unfolding in a sheltered spot, like a seed responding to the warmth of spring, becomes something closer to a Quaker 'inner light' encouraged by the circle of friends. But the 'trembling flame' is no campfire. In this idealist scenario friendship does not mean mixing, engaging, or adapting—this is not a Lockean consciousness being shaped by empirical experience. The poem creates a tension between

---

[16] Coleridge to Lamb, 28 Sept. 1796 (Griggs, 239).

[17] Coleridge to Charles Lloyd Sr., 14 Nov. 1796 (Griggs, 256); Coleridge to Poole, 24 Sept. 1796 (Griggs, 237). See above, pp. 198, 206.

[18] Charles Lloyd, *Poems on Various Subjects* (Carlisle: F. Jollie, 1795), 3.

what is opened out and what is secret and contained, so that the picture is less one of friendly exchange than of priests gathered round a sacred flame. At the very moment of celebrating his intimate circle of friends, Lloyd is investing in the virtue of secrecy, and the secrecy of virtue. Identities remain inviolate. Value and meaning are here intrinsic and private, and if given protection and encouragement will grow in defiance of any critical context ('heeds nor blame nor praise'). In Lloyd's fragile sonnet world the self is carefully nurtured, its potential for fulfilment recalling the idealist tradition of organicism discussed in Chapter 1 ('it shapes as it develops itself from within, and the fullness of its development is one and the same with the perfection of its outward form').[19] But there are also elements of Priestleyan vitalism here, as if Lloyd represents a precarious cultivar that needs a benign atmosphere in which to thrive. The closest analogy I can find to lines 5–7 is from Mark Akenside's *The Pleasures of Imagination* (1744) where Platonism and embryology (Akenside's two great intellectual interests) combine in picturing the unfolding powers of the soul:

> What high, capacious pow'rs
> Lie folded up in man; how far beyond
> The praise of mortals, may th'eternal growth
> Of nature to perfection half divine,
> Expand the blooming soul?[20]

By making 'fostering Friendship' a requirement for his version of this mystical process, Lloyd introduces an unstable factor not under his control. With his soul as a sacred trust that must be cherished and guarded, Lloyd is in danger of surrendering the initiative, and much of the responsibility, to his friend, while keeping his private inner world intact. And for Coleridge to be in attendance on Lloyd's 'trembling flame' was courting disaster.

As these examples of their sonnets suggest, some of the poems of Lamb and Lloyd at this time mount guard on identity and have an element of secrecy about them.[21] Rather than projecting a thought or attitude, they tend to contain and protect their meanings, as if there is a soul dwelling at the core whose truth cannot be betrayed. The words enshrine the idea. Their verse raises questions about the degree to which a poetic identity has to compromise, even contaminate itself, in expression. Lamb especially was unwilling to do this. In January 1797 he wrote to Coleridge about the sonnet

[19] *Coleridge's Shakespearean Criticism*, ed. T. M. Raysor, 2 vols (London: Constable and Co, 1930), i.224. See p. 16 above, note 6.

[20] Mark Akenside, *The Pleasures of Imagination* (1744), i.222–6. The lines are the same in the revised 1772 text. Akenside wrote his MD dissertation on 'The Origin and Growth of the Human Foetus'.

[21] For a reading of their verse which stresses the political context and discusses the radical songs in Lloyd's 1795 volume, see David Fairer, 'Baby Language and Revolution: The Early Poetry of Charles Lloyd and Charles Lamb', *CLB*, 74 (April 1991), 33–52. See also Burton R. Pollin, 'Charles Lamb and Charles Lloyd as Jacobins and Anti-Jacobins', *SiR*, 12 (1973), 633–47.

addressed to his sister Mary ('Friend of my earliest years, & childish days'), which he sent for inclusion in Coleridge's 1797 *Poems*. Lamb begins in apology but ends with a disarming resistance:

I am aware of the *unpoetical cast* of the 6 last lines of my last sonnet, & think myself unwarranted in smuggling so tame a thing into the book; only the sentiments of those 6 lines are thoroughly conginial to me in my state of mind, & I wish to accumulate perpetuating tokens of my affection to poor Mary.[22]

It is an admission of Lamb's fondness for secrecy ('smuggling') and for accumulating 'tokens' to preserve a lost moment or vanished scene. The fact that they are small, simple, and vulnerable increases their value as a part of himself that he locks away and treasures. In Lamb's non-Platonic idealism, a text's value lies in its power to contain the private associative idea/memory that already 'means' so much to him. It is therefore in tension with the organic procedures this book has been noticing, where meanings proliferate, adapt, and interrelate, or work through associative juxtaposition and superimposition. Lamb's meaning is not in the activity of the poem but in the idea it betokens. It is associative, but in the more limited sense of a personal association that cannot be experienced by the reader, an enshrined value rather than an articulated meaning:

> In my poor mind it is most sweet to muse
> Upon the days gone by; to act, in thought,
> Past seasons o'er, and be again a child;
> To sit, in fancy, on the turf clad slope,
> Down which the child would roll; to pluck gay flowers,
> Make posies in the sun . . . [23]

Throughout this poem ('Childhood') the scene never escapes from Lamb's mind. Such precious moments cannot be shared, and to return to the actual 'turf clad slope' would be dangerous. This is not a Wartonian revisiting, which would allow new things to be noticed, and bring fresh ideas and relations into play. Unlike Southey's 'The Retrospect', the text does not risk experiencing difference, growth, and change, which might open up organic possibilities. Instead, this would seem to be a genuine example of nostalgia, the word often carelessly used in criticism to label any thoughtful retrospect. Here in Lamb's lines, what might be channels for expansion and development (mind, thought, and imagination) in turn become containers that close down and internalise the scene: 'In my poor mind', 'to act, in thought', 'To sit, in fancy'. It is as though the poet needs reassurance that nothing will arise

[22] Lamb to Coleridge, 7–10 Jan. 1797 (see Marrs, 83, 87). Lamb's sonnet was published in the *Monthly Magazine*, 4 (Oct. 1797), 288, but not in Coleridge's 1797 volume (Marrs, 85). See n. 54 below.
[23] Charles Lamb, 'Childhood', 1–6 (1797 *Poems*, 227).

in the poem to spoil the view. He already has the image in his own memory and has made it his own.

But another friend entered the scene in January 1797 when Lamb had a surprise visit from Lloyd, who was staying in London while Coleridge settled into his new home at Nether Stowey. The first meeting of Lamb and Lloyd was evidently an emotional experience, and in reporting it to Coleridge Lamb included a newly written poem (intended for publication in 'our little volume'), 'To Charles Lloyd, An unexpected Visitor'. As a poem about a new friendship, it is disconcerting in its twists and turns. At the opening there are elements of doubt and suspicion: the men encounter one another as two strangers awkwardly contemplating a potential contract: 'Why seeks my Lloyd the Stranger out? | What offring can the Stranger bring... ?' (3–4).[24] The next movement sees Lloyd as 'a kindly loiterer' (12) who, it is suggested, is humouring Lamb and might really prefer to be back at home with Coleridge. Then comes a sudden explosion in the blood, with Lamb's joyful blushing and his 'o'ercharg'd bursting heart' that wants to respond to his new friend. But after this outburst of emotion Lloyd's impact is at once internalised and possessed. Although Lloyd is still with Lamb in London, he has already left the present:

> The voice hath spoke: the pleasant sounds
> In memory's ear, in after-time
> Shall live, to sometimes rouse a tear,
> And sometimes prompt an honest rhyme.   (21–4)

Paradoxically, by slipping into the past, Lloyd becomes a pledge for the future. This is a powerful idea; and as time stretches out, Lamb's feeling becomes more intense in recollection, and the sense more vivid for being 'cherish'd' in the memory. For Lamb in return, being recalled to Lloyd's mind will help confirm his own identity and self-worth, as the poem's ending says:

> Long, long, within my aching heart
> The grateful sense shall cherish'd be:
> I'll think less meanly of myself
> That Lloyd will sometimes think on me.   (29–32)

At their very first meeting Lamb is writing a memorial to their friendship. The poem ends with something like a bargain, a trust now shared between friends: each will be sustained in the other's thoughts. But we notice that the poem, although addressed to Lloyd, is a commentary on Lamb's thoughts and feelings rather than a direct expression of them. The role of the imagination appears to be to seal the moment, so that Lamb can carry it with him

---

[24] Lamb to Coleridge, 16 Jan. 1797 (Marrs, 92). The text of Lamb's transcription is identical, save for a few accidentals, to that printed in 1797 *Poems*, 238–40. I quote from the letter text.

'when the transient charm is fled, | And when the little week is o'er' (25–6). In place of a poetic image that realises their new friendship there is a 'perpetuating token' that Lamb can hold onto.

What we might call the associative *memento* is also at the heart of Lamb's relationship with Coleridge, whose letters become much more than communications: they are received as the equivalent of sonnets, domesticating with Lamb and becoming a part of his identity:

> I stared with wild wonderment to see thy well-known hand again . . . Before I even opened thy letter, I figured to myself a sort of complacency which my little hoard at home would feel at receiving the new-comer into the little drawer where I keep my treasures of this kind. You have done well in writing to me. The little room (was it not a little one?) at the Salutation was already in the way of becoming a fading idea! It had begun to be classed in my memory with those 'wanderings with a fair hair'd maid', in the recollection of which I feel I have no property.[25]

The little domestic drawer is the place where things of value are stored. It is Lamb's equivalent of his memory, a 'home' for the precious possessions that he longs to keep—until they are alienated from him. The sonnet 'Was it some sweet Delight of Faery' he feels he no longer owns, thanks to Coleridge. But his mental shrine to their friendship, his image of the other 'little room' at the Salutation and Cat, still survives as an idea, albeit fading with time. His letters to Coleridge often revisit that sociable space as a precious 'association' for him, and Lamb repeatedly recalls 'all its associated train of pipes, tobacco, Egghot, Welch Rabbits, metaphysics & *Poetry*'.[26] Coleridge's new letter will help to sharpen this image in his mind and prevent it from slipping away. Lamb's memory has this proprietorial aspect, and he loves to take out his treasures and review them. His 'little hoard' in his 'little drawer' represents what is imaginatively essential to him, something made treasurable by its very littleness. It is compacted, concentred, like the soul itself, the jewel in the casket. His precious sonnet, however, has been blurred and recoloured by someone else.

Lamb visited Coleridge at Nether Stowey in July 1797, an experience which, immediately on his return, became a valuable one. Lamb wrote apologising for his uncommunicativeness during his week's stay: 'I could not talk much while I was with you, but my silence was not sullenness . . . I know I behaved myself . . . most like a sulky child; but company and converse are strange to me. It was kind in you all to endure me as you did.' Now back in London, however, he registers a great deal: 'many a little thing, which when I was present with you seemed scarce to *indent* my notice, now presses painfully on my remembrance.' The memory of his visit has a physical weight of impression that the immediate experience did not:

---

[25] Lamb to Coleridge, 13 June 1797 (Marrs, 110).
[26] Marrs, 65. See also 18, 32, 78, 93.

'I forgot my "treasure's worth" while I possessed it,' he significantly adds.[27] Lamb's allusion is to the opening passage of Book 6 of Cowper's *The Task* ('not to understand a treasure's worth | 'Till time has stol'n away the slighted good') and it catches his own sense of spatiotemporal misalignment. The thought, which had lodged in Lamb's mind, is introduced a few lines earlier in Cowper's poem: 'How readily we wish time spent revok'd, | That we might try the ground again, where once | (Through inexperience as we now perceive) | We miss'd that happiness we might have found'.[28] Cowper's word 'inexperience' is telling, hinting at an inorganic unwillingness to engage, a shying away from experience until it can be fully possessed as idea.

But out of the occasion of Lamb's 1797 visit came the memorable poem in which he is given both 'company and converse', and which triumphantly overcomes a sense of 'miss[ing] that happiness we might have found'. Coleridge's 'This Lime-Tree Bower My Prison' gains from being placed in dialogue with Lamb's tendency to idealise and memorialise, and live in private retrospect. Coleridge is happy and engaged in the scene although absent, whereas Lamb was evidently disengaged and sullen although present. Coleridge's is an expansive poem exploring not only friendly sympathies and treasured associations, but also projected and shared identities. And it is a text which, although about a vicarious experience ('as though myself were there'), doesn't memorialise, but actively lives (not re-lives) the experience through the words in the text. Coleridge's poem is an organic one, not by any tendency to idealise or unify, but on the contrary through its exploration of continuities and associations, its openness to connecting, mixing, and adapting. 'This Lime-Tree Bower My Prison' opens out the private experience, the single identity, and brings it into conversation with the mind, senses, and emotions. In what follows I shall be discussing the earliest 55-line version transcribed in Coleridge's letter to Southey, 17 July 1797, a few days after Lamb's departure.

After the opening picture of Coleridge's enforced isolation and constraint, emphasised by the stress of 'Well—*they* are gone: and here must *I* remain' (my italics), the text begins its interesting, and interested, journey into a landscape of varying relationships and conjunctions. Individual identity is explored through appositions, in which things engage with each other in space and time, the composed and discomposed together:

> My friends, whom I may never meet again,
> On springy heath, along the hill-top edge,
> Wander delighted, and look down, perchance,
> On that same rifted Dell, where many an Ash
> Twists it's wild limbs beside the ferny rock,
> Whose plumy ferns for ever nod and drip
> Spray'd by the waterfall. (4–10)

[27] Lamb to Coleridge, 19 or 26 July 1797 (Marrs, 117–18).
[28] William Cowper, *The Task* (1785), vi.50–1, 25–9.

Immediately the keynote is responsiveness, with the buoyancy of the foot on the grass, and the nodding of the ferns to the waterfall. A sense of rhythm is created when he notices how the 'nod and drip' eternally alternate as the droplet pulls the fern down—weight and release, weight and release. After the static contortion of the tree's 'wild limbs', that tiny sequence sets extreme delicacy alongside tortured strength, and prompts us to think how small movements might be missed, while static power may seem animated.

The secluded dell becomes the appropriate place for Coleridge to intro-duce an aside. The poem's momentum is suspended while he turns to his friend:

> But chiefly Thou,
> My gentle-hearted CHARLES! thou, who hast pin'd
> And hunger'd after Nature many a year
> In the great City pent, winning thy way,
> With sad yet bowed soul, thro' evil & pain
> And strange calamity.—   (10–15)

Although there is sympathy in the difficult, impeded movement of this, we should also note that it is a parenthetical passage, inserted into the dynamic description of the landscape and halting the poem's progress (it could be omitted without affecting the metre). The poem seems to stop to accommo-date Lamb, insulating him from everything around.

After this, the resumed description brings a fresh sense of release, an exclamation in which the scene is gorgeously lit by the refracted sunset colours. Again the poem insists on how things variously enter our conscious-ness; angles turn, and the plane of vision shifts from the horizontal track to the downward look into the private place, and now out across to the 'slant beams' of the sun, kindling and enriching as they sink, giving everything new tints: 'Richlier burn, ye Clouds! | Live in the yellow Light, ye distant Groves! | And kindle, thou blue Ocean!' (18–20). There is what seems an unimpeded gaze; and it is at this moment of distant horizons that the text pauses, and makes its move from human spatial perceptions into the world of Idea. Taking an amicable risk, Coleridge trusts his friend Lamb to be our vantage point, and it is through his consciousness that we encounter the enigmatic all-sustaining 'presence' of the scene.[29] The Newtonian optics of refraction give way to Berkeleyan vision, according to which 'all Visible Things are equally in the Mind, and take up no part of the External Space'.[30] What follows, then, is nothing less than Lamb's expansive mental transfiguration:

---

[29] Like the previous Lamb passage, this could also be omitted without affecting the metre. For a reading of the poem as offering Lamb religious consolation in the 'One Life', see William A. Ulmer, 'The Rhetorical Occasion of "This Lime-Tree Bower my Prison"', *Romanticism*, 13 (2007), 15–27.

[30] George Berkeley, *An Essay Towards a New Theory of Vision* (Dublin: Jeremy Pepyat, 1709), 127.

> So my friend
> Struck with joy's deepest calm, and gazing round
> On the wide view, may gaze till all doth seem
> Less gross than bodily, a living Thing
> That acts upon the mind, and with such hues
> As cloathe the Almighty Spirit, when he makes
> Spirits perceive His presence! (20–6)

Lamb is given a potentially ecstatic, unbounded vision in which distance and 'presence' coalesce. From this Berkeleyan viewpoint, visual perception no longer conveys inferences about an external world, but itself constitutes reality and meaning. The subtitle of Berkeley's 1733 vindication of his *New Theory of Vision* is 'Visual Language, shewing The *Immediate Presence* and Providence of a Deity' (my italics), and this is the language Lamb's mind is experiencing: '[T]he true Nature of Vision', Berkeley maintains, is 'a Faculty of the Soul'.[31] At this point of his transcription Coleridge teases Southey with a footnote to the phrase 'wide view' (line 22), which reads: 'You remember, I am a *Berkleian*.' The note self-consciously highlights the philosophical element of the passage, reminding his reader that what might be the transcendent, 'spiritual' core of the text is also about the potential sublimity of experiencing one's own mental space.

But then, by way of Coleridge's shared delight in this visionary climax, we are recalled to the now and here, where the lime-tree bower, no longer constraining, takes on an equivalent animation. Within Coleridge's living prison is being performed his own miniature, domestic version of the glorious sunset:

> I watch'd
> The sunshine of each broad transparent Leaf
> Broke by the shadows of the Leaf or Stem,
> Which hung above it: and that Wall-nut Tree
> Was richly ting'd: and a deep radiance lay
> Full on the ancient ivy which usurps
> Those fronting elms, and now with blackest mass
> Makes their dark foliage gleam a lighter hue
> Thro' the last twilight. (29–37)

The reader is aware of being drawn back from ideal 'immediate' vision into the sensuous detail of the poem's activities, where once again all is relative and mediated. The light that remains is filtered and shared out, giving different effects as angles and alignments change. The scene is one of busy simultaneity; everything is being observed and characterised by relationship.

---

[31] George Berkeley, *The Theory of Vision, or Visual Language... Vindicated and Explained* (London: J. Tonson, 1733), 37. Seamus Perry shrewdly notes that 'the use to which Berkeley is put is actually rather tentative, the language clearly implying the continuing *materiality* of the landscape' (*Coleridge and the Uses of Division* (Oxford: Oxford University Press, 1999), 151).

Superimposition is a key idea, with the individual lime-leaves overlaying each other, remitting and mediating the light between them in impressionist collaboration. Surface effects are repeatedly given depth, with the walnut tree being 'richly ting'd', its transient colour seeming deep-dyed. And the phrase 'deep radiance' picks this up: the radiance of the direct beams appears to penetrate the ivy, with the tactile phrase 'lay | Full on' adding a sensuous hint. This is not just light catching a surface, or even overlaying it, but lying 'full on', intimate and palpable. In this scene of organic relationships, the ancient usurpation of the ivy with its mass of black appears to lend lightness to the elm tree, whose 'dark foliage' provides the final gleam as twilight sinks into night.

Michael O'Neill, in his fine analysis of the poem, remarks that in this passage 'the writing ripples with suggestions that never fall into the inertly emblematic, and decline the merely descriptive',[32] and indeed the lines seem to demand an intimacy of responsive reading, not a search for symbols. The dualisms of allegory/symbol and fancy/imagination seem themselves *inert* and *descriptive* from the exploratory viewpoint the poet gives us. This passage is about varied and modal experience, in which nothing appears to possess an independent, 'pure' identity, but takes its character from what it encounters. The impurities are wonderful. Once again the poem works not by unifying but by articulating its elements into a living scene. The *richness* of the experience is insisted on (the word is used twice), with the idea of depth or layering being important, like a rich mixture or rich colour, or food having a wealth of ingredients. 'Each faculty of sense' (43), we hardly need to be told, remains alert.

At this point in the poem, if we recall Lamb's apologetic thank-you letter (has Coleridge just received it?),[33] there seems to be another turn towards his troubled friend, this time with what seems like a specific reference to the Cowper allusion. If so, it is a secret only they can share:

>   sometimes
> 'Tis well to be bereav'd of promis'd good
> That we may lift the soul, & contemplate
> With lively joy the joys, we cannot share.   (44-7)

As well as returning to his own situation, Coleridge is giving Lamb a memento of his Nether Stowey visit: he intimates that ideas in contemplation can indeed be more rewarding than those of unreflecting experience. But through his organic text he shows how the words of a poem can be experiential, living in the act of reading. As a final token of sympathetic association, Coleridge offers his blessing on his group of friends, carried

---

[32] Michael O'Neill, *Romanticism and the Self-Conscious Poem* (Oxford: Clarendon Press; New York: Oxford University Press, 1997), 79.

[33] Mays makes the point that the poem 'might not have been drafted until after the Lambs had left' (ii.480).

homeward by a creature which mediates, and triangulates, his connection to them:

> when the last Rook
> Beat it's straight path along the dusky air
> Homewards, I bless'd it; deeming, it's black wing
> Cross'd, like a speck, the blaze of setting day,
> While ye stood gazing; or when all was still,
> Flew creaking o'er your heads...   (48–53)

With a brilliant moment of living geometry, Coleridge challenges the abstractions of Godwinian justice.[34] Here the human coordinates of the poem share in the richness of an experience that is simultaneously a solitary bird moving through the dusk, a black speck crossing a colourful sunset, and a creaking sound in the air above. The 'richness' of this is in its layering and its sharing. It is more than an idea or a symbol, rather a collection of perspectives, where truth and meaning are many-faceted.

If he valued his week's holiday in recollection more than he had at the time, Lamb did not treasure its commemoration in 'This Lime-Tree Bower My Prison', which in the expanded form of its first printed text (1800) he referred to as 'your *Satire* upon *me*'. Lamb's anger at the repeated epithet 'gentle-hearted' is well known and in some ways understandable;[35] but less easy to appreciate is his evident unwillingness to like the poem as a whole. Embarrassingly, he singled out for opprobrium the Berkeleyan passage over which he was made mystically to preside, referring to it as 'the unintelligible abstraction-fit about the manner of the Deity's making Spirits perceive his presence'. He added: 'God, nor created thing alive, can receive any honor from such thin, shew-box, attributes.'[36] In wishing to pay his tribute to Lamb's quiet, hidden soul, Coleridge had managed to project it publicly across a sublime landscape. Lamb's secret treasure appeared to become the world soul itself. And Coleridge's relational and overlaying details might seem too showy, and too presumptuous of others' experience. How easily a sympathetic superimposition could be thought an imposition.

After the great conversation poem, returning to Lamb and Lloyd means re-entering a context where purity, sincerity, and innocence are the overriding values, marked by a simple directness of expression that tends not to reach very far for its images. In their world the sociable has dangers, and organic mixture and adaptation tend to introduce difficulties. Both Lamb

---

[34] See pp. 78–80 above. Discussing the anti-Godwin arguments being developed at this time by Coleridge and his circle, Nicola Trott has shown how Godwin's theoretical disinterested benevolism could be countered by an emphasis on the immediate domestic affections. See Nicola Trott, 'The Coleridge Circle and the "Answer to Godwin"', *RES*, 41 (1990), 212–29.

[35] Lamb to Coleridge, 6 Aug. 1800 (Marrs, 217–18). Lamb's role in, and response to, the poem are analysed by Felicity James, 'Agreement, Dissonance, Dissent: The Many Conversations of "This Lime-Tree Bower"', *CB*, 26 (Winter 2005), 37–57.

[36] Lamb to Coleridge, 14 Aug. 1800 (Marrs, 224).

and Lloyd looked for the core of their personal identity to a distant remem-
bered spot that held meaning only for themselves. When the pair met in
January 1797 the immediate warmth of their friendship was strengthened by
this deeper bond in an ideal world, a lost domain of infancy associated with
a special place and its female presence—whether Priscilla Farmer's house or
Ann Simmons's cottage. Lamb's extraordinary, and rather disturbing, sonnet
'We were two pretty babes' (written in 1795) is best understood in this
context. It continues: 'the youngest she, | The youngest, and the loveliest
far (I ween) | And INNOCENCE her name' (1–3), and it suggests that since
reaching maturity he has felt only defilement and loss: 'my first love for
man's society, | Defiling with the world my virgin heart— | My lov'd
companion dropt a tear and fled' (8–10).[37] In Lamb's poem, experience of
the world can only introduce impurities.

Lloyd shared this ideal of a simple domesticity that might keep the wider
world of experience at bay. In his early 'Ode to Simplicity' he envisages an
enclosed retreat in which the pure and simple are combined: 'Methinks thou
lov'st to dwell | In some sequester'd cell | Where pure domestic bliss for ever
smiles; | Thou bid'st sensation shine | In tears of joy divine, | And inborn
virtue every hour beguiles'.[38] Lloyd's image of the divine at the heart of the
domestic, where 'inborn' virtue can be preserved, is recalled in 'The Dead
Friend', one of the poems about his grandmother where he shares Lamb's
deep-felt need to memorialise. Lloyd's opening lines form around the core
idea that guarantees his sense of himself:

> When I am quiet, and my centred soul
> Rests from its mortal working, it has seem'd
> As though the dead friend liv'd again, so sweet
> To me has been her memory.[39]

His soul is enjoying its sabbath, a day of *rest* when he can enter the special
place at the centre of himself, his internal identity. It is the focal point where
'soul' and 'memory' are joined, the immortality of the one helping to confirm
that of the other. (The idea is made explicit in another poem later in the
volume, where he speaks of 'the long sabbath of my centred soul'.[40]) Lloyd's
image of the sabbath as a moment/place that is an element of life's routine,
yet importantly set apart from it, is at the heart of his thinking about the
domestic. It is symptomatic that, when a child, Lloyd made himself a secret

[37] Charles Lamb, Sonnet VII: 'We were two pretty babes', 1797 *Poems*, 223. Lamb tran-
scribed it for Coleridge on 31 May 1796 (Marrs, 8). See Chapter 8, n. 26.
[38] Lloyd, *Poems on Various Subjects*, 23. Lloyd reported to his mother that Coleridge 'has
almost a child-like simplicity & purity of heart'. See Lynda Pratt, '"Perilous Acquaintance"?
Lloyd, Coleridge and Southey in the 1790s: Five Unpublished Letters', *Romanticism*, 6 (2000),
98–115 (101).
[39] *Blank Verse, by Charles Lloyd and Charles Lamb* (London: T. Bensley, 1798), 19.
[40] Charles Lloyd, 'Written the 12th of February 1797', ibid. 52.

garden within the sanctuary of his grandmother's house and each week transplanted there a flower ('he oft would gaze | With big-swoln heart, exulting at the thought | That he might call the spot belov'd *his own!*'). The idealised special place is also a spot of time set apart from the everyday and deserving of sanctification—''Twere not misnam'd if call'd a little Sabbath!', he concludes.[41]

When Coleridge entered Lloyd's life in 1796 he did so as the embodiment of this centre, as someone who could satisfy deep-rooted needs in Lloyd's personality:

> My COLERIDGE! take the wanderer to thy breast,
> The youth who loves thee, and who faint would rest
> (Oft rack'd by hopes that frensy and expire)
> In the long sabbath of subdued desire![42]

The 'sabbath' concept was clearly crucial for Lloyd as a calm space located at the heart of his character. The arrangement by which, for an annual payment of £80, Coleridge would allow Lloyd to live with him and would be his teacher and mentor, offered a role that Coleridge at first appreciated: 'Charles Lloyd wins upon me hourly,' he commented, 'his heart is uncommonly pure, his affections delicate, & his benevolence enlivened, but not sicklied, by sensibility.'[43] Coleridge offered Lloyd that emotional centre from which his powers could grow. But the stresses mounted, and beyond the well-known problem of his friend's illness we can sense the strain involved in having to embody Lloyd's ideal of a parenting friendship. In one copy of the 1797 *Poems*, alongside the four lines quoted above, Coleridge wrote: 'Too loving by Half! Am obliged to C.Ll. for his kind *wishes*, but would rather not! —S.T.C.—'.[44]

Lloyd's poetry of friendship during this period reveals how an idealising tendency can create tensions when it seeks its values in a perfect moment, a lost Eden, an elusive unity, a universal truth, or a transcendent reality. Life inevitably falls short, and the life of the poetry too can be restricted by an unwillingness to allow words their full associative range. When Geoffrey Hill writes that 'The Word has been abroad, is back, with a tanned look', the poet is allowing the word to have become something of a stranger, a traveller who has been mixing in different company. The Word, which went away as Logos, has come back incarnate, wearing its weathered human skin. It is ready to be the language of an exploratory poet who has (to use Hill's own

---

[41] Charles Lloyd, 'Lines written on a Friday, the Day in each Week formerly devoted by the Author and his Brothers and Sisters to the Society of their Grandmother', in *Poems on the Death of Priscilla Farmer* (1796), 21–2.

[42] The conclusion of 'Lines Addressed to S.T. Coleridge', included by Coleridge in 1797 *Poems*, 181.

[43] Coleridge to Poole, 24 Sept. 1796 (Griggs, 236–7).

[44] Coleridge's note alongside these lines in T. Hutchinson's copy. See Mays, i.277.

words) 'the willingness to lay the mind completely open to experience'.[45]
Lloyd's poetry of the 1790s evinces a degree of anxiety about allowing his
private meaning to enter the world of experience; but in doing so it gathers a
sinuous force, as if it is pursuing a strand of truth it mustn't let go. The result
is a narrowness, certainly, but also a sense of painful stretching that can be
very powerful. Where Lamb tends to cover and protect his precious ideas,
Lloyd exposes them like nerves. His whole volume, *Poems on the Death of
Priscilla Farmer*, is an exercise in agonised self-exposure.

We can see that there was an element of this in his idealising friendship for
Coleridge by looking at two sonnets evidently dating from August 1796
(though published only recently). Responding to the emotion of their first
meeting, Lloyd penned him a sonnet in which he recalls glimpsing what may
have been a momentary radiance from Coleridge's soul:

> I did fancy as mine eye met thine
> That there than erst e'er seen the social glow
> Intenslier dwelt—(I've wept in agony
> To think that glow the human face divine
> So scantily should radiate) if 'twere so—
> If 'twere a ray of soul remember me![46]   (9–14)

The thought clings on precariously through coiled Latinate inversion, then
parenthesis, then a tentative repetition. There is an urgent private meaning
here, which is being placed in his new friend's hands. It is as if Coleridge is
being asked to confirm this language, and supply the value of something
Lloyd himself cannot yet know. There is an uneasy fusion of the fragile and
the intense, a hesitation between the tenuous quality of the writing (with its
repeated 'if 'twere') and the full power of the emotion, which is conditional,
hanging on the precarious thread of Lloyd's 'fancy'. Momentary eye contact
suggests potential *dwelling*. A 'ray of soul' from his friend would be enough
to confirm that the private glance will bring the 'social glow' of which it is a
token. He thinks this human bonding may signify the radiance of the Elect.
There is a yearning for an organic connectedness here, but one premised on a
visionary moment. It is a difficult combination, and I think takes us to the
heart of Lloyd's dilemma and of his extraordinary tensile poetry.

Behind these notes of domestic transcendence is a longing to elide frater-
nity and spiritual election. It is a move that was confidently negotiated by the
author of 'Religious Musings', the Coleridge especially idolised by Lloyd
and Lamb. As we saw in Chapter 7, in the course of that poem human values

---

[45] Geoffrey Hill, 'Annunications', line 1; '"I in Another Place": Homage to Keith Dou-
glas', *Stand*, 6:4 (1963), 6–13 (13).
[46] Charles Lloyd, 'To Coleridge'. See Gurion Taussig, '"Lavish Promises": Coleridge, Charles
Lamb and Charles Lloyd, 1794–1798', *Romanticism*, 6 (2000), 78–97 (81). Taussig prints the
poem for the first time from BL MS Ashley 1005, fol. 13ʳ.

are superseded, and it reaches out with ease from the 'good man' to 'th'Elect, regenerate thro' faith' (99–101), from a universal brotherhood, which 'fraternizes man, [and] constitutes | Our charities and bearings', to that ideal 'SUPREME REALITY' in which all worldly coordinates have gone. As other critics have recognised, behind Coleridge's expansive idea is the unlimited 'ripple' effect of associative 'sympathy' as described in Hartley's *Observations on Man* (1749).[47] In Hartley's explication, it begins with 'A.'s supposition 'that he considered every man as his friend, his son, his neighbour, his second self, and loved him as himself; and that his neighbour was exalted to the same unlimited benevolence'. Thus, Hartley continues,

A, B, C, D, &c. would all become, as it were, new sets of senses, and perceptive powers, to each other, so as to increase each other's happiness without limits; they would all become *members of the mystical body of Christ*; all have an equal care for each other; all increase in love, and come to their *full stature*, to perfect manhood, *by that which every joint supplieth*: happiness would circulate through this mystical body without end, so that each particle of it would, in due time, arrive at each individual point, or sentient being, of the great whole, that each would *inherit all things*.[48]

It is a viral pandemic of empathy. Hartley's projected future (forming Proposition 68 of his 'Rule of Life') envisages a kind of universal transfusion through which personal self-consciousness is lost, and the boundaries of subject and object dissolve. He pictures something like an inherited world identity, effectively a single composite perception and memory—but without the Lockean power to forget.[49] Hartley's mystical organic*ism* takes its cue from our ability as human beings to make friends and thereby enrich ourselves and them. But in the process he looks beyond an articulated organisation of individuals to a surrendering of individuality in shared sensations and associations. This unifying is the apotheosis of the hypersensitised body of Sensibility, with the Universe as a single sensorium.[50] The motion becomes an ever-widening impulse that draws all people together into one consciousness. The result is the largest crowd in history, the supreme corporate unanimity, unbounded happiness.

---

[47] See, for example, Taussig, *Coleridge and the Idea of Friendship*, 215–18, and Richard C. Allen, 'Charles Lloyd, Coleridge, and *Edmund Oliver*', *SiR*, 35 (1996), 245–94 (265–8). Kelvin Everest discusses the Hartleian principles of Pantisocratic friendship in *Coleridge's Secret Ministry: The Context of the Conversation Poems 1795–1798* (Hassocks: Harvester Press; New York: Barnes and Noble, 1979), 78–84.

[48] David Hartley, *Observations on Man, his Frame, his Duty, and his Expectations*, 3 vols (London: J. Johnson, 1791), ii.287. Taussig discusses this passage in terms of friendship's ideals ('"Lavish Promises"', 79).

[49] It is reminiscent of John 'Walking' Stewart's panbiomorphic vision, but with God substituting for Nature. See pp. 53–4, above.

[50] This passage may underlie Yorick's eulogy to Sensibility as the 'great, great Sensorium of the world!' (Laurence Sterne, 'The Bourbonnois', in *A Sentimental Journey Through France and Italy* (1768)).

But the phrase 'individual...sentient being' is a nagging reminder of the utopian assumptions on which Hartley's infectious sympathy is predicated. Imagine the horror of being unable to access the system, of having, although yourself sentient and sympathetic, your identity declined:

> Coleridge my friend wherefore this long delay?
> Others have wrong'd me but methought thine eye
> Told me of friendship & of sympathy!
> And I have dreamt the lingering summers day
> Of all its lavish promises...[51]

Instead Lloyd now finds, he says, only 'cruel vacancy'. This second sonnet may have been written when he was waiting to hear if Coleridge would accept him as a pupil. To dwell with Coleridge, and to have him as friend and teacher, would be to experience something simultaneously domestic and transcendent. He could reach one through the other. Longing to be taken into Coleridge's family circle, Lloyd finds in that potential domesticity the key to his spiritual progress. But to cherish a perfect Idea in the heart runs the risk at any time of suddenly finding nothing there. The vacancy is total.

In his encouraging poetic response, 'To C. Lloyd, on His Proposing to Domesticate with the Author', Coleridge appears to be confronting his friend's idealising inwardness and his tendency to self-abasement (the above sonnet ends with a longing to be Coleridge's 'pensioner of meek regard'). In writing his poem Coleridge does everything Lloyd could have hoped for by welcoming him into the household, '[w]here smiling with blue eye DOMESTIC BLISS | Gives *this* the husband's, *that* the brother's kiss!', and he adds: 'She, whom I love, shall love thee'.[52] But before the reader comes to this little allegorical homecoming, in which Lloyd's perfect Idea is crystallised, we have to negotiate a rugged and variegated natural landscape reminiscent of Brockley Combe. As if to pull Lloyd out of his iconic meditation, Coleridge beckons him not only to *climb*, but to notice the different qualities of things around him while he does so. He uses variety of texture, colour, sound, and mood, to picture a more organic scene in which the elements mix happily together. It is, Coleridge insists, a place not only for climbing and aspiration, but also for wandering, observing, and relaxing:

> A mount, not wearisome and bare and steep,
> But a green Mountain variously up-pil'd,
> Where o'er the jutting rocks soft mosses creep
> Or color'd lichens with slow oozing weep;
> Where cypress and the darker yew start wild;
> And mid the summer torrent's gentle dash
> Dance brighten'd the red clusters of the ash   (1–7)

---

[51] Charles Lloyd, 'Sonnet 13: To the Same', 1–5; BL MS Ashley 1005, fol. 14ʳ, printed in Taussig, '"Lavish Promises"', 86. He suggests the sonnet was written shortly after 'To Coleridge', in Sept. 1796 before Coleridge agreed to tutor him.

[52] 1797 *Poems*, 114–15.

Different forms of life all have a part together: great and small, fast and slow, hard and soft, melancholy and cheerful. It is a living mixture. Far from being the steep route of a spiritual pilgrimage, nature's scene offers them a setting for conversation and quiet camaraderie: 'Seated at ease, on some smooth mossy rock; | In social silence now, and now t'unlock | The treasur'd heart; arm link'd in friendly arm' (24–6). The treasured memento in the heart can be released and communicated. The risk of obsessional fantasy is alleviated by observation and converse, and a friend's embrace.

The irony underlying the intense friendship subsisting among Coleridge, Lamb, and Lloyd at this time is the precariousness of the sensitive lines of communication between their personalities. What one admiring critic of Lamb's poetry called that 'little knot of pure and delightful sympathies' could be vulnerable because of its inherent delicacy and fineness.[53] In looking into the bond that linked these three men, it becomes evident that the ideal and the organic are being brought into uncomfortable proximity. It remains important to distinguish them. After all, the idealised friend and the good friend are very different notions, and over time it is the latter that will often prove more durable. Elements of the pure, the ideal, and the inviolate characterise the poetic language of Lamb and Lloyd in ways that make conversation tricky. Rather than working through juxtaposition, adaptation, collision, or overlap, the voice sustains a pure, almost statement-like singleness of meaning; its transparency becomes a refusal to taint or refract itself through any distorting medium. By resisting the image, the secret remains unembodied and unsullied.

In November 1797, the surface tension of these friendships was broken when Coleridge tossed a stone into the limpid water. His three 'Sonnets Attempted in the Manner of Contemporary Writers', signed 'Nehemiah Higginbottom', appeared without warning in the *Monthly Magazine*,[54] and in these, especially in the second ('To Simplicity'), Lamb and Lloyd were confronted by a language that not merely parodied elements of their own but seemed to mock their principles and ideals.[55] A year earlier, Lamb had presumed to urge Coleridge towards simplicity, not as a stylistic virtue but as an expressive integrity, a germination from the core, a pure spring welling up from the heart:

---

[53] Thomas Noon Talfourd reviewing Lamb's *Works* (1818) in *The Champion*, 16 May 1819 (313).

[54] See Lucy Newlyn, 'Parodic Allusion: Coleridge and the "Nehemiah Higginbottom" Sonnets, 1797', *CLB*, 56 (1986), 255–9; and Graeme Stones, 'The Ragged-Trousered Philanthropist: Coleridge and Self-exposure in the Higginbottom Sonnets', *CLB*, 100 (1997), 122–32. Coleridge described them to Cottle as 'three mock Sonnets in ridicule of my own, & Charles Lloyd's, & Lamb's, &c. &c.' (Griggs, 357). Lamb's sonnet to his sister, Mary, had appeared in the previous issue (see n. 22 above).

[55] Felicity James suggests that the sonnets were Coleridge's 'declaration of independence' from Lamb and Lloyd, partly in response to the reviewer in *The Monthly Visitor* (Aug. 1797) who identified them unfavourably as forming a 'Coleridgean School'. See her *Charles Lamb, Coleridge and Wordsworth: Reading Friendship in the 1790s* (Basingstoke: Palgrave Macmillan, 2008), 115.

Cultivate simplicity, Coleridge, or rather, I should say, banish elaborateness; for simplicity springs spontaneous from the heart, and carries into daylight its own modest buds and genuine, sweet, and clear flowers of expression.[56]

Such modest, sweet, and clear simplicity, as we have seen, is a key issue in the poetic language of Lamb and Lloyd, and in the opening lines of Lloyd's first sonnet to Coleridge, quoted from earlier, there is an almost painful directness and naivety: 'Coleridge, my soul is very sad to think | We seperate so soon, for tho unfit | To mould the prompt phrase with impetuous wit, | I love thee still'. It is clear that Coleridge's second 'Nehemiah Higginbottom' sonnet goes beyond parody to the heart of the matter:

> O! I do love thee, meek *Simplicity*!
> For of thy lays the lulling simpleness
> Goes to my heart, and soothes each small distress,
> Distress tho' small, yet haply great to me!
>
> . . . .
>
> *So* sad I am!—but should a friend and I
> Grow cool and *miff*, O! I am *very* sad!
> And then with sonnets and with sympathy
> My dreamy bosom's mystic woes I pall;
> Now of my false friend plaining plaintively,
> Now raving at mankind in general;
> But whether sad or fierce, 'tis simple all,
> All very simple, meek SIMPLICITY!

The thrust is deadly for both Lamb and Lloyd, because the element of simplicity and directness in their work carries so much truth, trust, and integrity with it. Their language has already been pared down and laid bare so that there is nowhere to hide, no irony or imaginative agility ('impetuous wit') in the writing to evade Coleridge's point. The potential cruelty of this tactic should not be underplayed. The surest touch is perhaps the way he exploits the connection between simplicity and friendship—the core of the experience from which his two friends wrote.

The story of estrangement, accusation, and suspicion that severed Coleridge from his two friends in 1798 has been often told, and Taussig writes especially well on the potential faultlines present in the friendships from the start.[57] From the perspective of this book, it is possible to see points of stress developing in the very ideals that Lamb and Lloyd brought with them. We have seen Coleridge keenly aware of their sensitivities, while himself having a more robust sense of his own varied and dynamic identity,

---

[56] Lamb to Coleridge, 8 Nov. 1796 (Marrs, 60–1).

[57] Taussig, *Coleridge and the Idea of Friendship*, 214–45. For Coleridge's analysis of the rupture with Lamb and Lloyd, see Coleridge to Lamb, (early May 1798) (Griggs, 403–5). On the strains in the Coleridge–Lloyd friendship, see Graeme Stones, 'Charles Lloyd and *Edmund Oliver*: A Demonology', *CLB*, 95 (1996), 110–21. See also James, *Charles Lamb, Coleridge and Wordsworth*, chap. 5.

which could accommodate (as his 1796 *Poems* did) inconsistency and disruption. Both Lamb and Lloyd, however, felt drawn to the Coleridge who aspired to be among the Elect, and both could write powerfully about the precariousness of their spiritual ideal. Ironically it was in the world of human converse, of gossip, misunderstanding, frustration, and impatience that their friendship with Coleridge broke down, and this was in itself a kind of betrayal.

Lamb's accusatory catechism, 'Theses Quaedam Theologicae' (written while staying with Lloyd in Birmingham in late May/early June 1798 and posted to Coleridge) is driven by a belief that he has been rejected at the human level by a being who is isolated in angelic perfection. Lamb's satiric questions include '6. Whether the Seraphim Ardentes do not manifest their virtues by the way of vision & theory? & whether practice be not a sub-celestial & merely human virtue?'[58] He feels estranged from his now seraphic friend, asking '[w]hether God loves a lying Angel better than a true Man?' Lamb finds it impossible to put the broken pieces of the icon together.

There is a similar sense of tragic alienation in what is perhaps Lloyd's finest poem, 'Written at Burton in Hampshire, August 1797'.[59] In an effective example of his sinuous stretching out of a painful idea, Lloyd pursues his baffled sense of loss as he wonders how a worshipped ideal can finally betray human feelings, and a living god become a lifeless replica:

> 'Tis true there are
> Who in the free convivial scene will ape,
> With most deceitful seeming, the full soul
> Of holiest virtue; and will sigh, or smile,
> As they her delicate vicissitudes
> Had keenly witness'd: but the ready mimic
> Plant in his *proper station*, and the *thing*
> (Though late so exquisitely organiz'd)
> Will stand the *statue of obduracy*,
> And scatter back, with strange inaptitude,
> Love's unadmissible radiance. Oh my God!
> Why is the fleshly heart so petrified?
> Why all its avenues clos'd, and the high swell
> Of infinite perfection disciplin'd
> To base manoeuverings, to the unnatural guilt
> Of intellectual murder?... (10–25)

The animated figure proves a stone statue and nothing more. In a betrayal of spiritual and intellectual ideals, the object ('the *thing*') refuses meaning and

---

[58] Marrs, 128.

[59] *Blank Verse*, 14–18. It is one of the poems written during summer 1797 when Lloyd found shelter with Southey and his wife at their house in Burton. Lloyd's residence with Coleridge had ended in April. The immediate trigger for the poem may have been Lloyd's frustrations in wooing Sophia Pemberton. See Allen, 'Charles Lloyd, Coleridge, and *Edmund Oliver*', 257–9.

spurns both divine perfection and human values. The lines of communication
are closed and lead nowhere. A being who was once 'so *exquisitely* organiz'd'
('Keenly sensitive to impressions; acutely susceptible of pain, pleasure, etc.;
delicate, finely-strung'[60]) is no longer a transmitter of sympathies and aspir-
ations. It is clear that the pain of realisation can be *exquisite* too.

But although full of tragic material, *Blank Verse, by Charles Lloyd and
Charles Lamb*, where Lloyd's poem first appeared, is a shared volume, an
assertion of friendship; and in his dedication to Southey, Lloyd has the
confidence to offer him 'many sensations of affection and virtue', trusting
that Southey will be responsive ('They...must certainly remain unclaimed,
if not acknowledged by you'). Such hope for acceptance and response was at
the heart of Lamb and Lloyd's friendship for Coleridge. Perhaps they
invested too much of their personal identity in him, and perhaps his sheer
radiance may have been too intense. If Southey did raise this issue with his
new friend in July 1794, then the answer he received was a portent of the
complex negotiations that friendship with Coleridge demanded.

Ironically, it is in Lloyd's philosophical novel *Edmund Oliver* (the publi-
cation of which in April 1798 effectively banished him from Coleridge's
circle) that we find a Coleridgean model of mutual friendship fully set out.
Dedicated to Lamb, Lloyd's novel concludes with its three families settling
together on neighbouring estates ('Basil, Edmund, and I, have taken lands
which lie contiguous to each other'[61]), where they set out to create among
themselves a kind of Pantisocratic society. In his Advertisement, Lloyd says
he has written his book 'with the design of counteracting that generalizing
spirit, which seems so much to have insinuated itself among modern philo-
sophers'. Instead he will focus on 'the domestic connections' according to
the principle that '[t]he human mind never will be led to interest itself with
regard to a *whole*, except it have been first excited by *palpable parts of that
whole*, which have addressed themselves to the wants and desires of its
constitution'. In stressing the 'palpable' in this mode of organisation,
Lloyd is now moving away from letting ideals take the lead, and from the
pursuit of what he terms 'indefinite benevolence'.[62] What is of lasting
constitutional value, he implies, must be earthed in experience. As Richard
Allen has persuasively shown, *Edmund Oliver*, with its principle of domestic
'connections' being at the heart of human progress, is in many ways the
'answer to Godwin' that Coleridge himself never wrote.[63] What Allen says
of the fictional friends at the close of Lloyd's novel is also a shrewd footnote
to the story told in this chapter: each of them, he says, 'embodies the
paradox that a stable self-identity requires the annihilation of selfishness,

[60] *OED*, s.v. 'exquisite', adj. 7.
[61] Charles Lloyd, *Edmund Oliver*, 2 vols (Bristol: Bulgin and Rosser, for Joseph Cottle,
1798), ii.292.
[62] Ibid. vol. i, pp. vii–ix.
[63] Allen, 'Charles Lloyd, Coleridge, and *Edmund Oliver*', 269.

for stability exists only in mutuality, and mutuality can flourish only when each has made room in the self for the other. The one identity they approximate exists in the reciprocity of affection both given and received'.[64] In place of abstract ideals, universals, and notions of perfection, radiance, and absorption, the best place to start would seem to be the more empirical one of making room for each other.

[64] Ibid. 293.

10   A Matter of Emphasis: Coleridge and Thelwall, 1796–7

'YOU AND I are very differently organized,' Coleridge told John Thelwall in December 1796, challenging his correspondent with an especially sublime passage from the Bible, though with little real hope of converting him to Christianity: '*You* may prefer to all this the Quarrels of Jupiter & Juno, the whimpering of wounded Venus . . . be it so (The difference in our tastes it would not be difficult to account for from the different feelings which we have associated with these ideas).'[1] Saving his friend's atheist soul and correcting his poetic taste had become a single enterprise, and issues of principle appear to have hung on personal memories and their emotional associations. For good or ill, much evidently depended on how one was 'organized', not least one's hopes of salvation; but Coleridge's correspondent might be excused for thinking that these subjectivities were not solid enough to be the foundations of belief. The story this chapter tells is of two men who debated questions of weight and substance—literally so—in the course of which the nature of poetic language came to be the crux of the matter. In the context of political and constitutional debate during the 1790s, what weight a man gave to words was much more than a stylistic choice. Mary Wollstonecraft deplored a situation where, she says, 'the judgment . . . is merely called into action to weigh the import of words rather than to estimate the value of things'.[2] But as someone whose life had rested on the power of words to carry weight, John Thelwall understood these seeming alternatives, of weighing words and valuing things, to be synonymous.

When Coleridge began corresponding with Thelwall in late April 1796,[3] he was conscious of squaring up to someone who valued commitment, principle, and action, a man who (in the words of Nicholas Roe) was 'the most prominent and active member of the democratic reform movement in Britain'.[4] In 1794 Thelwall had suffered for the cause as one of the British

---

[1] Coleridge to Thelwall, 17 Dec. 1796 (Griggs, 281).

[2] Mary Wollstonecraft, *An Historical and Moral View of the Origin and Progress of the French Revolution* (London: J. Johnson, 1794), 503.

[3] Of their earliest correspondence in April–May 1796, two letters are extant. Coleridge's introductory letter of late April (Griggs, 204–5) with a presentation copy of his *Poems* was followed by a missing 'voluminous' reply from Thelwall; Thelwall's second letter (10 May) is the only item to survive from his side of their correspondence. See Warren E. Gibbs, 'An Unpublished Letter from John Thelwall to S.T. Coleridge', *MLR*, 25 (1930), 85–90.

[4] Nicholas Roe, 'Coleridge and John Thelwall: The Road to Nether Stowey', in Richard Gravil and Molly Lefebure (eds), *The Coleridge Connection: Essays for Thomas McFarland* (Basingstoke: Macmillan, 1990), 60–80 (63).

radicals tried for high treason, held for months in solitary confinement, his life under threat. 'Citizen Thelwall' was a stirring popular lecturer, 'Tribune' of the people, a man who preferred, he said, the solid republican Doric order to the decorative imperial Corinthian.[5] In Coleridge's sonnet 'To John Thelwall', probably transcribed into the copy of the 1796 *Poems* that accompanied his April letter,[6] he pictured the radical activist in heroic pose 'mid thickest fire' leaping 'on the perilous wall', in contrast to those who fight imaginary battles in their closets. In its final couplet Coleridge hopes that his own verse will come to have Thelwall's manly, republican plainness, 'Blest if to me in Manhood's years belong | Thy stern simplicity & vigorous song'.[7]

In turning to Thelwall, whom he had never met, Coleridge was submitting himself to the judgment of someone for whom poetry was a test of honesty and integrity. In *Poems Written in Close Confinement in the Tower and Newgate, Under a Charge of High Treason* (1795) Thelwall had declared that the worth of a poem lay in the degree to which it was a genuine 'transcript' of the heart. It was a valuable artefact only to the degree that it embodied something true and real. Refusing 'to amuse the admirer of poetical enthusiasm', his Advertisement stated, 'I have spoken what I felt; not considered what I should speak'. Directness of speech continued to be Thelwall's main preoccupation throughout his career. Whether as a radical politician, poet, and public speaker, or later as a successful speech therapist and expert in techniques of voice-production, his key principle was to understand the natural mechanisms of the speaking voice, what had weight and what didn't, and to know where to place the emphasis. As someone who worked on remedying speech defects, he came to appreciate how, rather than forcing words into obedience or plucking them from the air, the stammerer could be helped by adapting to the natural rhythms of the diaphragm. Richard Gravil has pointed out that Thelwall used spoken verse 'for treatment of more psychologically induced speech defects as stammering and stuttering', and that his cure involved 'exercising the poetic rhythmus of "Pulsation and remission," his terms for the systole and diastole of the diaphragm'.[8] If Lear's daughter

---

[5] John Thelwall, 'On the Moral and Political Influence of the Prospective Principle of Virtue', lectures 1 and 2 (*The Tribune*, 1795–6, i.147–63, 222–36), in Gregory Claeys (ed.), *The Politics of English Jacobinism: Writings of John Thelwall* (University Park: Pennsylvania State University Press, 1995), 88–116 (97).

[6] Mays, i.264.

[7] The adjective 'perilous' in the text sent to Thelwall (Gibbs, 85) is omitted from the Cottle MS version first published by E. H. Coleridge. Coleridge himself never printed the sonnet. See Mays, ii.357–8. Thelwall quoted the sonnet back at Coleridge in 1817 as a reminder of his democratic principles: see Burton R. Pollin, assisted by Redmond Burke, 'John Thelwall's Marginalia in a Copy of Coleridge's *Biographia Literaria*', *Bulletin of the New York Public Library*, 74 (1970), 73–94.

[8] Richard Gravil, 'The Somerset Sound; or, the Darling Child of Speech', *CB*, 26 (Winter 2005), 1–21 (7). For a discussion of Thelwall's speech therapy in the context of public oratory, see Lucy Newlyn, *Reading, Writing and Romanticism: The Anxiety of Reception* (Oxford: Oxford University Press, 2000), 339–60. See also Susan Manly, *Language, Custom and Nation in the 1790s: Locke, Tooke, Wordsworth, Edgeworth* (Aldershot/Burlington VT: Ashgate, 2007), 89–99.

Cordelia had declared: 'I cannot heave | My heart into my mouth', for Thelwall easing the passage from heart into speech via the diaphragm was vital not only for fluent, expressive communication, but for the principles of honesty and truth.[9] It was his time in prison that made him recognise the often self-imposed constraints on what seems a simple and easy notion. Thelwall never took fluency for granted.

The ideal, as with Paine's revolutionary language, was transparency, a rhetoric that distrusted all but the clearest medium.[10] In Thelwall's concluding 'prison' sonnet, entitled 'The Crisis', expressive language itself (with its appeal to 'the partial ear') is rejected, and the reader is invited to look directly into Thelwall's breast 'with scrutiny severe' and inspect the emotions there.[11] At the critical moment, a window into the heart has to substitute for the potentially distorting medium of words. Thelwall's prison poetry, written in the Tower and Newgate between July and December 1794, responds to a world that has been closed down. He understands how constriction compromises natural expression, what imprisonment does to your language. The twelve prison sonnets show him repeatedly testing himself against the confines of the sonnet structure. He tries a different form each time, as if welcoming the discipline of the fresh rhyme scheme. Appropriately, in Sonnet 9, entitled 'The Cell', he even forces himself into octosyllabics, making what Wordsworth will call the 'narrow room' of the sonnet, even narrower. Here the voice is merely one of record: 'The damp foul floor, the ragged wall, | And shattered window, grated high', as if he is pacing out the restricted space. The tone is firm and defiant, refusing the subjective, and the poem stops at the point of potential self-exploration, when he '[l]ooks inward to his heart, and sees | The objects that must ever please'. In this poetic retrenchment, Thelwall's inner world is closed off from the reader, as if he cannot risk exposing himself. *Poems Written in Close Confinement* suggests a crisis of poetic expression, which comes from a refusal to access the inwardness to which he refers. Private feelings risk becoming tenuous and therefore vulnerable.

In his prison poems, therefore, rather than reaching for personal meanings, Thelwall articulates the power of the realised Idea, the embodied Truth, and he does so through personification. Ironically, Thelwall's influence on the prophetic language of Coleridge's 'Religious Musings' is suggested by many passages like this (in the sonnets as well as the odes), in which there is no room for exquisite shadings or intimate self-exploration:

---

[9] William Shakespeare, *King Lear*, I.i.91–2. Annotating his poem 'See where the heart', Thelwall notes: 'The sympathy between the Brain, Heart, and Lungs has long engaged the attention of Physiologists' (John Thelwall, *The Peripatetic*, ed. Judith Thompson (Detroit: Wayne State University Press, 2001), 148).

[10] See p. 78 above.

[11] John Thelwall, *Poems Written in Close Confinement in the Tower and Newgate, Under a Charge of High Treason* (London: Printed for the Author, 1795), 12.

> [A]t the call
> Of this eternal principle should wake,
>   As at th'Archangel's trump, the slumb'ring world;
>   And to the glorious standard, wide unfurl'd,
>   Of soul-ennobling Truth impatient throng;
>   While Civic-Virtue chaunts the martial song,
> And on their blood-stain'd Thrones fell Tyrants shake.[12]

In his Advertisement to the volume, Thelwall declares that '[t]hey who look for the sighs of personal regret, and the elegiac tenderness of complaint, will certainly be disappointed... the Patriot, immured in the walls of a bastille, is called upon, by important duties, to repel every enervating sensation' (iii). It is personification that allows him to turn away from personal feelings and stage himself publicly as a representative integrity. Thelwall projects himself as the voice of Liberty, as the embodiment of the Idea of 'Patriot Virtue', of indignation and opposition.

Coleridge was therefore rightly apprehensive about how the uncertain mixture of his newly published *Poems on Various Subjects* would be received by Thelwall: 'you will find much to blame in them—', he conceded, 'much effeminacy of sentiment, much faulty glitter of expression. I build all my poetic pretentions on the Religious Musings—which you will read with a POET's Eye.'[13] But this is just how Thelwall in 1796 tended *not* to read things. Ironically, he was closer to Shakespeare's sceptical Theseus, who lightly mocked 'the poet's eye in a fine frenzy rolling', particularly when it 'bodies forth the forms of things unknown'.[14] Coleridge was optimistic in thinking that Thelwall might value his 'Religious Musings'. He had taken the risk of applying Thelwall's own declamatory style to a subject on which the Godwinian atheist was bound to be opposed, and if Coleridge thought to make Thelwall growl, he succeeded. In his letter of 10 May (the only letter from his side of the correspondence to survive) Thelwall praised parts of the collection warmly; but—'Of your favorite poem', he wrote,

> I fear I shall speak in terms that will disappoint you. There are passages most undoubtedly in the Religious Musings of very great merit... but this praise belongs almost exclusively to those parts that are not at all religious. As for the generality of those passages which are most so, they are certainly anything in the world rather than poetry... They are the very acme of abstruse, metaphysical, mistical rant, & all ranting abstractions, metaphysic & mysticism are wider from true poetry than the equator from the poles. The whole poem also is infected with inflation & turgidity.

But Thelwall was not finished yet, and he went on to make a more detailed metrical point, which led to an exchange of views that underpins the theme of this chapter:

---

[12] John Thelwall, 'Ode I: The Universal Duty', in *Poems Written in Close Confinement*, 13.
[13] Coleridge to Thelwall, (late April 1796) (Griggs, 205).
[14] William Shakespeare, *A Midsummer Night's Dream*, V.i.12–15.

Before I wipe the gall from my pen, I must notice an affectation of the Della Crusca school which blurs almost every one of your poems—I mean the frequent accent upon adjectives and weak words—'Escap'd the *sore* wounds'—'Sunk to the *cold* earth'—'Love glittering, thro' the *high* tree . . .'—'When most the *big* soul feels'— 'Anon upon some *rough* rock's fearful brow' . . . all occur in the first 8 pages. Instances of this kind . . . give me, at least, the earache . . . 'Saw from her *dark* womb leap her *flamy* Child!'—*flamy* child!!!! 'For chiefly in the oppressed *good* Man's face'—etc.[15]

Responding to this on 13 May Coleridge found himself making a significant distinction:

Your remarks on the Della-crusca place of Emphasis are just in part—where we wish to point out the *thing*, & the *quality* is mentioned merely as a decoration, this mode of emphasis is indeed absurd—therefore I very patiently give up to critical vengeance *high* tree, *sore* wounds, & *rough* rock—but when you wish to dwell chiefly on the *quality* rather than the *thing*, then this mode is proper—& indeed is used in common conversation—who says—Good *Man*—? therefore *big* soul, *cold* earth, *dark* womb, & *flamy* child are [quite] right[16]

It may seem just a matter of emphasis; but a principle is involved here too, and one that Coleridge refuses to concede. Adjectives need not, as Thelwall thinks, always be '*weak* words', mere modifiers: they may be inherent in the nature of the *thing* as the poet perceives it, and a quality may itself be the essence of an idea. A fine point, perhaps, but a sign of the two men's more fundamental differences in philosophy and religion. In his *Essay, Towards a Definition of Animal Vitality* (1793), the materialist Thelwall had asserted that '*qualities* have no separate existence, nor can they even be conceived in the imagination, otherwise than as connected with the things of which they describe the shades or attributes: they are, in fact, solely and purely, modifications of matter'.[17] On this subject of poetic 'qualities', therefore, more was at stake than *metrical* stress.

As the epistolary debate between the men continued during the eighteen months that followed, other stresses would become evident, other qualities tested, and other modifications attempted and resisted. The issue of their

---

[15] Thelwall to Coleridge, 10 May 1796 (Gibbs, 87–8).

[16] Coleridge to Thelwall, 13 May 1796 (Griggs, 216). Anya Taylor, in 'Coleridge and the Pleasures of Verse', *SiR*, 40 (Winter 2001), 547–69, memorably characterises Coleridge's sensitivity to metre: 'Meter pulls Coleridge back from the chasm of idealism to the vivacious body that his spirit filled. Meter draws its power from both the disciplined will and the body's rhythmical energy; it spans the intersection of mind and body and reconciles head and heart, specifically the heart-beat' (548). This suggests that Bowles's responsive metrics were an important part of his poetry's appeal to Coleridge.

[17] John Thelwall, *An Essay, Towards a Definition of Animal Vitality* (London: T. Rickaby, 1793), reprinted in Nicholas Roe, *The Politics of Nature: William Wordsworth and Some Contemporaries*, 2nd edn (Houndmills: Palgrave, 2002), 101–19 (117). In this essay Thelwall denies the existence of a non-material 'spirit' that can modify matter: 'such *Spirit*, however subtle, however refined, must still be material' (116). All 'modifications', for Thelwall, are material.

respective organisations (personal and poetic) would grow less clear-cut during 1797, and the relationship between their poems would become more complex as their distinct, even polarised, identities threatened to overlap. Thelwall's acute sensitivity to the weighting of words developed in new expressive ways after his Nether Stowey experience that summer, a shift in verse-form and style shaped by what can be seen as a second crisis—this time not one of imprisonment and constriction, but one of release, of not being able to settle.

The Coleridge whom Thelwall eventually met in July 1797 was less the visionary dreamer than a young father at the centre of a domestic idyll. But Thelwall's glimpse of the possibility of an 'enchanting retreat' in Somerset brought their friendship to a crisis. Underlying the subtle shifts of commitment and motive there remained the question of where Coleridge finally stood, and what weight he was prepared to give to things of substance. As an individual, but also as a representative of political and moral principle, Thelwall challenged Coleridge's sense of what was material and what wasn't. In the end, the tragic curve of their relationship during 1796–7 would find its ironies in the poems that came out of Thelwall's Nether Stowey experience, and were shaped by it.[18]

By November 1796 it appeared that poetry would certainly not be a bridge between the two men, and Coleridge continued to emphasise the differences of principle that divided them. He writes: '[Y]ou & I, my dear Thelwall! hold different *creeds* in poetry as well as religion.' A few lines later the nature of this *creed* (not the most neutral word to use to Thelwall) becomes clearer: 'Bowles', he continues, '(the bard of my idolatry) has written a poem lately without plan or meaning—but the component parts are divine' (*idolatry, divine*—more incendiary words). An impression that Coleridge was taunting him can only have been reinforced by what follows: twenty lines transcribed from William Lisle Bowles's 'Hope: An Allegorical Sketch', ending with the phrase '[Hope] almost faints with Joy amidst the broad Day-light!' 'The last line', Coleridge adds provocatively, 'is indeed exquisite.' The letter continues with a declaration that 'Metaphysics, & Poetry, & "Facts of mind"—(i.e. Accounts of all the strange phantasms that ever possessed your philosophy-dreamers...) are my darling Studies'; and to illustrate his mood he offers Thelwall some new verses:

> Oft o'er my brain mysterious Fancies roll
> That make the Present seem (the while they last)
> A dreamy Semblance of some Unknown Past[19]

---

[18] For a full account of their 'sparring' relationship, see Gurion Taussig, *Coleridge and the Idea of Friendship, 1789–1804* (Newark: University of Delaware Press; London: Associated University Presses, 2002), 177–213.

[19] Coleridge to Thelwall, 19 Nov. 1796 (Griggs, 258–61).

Now, anyone who had read Thelwall would have known that *dreamy Semblances* were not his cup of tea; and his reply to Coleridge (not extant) was evidently forthright, since in his next letter of 17 December 1796, the letter quoted at the opening of this chapter (Griggs, 276–87), Coleridge accepts his friend's challenge with the words 'And now, my dear fellow! for a little sparring about Poetry'. Thelwall had apparently demanded to know just what his *dreamy Semblance* was, so Coleridge tells him: 'By "dreamy semblance" I *did* mean semblance of some unknown Past, like to a dream—and not "a semblance *presented* in a dream."' This *semblance*, Coleridge explains, is the déjà vu, a sudden intrusion of the past, acting 'so as to make Reality appear a Semblance'. It is nonetheless *real*, though it makes present reality seem dreamlike; 'this thought is obscure' (he adds patronisingly). Such usurping of a present reality by a shadowy past was something Thelwall had particularly inveighed against in *The Tribune*—what he had there called the 'malignant retrospective principle', with its tendency to bring 'despondency and lethargy'. For Thelwall this invasion by images of the past was a symptom of 'that debility into which persons sink from contemplating nothing but their own sensations'.[20]

Coleridge continues his 17 December letter unabashed, and after announcing 'I am a Berkleian' (thus allying himself with the philosopher's denial of material substance),[21] he goes on to answer what must have been an attack by Thelwall on the metrics of that 'exquisite' line of Bowles: 'As to Bowles, I affirm, that the manner of his accentuation in the words 'broad day-light' (three long Syllables) is a beauty, as it admirably expresses the Captive's *dwelling* on the sight of Noon—with rapture & a kind of Wonder'. The quality of the emotion, in other words, was primary here. With this point established, Coleridge makes it clear that he feels any attack on Bowles is wounding to himself: 'But that Bowles, the most tender, and, with the exception of Burns, the only *always-natural* poet in our Language, that *he* should not escape the charge of Della Cruscanism | this cuts the skin & *surface* of my Heart'.[22] On the next page Coleridge goes on to praise 'the *heart* and fancy of Bowles' (his italics), and near the end of this long Saturday-night letter he reveals to Thelwall that he has just edited a sheet of sonnets by himself and his friends to be bound up with those of his beloved Bowles—and a copy is on its way to him.[23] But about another volume of

---

[20] Thelwall, 'Prospective Principle of Virtue', 90, 108.

[21] Coleridge is being doubly aggressive here. It is clear from Thelwall's 10 May letter that he regards Coleridge's recent anti-Godwinian article in *The Watchman* (17 March) as an attack on himself. The article, 'Modern Patriotism', is a selection of points from Berkeley's 'Maxims Concerning Patriotism' (see *The Watchman*, 98–100). In these circumstances it seems Coleridge's remark also has a political edge to it.

[22] On the continuing importance of Bowles's 'natural language' for Coleridge, see James C. McKusick, *Coleridge's Philosophy of Language* (New Haven/London: Yale University Press, 1986), 13–18.

[23] S. T. Coleridge (ed.), *Sonnets from Various Authors* (1796). See Chapter 8 above.

poetry he hesitates: '(Shall I give it thee, Blasphemer? No. I won't—but) to thy Stella I do present the poems of my [Bowles] for a keep-sake.—Of this parcel I do intreat thy acceptance.' And so, in the Victoria and Albert Museum is a copy of the 1796 fourth edition of Bowles's *Sonnets, and Other Poems*, pointedly inscribed on the fly-leaf: 'Dear Mrs Thelwall— I entreat your acceptance of this Volume, which has given me more pleasure, and done my heart more good, than all the other books, I ever read, except-ing my Bible . . . Samuel Taylor Coleridge'.[24] In deliberately presenting it to Thelwall's wife, Coleridge implies that she, unlike her husband, will have a heart sensitive enough to appreciate it. It was an action that suggested he fell short of deserving Coleridge's wholehearted confidence.

In his missing reply, it seems that Thelwall asked Coleridge in his direct way whether he and Bowles were friends. Coleridge replied on 31 December: 'You imagine that I know Bowles personally—I never *saw* him but once; & when I was a boy, & in Salisbury *market-place*.'[25] Once again Thelwall could see the idea outrunning the actuality. But as if to re-emphasise his commit-ment to his poetic mentor Coleridge then transcribes some lines beginning: 'Such Verse as Bowles, heart-honour'd Poet, sang' (the *heart* again).[26] By this time Thelwall may have begun to wonder why he was having Bowles repeat-edly thrust at him. It could be that in a correspondence that seemed increas-ingly to be reaching across a divide, Coleridge felt he needed a poetic ally. Or perhaps he hoped Bowles would convert Thelwall away from his atheistic materialism, and lift his heart to what mattered? Whatever the reason, Bowles had become both an irritant and a point of honour between them, virtually an emblem of their disagreement over materiality. (What Thelwall eventually did materially with that 'keep-sake' volume of Bowles's verse we shall see in a moment.)

On 17 July 1797 Thelwall came to stay for ten days at Nether Stowey (just after Lamb's departure). He had been forced to give up public lecturing, having been threatened by mobs and constrained by the government's 'gag-ging' acts; his mail was opened, and he was being tracked by informers. He arrived at Coleridge's cottage as a man uprooted, vulnerable, isolated, holding to his democratic principles but now seeking refuge. Writing to his wife from Alfoxden on the following day, he suggests 'I have had serious tho[ughts] of a Cottage—Do not be surprised if my next should inform you that I have taken one.'[27] The verses he wrote the day he left Stowey, his 'Lines written at Bridgewater', are subtitled 'in quest of a peaceful retreat'.[28]

[24] Victoria and Albert Museum, Dyce 8° 1298 (Copy A). For the inscription, see Griggs, 287.
[25] Griggs, 293–5.
[26] Part of 'Fragments of an Epistle to Thomas Poole'. See Mays, ii.341–3.
[27] MS Pierpont Morgan Library MA77 (17). The letter is printed by Damian Walford Davies, *Presences that Disturb: Models of Romantic Identity in the Literature and Culture of the 1790s* (Cardiff: University of Wales Press, 2002), 294–7.
[28] Printed in Thelwall's *Poems chiefly written in Retirement* (Hereford: W. H. Parker, 1801), 126–32.

But for Coleridge, Poole, and the new star Wordsworth, Thelwall's plan to settle nearby was out of the question, and Coleridge's letters of August and October 1797 represented 'a rejection that went beyond their intellectual differences'.[29] Looking back, Thelwall saw this period as a time when 'Friendship (the last stay of the human heart)...has shrunk from its own convictions.'[30] Coleridge's letter of 14 October deals with practical matters first: 'I would to heaven', he tells Thelwall, 'it were in my power to serve you—but alas! I have neither money or influence...You have my wishes, & what is very liberal in me for such an atheist reprobate, my prayers.'[31] From that point on, the letter becomes insensitively blithe and idealising, even mystical; and Coleridge transcribes from 'This Lime-Tree Bower My Prison' the lines about imagining 'such Hues | As cloath th'Almighty Spirit, when he makes | Spirits perceive his presence!',[32] boasting to the materialist Thelwall: 'It is but seldom that I raise & spiritualize my intellect to this height.' (He chooses, in other words, the very passage from the poem that Thelwall will find most provocative.) To voice his desultory mood he also quotes from his new tragedy, *Osorio*, the moonlight reverie of Alhadra, who dreams of becoming utterly disembodied:

> would...that my soul
> Could drink in life from the universal Air!
> It were a lot divine in some small Skiff,
> Along some Ocean's boundless solitude,
> To float for ever with a careless course,
> And think myself the only Being alive![33]

In face of Thelwall's commitment to virtuous action in the world, this disembodied floating was the ultimate denial. Alhadra's longing to live on air alone reads like a parodic counterpart to Thelwall's concept of the 'vivifying principle', a material electric stimulus to thought and action that animates human life, and which is the subject of his published lecture on 'Animal Vitality'.[34] According to this materialist theory, what animates life is not the immortal soul, but a powerful electrical fluid that 'complete[s] the chain of connection between the divine immortal essence, and the dull inertion of created matter'. He considers the *'preliminary principles of life'* to be 'a *specific organization* and a *specific stimulus; the perfect contact of these* to be *the immediate cause*, and *life itself* to be *the state of action produced by this union'* (118). For Thelwall, therefore, life is not a spiritual drifting, but an energetic engagement of mind with organised matter, and its province is the physical world. Keeping the eyes focused on the real world

---

[29] Roe, 'Coleridge and John Thelwall', 76.
[30] John Thelwall, 'Prefatory Memoir', in *Poems chiefly written in Retirement*, xxxiv.
[31] Griggs, 349–52.
[32] A version of 'This Lime-Tree Bower', ll. 41–3. See p. 223 above.
[33] S. T. Coleridge, *Osorio*, V.i.53–8 (Mays, iii.135).
[34] John Thelwall, *Animal Vitality* (printed in Roe, *The Politics of Nature*, 119).

before you was the conviction that drove Thelwall's politics, and he measured actions and words, prose and verse, by the same standard. As he wrote in one of his *Tribune* lectures (1795–6): 'all virtue must be of an *active*, not of a *passive* nature, and, therefore . . . it is the duty of every individual to keep his eye steadily fixed upon that which is before him'.[35] What proved in effect to be Coleridge's letter of rejection seemed to be more interested in a dreamworld than in the practical future of Thelwall and his family.

Some time after returning from his stay with Coleridge at Nether Stowey, Thelwall picked up his wife's 'keep-sake' volume of Bowles's poetry, pen in hand, and began to read, mark, and annotate, in such a way as to continue his debate with Coleridge in the margins of the 'heart-honour'd' author. Thelwall's annotations are undated, but were probably done after November 1797 because they quote a line from the second of Coleridge's 'Nehemiah Higginbottom' sonnets, published that month. But an earlier dating is quite possible, given that Coleridge may have shown Thelwall his sonnet-parodies in manuscript, or if, as Duncan Wu has suggested, they had actually been 'written at Thelwall's instigation' during his visit (this is not unlikely, since one of the things they mock is the 'Della Cruscan' emphasis).[36]

Thelwall's markings and annotations begin on page 28 with Bowles's 'Sonnet XVII. To the River Cherwell' and they continue through the rest of the volume's opening section of twenty-seven sonnets, through the 'Elegy, Written at the Hotwells, Bristol' (pp. 41–6), the elegy 'On the Death of Mr Headley' (pp. 49–51), and the 'Verses on Reading Mr Howard's Description of Prisons' (pp. 55–62). After this point the annotations peter out, but there are a few markings to subsequent poems.

A preoccupation of the markings is the question of metrical emphasis about which he and Coleridge had differed in their correspondence during 1796. Thelwall marks certain lines to indicate what he takes to be their stress pattern, drawing particular attention to examples of the 'Della-crusca place of Emphasis'. Again and again he notes pairings of adjective and noun in which the adjective carries weight. It seems Thelwall cannot read Bowles without feeling the insistent way in which the qualities of things, their colour, temperature, or emotive potential, are being aurally registered. A typical example is his marking of the final lines of Bowles's 'Sonnet XXIV. May 1793':

---

[35] Thelwall, 'Prospective Principle of Virtue', 90. Judith Thompson has explored Thelwall's capacity 'to generate anxieties in Coleridge about the status and worth of his metaphysical interests relative to his friend's pragmatic activism'. See 'An Autumnal Blast, a Killing Frost: Coleridge's Poetic Conversation with John Thelwall', *SiR*, 36 (Fall 1997), 427–56 (440–1).

[36] Duncan Wu, 'Coleridge, Thelwall, and the Politics of Poetry', *CB*, 4 (Autumn 1994), 23–44.

[shrubs and laurels]
Shall put forth their green shoots, and cheer the sight!
But I shall mark their hues with sick'ning eyes,
And weep for her who in the cold grave lies!

Thelwall is an alert reader. He marks the two phrases that between them represent the sonnet's ironic juxtaposition of life and death, and in doing so he shows he is sensitive to the metrical echo of a speaker caught between *green shoots* and *cold grave*. However, given his argument to Coleridge in his letter of 10 May 1796, it is clear that Thelwall regards the adjectival stress as unwarranted (after all, most shoots are green and most graves are cold). Where Bowles offers a subjective impression, Thelwall sees only a commonplace observation. There is no marginal annotation here, but elsewhere in the volume Thelwall's accompanying notes reinforce this impenetrable barrier between the poet and his reader. We see him repeatedly resisting Bowles's subjective and affective register in favour of the objective and factual.

It becomes clear that for Thelwall the adjectival emphasis is only the symptom of a more radical weakness about Bowles's poetry. We begin to sense this in his response to the mysterious opening of 'Sonnet XX. November 1792':

There is strange musick in the stirring wind,
When low'rs the autumnal eve, and all alone
To the | dark| wood's | cold | covert | thou art | gone,

The heavy tread of the third line with its four successive stresses ('dark wood's cold covert') is of course a measured poetic effect, and Thelwall responds to it. He feels the slowness of the line, which he seems to hear as seven metrical feet rather than five. But his concern here is not just a technical one. As he reads, it is obvious that something else is troubling him, which the metre insists on emphasising. The very suggestiveness of Bowles's affective metrics, the way the poet lets the *dark* and *cold* weigh the line down, is part of the sonnet's deliberately disembodied opening, in which intangible qualities of mood and atmosphere are being evoked. The reader is made to feel the scene as vaguely *strange* and *stirring*, involving an unidentified ghostly 'thou'. The lines play on the reader's suggestibility and his readiness to have his imaginative sympathies aroused without the demands of fact and reason. It is therefore revealing (and typical of his annotations generally) that Thelwall underlines the word *thou* and writes in the margin, 'Who?' It is a small word, but an eloquent one. In a practical situation one would indeed want to know *who* had disappeared into the wood—it would be a sensible and necessary question for the rescue services.

The degree of Thelwall's resistance to Bowles, his rejection of the imaginative and emotional sympathies on which Bowles's poetry relies (and which Coleridge seemed so eager to grant), is evident in the rough handling he gives to 'Sonnet XIX. October 1792'. In this sonnet, which is entitled 'To a Friend' in later editions, the friendship bond itself becomes the model for the poet–reader relationship; but Thelwall will have none of it. He is too busy noticing other things. He underlines questionable phrases with a dotted line and footnotes them as follows:

> Go then, and join the distant city's throng!
>   Me thou dost[1] leave to solitude and tears,
>   To busy phantasies, and boding fears,
> Lest ill betide thee:[2] but 'twill not be long,
> And[3] the hard season shall be past: adieu!
>   Till then;—yet sometimes this forsaken shade
>   Rememb'ring, and these trees now left to fade;[4]
> Mayst thou, amidst the scenes of pleasure new,
> Think on thy absent friend: in heaviness
>   To me the hours shall roll, weary and slow,
>   Till mournful autumn past, and all the snow
> Of winter pale![5] the glad hour I shall bless,
> That shall restore thee from the croud again,
> To the green hamlet in[6] the peaceful plain.

>   1. While feeble expletives their aid do join!
>   2. So very simple sweet simplicity!!!
>   3. And for ere
>   4. Shrubs that she had to water I suppose.
>   5. Inversions that might break the neck of sense:
>   6. The green hamlet in the plain? Qy and?

In the first note Thelwall draws his comment from Pope's *Essay on Criticism* (a slight misquote[37]), and he predictably marks without comment the double emphasis of 'glad hour' in line 12. But it is notes 2 and 4 that catch the attention and hint at a deeper and more complex disenchantment, not merely with Bowles but with sympathetic friendship itself.

Bowles's 'Lest ill betide thee' (line 4), a relatively harmless antique phrase with a Spenserian cast,[38] evokes in Thelwall the gleeful comment: 'So very simple sweet simplicity!!!' This recalls the final line from 'To Simplicity', the second of the burlesque 'Nehemiah Higginbottom' sonnets,[39] and the exclamation marks reveal the obvious relish with which Thelwall drives his point home in Coleridge's own words. But why did that specific phrase in Sonnet XIX make Thelwall recall Coleridge's 'To Simplicity'? The answer may be that both sonnets are about the precariousness of friendship, and Bowles's concern for his friend, *Lest ill betide thee* ('lest evil should befall

---

[37] 'While *Expletives* their feeble Aid *do* join' (Pope, *An Essay on Criticism* (1711), 346).
[38] Cf. 'Lest worse betide thee' (Spenser, *The Faerie Queene*, II.iv.36).
[39] See p. 232 above.

you'), evidently brought to mind Coleridge's mocking lines about a lost
friend ('but should a friend and I | Grow cool and *miff*, O! I am *very* sad! |
And then with sonnets and with sympathy | My dreamy bosom's mystic
woes I pall... | All very simple, meek SIMPLICITY!'). In its original context,
that final line mocks not just a stylistic weakness, but a naive dependence on
a 'false friend'. With this added association, the text of Bowles's sonnet XIX
offers uncomfortable echoes to someone in Thelwall's situation in the winter
of 1797–8: ''twill not be long, | And the hard season shall be past: adieu! |
Till then;—yet sometimes this forsaken shade | Rememb'ring, and these trees
now left to fade; | Mayst thou, amidst the scenes of pleasure new, | Think on
thy absent friend' (4–9). Recovering what was in Thelwall's mind as he
annotated Bowles's poems can be nothing more than conjecture; but in
light of this, his response to line 7 of the sonnet is intriguing. The *trees
now left to fade* are for him obvious evidence of neglect. He notes: 'Shrubs
that she had to water I suppose.' With his practical emphasis, Thelwall cuts
through the words to the action—if the trees fade, then someone hasn't been
looking after them.

Thelwall is of course having fun, and he delights in subjecting Bowles's
melancholy to gleeful burlesque. In 'Sonnet XVIII', where Bowles sadly hears
'the carol of the matin bird | Salute his lonely porch', Thelwall's marginal
note suggests a more plausible alternative: 'The carrol of a bird saluting his
perch'. Throughout his reading Thelwall strongly resists anything that sac-
rifices clear description to vague evocation, and he particularly dislikes
images of evanescence, liminality, or transience. Since these are Bowles's
speciality the annotator's frustration shows. He repeatedly demands that
the text should explain itself and make clear what is going on—what is
there and what isn't. When Bowles describes the rocks of the Clifton Gorge
as they 'meet the earliest sunbeam of the sky', Thelwall responds: 'How
funny it would have been if they had met the sunbeam of the earth.' Bringing
Bowles down to earth is his aim. Any passage that evokes faint or fleeting
impressions will be ruthlessly interrogated. A poem, therefore, like the elegy
'On the Death of Henry Headley', where ideas of the fading and insubstantial
are appropriate (he died of consumption) is given a hard time. The line,
'Despair upon his fading smile was seen' is challenged: 'Despair <u>upon</u> a
fading smile?' There is a similar response a few lines later: 'Breath'd a sad
solace <u>on</u> his aching heart?' Affection breathing solace *on* a heart will not do.
Thelwall dislikes this playing over the surface of things. On the next page of
the poem he records two characteristic phrases, '<u>seem'd</u> to smile' and '<u>seem'd</u>
to suit', noting 'What a <u>seeming</u> poet this is'.

Thelwall demands clear and forceful images, and he enjoys testing out
their mettle, seeing what they're made of. Spoiling for a fight, he will
sometimes wrestle a poetic image to the floor until it begs for submission.
This happens with the first poem in Bowles's volume to carry his annota-
tions, 'Sonnet XVII. To the River Cherwell':

> CHERWELL, how pleas'd along thy willow'd edge
>   Erewhile I stray'd, or when the morn began
>   To tinge the distant turret's gleamy fan,
> Or Evening glimmer'd o'er the sighing sedge!
> And now reposing on thy banks once more,
>   I bid the pipe farewell, and that sad lay
>   Whose musick on my melancholy way
> I woo'd: amid thy waving willows hoar
> Seeking awhile to rest—till the bright sun
>   Of joy return, as when Heaven's beauteous bow
>   Beams on the night-storms passing wings below:
> Whate'er betide, yet something have I won
> Of solace, that may bear me on serene,
> 'Till Eve's last hush shall close the silent scene.[40]

This sonnet to the river of Bowles's youth, like its partner 'To the River Itchin', evokes atmospheric memories that are suggestive rather than distinct. Thelwall crowds the foot of the page with his comments, rather like a headmaster demanding an explanation from an obtuse schoolboy:

The gleamy fan of a turret?—Does he mean the sail of a windmill? Wooing the music of a sad lay? The lay then makes the music, or perhaps the lay & the music are the song, & the same, & he woo'd the tune only because the song itself was sad stuff, & not worth remembering. Heaven's beauteous bow beaming on the wings of the night-storm!!! (This must have been a lunar rainbow in spite of the bright sun.) A hush closing a scene!!!

Despite its turn from past to future (a turn Wordsworth would make more confidently in his Tintern Abbey 'Lines'[41]), Bowles's sonnet seems unable to leave the lingering mood of sadness behind. It is not hard to see his gentle nostalgia becoming for Thelwall the embodiment of what he called 'the desponding, listless, melancholy misanthropy of the retrospective principle . . . the system of brooding over the past'. For him, retrospection is not an innocent subjective mode, but a *system*, an interlocking fabric sanctioned by the Burkean romance of prejudice and 'Superstition, with her hood and cowl'.[42] In his confrontation with Bowles, as in his own prison poems, Thelwall aims for something like Paine's 'transparency' of meaning. In his iconoclastic annotation he strips away all Bowles's non-material modifiers of mood, colour, and sound, to expose the no-meaning behind the elegiac tinges, the gleams and glimmers, the hushed sighings.

With relish Thelwall disorganises this intangible system into its component parts. At the foot of page 45 containing four stanzas from the *Elegy*,

---

[40] In his jottings on this sonnet, Thelwall marks the alliterations, which he evidently thinks excessive, e.g. 'sighing sedge', 'woo'd . . . waving willows', 'beauteous bow | Beams', and 'silent scene'.

[41] See Chapter 4 above.

[42] Thelwall, 'Prospective Principle of Virtue', 92, 90.

Written at the Hotwells, Bristol, he itemises some of their phrases so that they become an incongruous bundle (the italics are mine): 'Lawns of early life, and springtide plains, and transports bland, & *hearing bells for the last*, and detaining glistening tears.—Drivelling enough for one page, at any rate', he concludes. Thelwall knows how to destroy Bowles because he understands the tenuous nature of his meanings; he sees that they depend on a finely (thinly?) spun mood, which can be easily cut through, and which relies on the reader's sympathetic attunement to sustain its effect. Bowles's early poems are about granting, and accepting, sympathy (this is frequently their subject), and with this in mind they deliberately make themselves vulnerable ('smokeable' would be Keats's word[43]). In one of those problematic stanzas from the Hotwells elegy Bowles watches the consumptives emerge for their morning walk, and he recalls his dead friend, the poet Thomas Russell, whom he last saw there:

> He heard the whispering winds that now I hear,
>   As, boding much, along these hills he pass'd;
> Yet, ah! how mournful did they meet his ear
>   On that sad morn he heard them for the last!

'Heard them for the last'—in isolation the phrase is nonsense (though Thelwall's '& hearing bells for the last' conflates this with the next stanza where Bowles contrasts the 'merry bells' of their Oxford days); but in context the silence into which the curtailed phrase moves is eloquent—at least, it is to a reader prepared to hear what isn't there.

Thelwall refuses this trust in the impalpable. It is the 'heart' of Bowles, and in the autumn of 1797 it was becoming the heart of Coleridge too. In the interval between his two chilling letters of 21 August and 14 October discouraging Thelwall from settling at Stowey, Coleridge walked to Shaftesbury in Dorset to visit Bowles.[44] Clambering on the barricades with Thelwall and matching his 'stern simplicity and vigorous Song' was no longer on the agenda. It was at this time, as Nicholas Roe has argued, that Coleridge began the process of effacing the 'realities' (about himself and the world) that Thelwall represented to him,[45] and from Thelwall's notes in the presentation copy of Bowles we have picked up hints of the bitterness and disillusionment generated in the autumn following his July visit. Underlying Thelwall's mockery of the bard of Coleridge's 'idolatry' is an aversion from a disembodied poetic language that appears to privilege things that *seem* over things that *are*. In putting Bowles to the test, Thelwall was continuing his argument with Coleridge, whose friendship had finally shown, in Gurion Taussig's

---

[43] Keats to Woodhouse, 21–2 Sept. 1819 (*The Letters of John Keats 1814–1821*, ed. Hyder Edward Rollins, 2 vols (Cambridge MA: Harvard University Press, 1958), ii.174).
[44] He set off on 6 Sept. 1797 (Griggs, 344).
[45] Roe, 'Coleridge and John Thelwall', 78–9.

words, 'a disconcerting gap between the Idea and its embodiment'.[46]
Thelwall detects in Bowles's verse a lack of robustness, an inability to take
the pressure. The poet's weightlessness is exposed as an inability to carry
weight.

One annnotation, however, suggests that resisting the 'heart-honour'd'
Bowles may not have been so easy for Thelwall, and that his reading was a
test for him too. In the wake of the treason trials and the gagging acts,
political apostasy might come, not from disenchantment, but from enchant-
ment itself—a more subtle and tempting enemy. The danger would be to
indulge in private sympathies, and default on future action by cherishing
personal retrospection, to 'consume our faculties in unavailing lamenta-
tions, which can never undo the acts that are past, but which have too
powerful an influence to unfit us for what is to come'.[47] One passage in
the Bowles volume that tempted Thelwall to indulge his own sensibilities is
from the 'Verses on Reading Mr Howard's Description of Prisons'. Given
Thelwall's experience in 1794 its picture of the reformer John Howard
visiting a man in solitary confinement might be expected to have struck a
sympathetic chord:

> Despairing, from his cold and flinty bed,
> With fearful muttering he hath rais'd his head:
> "What pitying spirit, what unwonted guest,
> Strays to this last retreat, these shades unblest?
> From | life and | light | shut | out, | beneath this cell
> Long have I bid hope's cheering sun farewell

Thelwall homes in on the vivid penultimate line, but only to resist its
emotional appeal. Where Bowles stirs recollections of Milton's blindness
('Nature's works to mee expung'd and ras'd, | And wisdom at one entrance
quite shut out'[48]) Thelwall marks up the 'Della Cruscan' emphasis. But he is
also irritated by the last three words of that line:

How did the prisoner get beneath his cell to bid farewell to anything? But I forgot he
tells us in the same line that he is shut out from life (i.e. is dead) & then to put him (i.e.
to bury him) under the cell was a cheap way of disposing of him: but after being so
disposed of, it was very civil of him to make such a speech to Mr Howard?

The obtuseness of this is startling. No poetry can survive such literalisation
of meaning, such a withholding of imaginative sympathies. But perhaps
Thelwall is right: how could a good poet possibly write *beneath this cell*?

An answer had already been given by Thelwall himself at the climax of his
speech to the jury when on trial for his life:

---

[46] Taussig, *Coleridge and the Idea of Friendship*, 212.
[47] Thelwall, 'Prospective Principle of Virtue', 90.
[48] John Milton, *Paradise Lost*, iii.49–50.

I have been destined to the vilest dungeon of Newgate—a miserable hole almost impervious to a ray of light...a charnel house, whose ragged walls, and old hereditary filth might persuade the wretched inhabitant that he was already buried.[49]

Thelwall knew too well the import of Bowles's line—the sense of being not just *in* a cell, but *beneath* it.

In annotating the 'keep-sake' volume of Bowles, Thelwall was putting to the test a principle which had guided him as a public figure, and which had defined the oppositional nature of his friendship with Coleridge: 'the opinions of six moments and of six thousand years...stands precisely upon the same basis, the basis of reason and argument; and, therefore, must be brought to the same test of experimental investigation'.[50] What he demanded of poetry was what he demanded of himself, and of others.

To judge from the poetic 'sparring' with Coleridge and its follow-up in his angry annotation of Bowles, we might think that Thelwall had abjured any kind of poetry expressive of personal feelings, especially retrospective ones. But the truth is just the opposite. The verse Thelwall wrote during the weeks following his Somerset visit in July 1797 shows him exploring those subjective responses that the prison-poet had rejected. It is remarkable that not only did he find a new expressiveness in his poetry, but that he did so with an immediate mastery of the subtle rhythmic demands of blank verse. There is a degree of contradiction here, but Thelwall's shift in style confirms the sense of release that his experiences in Nether Stowey gave him. Hearing Wordsworth and Coleridge reading their poetry under the trees clearly made an impression on him, and encouraged him to experiment for himself with the sounds of friendly poetic converse. He at last found a poetic mode that gave scope to his finely tuned ear with its responsiveness to degrees of metrical emphasis.

Thelwall's poetry of the late summer and autumn of 1797 shows a new discursive confidence and flexibility, as if he is eager to accommodate himself to Coleridge's more conversational poetic tones, and enter into dialogue with his friend. These poems have rightly been viewed as responsive to, and in their turn influential on, the development of the Coleridgean 'conversational' poem.[51] By turning to blank verse and endowing it with what he would later call 'the melodies of conversation'—'more temperate in their compass than those of public declamation'—Thelwall was able to employ a responsive 'Flexure of Tone' (his phrase) that had its own quieter rhetoric,[52]

---

[49] John Thelwall, *The Natural and Constitutional Right of Britons* (London: For the Author, 1795), in Claeys (ed.), *The Politics of English Jacobinism*, 60. The speech, on his counsel's advice, was not delivered in court.

[50] Thelwall, 'Prospective Principle of Virtue', 89.

[51] See especially Thompson, 'An Autumnal Blast' (n. 35 above); Davies, *Presences that Disturb*, 210–40.

[52] *Selections and Original Articles for Mr Thelwall's Lectures* (Birmingham, 1806), n.p., quoted by Gravil, 'The Somerset Sound', 11. On Thelwall's 'poetic dialogue' with Coleridge and Wordsworth, see Davies, *Presences that Disturb*, 210–40.

although, as we shall see, matters of emphasis remain important in this more muted context. But other dramatic elements were also released by Thelwall's Somerset idyll, which suggest that the opportunity to 'loose the world in this scene of enchantment' had served to heighten his awareness of past horrors.[53] In his poem 'Maria. A Fragment', written in October 1797, he revisits his confinement with a keen sense not just of the prison cell, but of the emotional self-censoring it brought. In retrospect he sees how

> by the watchful eyes,
> And ears, and prying insolence of guards
> Check'd and imbitter'd, have I heav'd the sigh,
> And felt the anxious wish, that yet the tongue
> Disdained to utter, or the throbbing breast
> To own, uncheck'd...[54]   (12–17)

We can detect a Cordelia-like guardedness in these words. The active verbs are almost hidden away. Heart and tongue turn in on themselves and refuse to communicate. The verse from this point of the poem keeps checking itself (like the double negative in the last two lines), capturing the effects of time and space that such constriction (and enforced self-constriction) brings.

But while space cramps him physically, time stretches shapelessly. At those moments in prison when he could expect a visit from his family, time slowed to an especially 'tardy pace' (45). The verse becomes hesitant, almost recalcitrant and uncooperative, as if it is waiting for some rhythmic impetus. The speech therapist in Thelwall conveys an effect of constriction under which someone labours to release their language into eloquence. In the following passage from 'Maria' the repeated awkward 'then's, 'when's, and 'only's, along with the dashes and audible sighs, all conspire to suggest how difficult human communication and family feeling (what he incongruously calls 'the social banquet') might become in the context of the prison cell:

> Chiefly then
> When, with a tardy pace, the wish'd-for hour
> Approach'd, that to a husband's, father's sight
> Promis'd the social banquet. Then—ah! then,
> When thro' my grated dungeon I have gaz'd,
> With straining eye unmov'd, upon the gate
> Thro' which the partner of my soul should pass—
> And this, my only babe:——my only, then,
> And still my best beloved!—ah! how high
> (With what a tide of fervour thro' my breast)
> Swell'd the fond passion—for Thee, babe belov'd!—   (44–54)

---

[53] Thelwall to Stella Thelwall, 18 July 1797 (Davies, *Presences that Disturb*, 297).
[54] Thelwall, 'Maria. A Fragment', in *Poems chiefly written in Retirement*, 143.

This is not the kind of poetry Thelwall could have risked writing in Newgate. The movement of the lines is hesitant, the pulse unsettled. The most dynamic line (53), with its *tide of fervour*, is placed in parenthesis, and serves only to check the natural impetus of 'how high swell'd the fond passion'. The visual fixation is effective too. The 'straining eye unmov'd' gains irony from its sense of total concentration. The lines place the focus and the emphasis exactly, with certain words carrying full weight: *grated, gaz'd, straining, gate*, pinpointing for us the coordinates of the prisoner's constricted world. The final line of the passage struggles to assert its own stresses and shatters the iambic pentameter: 'Swell'd the fond passion—for Thee, babe belov'd!—'. The emphatic pause between '*substantive* monosyllables' (here 'thee' and 'babe') was something that Thelwall the prosodist always insisted on.[55] Substance is the key—very different from the limp and affected Della Cruscan emphasis.

Such a level of verbal responsiveness gives these post-Nether Stowey poems a new and distinctive voice, and one more organic in character. The contrast with *Poems Written in Close Confinement* is stark. In his prison poetry, as we saw earlier in this chapter, Thelwall had clung onto reified abstractions in unrelentingly heroic tones that kept more shaded personal experience out of the picture. As poems of resistance they exploited a public voice fitted for declaring justice, truth, and right. The result, in both sonnets and odes, was a series of pageants in which Liberty, Freedom, and Virtue are set against Tyranny, Oppression, Power, Luxury, and Vice. In the prison poems, the voice of William Collins's odes predominates (severe, classical, frieze-like), but without Collins's more enigmatic symbolism and some of his pathos. The effect as we read is of Citizen Thelwall projecting Truth and Virtue in all their clarity of outline. In this he becomes a Flaxman of words ('O for the Spartan Fife, to pierce the ear | Of slumbering Virtue, and again restore | Those ancient Manners—simple and severe, | That aw'd encroaching Tyranny!').[56] The language is declaratory and visionary, not personal and explorative.

In the new blank verse, however, Thelwall risks being a voice of Sensibility. In 'Maria. A Fragment', tone and rhythm are modulated so as to be responsive to layers of thought; and the reader is aware of a verbal medium in which ambivalence, uncertainties, and elements of tension or relaxation can register. Instead of declaring ideas and principles, the poems embody experience and are more attuned to human discourse. Thelwall's post-Nether Stowey poetry reads as if something has unblocked the restrictions on his own speech, and they suggest he is trusting words to convey more mixed personal thoughts and feelings. During his stay with the Wordsworths and Coleridges Thelwall became for a short time part of a sympathetic

---

[55] See Gravil, 'The Somerset Sound', 9–10.
[56] John Thelwall, Sonnet IV: 'To Simplicity of Manners', in *Poems Written in Close Confinement*, 4. Cf. 'Who shall awake the *Spartan* Fife?' (Collins, 'Ode to Liberty', 1).

reading community. One suspects the impact was considerable, and that he heard and felt poetry, especially the subtle inflections of blank verse, in ways he had not experienced before.

The poem Thelwall composed immediately after waving goodbye to his friends was 'Lines, written at Bridgewater, in Somersetshire, on the 27th of July, 1797; during a long excursion, in quest of a peaceful retreat'.[57] A more conversational, philosophical tone predominates here, reminiscent of his friend's 'Effusion 35' and the recently written poems 'To the Reverend George Coleridge', and 'This Lime-Tree Bower'. But the verse also draws on earlier voices, ranging from the intelligent variousness of Thomson and Cowper, to Miltonic exposition, and elements of Horatian balance worthy of Pope. But here again Thelwall appears to be weighing and testing his phrases, conscious of how variations in stress express the mental and emotional dynamics behind the words. In the extraordinary opening section of 'Lines, written at Bridgewater' (ll. 1–69) we move through a variety of eighteenth-century poetic modes, here almost mood-interludes, which the fluid blank verse somehow manages to accommodate into one long organic paragraph, taking in successively the satiric, the picturesque, the romantic, the patriotic, the mystical, the sociable, the sublime, and even finally the georgic. At this point, line 70, the exclamation that has begun the poem ('Day of my double Birth!') is repeated, recalling him back to the uncomfortable present: 'my soul | Is sick of public turmoil—ah, most sick | Of the vain effort to redeem a Race | Enslav'd, because degenerate' (71–4).

Only in the third paragraph, after this angry outburst, does the longed-for image of retreat finally establish itself in full-throated ease:

> Ah! let me, far in some sequester'd dell,
> Build my low cot; most happy might it prove,
> My Samuel! near to thine, that I might oft
> Share thy sweet converse, best-belov'd of friends!—
> Long-lov'd ere known: for kindred sympathies
> Link'd, tho far distant, our congenial souls.   (85–90)

Here the relaxed rhythmic negotiations of Thelwall's blank verse recall the easy human converse in Milton's Paradise, where angels stay for lunch. The quiet but firm emphases convey a sense of interlinked identities (*belov'd, lov'd, link'd*), where distance and secrecy are conjoined with proximity and intimacy; and the bonding words (*share, kindred, congenial*) allow him to elide past and future into a single contemplative present. The effect, in that sense, is a pastoral one. The organisation of these lines, with their composed picture of 'philosophic amity' (92), could hardly be more different from the prison description in 'Maria'. There is even room for a friendly Della Cruscan emphasis ('low cot', 86).

---

[57] Printed in *Poems chiefly written in Retirement*, 126–32.

As the scene develops in 'Lines, written at Bridgewater', Thelwall pictures himself and Coleridge in the Pantisocratic primal scene; but although levelling implications are hinted at, the pair slip into friendly enquiry and debate, seeking wisdom rather than instigating action. The polite tone and polished phrases, like the two men, are well matched:

> and it would be sweet,
> With kindly interchange of mutual aid,
> To delve our little garden plots, the while
> Sweet converse flow'd, suspending oft the arm
> And half-driven spade, while, eager, one propounds,
> And listens one, weighing each pregnant word,
> And pondering fit reply   (94–100)

The lines achieve a fine balance of weight and ease, like the men pausing in their labour. As talk flows and bodies become still, there is simultaneously motion and stasis ('Sweet converse flow'd, suspending oft the arm'). Relaxation rather than tension comes from the light caesuras and the very neat chiasmus ('one propounds, | And listens one') which enacts the balanced reasonableness of their debate. This is a community in which Thelwall's thoughts can be picked up and returned to him with interest. The shared scene is not combative and provocative, but natural, somehow patient without the strain of patience. Even the passage that follows, where 'knotty' philosophical argument takes over, has an ease and clarity in the way the phrases fold round the line endings and weave a thoughtful fabric. The Adamic digger gives way naturally to the ruminative philosopher, as if Raphael is listening:

> that may untwist
> The knotty point—perchance, of import high—
> Of Moral Truth, of Causes Infinite,
> Creating Power! or Uncreated Worlds
> Eternal and uncaus'd! or whatsoe'er,
> Of Metaphysic, or of Ethic lore,
> The mind, with curious subtilty, pursues—
> Agreeing, or dissenting—sweet alike,
> When wisdom, and not victory, the end.   (100–8)

The terms run with surprising ease and speed, allowing argument to be guided by a civilised curiosity. Such well-balanced verse, we feel, could never be dogmatic. Thelwall has been seeking an element of metrical poise and reassurance, and seems to have found it.

But the drama of the poem is only suspended; and an exclamation returns him to the reality of the present, to the 'fateful Day!', as he calls it (the coincidental day of his birth and marriage) on which the poem had begun. In true Thelwall fashion he realises the difference between hard reality and the fictional page of romance, which his imagination has been filling, he admits, with 'Fancy's glowing characters' (158). The next passage negotiates this move towards reality with a strong sense of the emphasis being held back, the pulse of the verse somehow apprehensively muted until the crucial word finally comes (my italics):

> Ah, fateful Day!
> If that the Year thou lead'st (as fain my soul
> Would augur, from some hours of joy late past,
> And friendship's unexpected)—if the Year
> Thou usherest in, has aught, perchance, in store
> To *realize* this vision, welcome most——
> Ah most, most welcome! for my soul, at peace,
> Shall to it's native pleasures then return ...   (164–71)

After the emphatic enunciation of *realize*, on which all this hangs, there is a brief emotional flutter, then composure again with the reassuring word 'return'. He understands the import of the 'real', and what the realisation of his hopes depends on. Thelwall's blank verse is alive not only to the movements of mind and feeling, but to the valence of words themselves, their force and significance.

In early October 1797 Thelwall sent some of this new poetry to Coleridge, with a letter (now lost) in which he evidently reminded his friend of his wish to settle in the neighbourhood, and find refuge there. In reply he received the 'I would to heaven, it were in my power to serve you' letter of 14 October discussed earlier, which also contained brief comments on the poems.[58] One of them was evidently a shorter version of 'To the Infant Hampden.— Written during a sleepless night. Derby. Oct. 1797',[59] a text in which Thelwall's influence on Coleridge's verse, specifically on 'Frost at Midnight' and 'Dejection', can be fully appreciated;[60] but what concerns us here is Thelwall's continuing search for poise and stability, and his metrical commitment to what carries weight. In 'To the Infant Hampden' his sleeping child (not yet weighed down by the import of his name) acts as a point of stillness and silence, which only heightens the storm and stress around him. The 'pelting storms | Of cold unkindness' have rightly reminded critics of Lear on the heath; but the possibility of a miracle is surely held out by the equally strong recollection of Pericles and Marina: 'Ill-omen'd babe! | Conceiv'd in tempests, and in tempests born! | What destiny awaits thee?' (23–5). Is the genre to be tragedy or romance? In sending the poem to Coleridge at that moment he was leaving the issue open.

Once again we seem to be hearing Thelwall—and his verse—searching for a place to rest, rhythmically and emotionally:

---

[58] Griggs, 348–52.

[59] Coleridge's letter implies that he has seen a 25-line version of 'To the Infant Hampden' (44 lines in its printed version), which Thelwall has provocatively described as a sonnet (Griggs, 351).

[60] Thompson, 'An Autumnal Blast'.

> Ah! sleep secure:
> And may thy dream of Life be ne'er disturb'd
> With visions such as mar thy father's peace—
> Visions (Ah! that they were but such indeed!)
> That shew this world a wilderness of wrongs—
> A waste of troubled waters: whelming floods
> Of tyrannous injustice, canopy'd
> With clouds dark louring; whence the pelting storms
> Of cold unkindness the rough torrents swell,
> On every side resistless. There my Ark—
> The scanty remnant of my delug'd joys!
> Floats anchorless; while thro' the dreary round,
> Fluttering on anxious pinion, the tired foot
> Of persecuted Virtue cannot find
> One spray on which to rest; or scarce one leaf
> To cheer with promise of subsiding woe.   (29–44)

The stormy rhetoric of the long first sentence, with its almost suffocating tautology ('troubled waters', 'whelming floods', 'rough torrents'), reaches its climax in the emphatic phrase, 'On every side resistless'. As everything closes in, the sudden glimpse, '*There* my Ark', appears both precarious and distanced, as if his hopes are floating away from him (how much weaker would '*and* my Ark' be here). The various stormy nouns combine into that single decisive verb *delug'd*; but simultaneously there is suspension and drifting: 'There my Ark . . . | . . . Floats anchorless'. The poem ends on a note of exhaustion ('dreary', 'tired') and an almost baffled anticlimax. The last line is lamely abstract ('To cheer with promise of subsiding woe') and it would sound almost jaunty did not the word 'subsiding' carry its freight of implication. And metrically too, the closing lines seem to have lost their impetus. Line 41 is in effect distressed, its syllables hardly knowing where to settle: 'Fluttering on anxious pinion, the tired foot'. The phrase 'tired foot', practically Della Cruscan in emphasis, describes exactly what it is, physically and metrically.

Coleridge was evidently disappointed with Thelwall's poem, and in his 14 October letter he comments: 'The last line & a half I suppose miswritten—what can be the meaning of "or scarce one Leaf To cheer etc. &c.– "?' Having in this chapter followed Thelwall's provocative engagement with matters of emphasis, and with the tendency, as he thought, in Coleridge and Bowles to place it wrongly, we can appreciate the implications of this ending: Thelwall believes that in his drowned world where his ark floats aimlessly there is nowhere to anchor and nothing to which he can cling, not the smallest spray or even a single leaf on which he can place any weight. We have seen that in Thelwall's moral metrics, matters of priority and principle were firm. But if he was looking to Coleridge to be his Mount Ararat, then he was disappointed. At this moment, with almost painful irony, he found himself seeking support from someone who, in this very same letter, with Thelwall's terrifying image of potential drowning in front of him, was able to write:

I should much wish, like the Indian Vishna, to float about along an infinite ocean cradled in the flower of the Lotos, & wake once in a million years for a few minutes—just to know that I was going to sleep a million years more.

When he received this letter, I suspect Thelwall knew the game was up.

11 Returning to the Ruined Cottage

We in our sweet sequester'd Orchard-plot
Sit on the Tree crook'd earth-ward; whose old boughs,
That hang above us in an arborous roof,
Stirr'd by the faint gale of departing May
Send their loose blossoms slanting o'er our heads

—S. T. Coleridge, 'Dedication. To the
Reverend George Coleridge', ll. 57–61

SO FAR IN this study of poetic organisation little has been said about nature, which has always featured strongly in studies of Romantic organicism, whether in terms of a pantheistic 'One Life', or as the master metaphor for ideas of germination and growth.[1] It will long ago have become clear that the eighteenth-century organic tradition I am tracing into the 1790s is one to which holistic or teleological concepts are alien. Unifying Ideas that privilege notions of transcendence, completion/perfection, or the eternal/timeless gain no meaning from a spatiotemporal context in which all boundaries tend to be permeable. Things encroach and overlap; situations alter; directions may be diverted; and categories may be blurred or extended. This means that the core issue here is an organisational one, of finding coherence and continuity in human experience, within the constraints of time and space—and, of course, human mortality. Given these organic features, nature's function is not to preside over the world, to set paradigms for us, or to imbue life with a spiritual purpose, but to be what it is: an infinitely various living continuity within whose terms and through whose energies humanity is able to survive.

In the language of the biblical story, we are dealing here with 'fallen' nature, in which time, decay, and death coexist with beauty, growth, and power. Humanity's position within it is at best one of collaboration. But to conceptualise 'Nature' as a single force, rather than as ever-changing modes through which forces work, risks making 'it' a purposeful system rather than an endlessly varied process that takes different forms. When Coleridge sits on the deformed old fruit tree in his orchard at Nether Stowey on 26 May 1797 he is caught for a moment in an emblematic natural situation, with the

---

[1] On the 'One Life', see Jonathan Wordsworth, *The Music of Humanity* (New York/ Evanston: Harper and Row, 1969), 184–201; and William A. Ulmer, 'Wordsworth, the One Life, and *The Ruined Cottage*', *SP*, 93 (1996), 304–31. On Coleridge's complex developing involvement with nature, see Raimonda Modiano, *Coleridge and the Concept of Nature* (Tallahassee: Florida State University Press, 1985).

old, bent tree 'crook'd earth-ward' while its youthful blossoms are shed overhead. The tree is simultaneously old and young. In Philip Larkin's fine words, 'its yearly trick of looking new | Is written down in rings of grain'.[2] This is the organic quality, the Lockean 'one common life' that connects the gnarled trunk, bent by the weight of humanity, to the repeated process by which 'new particles of matter' are 'vitally united to the living plant, in a like continued organization'. In his dedicatory verses, 'To the Reverend George Coleridge, of Ottery St. Mary, Devon',[3] from which my epigraph comes, Coleridge is exploiting nature's human accommodations as a context for negotiating the renewal of the family bonds that in recent years have become severely strained, hoping to reconcile rooted age and 'loose' youth. In this early 'conversation poem' Coleridge is heavily invested in reconnections, in finding a mode of converse through which to reconnect himself to his family and establish continuities with his Ottery childhood and with the brother who had become the father-figure of his teenage years.[4]

The poem thus stages a return to his childhood home:

> A blessed Lot hath he, who having past
> His youth and early manhood in the stir
> And turmoil of the world, retreats at length,
> With cares that move, not agitate the heart,
> To the same Dwelling where his Father dwelt;
> And haply views his tottering little ones
> Embrace those aged knees and climb that lap,
> On which first kneeling his own Infancy
> Lisp'd its brief prayer...   (1–9)

We are struck by the simple emblem of generations coming together, of youth in the lap of age, before we quite realise the complex layerings of the picture—that it can be neither Coleridge's own homecoming nor his brother's current domestic scene (their father had died when Coleridge was eight, and George is now in his place). It is rather a set of superimposed images that articulate what might have been, in which the prodigal's return to the paternal dwelling merges into the image of George and his children. In the ghostly palimpsest three generations are present: Coleridge imagining George watching his children embracing their (dead) grandfather.

After these lines, the picture immediately expands to accommodate their other brothers into the scene of mutual happiness: 'Such, O my earliest Friend! | Thy Lot, and such thy Brothers too enjoy, | ... | Yet cheer'd and cheering: now fraternal Love | Hath drawn you to one centre' (9–13).

---

[2] Philip Larkin, 'The Trees', in *High Windows* (London: Faber and Faber, 1974), p. 6, ll. 7–8.

[3] S. T. Coleridge, 'To the Reverend George Coleridge, of Ottery St. Mary, Devon', 1797 *Poems*, vii–xii. The poem is dated 'May 26th, 1797. *Nether-Stowey, Somerset*'.

[4] Coleridge's hopes for his brother's acceptance were not fulfilled. He noted in one copy: 'to Posterity, let it be known, that the Reverend George Coleridge was displeased and thought his character endangered by this Dedication!!' (Mays, i.326).

Coleridge feels himself uprooted from this special (though by now rather crowded) place. In the poem's continuing language of trees, he has become 'like a Tree with leaves of feeble stem' (22); and although some sheltering friends have turned into poisonous 'Manchineels' (the legendary poison tree), one man has proved to be a steadfast 'Oak' (Tom Poole). He himself, Coleridge realises, has lost touch with his home ground where he might have flourished: 'Me from the spot where first I sprang to light, | Too soon transplanted' (17–18). Conscious of how far his political activities might have alienated him, Coleridge hopes through the poem's amicable converse to renew his family ties. Or to use the poem's own arboreal imagery: the rebellious scion offers to re-engraft himself onto the family stock.

By employing the georgic motif of engrafting in relation to what appears a simple pastoral picture, I want to introduce a distinction important for this chapter, where the forces of nature make demands on humans and introduce interpretive complications that break the limits of the pastoral world. In 'To the Reverend George Coleridge', for example, the field of reference might seem confined to Virgil's first *Eclogue*, with the poet hopefully picturing himself as the Tityrus figure, returning to claim his paternal acres that have been restored to him, while perhaps fearing that he will remain Meliboeus, sent into exile from his alienated home. In Virgil's pastoral world these two forces of repatriation and exile are beautifully poised through the harmony of bucolic song. But Coleridge knows his position is more conflicted, and that he really belongs in the troubled world beyond. He may be offering his brother 'various songs, | Which I have fram'd in many a various mood' (69–70), but this comes with a warning to expect 'deeper notes, such as beseem | Or that sad wisdom, folly leaves behind; | Or the high raptures of prophetic Faith; | Or such, as tun'd to these tumultuous times | Cope with the tempest's swell!' (64–9). This is no pastoral singer, then, but a voice of generic instability and heroic potential, a man who knows he lives in the world of experience, not innocence. In this context, his rueful phrase 'too soon transplanted' (18) now begins to sound like a georgic warning that might have come from Christopher Smart's *The Hop-Garden*, or John Philips's *Cyder*.

This is because, unlike the pastoral scene, the georgic landscape is located east of Eden, in the fallen world of time and change where nature offers a constant challenge to human strength, skill, and wisdom.[5] The georgic poem is therefore a genre in which the concept of organisation (as opposed to structure) is crucial, and human experience (Virgil's *usus*) is at a premium. For all its seemingly sprawling character, the georgic is primarily interested in matters of 'economy' in the wider eighteenth-century sense of putting materials to productive use, harnessing energies effectively, and exploiting

---

[5] For a fuller discussion see David Fairer, *English Poetry of the Eighteenth Century, 1700–1789* (London: Longman, 2003), 79–101.

resources with skill. 'Organising Poetry', indeed, could be an appropriate title for a study of georgic itself. Whether the setting is the orchard, the market garden, Coalbrookdale, St Kitts, or Birmingham, in the georgic careful organisation is needed, and all theories have to be tested. The natural world, subject to the endless cycle of the seasons, is harsh but bountiful and will respond to ingenuity and practical experience. The georgic is informed by natural processes that need to be directed, whether it is the economy of the human body, the organisation of a sugar plantation, the functioning of coalmines, or the conduct of the nation's woollen industry.[6]

The adaptable eighteenth-century georgic had settled the postlapsarian landscape in which human life persists 'through the varied tenour of perpetual decay, fall, renovation and progression'.[7] Although the formal blank-verse georgic fell out of fashion in the 1760s, its elements were easily transfused into the topographical poem, the progress poem, and the descriptive/meditative poem of the later decades, in which georgic episodes and motifs are common.[8] Landscape poetry, especially celebrating a local area, is often conscious of land use and other practical concerns, and historical landmarks and the traces of past events may also be incorporated.[9] The character of a scene frequently has a temporal dimension. As they were for Hesiod and Virgil, the contingencies of time and place are crucial for later georgic. The genre offers us, in Thomson's words, 'a broken World' where 'all is off the Poise', so that success or failure can depend on local conditions of soil, geology, or weather. The universalised always must cede to the particular context, and allowance be made for 'ever-changing Views of Good and Ill, | Form'd infinitely various'.[10] Georgic organisation is thus closely bound up with the seasonal round or routines of one kind or another, and at its heart is the motif of the cycle or return, what Stephen Duck the Thresher called 'the Toils of each revolving Year'.[11] Unlike the more reassuring repetitions of pastoral, georgic's returns impose fresh constraints and are seldom free of challenge or the need to adapt. If pastoral endlessly revisits a

---

[6] John Armstrong, *The Art of Preserving Health* (1744); James Grainger, *The Sugar-Cane* (1764); John Dalton, *A Descriptive Poem, Addressed to Two Ladies, At their Return from Viewing The Mines Near Whitehaven* (1755); John Dyer, *The Fleece* (1757).

[7] Edmund Burke, *Reflections on the Revolution in France* [1790], ed. Conor Cruise O'Brien (Harmondsworth: Penguin, 1986), 120. See p. 77 above.

[8] Georgic motifs and episodes play an important part in poems like Richard Jago's *Edge-Hill* (1764), Henry James Pye's *Faringdon Hill* (1783), and most popularly Cowper's *The Task* (1785). Alan Bewell has revealed Wordsworth's indebtedness to the eighteenth-century progress poem. See *Wordsworth and the Enlightenment: Nature, Man, and Society in the Experimental Poetry* (New Haven: Yale University Press, 1989).

[9] Two characteristic examples are Anne Wilson, *Teisa: A Descriptive Poem of the River Teese, Its Towns and Antiquities* (Newcastle: Printed for the Author, 1778); and Thomas Maude, *Verbeia; or, Wharfedale; A Poem, Descriptive and Didactic, with Historical Remarks* (York: W. Blanchard, 1782).

[10] James Thomson, *Spring* (1728), 318, 278, 298–9.

[11] Stephen Duck, *The Thresher's Labour* (1730), 8.

primal world (and can draw satirical/political ironies from this pattern), georgic has to retrieve repeatable strategies from sites of experience, trial and error, where change is a fact of life.

It is this motif of the *return*, as a point where pastoral and georgic possibilities meet, which is the chief concern of the present chapter. In the 1790s, against a background of rapid change, disorganisation, and uncertainty, the act of revisiting is potentially a highly charged one. It can offer scenarios where the pull between idealism and pragmatism is played out across a landscape in which pastoral and georgic elements create tensions. In the post-Bastille years, the levelled scene of Adamic pastoral developed its revolutionary potential (in Southey's *Eclogues*, for example), while the georgic's practical accommodations and hard-won continuities offered models for endurance and survival. The 'iron times' of Virgilian georgic, with its context of civil war, social conflict, and economic pressures,[12] had special resonance during this decade, but in response there was an appeal to strategies of self-contained 'local attachment' or self-reliant cottage economy that might also have pastoral suggestions.[13]

It is clear that Coleridge at this time was aware of these alternatives as fundamentally incompatible, and requiring a choice of direction. His poem 'Reflections on Having Left a Place of Retirement' creates a dramatic scenario out of the move from his Edenic Clevedon retreat into the public world.[14] By an act of willed self-expulsion, he sets a distinctly pastoral stereotype ('the little landscape round | Was green and woody, and refresh'd the eye. | It was a spot, which you might aptly call | The VALLEY of SECLUSION!') in opposition to the bracing appeal of 'honourable toil' in the world beyond. There is no overlap or ambivalence here; and even when he contemplates his future recollection of the scene, it will be a nostalgia limited to those moments 'when... | Rests the tir'd mind, and waking loves to dream'. Although Coleridge declares '*My Spirit shall revisit thee*, dear Cot!' (my italics), the daydream will bring neither nourishment nor rededication. Instead he will 'sigh fond wishes' for his former 'sweet Abode', his own lost Auburn. In contrast, Wordsworth's well known lyrical version of this idea, 'How often has my spirit turned to thee!', suggests a deep need to reconnect himself to a source of energy and refreshment. Indeed, it is in Wordsworth's handling of the re-visiting motif that the more nuanced implications of these landscapes are explored. In his hands

---

[12] Virgil, *Georgics*, trans. L. P. Wilkinson (Harmondsworth: Penguin, 1982), i.498–514. The notion of the 'iron times' of the present goes back to Hesiod's *Works and Days*. See M. L. West (trans.), *Theogony and Works and Days* (Oxford: Oxford University Press, 1988), 42.

[13] See Richard Polwhele, *The Influence of Local Attachment, with Respect to Home. A Poem* (London: J. Johnson, 1796; enlarged 2nd edn 1798). Idyllic cottage life is the subject of Joanna Baillie's 'A Winter Day' and 'A Summer Day', *Poems* (London: J. Johnson, 1790), 1–33.

[14] The poem first appeared in the *Monthly Magazine* for Oct. 1796 and was included in 1797 *Poems*, 100–4.

their generic associations have the effect of complicating the argumentative texture. In Wordsworth's poetry during 1797–8 various 'returns' are enacted in ways that suggest he has an acute sense of their subtler possibilities.

In this context, it is now time to revisit his 'Lines written a few miles above Tintern Abbey, on revisiting the banks of the Wye during a tour, July 13, 1798'. The green pastoral landscape that greets us at its opening (revived again after the length of seven long chapters) has often been viewed in terms of composure and unity. In Alan Grob's philosophical reading, the 'idealized prospect' conveys 'a deep and abiding calm and a coalescence of particulars into a single, interlocking and indivisible pattern of harmony' where 'products of human agency... unite readily into an almost uniform composition, harmonious and silent'.[15] But the critic's rapt response, I would suggest, risks substituting a contemplative Idea for the spoken words of the poem as we actually hear them. It is a quiet voice, certainly, but a discriminating one, matched to a restless eye, and a mind that won't quite let things be, but likes to adjust and slightly qualify what it sees. The result, if we think of it in these more spatial and conversational (rather than contemplative) terms, is a little more unsettled. The greenness of the scene is insisted on, but in such a way that hovers between a reassuring pastoral innocence and something that could be disturbing if we looked at it from a different angle:

> These plots of cottage-ground, these orchard-tufts,
> Which, at this season, with their unripe fruits,
> Among the woods and copses lose themselves,
> Nor, with their *green* and simple hue, disturb
> The wild *green* landscape. Once again I see
> These hedge-rows, hardly hedge-rows, little lines
> Of sportive wood run wild; these pastoral farms
> *Green* to the very door[16]

This repeated *green* (my italics) seems like the timeless green of pastoral—the green world of *As You Like It*, the 'green thought in a green shade' of Marvell's inviolable inner universe, or Dylan Thomas's memories of his Welsh childhood, 'young and easy under the apple boughs | ... and happy as the grass was green'.[17] The pastoral is certainly there in Wordsworth's poem, wearing its emblematic 'green and simple hue'. This is not Thomson's minutely observed georgic palate that catches the specific 'wan declining green' of an autumn twilight, but a simple pastoral greenness[18]—until, that

---

[15] Alan Grob, *The Philosophic Mind: A Study of Wordsworth's Poetry and Thought, 1797–1805* (Columbus: Ohio State University Press, 1973), 14.

[16] William Wordsworth, 'Tintern Abbey', in *Lyrical Ballads, with A Few Other Poems* (Bristol: Biggs and Cottle; London: Longman, 1798), ll. 11–18.

[17] Dylan Thomas, 'Fern Hill', 1–2 (*Dylan Thomas: The Poems*, ed. Daniel Jones (London: J. M. Dent, 1971), 195).

[18] James Thomson, *Autumn* (1730), 951–2.

is, we begin to sense the voice's knowingness: the extent to which it appreciates that at this point of the season the 'unripe' fruits, being themselves green, merge into the foliage; how it understands the way growth can easily 'sport' if not properly tended.[19] If we read the scene from a georgic perspective, its Edenic innocence becomes disturbed by questions about the relationship between nature and culture and the role of human activity in cultivating nature's resources. There is a hint in the word 'disturb' itself, which is uttered only to be denied ('Nor, with their green and simple hue, disturb | The wild green landscape'), as if something potentially disturbing (ripened fruit perhaps?) is being held at bay.

If we try registering it in terms of a georgic landscape, the concept of 'pastoral farms' becomes an oxymoron: is no one on the farms working? If this is a farming landscape, then where is the cultivation? The hedges are evidently neglected and have got out of hand, becoming those playful 'little lines | Of sportive wood run wild'. What for the pastoral eye is a unified harmonious scene arouses an observant georgic curiosity. The orchard trees, in fact, are contrary to best practice as detailed in John Philips's *Cyder*, which celebrates 'well rang'd Files of Trees' each with its 'circling Trench' kept well watered, especially in July ('when the Sun in *Leo* rides').[20] Wordsworth's are mere 'orchard tufts' clustered closely together and disappearing in the overgrowing woodland. And as for the farmhouses being '[g]reen to the very door', has no one been weeding the paths? Are the cottages even occupied? A rural economy under wartime pressure in 1798, a year of desperate shortages, vagrancy, and poverty, is seemingly being reclaimed by nature.

When human activity is detected it is hidden away as if mysterious and illicit. The poet sees:

> wreathes of smoke
> Sent up, in silence, from among the trees,
> With some uncertain notice, as might seem,
> Of vagrant dwellers in the houseless woods   (18–21)

The business of humanity, emptied from the farming scene, emerges in disembodied form through what could qualify as the vaguest line in English poetry: 'With some uncertain notice, as might seem'. *Uncertain notice.* Throughout this passage the poet's mind is eddying between uncertainty and noticing. Once again the oxymorons register, here in the suggestion of *vagrant dwellers.* What might be the georgic activity of charcoal-burners is turned into an idea of pastoral uneasiness, one that will soon be sublimated into a spiritual 'presence that disturbs'. But in the opening scene of the poem,

---

[19] Virgil recommends that unfruitful, sportive growths, 'if grafted or transplanted | To the care of well-dug trenches, will discard | Their wildwood spirit and by discipline | Be trained' (*Georgics*, ii.47–52, p. 78).

[20] John Philips, *Cyder. A Poem. In Two Books* (London: Tonson, 1708), ii.61; i.126–36.

positioned between notions of dwelling and vagrancy, between the pastoral and the working farm, between what he notices and the surrounding uncertainty, Wordsworth is ambivalent about the kind of nature to which he has returned.

Some critics, of course, as mentioned in Chapter 4, have seen Wordsworth's Wye Valley 'Lines' as marking a retreat from radical politics into nature; others from a New Historicist perspective have focused on its exclusions of 'social reality'; but rather than stress retreat or exclusion, I am interested in the poem's engagement with the ambivalence of nature and in the ambiguity of that insistent greenness. The differences in implication between a pastoral nature and a georgic nature can help us gauge the consciousness, the conscience even, that characterises Wordsworth's poems of the late 1790s. It suggests a relationship between what we think of today as a politics and an ecology, or, as suggested earlier in this book, a biohistory in Wordsworth himself.

That opening descriptive passage from the poem has been interpreted from an eco-critical perspective by James McKusick in an essay on the ecology of Romantic poetry. But his reading is disconcertingly coloured by the vocabulary of twenty-first-century 'green' politics. 'The opening lines of the poem', he remarks,

depict a human community dwelling in harmonious coexistence with nature; the local farmsteads are 'green to the very door', and the local farmers have acted to preserve a remnant of the primordial ecosystem of that region by allowing their hedgerows to run wild. Considering the increasingly destructive activities of the nearby charcoal-burners, however, it remains an open question whether such an environmentally benign mode of agriculture can be sustained in the long run.[21]

A problem with this reading is the way it erases nuanced historical meanings in favour of a bland celebration of 'harmonious coexistence with nature', as if the model might be to recover Goldsmith's threatened Auburn, that 'sweet smiling village, loveliest of the lawn'.[22] The suggestion that the eco-friendly farmers of the Wye Valley are working to preserve their environment assumes a pastoral ideal, and in doing so, insulates it from the challenges posed by georgic nature in a time of economic stringency. A productive, organised landscape has room for the charcoal-burners and their coppicing.

A georgic scene can certainly 'smile' but only after a lot of hard work has been put into it. To quote Virgil's words in the first Georgic: 'The Father himself | Willed that the path of tillage be not smooth, | And first ordained that skill should cultivate | The land, by care sharpening the wit of mortals'; hence the importance of continuing the skills and precepts of the past (*veterum*

[21] James McKusick, *Green Writing: Romanticism and Ecology* (New York: St Martin's Press, 2000), p. 68.
[22] Oliver Goldsmith, *The Deserted Village, A Poem*, 2nd edn (London: W. Griffin, 1770), l. 35.

praecepta).[23] In the face of potential loss and frustration, the georgic seeks continuities between the wisdom of the past and the challenge of the future, and sustainability and connectedness become key concerns. With this in mind it is possible to speak of a georgic consciousness underlying the pastoral opening of Wordsworth's poem. The man who returns to the Wye Valley after five years' absence might long to find an unchanged primal scene; but, as I've suggested, its pastoral green language is ambiguous in that it also makes organic growth visible, and the poet begins to find that his own history is becoming readable. This is what the rest of the poem proceeds to explore. We discover that the speaker of the poem does not want to be the newly awakened Adam, in at the beginning, but instead is happy to locate a maturing consciousness through which he is able to reconnect his memories to his hopes. The poem makes that connection. The sheer repeatability of the experience becomes a reassuring token that, although his character has changed, his own integrity survives. What has proved to be repeatable will, he trusts, finally become habitual, and thus, in an organic way, bring meaning and value together.

That Wordsworth was coming to understand how human beings should be judged not by Idea, but by their own inner grain, their settled habits, is clear from the unfinished draft essay he attempted at this time (1798), known starkly as the 'Essay on Morals'. In this fragment he attacks the systematic moral reasoning of Godwin and Paley in favour of an organic judgment, which accommodates individual human character and experience. Those theoretical moralists, he declares in a remarkably Burkean image, 'attempt to strip the mind of all its old clothing', and thus ignore 'that part of our conduct & actions which is the result of our habits'. Wordsworth continues:

Now, I know no book or system of moral philosophy written with sufficient power to melt into our affections, to incorporate itself with the blood & vital juices of our minds, & thence to have any influence worth our notice in forming those habits of which I am speaking.[24]

Nothing could be further from a notion of The Elect, or of Godwin's 'single and uniform' truth.[25] A *system* is clearly involved here, but it is a practical one that 'incorporates' human experience to the extent that it becomes an organised expression of humanity itself.

Something of this very nature is happening in another poem of 1797–8, 'The Old Cumberland Beggar, A Description', a text focused on a figure of repetition who is able, by being at the centre of a little social ritual, to knit

---

[23] Virgil, *Georgics*, i.121–4, 175, pp. 60, 62.
[24] William Wordsworth, 'Essay on Morals', in *The Prose Works of William Wordsworth*, ed. W. J. B. Owen and Jane Worthington Smyser, 3 vols (Oxford: Clarendon Press, 1974), i.103–4. On the Burkean language of Wordsworth's 'Essay', see James K. Chandler, *Wordsworth's Second Nature: A Study of the Poetry and the Politics* (Chicago: Chicago University Press, 1984), 81–2.
[25] See p. 79 above.

his society together.[26] These two impulses, the habitual and the integrative, run through the poem, and help to organise it around the picture of how a wider 'common life' may be sustained by even the most tenuous life force. Wordsworth's headnote records that the 'class of Beggars' he describes 'confined themselves to a stated round in their neighbourhood, and had certain fixed days, on which, at different houses, they regularly received charity'. With this revisiting motif at its core, the poem shows how individual acts and responses become part of a social fabric. In Kenneth Johnston's telling phrase, 'his movement through the parish stitches it together into human community'.[27] We soon find that the poem is not interested in unity, but in how scraps and bits might combine into a larger picture:

> [F]rom a bag
> All white with flour, the dole of village dames,
> He drew his scraps and fragments, one by one,
> And scann'd them with a fix'd and serious look
> Of idle computation...
>
> .   .   .   .
>
> And ever, scatter'd from his palsied hand,
> That still attempting to prevent the waste,
> Was baffled still, the crumbs in little showers
> Fell on the ground, and the small mountain birds,
> Not venturing yet to peck their destin'd meal,
> Approached within the length of half his staff.   (8–21)

It is an untidy, seemingly disorganised scene. The old man puzzles over his fragments, unable to control them. He is clearly in the uncomfortable world of georgic nature, where entropy threatens to frustrate human energy. Indeed, in economic terms, he is a figure of waste, idleness, dissipation, and frustrated intentions. What is 'fix'd and serious' proves to be wholly ineffectual, almost comic, and we are given a little satiric emblem of the 'trickle-down' economy of 1790s charity, as celebrated in charity sermons of the period. But the poem throughout refuses to be embarrassed by the piecemeal, and by its own many repeated phrases, which reappear and nudge the text along, as if a porous memory is reminding itself of a purpose.[28] The poem shares the beggar's patience in the way it builds up identity and meaning out of discrete details. This is evident in so simple a thing as the stone on which the old man sits, which we piece together in stages as we return to it, noting its elements: 'A low structure of rude masonry | Built at

---

[26] First published in the second edition of *Lyrical Ballads* (1800), ii.151–62. On the poem's engagement with contemporary theories of political economy, see Philip Connell, *Romanticism, Economics and the Question of 'Culture'* (Oxford: Oxford University Press, 2001), 19–30; on the poem's links to the 'Essay on Morals', see Chandler, *Wordsworth's Second Nature*, 84–9.

[27] Kenneth R. Johnston, *Wordsworth and the Recluse* (New Haven: Yale University Press, 1984), 41.

[28] The poem's larger point is that a wider purpose need not appear purposive.

the foot of a huge hill' (3–4); 'the broad smooth stone | That overlays the pile' (7–8); 'upon the second step of that small pile' (13). The poem seems to be constructing it as we watch.

Wordsworth's poetic organisation is daring in this and other ways. The speaker begins with a simple 'I saw' recalling a particular occasion; but then suddenly the curious figure of the opening paragraph is made familiar ('Him from my childhood have I known', 22), and the next moment the writing changes tense to the 'habitual present'. The ensuing description is constructed out of innumerable encounters over many years, the overlaid memories coalescing into a single scene (featuring the horseman, the toll-gate keeper, the post-boy, etc.) so that it has the odd effect of forming a *picture* out of a *habit*. Repeated sightings of the old man are subsumed into the present tense because he has by this time been absorbed into the speaker's heart. He has become, in other words, a *presence*, in a process which at the poem's close, as at the end of the Wye Valley 'Lines', turns naturally, with only the slightest tonal modulation, into an act of blessing.

Set in motion, the old man hardly sees anything, but seems to be tracking the ground intently, as if measuring his grave-plot as he goes:

> On the ground
> His eyes are turn'd, and, as he moves along,
> *They* move along the ground; and evermore,
> Instead of common and habitual sight
> Of fields with rural works, of hill and dale,
> And the blue sky, one little span of earth
> Is all his prospect. Thus, from day to day,
> Bowbent, his eyes for ever on the ground,
> He plies his weary journey, seeing still,
> And never knowing that he sees, some straw,
> Some scatter'd leaf, or marks which, in one track,
> The nails of cart or chariot wheel have left
> Impress'd on the white road, in the same line,
> At distance still the same.   (45–58)

These unremarkable, even dogged, lines, repeatedly go over the same *ground* (a word used three times in the passage) in a way that conveys the 'habitual' repetitiveness of this worn track. At one level it echoes the endless routines of georgic, specifically Virgil's remark that 'the farmer's labour is a treadmill: | All round the year he treads in his own tracks'.[29] But beyond the economic dimension lies a philosophical one. The old man seems to be clinging onto his human identity, hardly perceiving or recollecting, his mind literally going through the motions. With reference to the mechanisms of empirical perception, he is 'seeing still, | And never knowing that he sees'. There is an element of pathos here in the way the vocabulary of Lockean association, with its stress on

---

[29] Virgil, *Georgics*, ii.401–2, p. 90.

mental habits (impression, mark, track, road), finds an emblem in this 'one track' consciousness.[30] But tricks are played with the reader's consciousness too, and we are made to think about how we compute sensations and process information from them. Wordsworth is intrigued by the ways in which repetition works in terms of the reader's perceptions, particularly how we experience ideas of succession, simultaneity, and duplication. Of the man's eyes, for example, we are told, with great risk of naivety: 'as he moves along, | *They* move along'. What is simultaneous is registered for us as repetition. With similar effect the poet describes the wheel-marks on the road, reminders of previous journeys and innumerable other travellers, which run 'in the same line, | At distance still the same'. The poet labours to tell us that the tracks of carts or chariots are always the same distance apart. It is such an obvious point that we are prompted to ask why he can't just say 'parallel lines'. But the simple notion is figured like a philosophical riddle about an identity that is not a unity, and which leaves 'one track' that is double. The suggestion is reinforced in the next line (59) which shifts to the beggar, whose 'staff trails with him' (not 'after'), so that he too, one assumes, is leaving a dual track. But in his entirely human case, 'scarcely do his feet | Disturb the summer dust'. While we are being made to wonder if his feet even mark the ground, it may occur to us that what the old man leaves behind him, the richness of his impression, is in fact the subject of the poem.

Wordsworth, in a sudden change of tone, confirms this with a public challenge to those 'Statesmen' who might want to sweep away the traces of such a figure: 'ye | Who have a broom still ready in your hands | To rid the world of nuisances' (68–70). The apostrophe is awkward and disruptive, but tactical. The Miltonic tones here ('Of forms created the most vile and brute', 75) give way to an intense, reassuring repetition, now a justified insistence, that nothing in nature, not even 'the meanest of created things',

> should exist
> Divorced from good, a spirit and pulse of good,
> A life and soul to every mode of being
> Inseparably link'd. (76–9)

The word 'pulse' confirms the poem's concern with distinct, repeated things that become a continuing attachment, and thus a pledge of continuity. That decisive phrase, 'Inseparably link'd', confirms how the text is avoiding a theoretical unity in order to forge firm and enduring bonds. It asserts that being good is not an Idea of goodness but reiterated actions, the 'pulse of

---

[30] Cf. 'Custom settles habits of thinking in the understanding, as well as of determining in the will, and of motions in the body; all which seems to be but trains of motions in the animal spirits, which, once set a-going, continue in the same steps they have been used to, which, by often treading, are worn into a smooth path' (John Locke, *An Essay Concerning Human Understanding*, ed. Peter Nidditch (Oxford: Clarendon Press, 1975), II.xxxiii.6). Locke's words are closely echoed in the opening chapter of *Tristram Shandy*.

good', just as life is sustained by the blood repeatedly revisiting the heart. The old man is himself an organic text, a Burkean connective memory: 'a record which together binds | Past deeds and offices of charity | Else unremember'd, and so keeps alive | The kindly mood' (81–4). The beggar's role is simply to 'keep alive', both transitively and intransitively. As he 'takes his rounds' he becomes, like the heartbeat, a token of repetition as continuity.

In this poem, 'habit does the work | Of reason' (i.e. what 'reason' itself would call tautology or duplication), and the text is organised simply around our consciousness of the beggar. He is not symbolic of anything, just an old man with the shakes, but he organises something of value as he goes. He hardly moves things around him, but he does move them. The poem shows how active good can 'live, and spread, and kindle ... | ... from this solitary being' (101–2). There is a pattern, then, but not one imposed as the 'thought' of the poem. There is no template or paradigm. It is in this sense organic, not a structure but both a temporal pattern and a spatial arrangement. Out of the poet's pieced-together recollections of the old man come an organic identity and an organic history, in which memory, association, and narrative combine.

'The Old Cumberland Beggar' suggests that Wordsworth's concept of the 'One Life', which generated his ambitions for 'The Recluse', was at the beginning something much closer to Locke's accretive notion of 'one common life', a living organisation sustained through time and space, embracing change, and accepting loss.[31] The old man's surroundings, from the tracks on the road to the 'smooth' worn mounting-stone on which he sits, empha-sise how time marks, alters, and erases human traces. He himself, it is suggested at the end of the poem, will become absorbed into nature, not in any transcendent way but as an element of life that finally relapses back into the stream of things, like the rise and fall of a single breath: 'As in the eye of Nature he has liv'd, | So in the eye of Nature let him die' (188–9).

These words would make an appropriate motto for georgic writing, in which the natural processes of growth and decay always work jointly, not least in the way the soil is improved by rotting matter.[32] 'Nature' (as it did for John 'Walking' Stewart) can thus function as a kind of layered history, building up experience and memory, which can be passed on through generations. Georgic's capaciousness allows it to be both enriched and disturbed by such returns. The moment at the end of the first Georgic (493–7) when Virgil imagines the farmer of the future turning up with his plough the mouldering spears and helmets of a battlefield becomes an emblem for later georgic writers of the sobering capacity of history to

---

[31] See Chapter 2 above.
[32] The use of decaying materials to fertilise the soil is a staple topic of georgic (Virgil, *Georgics*, ii.346–8). See Juan Christian Pellicer, 'The Georgic at Mid-Eighteenth Century and the Case of Dodsley's "Agriculture"', *RES*, 54 (2003), 67–93 (77–8).

disturb the surface and bring things to light.[33] As Kevis Goodman argues (in opposition to Alan Liu) georgic poems do not attempt to bury history, but on the contrary, make it uncomfortably present. She writes: 'the problem is sometimes not that the plough or the pen buries what should be disclosed, but that the critic's predicament, like that of the farmer and the poet, is the difficulty of recognizing the historical meanings of what does get turned up, not under, by their lines.'[34] The natural cycle continues, somehow incorporating all that has gone before.

The 'indifference' of nature's resumptions to the fact of human suffering has been seen as one of the leading ideas of Wordsworth's *The Ruined Cottage*, specifically the revised 'D' text,[35] a poem that stages a series of returns, and returns within returns, almost of a compulsive nature.[36] It is a text in which a human tragedy is played out amidst what the poet refers to as 'the calm oblivious tendencies | Of nature' (504–5). There is a persistent critical tradition that focuses on that word *oblivious* and reads nature's detailed activities in the poem as uncaring and implacable, and to that degree having interests incompatible with the human. In Jonathan Wordsworth's powerful reading, its processes are from a human point of view 'inexorable', almost as if nature were gaining strength through her weakness: 'active Nature, though if correctly viewed not hostile to Margaret, is at least implacable, and through its encroachment brings about her death'.[37] Other critics of the poem have taken this further: for Evan Radcliffe, 'nature becomes an obliviously destructive force', and Karl Kroeber questions our response as readers to 'the indifferent destructiveness of natural processes'.[38] Peter Larkin's more thoughtful reading speaks of 'the poem's vision of inexorable natural processes calmly (perhaps seductively) oblivious of human suffering'.[39] His parenthesis is suggestive, and I'm specifically interested here in the text's more literal potential to *seduce*, repeatedly to 'lead aside or away',[40] in order to stage its returns.

---

[33] The image is echoed, for example, in Philips, *Cyder*, i.238–42; and Jago, *Edge-Hill*, iv.563–9.

[34] Kevis Goodman, *Georgic Modernity and British Romanticism: Poetry and the Mediation of History* (Cambridge: Cambridge University Press, 2004), 3. See also Alan Liu, *Wordsworth: The Sense of History* (Stanford: Stanford University Press, 1989), 18–19, discussed by Goodman, *Georgic Modernity and British Romanticism*, 1–5.

[35] The 'D' text (1799) of the poem occupies ff. 46^r to 56^r of MS D (Dove Cottage MS 16). See William Wordsworth, *The Ruined Cottage and The Pedlar*, ed. James Butler (Ithaca: Cornell University Press, 1979), 282–325. The reading text is 43–75.

[36] Karen Swann remarks on the 'compulsiveness' of the poem's 'observing consciousness' ('Suffering and Sensation in *The Ruined Cottage*', *PMLA*, 106 (1991), 83–95 (88)).

[37] Wordsworth, *The Music of Humanity*, 108, 120.

[38] Evan Radcliffe, '"In Dreams Begins Responsibility": Wordsworth's Ruined Cottage Story', *SiR*, 23 (1984), 101–19 (114); Karl Kroeber, *Ecological Literary Criticism: Romantic Imagining and the Biology of Mind* (New York: Columbia University Press, 1994), 50.

[39] Peter Larkin, 'Relations of Scarcity: Ecology and Eschatology in *The Ruined Cottage*', *SiR*, 39 (2000), 345–64 (349).

[40] *OED*, s.v. 'seduce', 1.

But once again the assumed pastoral character of the poem has tended to limit readings, in this case to certain thematic expectations centred on the 'tragedy' of Margaret. It is true that in the tradition of pastoral elegy, the yearly renovations of nature highlight the tragic irony of the human being's inability to return to life, an ancient theme set by Moschus' pastoral lament for Bion: 'each with Verdure fresh | Renew their Bloom, and with the Spring return. | But Man . . . etc.'.[41] It is a topos of the indifference of nature that has been a powerful motif in elegy for centuries,[42] and it makes its presence felt in *The Ruined Cottage*. But the poem is more mixed in genre, and its pastoral/elegiac elements are subsumed into a complex descriptive narrative mediated to us through the experience of both the old man and the poet. The life of nature reaches us through layers of human consciousness. Not least, the poem's insistent motif of departure and return establishes the natural scene as something interfused with human thoughts and feelings. It is a poem about place as much as about people, in which 'Earth's returns' (to reapply Browning's beautiful phrase[43]) accompany the human ones, and draw power, not always ironically, from those connections and continuities.

At first, the restless poet who enters the scene is unable to find a sure footing on the earth at all. As he makes his way 'across a bare wide Common' his feet are 'baffled' by 'the slipp'ry ground',

> and when I stretched myself
> On the brown earth my limbs from very heat
> Could find no rest nor my weak arm disperse
> The insect host which gathered round my face
> And joined their murmurs to the tedious noise
> Of seeds of bursting gorse that crackled round.   (21–6)

No resting on the 'lap of Earth' for him. A potentially pastoral attitude brings a georgic reminder that nature in this poem does not shape itself to human contours and has its discomforts and predations ('Myriads on Myriads, Insect-Armies waft | Keen in the poison'd Breeze' is Thomson's phrase).[44] So much, too much, life is going on around him; but this restlessness, discomfort, and annoyance make the meeting with his friend all the more effective as a kind of calming and settling of himself in a moment of

[41] Thomas Warton, 'A Pastoral on the Death of Bion. From the Greek of Moschus', printed in his father Thomas Warton the Elder's *Poems on Several Occasions* (London: R. Manby and H. S. Cox, 1748), 197–208 (205–6).

[42] See, for example, Petrarch's sonnet 269, *Zephiro torna* ('the west wind returns'), one of the sources for Gray's sonnet to Richard West, which centres on this theme, as does West's own elegiac version in 'Ad Amicos': 'Unknown and silent will depart my breath, | Nor nature e'er take notice of my death' (*Correspondence of Thomas Gray*, ed. Paget Toynbee and Leonard Whibley, 3 vols (Oxford: Clarendon Press, 1935), i.63).

[43] Robert Browning, 'Love Among the Ruins', 80 (*The Poetical Works of Robert Browning*, vol. 5, ed. Ian Jack and Robert Inglesfield (Oxford: Clarendon Press, 1995), 8).

[44] Thomson, *Spring*, 121–2. The original description of annoying flies is Virgil, *Georgics*, iii.146–56.

recognition, since it is of course a fortunate *re*-encounter with the man who had been his 'fellow-traveller' two days earlier. The person who will be the narrator of Margaret's story is offered as a contrasting figure at this point: 'the venerable Armytage' rests in the shade with his eyes closed; and the poet greets him (rather oddly, unless placed in a context of departure and return) as 'a friend | As dear to me as is the setting sun' (38–9). We might expect the *dawning* sun here, given the welcome that the poet is about to make him, but in this poem things become dear by *leaving*. The promise of *return* is the poem's animating principle throughout, and it is through the departures and returns of Armytage, the wanderer-figure, that the poem charts the story of Margaret and her cottage.[45]

The poet has his local returns also; and before the conversation can begin he rises for a second time in order to drink from the well, 'half-choked with willow flowers and weeds'. 'I slaked my thirst', he says, 'and to the shady bench | Returned' (64–5). Of course, for these *returns* to have their full effect, the poem has to locate itself in a *here* and a *now*. The poet, and the reader too, have to feel the rootedness of this spot, and the opening passage of the poem is focused on establishing this idea of increasing familiarisation. As we read on, we too are given details to which we can repeatedly return, so as to build up our own sense of attachment to this place, just as a few lines later we return to the well, this time with the detail of the spider's web that 'hung to the water's edge' (89). In every corner of the scene, life of some kind is continuing.

The poet's, and our, first glimpse of the cottage establishes how the poem will combine a language of alienation and loss with one of growth and continuity. The ruined structure is introduced by the words: 'I rose and turned towards'. The phrase *turned towards* signals that from this point on, each 'turn towards' this spot will be a *return*:

> I rose and turned towards a group of trees
> Which midway in that level stood alone,
> And thither come at length, beneath a shade
> Of clustering elms that sprang from the same root
> I found a ruined house, four naked walls
> That stared upon each other.   (27–32)

---

[45] The word 'Pedlar' is not used for Armytage in the 'D' text of the poem, and in avoiding the term I want to distinguish him from the figure who features in the earlier MS 'A', and whose 'One Life' philosophy Wordsworth was soon to develop at greater length. The pantheistic 'One Life' for which the Pedlar stands was, James Butler argues, omitted when Wordsworth began thinking about *The Ruined Cottage* as a separate poem. Butler points out that 'Despite its 1799 date, *Ruined Cottage* MS D is more closely related to the original 528-line poem of early 1798, and to what Coleridge and Lamb heard in 1797, than to the combined version of the revised MS B text. Wordsworth, perhaps uneasy about what his poem had become, in MS D separated the history of the Pedlar from what he now considered, and entitled, *The Ruined Cottage*' (*The Ruined Cottage*, ed. Butler, 23). On this, see Ulmer, 'Wordsworth, the One Life, and *The Ruined Cottage*', 316.

The contrast between the elms and the house is a stark one. The elms, viewed at first as standing *alone*, are on closer view seen to be a sociable family, growing together, *clustering*, joined to *the same root*, whereas the cottage, at this stage, appears divided, alienated from itself: 'four naked walls | That stared upon each other', like Adam and Eve after the fall, estranged, staring at each other's nakedness.

But only a few lines later, in Armytage's speech, we ourselves return to the cottage, our first return of many, and there is a moment of recognition; but now the scene has accrued some telling details:

> 'this poor hut,
> Stripp'd of its outward garb of houshold flowers,
> Of rose and sweet-briar, offers to the wind
> A cold bare wall whose earthy top is tricked
> With weeds and the rank spear-grass.'   (104–8)

The poet, and we, are already seeing things differently, noticing more. As an image of a *poor* human form, *Stripp'd of its outward garb*, the cottage is beginning to develop an *earthy top* that can support life, albeit *weeds and the rank spear-grass*. The word *rank* (meaning 'vigorous') insists on the capacity of things to flourish in the most meagre soil; and the principle of natural growth is emphasised at the expense of mere picturesque decoration. At this point in the poem we are introduced to what will soon become a familiar scene, at the centre of which is the cottage-garden:

> It was a plot
> Of garden-ground, now wild, its matted weeds
> Marked with the steps of those whom as they pass'd,
> The goose-berry trees that shot in long lank slips,
> Or currants hanging from their leafless stems
> In scanty strings, had tempted to o'erleap
> The broken wall.   (54–60)

Tempted to o'erleap—the language is that of a violated Eden, its fruit hanging, but not with the full richness of Paradise. It still offers a temptation, and the wall has been broken down by those who have entered it, with as much ease as Satan in *Paradise Lost* entered the garden: 'at one slight bound high overleap'd all bound | Of Hill or highest Wall'.[46] The Miltonic echo makes it clear that the poem's location is not a pastoral one, evoking the temperate poise and innocence of the original garden. There was once an Edenic quality to the place, but as Armytage's story unfolds, the scene moves irreversibly into the challenging landscape of the georgic, a genre located in the fallen world of decay, disease, war and death, the changing seasons, the pressures of time, and the precariousness of human labour. As if to signal

---

[46] Milton, *Paradise Lost*, iv.181–2.

this, all those things that the pastoral holds at bay now crowd together into the poem. The old man recalls 'Two blighting seasons when the fields were left | With half a harvest', a situation made worse by 'the plague of war':

> ' 'Twas a sad time of sorrow and distress:
> A wanderer among the cottages,
> I with my pack of winter raiment saw
> The hardships of that season...' (138–41)

The convalescent Robert, however, still thinks he is in a pastoral. We are given a picture of him standing at the cottage door, whistling 'many a snatch of merry tunes' (163) and carving heads on sticks. In the georgic, as Hesiod, Virgil, and their eighteenth-century successors knew, work must be regular and well organised, each job completed *in the proper season*. 'You should embrace work-tasks in their due order', Hesiod admonishes, establishing a whole tradition of regular labour at the appropriate times.[47] There are spring jobs and autumn jobs, and important jobs for winter evenings ('then an industrious man may do much for his household'). At that season Virgil specifically recommends basket-weaving, fencing, burning briar-thickets, or cleaning gutters.[48] As Stephen Duck knows in *The Thresher's Labour*, regular routines are vital: 'the same Toils we must again repeat: | To the same Barns again must back return, | To labour there for room for next Year's Corn. | Thus, as the Year's revolving Course goes round, | No respite from our Labour can be found' (275–9). The yearly *returns* of georgic have to be worked for within the cycle of the returning seasons. Virgil stresses the importance of small 'humdrum tasks' (*tenuisque curas*), which can make the difference between success and disaster if properly carried out at the right time (i.177). But Robert's casual attitude is just not good enough:

> '[He] idly sought about through every nook
> Of house or garden any casual task
> Of use or ornament, and with a strange,
> Amusing but uneasy novelty
> He blended where he might the various tasks
> Of summer, autumn, winter, and of spring.' (166–71)

Such *casual* indifference to the individual seasons in a world that is 'off the poise', combined with an inability to distinguish between *use* and *ornament*, suggests a lack of that purposiveness that georgic nature demands. In Milton's garden Adam and Eve could afford to be casual about their tasks (indeed the Fall is first intimated when Eve decides that the two of them have to get organised), but in the georgic scene organisation, energy, and direction are required. It is a serious point, and Wordsworth understands it all too well. *The Ruined Cottage* moves into the rigorous landscape of

---

[47] Hesiod, *Works and Days*, 46.
[48] Virgil, *Georgics*, i.259–74, p. 65.

georgic, but in doing so it suspends human labour and reclaims fallen nature as a power in and of itself, no longer harnessed to human energies. In the first of Virgil's *Georgics* the farmer is seen as resisting the general tendency in nature towards degeneration and reversal: 'So it is: for everything by nature's law | Tends to the worse, slips ever backward, backward'.[49] As the first part of Wordsworth's poem draws to a close, this entropic principle has been set in motion; but against it, another counter-motion will begin to register, and we sense it when Armytage pauses as the poem stages a return to the here and now of the elm trees:

> '"Every smile,"
> Said Margaret to me here beneath these trees,
> "Made my heart bleed."' At this the old Man paus'd
> And looking up to those enormous elms
> He said, ''Tis now the hour of deepest noon . . .'   (183–7)

The narrative breaks just at a moment when our minds are full of impending change and loss. There is a sudden return to the *here* and the *now*, and we are made to look up at an image of endurance, as the elms tower above us. This return is crucial in giving us the continuing life of nature. The annoying flies also return, but now we encounter them through the consciousness of the old man, for whom they '[fill] all the air with happy melody' (191). The voice of experience, we find, asks more searching questions:

> 'Why should a tear be in an old man's eye?
> Why should we thus with an untoward mind
> And in the weakness of humanity
> From natural wisdom turn our hearts away,
> To natural comfort shut our eyes and ears,
> And feeding on disquiet thus disturb
> The calm of Nature with our restless thoughts?'   (188–98)

Simply to 'turn our hearts away' is a gesture the poem disallows as somehow incomplete, and the rhetorical question hangs in the air as the First Part ends. By reacquainting us with the familiar spot the poet breaks into the narrative, but only to allow a return, and with it an idea of *resumption*. But before this happens, the poet too must take a time-out. Yet again there is a rising, a turning away, a look round, then a return, and a resumption—it is a sequence at the heart of the poem's narrative procedure (my italics):

> I *rose*, and *turning* from that breezy shade
> Went out into the open air and stood
> To drink the comfort of the warmer sun.
> Long time I had not stayed ere, *looking round*
> Upon that tranquil ruin, I *returned*

---

[49] Virgil, *Georgics*, i.199–200, p. 63.

> And begged of the old man that for my sake
> He would *resume* his story.   (214–20)

There is a fresh urgency, a sharp interest now, as we return to the main body of Armytage's tale, which is structured round four departures and four returns; and after each of them the familiar spot of the cottage, and the elm trees above it, reappear. The first return is briskly done:

> 'It was my chance
> To travel in a country far remote.
> And glad I was when, halting by yon gate
> That leads from the green lane, again I saw
> These lofty elm-trees. Long I did not rest:
> With many pleasant thoughts I cheer'd my way
> O'er the flat common. At the door arrived,
> I knocked.'   (239–46)

At this first return he learns that Robert has left unannounced, and has gone abroad to fight. 'The tidings came', says Margaret, 'that he had joined a troop | Of soldiers going to a distant land. | He left me thus' (266–9). The power of this idea is reinforced by the fact that of the poem's many departures, this one has no return. As Armytage's own movements away from and back to the scene succeed each other, the failure of Robert to return becomes more painful, and Margaret herself begins to wander off from the cottage, and then return, repeatedly re-enacting a departure in order to come back again.

It is a pattern of frustration, of apparently pointless motion, away and back, and one reader found this memorably frustrating himself. It has to be said that Thomas De Quincey didn't really enter into the spirit of the piece. For him, at this point, decisive action was needed to find the truant husband and force him to return. The narrator, he says, could have made enquiries: 'That same night he would have written to the War-Office: and in a very few days, an official answer, bearing the indorsement *On H.M.'s Service*, would have placed Margaret in communication with the truant.'[50] In such a way Robert's return might have been achieved, and the tragedy avoided. The poem's many tentative tracings could be replaced by a single determined and practical *tracing* of the fugitive. De Quincey's sheer practicality (that most praised of georgic qualities) itself makes a telling point about the capacity of the poem to frustrate its georgic implications.

The old man's second return occurs after a long and complex journey. It was, he tells the poet, 'o'er many a hill and many a dale ... | ... Through many a wood, and many an open ground' (289–91). The sweep is wide, the

---

[50] Thomas De Quincey, 'On Wordsworth's Poetry', in *The Works of Thomas De Quincey*, vol. 15, ed. Frederick Burwick (London: Pickering and Chatto, 2003), 232. The passage is quoted by Wordsworth, *The Music of Humanity*, 85.

terms vague and generalised, his thoughts brief and unremembered ('many a short-lived thought that pass'd between | And disappeared', 297–8), until he reaches the spot that has now become home, for him and for us, when the *now* brings the focus back to the sharp details of the present scene: 'When I had reached the door | I found that she was absent. In the shade | Where now we sit I waited her return' (302–4). He notices the familiar honeysuckle crowding round the door, but also

> 'knots of worthless stone-crop started out
> Along the window's edge, and grew like weeds
> Against the lower panes. I turned aside
> And stroll'd into her garden.—It was chang'd'   (310–13)

In this particular spot every detail registers. Of course the *turn aside*, into the garden, allows him to stage a return: 'Back I turned my restless steps' (321); and we turn with him, this time to encounter a passing stranger with news of Margaret; then, after a few lines, Margaret herself: 'I turned and saw her distant a few steps' (337). Each of the poem's turns and returns makes us increasingly observant, ready to catch something more. They allow us repeatedly to re-encounter the special place, mark the changes, and appreciate its continuing interest for us as the associations accumulate. In this way our own perceptions are beginning to mimic the tracings of organic history. We notice how vegetation of various kinds is spreading and reclaiming space for itself. In the garden 'Daisy and thrift and lowly camomile | And thyme— had straggled out into the paths' (318–19). The scene is evolving and its forms slowly loosening as meandering lines respond to organic developments, like those that delighted Piranesi and Dyer among the ruins of Rome.[51]

At his third return, the old man revisits the garden and looks at the weeds and 'knots of withered grass' (415), noticing that a young apple tree is being nibbled at by the sheep who have found their way in. The signs of former georgic husbandry only emphasise the neglect: 'a chain of straw | Which had been twisted round the tender stem | . . . lay at its root' (419–21). Boundaries and structures are crumbling. In the final passage leading up to Margaret's death the narrative offers a series of individual glimpses of her, each one placed in relation to an eloquent gesture of bending or turning. The thread of her flax-spinning confirms Wordsworth's fascination for tracing her movements:

> 'Seest thou that path?
> (The green-sward now has broken its grey line)
> There to and fro she paced through many a day
> Of the warm summer, from a belt of flax
> That girt her waist spinning the long-drawn thread
> With backward steps'   (457–62)

[51] See Chapter 3 above.

The green-sward now has broken its grey line. It will soon, we realise, be
'green to the very door'. Rather than marking a reversion to a pastoral idea,
such growth is offering a challenge to humanity that is not being met. From
an ecological perspective the poem exemplifies Lawrence Buell's remark that
'human history is implicated in natural history',[52] and there is something
of that here, but of an ambiguous kind, as if the boundary between the two
were being broken down. Nature's persistence makes Margaret's absence
the more felt and immediate, but it offers a living presence too, small signs of
life continuing and enduring, a toadstool or a patch of grass encroaching onto
the path. It is this sense of earth's small returns that gives *The Ruined Cottage*
its particular power as a human document, while placing the human within
the broader rhythms of life. Against those critics who see the poem as
recording an 'indifferent' nature, I would urge the georgic principle that we
are living in nature's context, not vice versa. By the end of the poem, with all
our returns, the scene has become imbued with life, something to which the
figure of Margaret has contributed but which continues after her.[53]

But the poet has one final turn and return to make. What has become a
moving ritual of movement, turning aside and returning, reaches its climax.
It is as if the emotive force of returning, what Robert and Margaret can never
do, has to be insisted on:

> The old Man ceased: he saw that I was mov'd;
> From that low Bench, rising instinctively,
> I turned aside in weakness, nor had power
> To thank him for the tale which he had told.
> I stood, and leaning o'er the garden-gate
> Reviewed that Woman's suff'rings, and it seemed
> To comfort me while with a brother's love
> I blessed her in the impotence of grief.
> At length [towards] the cottage [I returned][54]
> Fondly, and traced with milder interest
> That secret spirit of humanity
> Which, 'mid the calm oblivious tendencies
> Of nature, 'mid her plants, her weeds, and flowers,
> And silent overgrowings, still survived.   (493–506)

It is here, among the *silent overgrowings*, that we finally recognise how *The
Ruined Cottage* has been organised around a persistent tracing and retracing.

[52] Laurence Buell, *The Environmental Imagination* (Cambridge, MA: Belknap Press of
Harvard University Press, 1995), 7.
[53] In relation to the 'tragedy' of Margaret, Jonathan Bate concludes that as readers 'what we
do sense is that since the vegetation lives beyond, lives on, her spirit somehow survives too'
(*Romantic Ecology: Wordsworth and the Environmental Tradition* (London: Routledge, 1991),
34). In Kurt Fosso's reading, the poem finally forges 'a bond of community' through mourning
('Community and Mourning in William Wordsworth's *The Ruined Cottage*, 1797–1798', *SP*, 92
(1995), 329–45).
[54] Missing words supplied from the text of MS 'E'. See Butler edn, 73 n.

It is what we readers have been doing throughout, what Piranesi does with his engraved lines, what Wartonian poets do with their poetic recoveries, what Dyer does with pen and brush.[55] The repeated *'mid* (504–5) implies that the *secret spirit* of the poem is not something that can be located 'within' or 'beyond' things, but rather between and amongst them, along their lines of connection. Wordsworth's poem has explored a living history that is not in any way mystical or transcendent.[56] It is the ordinary endless process of life, which, with each of our returns to the scene, draws our attention more and more. The poem has developed a silent dialogue between the human and the natural, until they begin to speak the same language. To single out one death amidst all this life pushes against the momentum of the poem; and to speak of nature's 'indifference' seems such a blank idea for something that works its way into every nook and cranny of the poem. This sense of what Coleridge calls 'the numberless goings-on of life' suggests a notion of the 'one life' that is rooted in biological existence.[57] It is an image of vital growth linking past and future, one embedded in decay and death, but somehow drawing life 'from ruin and from change' (521).

A scene close to this in implication is Caspar David Friedrich's painting, 'Monastery Ruins at Eldena' (Figure 10), where we seem to be revisiting the organic history of Piranesi. In this haunting picture the church is finding another identity as a collapsed skeletal form. If there is a 'spirit' here, it is no longer contained in the sacred body of the building, now a series of broken ribs, nor is it somewhere beyond; rather it can be sensed at play among the traced lines as they work to pull the structure back into the shapes of nature. The fragmented masonry is crumbling into new colours and textures; leaves are superimposed across stone and brick; branches mimic columns, creating lively visual rhythms. Smooth surfaces roughen; old proportions are distorted, and clean lines are broken and twisted. A 'gothic' language is still evident in the vertical shafts that reach up on the right, now no longer branching out into the ribs of a vault but becoming almost continuous with the trees, pointing into the air, mimicked by the vagaries of the foliage. In this sentimental visual language, something that we might too easily categorise as an emblem of tragedy (the monastery was destroyed during the Thirty Years' War) gains a new aesthetic and emotional register thanks to the artist's bravura handling of his medium, where materials are overlaid and combined in creative ways; and thanks also to what we discover at the heart of the scene. Huddled in the roofless nave is a cottage, with its hint of green cultivation, and two human figures who seem oblivious of the portentous

---

[55] Cf. Dyer's fascination with 'a certain disjointedness and moulder among the stones' (p. 69 above).

[56] William Ulmer sees the poem's 'organic processes' as representing 'an ultimate transcendence of human mutability and finitude' ('Wordsworth, the One Life, and *The Ruined Cottage*', 318).

[57] S. T. Coleridge, 'Frost at Midnight', 12.

10. Caspar David Friedrich, 'Monastery Ruins at Eldena' (1824–5); oil on canvas; 35 × 49 cm. bpk/Nationalgalerie, Staatliche Museen zu Berlin. Photo: Jörg P. Anders.

setting, caught in the routines of their day. When the scene was painted in 1825 this 'cottage' was a warehouse used for storing building materials.

Life goes on. The *Georgics* end with the honey-bees, tokens of a sweetness to come, who emerge miraculously from the putrifying flesh of the sacrificed oxen, 'buzzing, swarming, and bursting', says Virgil, 'out of their ruptured flanks'.[58] As things break down and crumble, new possibilities arise. In this context, georgic is not about stability and order, but about struggle and uncertainty, and sustaining hopes for the future. Virgil's poem (strictly an 'Octavian' rather than an 'Augustan' one) is a text about re-growing a culture from the waste and dereliction that lies around; about locating an old wisdom, and evolving the new from the old. Pastoral forms are no longer appropriate for this poetry of practical resourcefulness. In *The Ruined Cottage* Wordsworth is conscious of this generic shift, exploits it, and understands what the human implications are. The distinctive character of the poem can be found in the way in which pastoral tragedy is embraced by a kind of georgic stoicism.[59] And if we pick up a political inflection in this, it is perhaps less one of a stark contrast between a radical pastoral and a conservative georgic, than a more complex poetic response to a shift in the political landscape, in which a leap for the new appears less attractive than finding continuity and commitment at a time of disorganisation and uncertainty.

[58] Virgil, *Georgics*, iv.554–8.
[59] Paul D. Sheats has written well on the poem's 'discipline of hope by empirical experience' and on the 'chastened empiricism' of its physical details ('Cultivating Margaret's Garden: Wordsworthian "Nature" and the Quest for Historical "Difference"', in Peter Kitson (ed.), *Placing and Displacing Romanticism* (Aldershot: Ashgate, 2001), 16–32 (25)).

12 'Look homeward Angel now': Prospects and Fears in 1798

... whether thou to our moist vows deny'd,
Sleep'st by the fable of *Bellerus* old,
Where the great vision of the guarded Mount
Looks toward *Namancos* and *Bayona's* hold;
Look homeward Angel now, and melt with ruth,
And, O ye *Dolphins*, waft the hapless youth.

—John Milton, *Lycidas* (1638), 159–64

ON 20 APRIL 1798 King George III issued a call for the nation to organise itself and prepare for the imminent invasion. In a formal message delivered to Parliament and printed in newspapers throughout the kingdom he announced what many already recognised, that the country was under a potentially coordinated threat, from without and from within. He had been advised that along the Channel coast of 'France, Flanders, and Holland' active preparations had begun for the embarkation of French troops and supplies; and in response, in accordance with the powers granted to him, he had begun mobilisation by 'embodying a provisional force of Cavalry'. But he warned that the enemy's design was being encouraged by 'communication with treacherous and disaffected persons in these Kingdoms'. For that reason,

he deemed it indispensibly necessary to recommend it to the House of Commons to consider without delay of such farther measures as might enable his Majesty to defeat the wicked machinations of disaffected persons within this realm and so guard against the designs of the enemy either abroad or at home.[1]

Invasion from without and treason within, it was suggested, were in collaboration. Eleven leaders of the so-called 'United Englishmen' arrested in Manchester the previous week had been brought to London for questioning.[2] The invasion threat which had hovered over the country since February 1797 when a small French force landed at Fishguard finally seemed about to materialise.[3]

---

[1] *The Times*, 21 April 1798. In fact Bonaparte was already considering an expedition to invade Egypt, as *The Morning Chronicle* reported on 23 April.

[2] Modelled on the United Irishmen, these divisions totalling approximately 1,000 armed men had attempted to win over troops in the North-west of England. See Edward Royle, *Revolutionary Britannia? Reflections on the Threat of Revolution in Britain, 1789–1848* (Manchester: Manchester University Press, 2001), 26–35.

[3] See the account by Nicholas Roe, 'Coleridge, Wordsworth, and the French Invasion Scare', WC, 17 (1986), 142–7; and his *Wordsworth and Coleridge: The Radical Years* (Oxford: Clarendon Press, 1988), 248–62.

Since October 1797 Britain had known it was the target for a full-scale invasion, and in recent months General Bonaparte's troops (the 'Army of England') had been encamped along the Channel coast waiting for what would surely have to come.[4] Britain's former allies, Austria and Prussia, had been neutralised, so that the way seemed clear and inviting.[5] Only a strip of hazardous water separated the successful armies of revolutionary France from a country ripe for liberation. On the next day, 21 April, the back page of the *Bristol Journal* was given over to the 'Official Papers respecting the Invasion, and Plan of Defence', with detailed instructions for disrupting the enemy's mobility and food supplies; and it advised its readers 'carefully to preserve these Official Documents to guide and direct their operations in the hour of attack'. Graphic reports of French atrocities in Germany were in all the papers.

The situation called for national unity; but George's phrase, 'abroad or at home', reveals the dual focus that complicated singleness of purpose. Where should people direct their attention—abroad or at home? Drawing a contrast with the later invasion threat of 1803, Mark Philp concludes that in 1798 'propaganda was directed as much against forces within Britain as it was against outsiders'.[6] Given this pull between domestic and international concerns, I want to explore what it meant to be aware simultaneously of internal and external pressures at a moment when the call was for 'unity'.

The 25-year-old Coleridge is an intriguing case-study in this respect, given the tradition of talking about his work at this time in the vocabulary of 'retreat' (away from his earlier radicalism) and 'unity' (what in *Biographia Literaria* he will call the 'struggle to idealize and to unify'). In a specific wartime situation in which both *retreat* and *unity* are taking on a strategic character, it should be useful to place Coleridge in that context and to raise questions about how his poetry handles these two ideas. Coleridge in the spring of 1798 continues to be concerned with adaptability, variety, and mixture, and the particular strains these accommodations impose on matters of personal and political integrity. These are large issues, especially given my narrow focus on the events of April 1798; but I want to suggest that Coleridge's political relocation at this time was not a betrayal of principle; and that the two substantial poems he wrote during this month, 'The Recantation' (soon to be re-named 'France: An Ode') and 'Fears in Solitude', are in their different ways both tactical and principled in responding to the immediate national situation.[7] The rhetoric of these poems is best understood in terms of the public rhetoric of April 1798.

[4] The 'Army of England' was encamped on the Channel coast from October 1797 until May 1798. See Clive Emsley, *British Society and the French Wars, 1793–1815* (London/Basingstoke: Macmillan, 1979), 65.
[5] The Treaty of Campo Formio between France and Austria (17 Oct. 1797) marked the collapse of the First Coalition. By the Decree of 5 Brumaire Year 6 (26 Oct.1797) 'the Army of England' was formally constituted under Bonaparte's command.
[6] Mark Philp (ed.), *Resisting Napoleon: The British Response to the Threat of Invasion, 1797–1815* (Aldershot: Ashgate, 2006), 7.
[7] In autumn 1798 the two poems were collected, along with 'Frost at Midnight', into the composite volume, *Fears in Solitude, Written in 1798, During the Alarm of an Invasion, To*

Nationally, what in fact proved possible in terms of organisation was less a strict 'unity' than a temporary alignment of various interests conscious of the pressures of the moment and of what was expected of them. In this crisis, the concept of unity (a word that in politics is always more hortative than descriptive) was not a simple one. Was the unifying factor to be the physical embodying of the nation, with 116,000 armed volunteers already organising round the country,[8] or did it lie in a national 'spirit', a less tangible power of resistance? How was the nation being organised at this moment? In many minds during the days that followed there was a nagging ambivalence, not about resisting the invader but about the nature of the country that everyone sought to defend. It was agreed that aggression and hostility were to be directed outwards, but in the other direction the mix of anger and fear was far less simple. Thoughts of home, as we shall see, included protectiveness and anxiety but were mingled also with elements of guilt and doubt. What should be directed abroad was simple; but looking homeward was much more complicated.

For Coleridge, this dual scenario of the early months of 1798 gave him both a political and a poetic opportunity. The emergency situation offered the national equivalent of tensions that we have noticed in his verse, where the prophetic public voice alternates with a more ambivalent language of private experience. Over the previous two years his broadcast sublimities had ceased to make headway, and a poetry of friendship and thoughtful converse developed. The 'higher' ode and rapt meditation, with their big Ideas and impetuous precipitancy, sat uneasily alongside the more exploratory and thoughtful blank-verse poem in which wonderings and noticings replaced declamatory vision. The confident new direction he took in 'Religious Musings' had been continued with the buoyantly idealist *Ode on the Departing Year* (December 1796), an allegorical mixture of prayer and prophecy,[9] and with his attempts to develop his *Joan of Arc* material in which nations are guided by a spiritual destiny.[10] But confidence seemed to be lacking, and after publication of the fragmentary 'Visions of the Maid of

which are added, France, An Ode; and Frost at Midnight. By S.T. Coleridge (London: J. Johnson, 1798).

[8] A volunteer force for national defence was formed in 1794. Between April and July 1798 it grew from 54,600 to 116,000 men, rising to 146,000 in 1801, almost a quarter of whom were cavalrymen. See J. E. Cookson, *The British Armed Nation, 1793–1815* (Oxford: Clarendon Press, 1997), 71; and Austin Gee, *The British Volunteer Movement, 1794–1814* (Oxford: Clarendon Press, 2003), 11.

[9] In his dedication Coleridge speaks of 'that Impetuosity of Transition, and that Precipitation of Fancy and Feeling, which are the *essential* excellencies of the sublime Ode' (*Ode on the Departing Year* (Bristol: N. Briggs, 1796), 4), and he adds: 'although I prophesy curses, I pray fervently for blessings'.

[10] 'If there be Beings of higher class than Man, | I deem no nobler province they possess | Than by disposal of apt circumstance | To rear up kingdoms' ('Visions of the Maid of Orleans', 1–4). The *Joan of Arc* materials were subsumed into 'The Destiny of Nations' of *Sybilline Leaves* (1817). See Mays, i.279–80.

Orleans' in *The Morning Post* on 26 December 1797 these more epic
ambitions for 'The Destiny of Nations' ran into the sand.

But the nation's precarious destiny in April 1798 offered a fresh challenge,
and Coleridge announced himself in the most public way possible. On the
16th, more than a full column of *The Morning Post* was occupied by 'The
Recantation, An Ode. By S.T. Coleridge', introduced by its own editorial in
which the paper warmly endorsed the poem's message: 'The following
excellent Ode will be in unison with the feelings of every friend to Liberty
and foe to Oppression,' it began. With the news of France's outrageous
invasion of Switzerland in March, it was at last possible to identify oneself
in those binary terms without being a self-declared Jacobin. The language of
politics was taking on a refreshing ambiguity and the old labels were
becoming less useful. Coleridge's sublime ode uses this potential irony, as
the *Post* recognised, to cast itself as in effect an ode to Liberty. It reads less
like a recantation than a self-justification, celebrating an elemental principle
to which he has remained constant.[11] The poet's words are projected out
into the air from his precarious vantage point on a 'sea-cliff's verge', al-
though the poem is framed not by the forces on the other side of the Channel,
but by the eternal living powers around and above him. The first section
takes the form of an oath sworn on this divine testament, the Book of
Nature:

> O ye loud waves, and O ye forests high,
> And O ye clouds, that far above me soar'd!
> Thou rising sun! thou blue rejoicing sky!
>   Yea, every thing, that is and will be free,
>   Bear witness for me, wheresoe'er ye be,
> With what deep worship I have still ador'd
> The spirit of divinest Liberty!   (15–21)

But after this ringing declaration, when Coleridge turns to the recent events
that tested this belief, they are introduced in such a way as simultaneously to
sensationalise and fictionalise them. We seem to enter a world of childhood
enchantment. The pictures of the French Revolution and the ensuing Euro-
pean war shrink to a chapbook romance, where France 'in wrath her giant
limbs uprear'd, | And with that oath, which smote earth, air, and sea, |
Stamp'd her strong feet and said, she would be free' (22–4). In the lines
that follow Coleridge cheers France on in her struggle against the Coalition
forces (those 'fiends embattled by a wizard's wand'): 'Yet still my voice
unalter'd sang defeat | To all that brav'd the tyrant-quelling lance' (36–7).
Coleridge's language here catches the simple, trusting responses of a child

---

[11] Paul Magnuson links the poem to Daniel Stuart's editorial policy in *The Morning Post*
(*Reading Public Romanticism* (Princeton: Princeton University Press, 1998), 73). See also,
Morton Paley, *Apocalypse and Millennium in English Romantic Poetry* (Oxford: Clarendon
Press, 1999), 131–2.

reading *Jack the Giant-Killer*. What was at the beginning of the poem a declaration of belief now shades into an admission of credulity.

The third section continues this fairytale mode with its lurid allegorical picture of Jacobin repression in France itself: 'DOMESTIC TREASON, crush'd beneath her fatal stamp, | Writh'd, like a wounded dragon in his gore' (56–7). So much for the Vendée massacres. The disingenuousness culminates in the vision of enforced universal happiness, welcomed in terms that scarcely disguise the childish fantasy of the Idea: '"soon . . . | . . . Shall FRANCE compel the nations to be free, | 'Till LOVE and JOY look round, and call the earth their own!"' (59–63). The daring of Coleridge's approach to this point, which has verged on self-parody, becomes clear in the very next line, which opens section IV by at last introducing the recantation itself: 'Forgive me, Freedom! O forgive those dreams!' (64). The poem recalls itself from romance fantasy to relative realities, hearing the 'loud lament' from the distant Alps and imagining the fleeing Swiss as they 'spot the mountain snows | With bleeding wounds' (69–70). It is Switzerland where the 'shrine of Liberty' is to be found, he suggests.[12] But the wider impression the poem gives is that her true home is found neither in states nor in institutions. Liberty and human power are finally incompatible: 'Divinest Liberty! . . . thou nor swell'st the victor's strain; nor ever | Didst breathe thy soul in forms of human pow'r' (89–92). Coleridge's ode ends with the recognition that when embodied like this, Liberty is easily betrayed; but as a personal living force it can remain to animate us. In the final lines the 'spirit' escapes into the air, 'to live amid the winds, and move upon the waves!'

> And *there* I felt thee—on that sea-cliff's verge,
>   Whose pines, scarce travell'd by the breeze above,
> Had made one murmur with the distant surge.
> Yes! while I stood and gaz'd, my temples bare,
> And shot my being thro' earth, sea, and air,
>   Possessing all things with intensest love,
> O Liberty, my spirit felt thee there!   (99–105)

There is a sense of elemental refreshment here, of being able to breathe easily. Liberty is at last discovered to be an informing spirit, not a structure or system, or a reified abstraction. But these concluding lines of Coleridge's ode also suggest his uneasiness with Idea itself and how its universals can be contemptuous of specific human experience. After all, a crushed dragon is less troubling than thousands of murdered women and children. The tumid

---

[12] Weeks after the French invasion, the 'Helvetic Republic' was founded on 29 March 1798. In April Geneva was annexed to France, and the remainder of Switzerland incorporated into the new Cisalpine Republic. See G. Bonnard, 'The Invasion of Switzerland and English Public Opinion (January to April 1798): The Background to S. T. Coleridge's *France: An Ode*', *English Studies*, 22 (1940), 1–26. Bonaparte's capture of the Venetian Republic in 1797 had ended a thousand years of Venice's independence.

language of the earlier part of 'The Recantation' in fact echoes that of the French Directoire itself, with its fondness for inspirational allegories that toyed with the sublime. The French proclamations of this time (printed in the British newspapers) regularly featured 'The Genius of Liberty' who, it was announced, would accompany the invading force personally. In the Decree of 5 Brumaire Year 6 (26 October 1797) General Bonaparte and his army were charged to:

Crown your exploits by the Invasion of an Island whither you carried slavery under William the Conqueror, and on the contrary, now conduct there the Genius of Liberty, which it will import at the landing of the French.[13]

It reads like the stage direction for a pageant. On 11 December Bonaparte told the Directoire that as a result of his recent Italian conquests 'the two finest Countries of Europe' can now 'see the Genius of Liberty rise from the tombs of their ancestors'.[14] After reporting his address, the British newspapers printed Barras's eloquent speech of reply, in which he urged the general to carry out the invasion plans for Britain as if it were an extravagant opera production. The Ocean, Barras assured him, would fight on his side:

Go, ye, greater than [Pompey], and chain up that gigantic Buccaneer, who tyrannizes over the Sea; go, and punish in London outrages which have been too long unpunished. Numerous votaries of Liberty await you there. You are the Deliverer whom outraged Humanity calls for with plaintive cries. No sooner shall the Tri-coloured Standard wave upon its ensanguined shores, than an unanimous shout of benediction shall announce your presence; and that generous Nation, perceiving the first dawn of happiness, shall embrace you as Deliverers[15]

It is a heroic scene waiting to be set to music, perhaps by Méhul as a follow-up to Le Chant du Départ, the famous revolutionary war-song of 1794 ('Liberty guides our steps...Battles are your holidays...Let our heroes return embellished with Glory and Liberty. Let their blood be spilt for Equality').[16] Reified Ideas make an invasion sound smooth and painless. War is a spectacular pageant played out in front of a chorus of *votaries of Liberty* and *outraged Humanity*. For Barras, the only *cries* are those of the British nation longing for Liberty. And the poetic tint of 'ensanguined shores' nicely sets off the colours of the revolutionary tricolor. If all you need do is chain up a giant pirate, then the adventure will not be complicated by moral issues, and you can ensure a triumph scene at the end. The blood won't be real.

[13] *Lloyd's Evening Post*, 6 Nov. 1797. See note 5 above.
[14] Bonaparte's address to the Directoire, 10 Dec. 1797; quoted in *The London Packet*, 15 Dec. 1797.
[15] *The True Briton*, 21 Dec. 1797.
[16] *Le Chant du Départ* was first performed on 14 July 1794, with words by the Jacobin dramatist, Marie-Joseph Chénier (1764–1811), and music by Étienne Nicolas Méhul (1763–1817), the opera composer.

By April 1798, thanks to French propaganda like this, the language of the universal Idea was developing chilling associations. It was too easily becoming the lingua franca of warlike posturing. It is clear that in his 'Recantation' ode Coleridge is aware of the embarrassment of being considered one of those 'votaries of Liberty' waiting to welcome Bonaparte. But however he tries to refocus his Idea of Freedom as a continuing inspiration, it tends to remain in its allegorical context. In the end, the reader may wonder, is human freedom better served by announcing it from a lofty cliff, or in letting it work from within? Coleridge's expansive final image doesn't quite resolve the question, perhaps even tries to have it both ways. He wants to rescue the Idea of Liberty from the spirit of warlike enmity that seems to be everywhere, and to relocate it as a spiritual force that will 'possess all things with intensest love'.

As a public 'recantation' the poem gave notice on its own behalf, and on behalf of *The Morning Post*, that British reformist opinion felt thoroughly betrayed by France. The newspaper was at this moment repositioning itself politically in response to the invasion threat, and Coleridge's ode was in tune with its new attitude.[17] Indeed a reader might think 'The Recantation' had been written in immediate response to the extended editorial leader of 14 April, in which the paper announced its own kind of recantation. One point on which the *Morning Post* leader is clear is that liberty is not something to be imposed on a nation, as it has been on the newly created Cisalpine Republic ('that mockery of freedom!'). She has been told by France 'that her liberty is established, her independence affirmed. Does she exercise the right of discussion? "Oh no," says France, "we give you perfect freedom—to do as we like."' Coleridge's phrase 'Shall FRANCE compel the nations to be free' carries the same bitter implication.[18] The new situation in the wake of the Manchester arrests has convinced the paper that 'the Country is in danger'. It is fearful that the dual threat is genuine, and the national situation 'very perilous':

What is the duty of an Englishman at the present moment? To unite in arms against the French. That is his most pressing duty; a duty perfectly compatible with the principles of all parties... Surely they who have united in opposition to domestic oppression, will not hesitate in uniting against foreign tyranny.

The word *unite* is reiterated, but in the context of national defence; and it is undercut by the reminder of a *united opposition*. It is clear that this unity is a pragmatic embodying of the nation, not a spiritual union. The paper goes on to declare that its long-standing political sentiments have not altered, and that its announcement is not to be regarded as a recantation of *principle*:

---

[17] See Magnuson, *Reading Public Romanticism*, 72–4.

[18] *The Morning Post*, 14 April 1798. The leader continues: '[W]ould [France] come only to give us Liberty? Absurd supposition. She comes for plunder and conquest.' Richard Brinsley Sheridan would rework this rhetorical question in his speech of 20 April.

'And are we to be told that we have recanted our former sentiments? No, we follow them up; we are acting in strict uniformity with them.' The title 'Recantation' attached to Coleridge's ode two days later bears a similar ironic relationship to his own views, and he is able to publicise them in the knowledge that he can still adhere to *The Morning Post*'s unwavering reformist position. The paper goes on to stress that its appeal for national unity is not an endorsement of the government, but is temporary and conditional:

To the present Ministers of Great Britain we impute our present situation; we detest their principles, abhor their practice, and view them as the prime authors of our present calamities.... But our first duty is to resist and repel the French. Then, having deserved to be free; then, if we are wise, we shall correct our domestic abuses, punish our domestic oppressors, establish our rights, affirm our liberties, and make the Constitution what it ought to be.

The paper finds a way of accommodating its concerns: blaming the government while suspending its opposition, and adjusting its political line while sticking to its principles. An indignant defiance of the French makes the headline simple; but underneath are two nagging doubts: a suspicion that the *domestic oppressors* may finally be harder to deal with; and the thought that the nation itself must finally *deserve to be free*. All was still not well at home. The patriotism on show here is not a simple unifying Idea, but a complex, pragmatic mixture of fear, anger, patience, hope, and prayer. It suggests how we might view Coleridge's political position during these days as being a more mixed and conditional one of this kind.

Nevertheless, at the end of the paper's 14 April editorial there is an organic hope struggling to emerge, in which Britain will eventually be constituted differently. Calls for 'unity' will then be more than a slogan in a crisis, and will express a genuine national integrity in which everyone can partake:

make the Constitution what it ought to be—not a black and bloated mass, cumbrous and unwieldy, enfeebling, cankering, and corrupting every thing; but a living and protecting Spirit, animating and invigorating the land, and diffusing through the whole body, health, and happiness, and joy.

The present Burkean constitution, it suggests, is organic only in its corruption and decay. It lacks the animating principle that ought to sustain it. At this moment of crisis, *The Morning Post* is voicing its wish not for a revolution, but for a thorough constitutional reform in which the whole of society can play a part, something that will genuinely represent the life of the nation. The spirit of 'Liberty' in the final lines of Coleridge's ode is perhaps his version of this *living and protecting Spirit, animating and invigorating the land*.

'The Recantation, An Ode' is a confident, perfectly timed public intervention, which seizes its moment to make common cause with *The Morning*

Post and with reformist opinion throughout the country. Its message is a national one, projected across the land in a declamatory way, and its personal qualms are not developed beyond the ironies that edge it towards parody. But the poem is finally limited by its Pindaric character: the requisite bold onrush and urgency of tone preclude elements of introspective questioning that might have complicated its topic of second thoughts. The result is that Coleridge's commanding rhetoric ends up being uncomfortably similar to the bellicose sublimities he is trying to distance himself from. The ode is projecting a voice of national unity, which inevitably compromises personal integrity. To explore the latter, and the strains under which it was working at this time, Coleridge would need a less unified and more organic text—one that did not simply project itself in one direction, but which faced both ways, so to speak. A more localised poem, looking both outward and homeward, might in the end do more justice to the national situation in these anxious weeks. 'Fears in Solitude' (first published in Coleridge's composite volume of that name[19]) may seem a poem that juggles awkwardly its public oratory and its personal reflection; but many thousands of intelligent people were in April 1798 attempting to bridge that very gap. At this time, individual voices were locating themselves within a national strategy that needed to win every neighbourhood to its cause. During the state of emergency people were facing local fears and home truths.

This is not to say that Bristol and its environs did not share in the sense of enthusiastic national organisation. Like other cities and towns, it made a showing in the 'voluntary subscription' scheme, which across the land allowed every individual from a duke to a manservant to contribute to the cause. *The Bristol Journal* recorded that the Duke of Marlborough had given £5,000, and Percival Stockdale's servant 1 guinea (the same sum, as it happens, as one J. Cottle).[20] On 2 March the Bristol Theatre staged *Cymbeline; or the Invasion of Britain*, followed by a comical interlude, *Voluntary Contributions*, in which 'the first scene representing all classes crouding to pay in their mite' was acted to 'unbounded and incessant' applause.[21] This special performance was honoured by the 'personal attendance' of 'the Gentlemen Troop of *Bristol Volunteer Yeomanry Cavalry*'. Such national gestures, it is clear, were also outbursts of local pride and solidarity. As Mark Philp has shown,

The evidence suggests a deep localism to the volunteer movement: people were willing to defend their localities, but had no desire to serve outside them—and

---

[19] See n. 7 above.
[20] *The Bristol Journal*, 10 Feb. and 3 March 1798.
[21] Ibid. 3 March 1798. Walsh Porter's 'occasional interlude' was never printed, but survives as Huntington Library Larpent MS 1197. The double bill was a repeat in Bristol of the performance at the company's sister theatre, the Theatre Royal Bath, on 27 Feb. See Valerie Wayne, '*Cymbeline*: Patriotism and Performance', in Richard Dutton and Jean E. Howard (eds), *A Companion to Shakespeare's Works*, vol. iv (Oxford: Blackwell, 2003), 389–407.

were not reluctant to say so … the final totals mask the complex stories that underlay the particular histories and conditions of each of the local units. These more particular stories offer an important counterweight to the view that there is at work a process of national identification and commitment to the country.[22]

Specific individual narratives might complicate the national picture, and the politicians knew this. In the words of Linda Colley, War Secretary Dundas's questionnaire for all able-bodied volunteers 'demanded … details of what service, if any, each man was prepared to offer to the state', and it was acceptable for a volunteer to limit his commitment to the nearest town and its locality. J. E. Cookson concludes that 'corps remained firmly anchored in local communities, often resisting strenuously attempts to amalgamate them in larger units based perhaps on groups of parishes'.[23]

In 'Fears in Solitude' Coleridge takes on the difficult challenge of speaking simultaneously *to* and *for* the nation in April 1798, while projecting himself as a man with strong local affiliations and domestic commitments. In order to straddle these points of reference a more mixed and personal topography was needed. Instead of the emblematic gesture of being a prophetic voice on a coastal cliff-top, the poet places himself in a specific situation in time and space, as someone who is writing when the local landscape (and especially his own local landscape, as it happens) has become newly politicised. Critics of the poem have noted that Coleridge is revisiting the site of his 'Reflections on Having Left a Place of Retirement'.[24] He does so, however, in the knowledge that a small-scale picturesque spot of countryside, which in early 1796 had symbolised pastoral retirement (rejected for a life of urban engagement), has moved centre stage in the national struggle. A 'close country' of more intimate spaces, wooded combes, and secret places was now being viewed as ideal for resisting an invader.[25] Guerrilla resistance would be the ideal strategy, and in this situation local guides who knew their patch of ground intimately would be needed.[26] Pitched battle would be less effective than the village skirmish. Part of the plan was to evacuate

[22] Philp (ed.), *Resisting Napoleon*, 7.

[23] Linda Colley, *Britons: Forging the Nation 1707–1837* (New Haven/London: Yale University Press, 1992), 289–90; J. E. Cookson, 'The English Volunteer Movement of the French Wars, 1793–1815: Some Contexts', *Historical Journal*, 32 (1989), 867–91 (872).

[24] See Kelvin Everest, *Coleridge's Secret Ministry: The Context of the Conversation Poems 1795–1798* (Hassocks: Harvester Press; New York: Barnes and Noble, 1979), 270–4; and C. R. Watters, 'A Distant "Boum" among the Hills: Some Notes on "Fears in Solitude"', *CLB*, 59 (July 1987), 85–96 (88).

[25] This was the conclusion of Gen. Henry Lloyd in *A Political and Military Rhapsody, on the Invasion and Defence of Great Britain and Ireland*, 5th edn (London: Egerton and Debrett, 1798), quoted approvingly by *The Bristol Journal*, 27 Jan. 1798.

[26] 'A Corps of Guides … on horseback and on foot, consisting of those who are best acquainted with the Roads, Lanes, Footpaths, Bridges, Creeks, Rivers, Fording Places, and other Communications … should be selected in the maritime counties' (*A Plan … for Rendering the Body of the People Instrumental in the General Defence*, 5; rpt. in *The Bristol Journal*, 21 April 1798).

non-combatants from the vicinity of the coast, which meant there would be a simultaneous two-way traffic of people, with the retreating evacuees using smaller lanes and trackways, thus avoiding the turnpike roads down which the troops would be marching coastward to face the enemy. Villages and small towns within reach of the sea were finding themselves in the front line. The able-bodied with spades and pickaxes were encouraged to sign up as pioneers, or to contribute their implements to the local stockpile.[27] Every parish should agree on an appropriate 'place of rendezvous'.

On 12–13 February 1798 all the national newspapers had carried the newly discovered (or released) plans for the abortive French 'invasion' the previous year.[28] These make it clear that Colonel Tate's instructions had been to land his force on the southern shore of the Bristol Channel and move up the River Avon by night, with his first priority an attack on Bristol ('The destruction of Bristol is of the very last importance, and every possible effort should be made to accomplish it'). The focus was suddenly on the south-west once again; and as Nicholas Roe has shown, the dispatch of an experienced government spy, James Walsh, in August 1797, to investigate the 'emigrant family' living at Alfoxden (who walked around the vicinity equipped with camp-stools and showed interest in a nearby river) is evidence of the concern of central government for this small patch of England. Suddenly the little circle of the Wordsworths, Coleridges, and Tom Poole had become linked to the national fear of treason and plot.[29]

Coleridge's 'Fears in Solitude' can be read as in some ways equivalent to this uneasy convergence of national and local allegiances. The poem places its local voice and situation at the service of the nation, and daringly uses the image of retreat as a pledge of commitment. Only at this time might such seemingly contradictory gestures make sense. The poem's full title, 'Fears in Solitude. Written, April 1798, during the Alarms of an Invasion', draws attention to the state of crisis in which it was composed, but it does so in a way that is conscious of working both with and against the national grain. The title's emphasis on inward concerns would normally risk the implication of cowardly retreat at a juncture when everyone is being urged to stand firm and commit themselves; but here it signals a genuine 'fear', an emotion which at this particular time was being read as a patriotic response to the invasion threat. Although 'Fears in Solitude' comes out of a moment when poetic 'solitude' seemed to have been removed from the national agenda, it touches on questions of personal integrity that were being aired in the political arena.

---

[27] Ibid. 4–6.

[28] The *Instructions* were first printed in *The Anti-Jacobin*, 12 Feb. 1798. They were published in full as *Authentic Copies of the Instructions Given by Gen. Hoche to Colonel Tate, Previous to His Landing on the Coast of South Wales, in the Beginning of 1797* (London: J. Wright, 1798).

[29] See Roe, *Wordsworth and Coleridge: The Radical Years*, 248–62.

The poem is also an oratorical text; but it is manifestly, indeed resolutely, not a unified one, something that has lowered its evaluation in Coleridge studies. The most helpful criticism of the poem acknowledges this. Mark Rawlinson, for example, shows how the poem's apprehension of war's horrors 'lends itself both to opposition to war and violent opposition to an enemy'. 'It is not so much that Coleridge's poem turns on its head', he adds, 'as that what it imagines can face two ways.'[30] I want to develop this insight, specifically in relation to the critical situation on 20 April, when *facing two ways* was a national phenomenon. But where Rawlinson understands this in binary terms and moves into a critique of what he judges to be 'the poem's worrying intellectual apostasy', I shall argue that 'Fears in Solitude' is far from evincing a desertion of faith or principle, but is an intelligent move that sees beyond theoretical polarities to what is immediately practical; that it recognises and responds to uncomfortable experience. At this point in time, an Idea could no longer bear the weight of events. Being in two minds somehow gave Coleridge a more organic understanding of the political choices that had to be made. When placed in the immediate context of its writing, the poem expresses a struggle for integrity, in which an unqualified 'unity' is not on the agenda. It is a poem that is finally prepared to await the outcome, biding its time, ready for war while possessing its soul in peace. It does not shape an Idea, but allows itself to be shaped by experience.

The poem articulates a succession of emotional states and intellectual positions, which express the varied tensions of patriot, libertarian, preacher, cottager, parent. Some readers find the public and private elements pulling against each other to produce a hybrid that is partly an oratorical declamation, partly a more intimate conversation poem, while some develop readings that elide the two.[31] Others examine it as a critique of a debased public rhetoric: Paul Magnuson has highlighted its condemnation of a national 'scheme of perjury'.[32] In Michael Simpson's deconstructive approach, the oratory of the poem is turned against itself: what he terms its 'corrupt semiosis' is the equivalent of an omnipresent public corruption; and the text makes 'itself and us...complicit in this rhetoric, by its sweeping public address'. The poem, he argues, 'invites its readers to sift the graven images of rhetoric from the authentic inspiration of poetry'.[33]

---

[30] Mark Rawlinson, 'Invasion! Coleridge, the Defence of Britain and the Cultivation of the Public's Fear', in Philip Shaw (ed.), *Romantic Wars: Studies in Culture and Conflict, 1793–1822* (Aldershot: Ashgate, 2000), 110–37 (121).

[31] See, for example, Carl R. Woodring, *Politics in the Poetry of Coleridge* (Madison: University of Wisconsin Press, 1961), 189–90; in response, Kelvin Everest argues that 'Coleridge sustains his public style because the poem in a sense supposes simply the conversational audience, family and friends, on a national scale' (*Coleridge's Secret Ministry*, 279).

[32] Magnuson, *Reading Public Romanticism*, 67, 74–5.

[33] Michael Simpson, 'The Morning (Post) After: Apocalypse and Bathos in Coleridge's "Fears in Solitude"', in Tim Fulford (ed.), *Romanticism and Millenarianism* (New York/Houndmills: Palgrave, 2002), 71–86 (74, 78).

It is an age-old binary of 'false' rhetoric and 'genuine' poetry. But these various comments tend to assume that the public language of the poem is throughout a debased one, a patriotic 'zeal' that can't avoid compromising itself with the warlike 'clamour' it attacks. In the case of 'The Recantation' I have taken a similar view; but 'Fears in Solitude' written a few days afterwards has, I would argue, a different and more subtle character. Through its mixed form it not only sets the personal and the public in a complex relationship to each other, but makes critical distinctions between different kinds of public rhetoric. Most readers will agree that 'Fears in Solitude' exposes the difficulty of finding in 1798 a patriotic language that is free of the bad faith and violent 'war-whoop' against which it speaks;[34] but I want to argue that there was such a public rhetoric available to Coleridge at this moment, and one with which he might wish to be associated. We have looked at how closely Coleridge's 'Recantation' ode reflected the strategic shift in policy of *The Morning Post*. 'Fears in Solitude' builds on this in ways that align his poem with the contribution made to the current debate by the leading parliamentary orator of the time, Richard Brinsley Sheridan.

No one seems to have linked Sheridan to 'Fears in Solitude', which is a little odd given the critical interest in its politics, and one reason may be Coleridge's severe soreness over Sheridan's rejection of *Osorio* for Drury Lane the previous November. But this did not become anger and disillusionment until January 1800 (when he wrote to Southey: 'This Sheridan!—Is he not an *arch* Scoundrel?'). In April 1798 Coleridge could perhaps separate the patriot and orator from the theatre-manager.[35]

The oratory of 'Fears in Solitude' is framed by lyric descriptions of the natural world at peace; and the poem's move from an extreme stillness, where the most delicate sensitivities can be registered, to a manly, zealous, public declaration ('Stand forth! be men! repel an impious foe', 136) is jarring, disconcerting, itself *invasive*. Coleridge soon came to think that these two voices compromised his poem by making it a generic hybrid. Transcribing it about a year later he added a postscript: 'N.B. The above is perhaps not Poetry—but rather a sort of Middle thing between Poetry & Oratory— Sermoni propior.'[36] Michael Simpson has demurred: 'It seems to me', he writes, 'that the text is not in fact able to become a middle thing'; the reader's experience, he says, is one of being 'shunted between, on the one hand, a depiction of the dell and the speaker's response to it, and, on the other, his

---

[34] The term 'war-whoop' (cf. l. 86), first used for the blood-curdling cry of Native Americans (1739), had recently been used in *The True-Briton* (1 Dec. 1797) to deplore 'the war-whoop of sedition sounded throughout [Ireland]'.

[35] Coleridge to Southey, 25 Jan. 1800 (Griggs, 564). On 14 May 1798 he reported a fresh promise from Sheridan to stage *Osorio*, adding: 'which promise he will...certainly break' (Griggs, 409).

[36] Mays, i.469.

publicly phrased admonitions'.[37] My argument here is that political language
during these weeks was itself simultaneously facing in two directions: confi-
dently outward towards the enemy, and more circumspectly inward to ideas of
home and domesticity. National 'unity' was becoming entangled with personal
integrity, and the management of strategic retreat was suddenly an urgent
topic. In April 1798, the elements of retreat in Coleridge's poem are, I would
suggest, better understood in terms of the political and military organisation of
the time—not as a shying away from commitment but committing himself in
quite a particular way. The extreme dynamics of the text convey a sense of
crisis; and however successfully or otherwise the language works, it would be
misleading to split off the private meditation from the public oratory. The
poem's conflicted rhetoric articulates the issues in the air.

Certainly the poem's opening location, the 'quiet spirit-healing nook' in the
Quantock Hills, is one that seems deliberately to refuse the national vantage
point. The setting could not be more localised, with an insouciant nature
performing its everyday wonders and filling the poet's attention. But as so
often with Coleridge the silence is full of potential sound, the stillness of
potential movement, the solitude of potential company: each makes us listen
and look more intently. And one particular sound increasingly makes itself
heard, as if it is insisting there is another dimension beyond this enclosed spot:

> A green and silent spot amid the hills!
> A small and silent dell!—O'er stiller place
> No singing sky-lark ever pois'd himself!   (1–3)[38]

The skylark's accompaniment, indeed company, registers; and it does so
again in line 18 as 'the singing lark (that sings unseen | The minstrelsy
which solitude loves best)'; and once more at the end of the opening para-
graph, when a great deal is beginning to happen for the young man: 'his
senses gradually wrapp'd | In a half-sleep, he dreams of better worlds, | And
dreaming hears thee still, O singing lark! | That singest like an angel in the
clouds' (25–8). We note simultaneously the man's lapse into unconscious-
ness and the poem's stirring consciousness. The promise of *better worlds* has
a double connotation here: the private daydream, and the heavenly messen-
ger. The text holds the two contrasting possibilities together.

The thought that suddenly invades the dell's 'meditative joy' (23) is
nonetheless disturbing, especially for one 'who would full fain preserve |
His soul in calmness' (30–1), and it is increased by his immediately super-
imposing it onto the *now* of his text:

> O my God,
> It is indeed a melancholy thing,
> And weighs upon the heart, that he must think

---

[37] Simpson, 'The Morning (Post) After', 72.
[38] The text quoted is the first printing in the composite *Fears in Solitude* volume, 1798, 1–12.

> What uproar and what strife may now be stirring
> This way or that way o'er these silent hills—
> Invasion, and the thunder and the shout,
> And all the crash of onset... (32–8)

'This way or that way'—is this just invasion or also insurrection? What direction is the threat coming from? The urgent question is marked by a nice oratorical touch: he ends with an extended version of the classic triplet, or *tricolon auctum* ('*Invasion*, and the *thunder* and the *shout*, | And all the *crash* of *onset*'; my italics). Perhaps we have to hear the 'crash' of language so that what is distant can be brought home *now*: not just the obscenity of war but the nation's own guilt. There is dramatic effect here, and perfect timing. The two voices—the localised stillness and the loud international war cry—are made to collide, to compete for the same space.

At this moment, the public rhetoric of the poem makes the reader uneasily aware of different directions, and from neither quarter can we take comfort. We discover this is no national rallying cry, but a cry of a different kind:

> We have offended, O my countrymen!
> We have offended very grievously,
>
> . . . .
>
>   have we gone forth
> And borne to distant tribes slavery and pangs,
> And, deadlier far, our vices, whose deep taint
> With slow perdition murders the whole man,
> His body and his soul! Meanwhile, at home,
> We have been drinking with a riotous thirst
> Pollutions from the brimming cup of wealth (42–56)

Both abroad and at home, we have been committed, he says, to a national scheme of cruelty, blasphemy, and perjury. This is very much in the spirit of the Dean of Bristol's sermon, delivered in the city on the day of the National Fast on 7 March, on the subject of 'the abominable viciousness and depravity of the present times' and 'the threatened judgment which seems to hang over us'.[39] In light of this spiritual scrutiny, the poem's double landscape of inner peace and public conflict, the spirit-healing nook and sounds of encroaching battle, turns potential retreat into a spiritual advance, a necessary and vital self-regeneration which is the only thing that will save us. At this time of threatened invasion, it implies, we must look homeward.

Coleridge was not alone at this moment in writing a poem with two such voices. In order to clarify the context of 'Fears in Solitude' and find a fresh perspective on its public rhetoric, I want to introduce another substantial poem of that year which similarly interrupts a subjective meditation on nature's peace with a central oratorical section on state corruption and the

---

[39] *The Bristol Journal*, 10 March 1798.

violence of war. The setting for this poem is St Michael's Mount on the south
coast of Cornwall, a fortified promontory/island which looks across the
western Channel to France and the Bay of Biscay. Guarding the approaches
to Plymouth, this was a strategic location in 1798, and one with a proud
history as the beacon from which the invading Spanish Armada was first
sighted in 1588.[40] From this vantage point the poet will turn in two direc-
tions: towards corruption at home and war abroad. This is a little known
text, so extended quotation is needed to convey its character and argument.
As in Coleridge's opening, before the disturbing visions invade his world, the
poet offers a scene of nature's utter peace and silence, highlighted by the
sound of a bird:

> Amid the arch of Heav'n, extended clear,
> Scarce the thin frecks of feathery cloud appear!
> Beyond the long curve of the lessening bay
> The still Atlantic stretches its bright way,—
> The tall ship moves not on the tranquil brine!
> Around, the solemn promontories shine!
> No sounds approach us, save, at times, the cry
> Of the grey gull, that scarce is heard so high!
> The billows make no noise, and on the breast
> Of charmed Ocean, Silence sinks to rest!
>   O might we thus from Heav'n's bright battlements
> Behold the scene Humanity presents;
> And see, like this, all harmonis'd and still,
> And hear no far-off sounds of earthly ill;
> Wide landscape of the world, in purest light
> Array'd—how fair, how chearing were the sight!

No sooner has this panorama of universal peace been established than from
opposed directions come two apocalyptic visions. Looking homewards the
poet sees a riotous Belshazzar's Feast of vice and dissipation, which indicates
a corrupt nation for whom the writing is on the wall:

> We hear the clangors and the cries, that shake
> The mad world, and their dismal music make!
> We see gaunt Vice, of dread enormous size,
> That fearless in the broad day sweltering lies
>
> .   .   .   .
>
> We see Intemperance his goblet quaff;
> And mocking Blasphemy, with mad loud laugh,
> Acting before high Heav'n a direr part,
> Sport with the weapons that shall pierce his heart!

[40] General Lloyd considered Plymouth as the most likely first target of a French invasion (*A Political and Military Rhapsody*, 25–6).

But then, looking out across the sea to France the poet views the other half of
this nightmare diptych, where the Leviathan of War has been unleashed like
a furious animal, intimating the end of the world. Caught between the two
scenarios, at home and abroad, the poet can only ask in a personal prayer to
be lifted up out of the human world entirely:

> If o'er the southern wave we turn our sight,
> More dismal shapes of hideous woe affright!
> Grim-visag'd War, that ruthless as he hies,
> Drowns with his trumpet's blast a brother's cries
>
> .   .   .   .
>
> O'er a vast field wide heap'd with festering slain,
> Hark how the Daemon Passions shout amain,
> And cry, exulting, while the death-storm low'rs,
> 'Hurrah, the kingdoms of the world are ours!'
> O GOD, who madest man, I see these things,
> And wearied, wish for a fleet Angels wings,
> That I might fly away—and hear no more,
> The surge that moans along this mortal shore![41]

This is William Lisle Bowles exploring his own 'fears in solitude' from the
top of St Michael's Mount, the title of his meditative poem of 335 lines
published not long after April 1798. Placed against Coleridge's, Bowles's
geography offers a loftier, heavenly perspective on the Europe of 1798, but
also a higher sanction for his rhetoric. The poet speaks from the vantage
point of St Michael, the angel who once was seated in 'St Michael's Chair',
'on the highest turret of the castle'. 'O might I now, amid the frowning
storm, | Behold, great Vision of the Mount, thy form' (247–8). He longs for
Milton's vision in *Lycidas*, the 'great vision of the guarded Mount'; but as
Bowles clambers up to 'the watch-tow'r's loftiest platform', he discovers the
place is empty: 'Departed spirit, fruitless is the pray'r. | We see alone thy long
deserted chair' (254–6).[42]

Coleridge, however, speaks from within his private dell; his angel is the
skylark singing far above him 'like an angel in the clouds' while he is
observing the 'half-transparent stalks' of the 'unripe flax', close-up details
of the moment. Only at the close of Coleridge's text is there a 'burst of
prospect', but this comes when the rhetorical burst is over. We have the odd
sense, up to that point, of a resounding public declaration being made in 'a
quiet spirit-healing nook' hidden within the folds of the Quantocks. For his
sermo Coleridge has no saintly pulpit, and no panorama across which to

---

[41] William Lisle Bowles, *St. Michael's Mount, A Poem* (Salisbury: Adams and Dilly, 1798),
ll. 279–322.
[42] As Bowles points out in a footnote, it was his mentor Thomas Warton who first explained
Milton's enigmatic lines 'Look homeward Angel' (previously interpreted as addressing Lycidas
himself). Warton's admired note appeared in his edition of Milton's *Poems upon Several
Occasions, English, Italian, and Latin, with Translations* (London: J. Dodsley, 1785), 27–30.

project his equivalent of St Michael's voice. Bowles locates his visionary rhetoric by invoking the figure who is simultaneously the warrior angel, the guardian who should be watching over the land, and the voice that in *Paradise Lost* mediates history's providential course to humanity. In Coleridge, the 'St Michael voice' lacks these carefully placed markers that help Bowles to direct his public address across the nation.

But there is another supporting figure standing beside Bowles in this passage, who materialises at the pivotal point where the speaker turns from vice and blasphemy at home to the cruelties of war emanating from Revolutionary France. Bowles's footnote (on p. 23) reads:

Every English heart must rejoice at the open, manly manner in which Mr. Sheridan avowed his sentiments upon this subject in the House of Commons, April 20, 1798.

That date brings us back to Coleridge's 'Fears in Solitude', which is inscribed at the end: 'Nether Stowey, April 20th, 1798', the date with which this chapter began. Unlike the two other poems in the 1798 volume this text is linked to a specific day. In the Bollingen edition J. C. C. Mays notes that it 'appear[s] to have no special significance in political history',[43] and indeed it has always been taken to be the date of composition; but I want to suggest that Friday 20 April 1798 did have significance for Coleridge—and for the nation as a whole; that it is not a private record, but part of the public voice of the poem; and that by ending his text with it he was implicitly associating his sentiments (as Bowles explicitly did) with Sheridan's House of Commons speech, and the other events of 20 April.

Sheridan's performance on that day was the talk of the land. It was immediately printed in newspapers throughout Britain: *The Times* cleared the front page and gave it three whole columns, and the *Bristol Journal* awarded it pride of place on the back page—a tenth of the whole paper.[44] Its immediate context could hardly have been more dramatic. Dundas, the Secretary for War, brought to the Commons that message from His Majesty with which I began, confirming that invasion was imminent and seeking an appropriate response. A loyal address to the King was proposed, and Sheridan (who, with Fox's withdrawal from parliament, was de facto leader of the tiny but tenacious opposition to the Ministry[45]) immediately rose to give his wholehearted support to the motion. At this critical juncture Sheridan's move was more than symbolic: it announced unanimity as a patriotic duty for all Britons, and the shelving of party differences in response to the invasion threat. It seemed to many that 20 April 1798 was the day the nation, as constituted in parliament, finally came together. In the words of *The Morning Post*, 'Perhaps there never was a speech delivered

---

[43] Mays, ii.593, notes that the date is changed in *Sybilline Leaves* (1817) and later texts to 28 April ('probably an error').

[44] *The Bristol Journal*, a weekly, printed it on 28 April.

[45] See Lewis Gibbs, *Sheridan* (London: J. M. Dent and Sons, 1947), 204–23.

with more animation, heard with more attention, more in unison with the feelings of every man who heard it, or received with more enthusiastic approbation.'[46]

The sentiments Sheridan went on to declare set the whole House cheering and applauding. The speech took upon itself to be the voice of the country, and the papers treated it as such. I'm not suggesting that 'Fears in Solitude' is directly modelled on the speech, but that it can be read as Coleridge's response to Sheridan's call, and that in several ways the speech prompted him and gave him confidence to write his own oratorical poem. Sheridan's aim is to project his words beyond the chamber of the House of Commons, beyond ministers and parties, and to address the people. He declares that his purpose is to rouse the energy and spiritual zeal of the kingdom (the transcript used here is that of *The Bristol Journal*[47]):

What I wish ... is, to see a superior zeal to animate the country; a zeal which it is not in the power of any Minister to call forth. Sir, in times like these, a common spirit will not do ... In God's name, if the enemy are to be resisted, let us do it effectually. ... to say that we will not pledge ourselves but in the last extremity, is pledging ourselves only as a modified opposition, and to a diluted spirit ... On these grounds it is, that I wish to behold a higher zeal manifested than at present seems to pervade the country, though, I am happy to confess, I see such a zeal rising.

(When Coleridge read those last words he may have thought momentarily of *The Morning Post*, and of his 'Recantation' published four days earlier.) Sheridan calls for all Britons to *pledge* themselves, to express not just spirit, but a *higher zeal* (in this *Bristol Journal* version he repeats that word, with its religious overtones, again and again). 'Fears in Solitude' shows us Coleridge pledging himself to his country, and indeed doing so with a zeal that *rises* about as high as he can make it. 'Nor deem my zeal or factious or mistim'd' (153), Coleridge says, as if to stress that his words are both unifying and timely.

Unanimity is Sheridan's keynote; but he is careful to distinguish it from party. He repeatedly declares that he will not, as many other opposition Whigs had done, enter into the spurious unity of a coalition. He is focused on the nation, and this allows him to hint at selfish motives in those who are rallying round more predictably at this time. What others might see as his apostasy from the radical cause is recast as a true political liberty that remains firm in its principles:

---

[46] *The Morning Post*, 21 April 1798.
[47] *The Bristol Journal*, 28 April 1798. Their transcript is identical with that in *The Morning Post* and *The Star* (both 21 April). Versions in other papers have less oratorical force: *The Times* (21 April) offers reported speech: 'What he wished to see ... was, superior spirit and unanimity in every class of the community; and he thought he saw that spirit rising through the country at that moment'; likewise *The True Briton* (21 April): 'What he wished was this, that there should be added that superior spirit and zeal, which, he was sorry to say, had not been manifested so much and so soon as it ought to have been. A common spirit would not now do ... He rejoiced to see that that spirit was at length rising.' *The Oracle* produced yet another version.

With regard to the principle on which I would recommend unanimity, I hope and trust that no man will understand, that I mean to recommend a jobbing, shifting union with the present Administration—No, sir, no! There are sins on this subject which I will not now rehearse, but which I never shall forget. The unanimity I wish, is against the French, and it is the only unanimity which can be successful.

He throws in the word 'French', and the pores tingle. The 'sins' of ministers and former allies are alluded to darkly, but held back, as they will be throughout the speech. That, he suggests, is material for another time; meanwhile his opposition is only suspended.

The message Sheridan's address has for someone like Coleridge is that this is a moment when patriotism and principle can be reconciled, and that it is *fear* that binds the two together. For Sheridan, the fears of invasion are very important. He attacks those who 'seem to wait for it as a show, rather than dread it as a peril', as a 'real danger that surrounds us'. Sheridan succeeds in making fear both courageous and stirring. This is a time, he suggests, when fear is patriotic.[48] Someone who might be thought to have less to fear than many from a Napoleonic takeover shows himself anxious to share the country's alarm. The fact that Coleridge too stresses fear in his poem is a signal that he also is 'on side' at this moment, and has as much to lose as anyone.

Sheridan poured scorn on the idea that the invading French (as their publicity had announced) would 'secure peace to every cottager'; and indeed the newspapers featured vivid accounts of the revolutionary army's atrocities against humble cottagers and their families. A widely circulated pamphlet, *A Warning to Britons against French Perfidy and Cruelty*, describing the French invasion of Swabia in 1796, emphasised how the soldiers

attacked the cottages and habitations of the peasantry (to whom they had promised liberty, equality, and affluence)... | ... mad with wine, [they] rushed into the houses with the most hideous war-whoop, and had immediate recourse to their well-known system of plunder... even infants were vehemently dragged from their cradles... In whole villages there was neither maiden, wife, nor widow, who was not forcibly and repeatedly dishonoured.[49]

---

[48] This is the primary message of the anonymous epistolary novel, *The Invasion; or, What Might have Been*, 2 vols (London: H. D. Symonds, 1798), where Fanny Seagrove's mockery of the fears of invasion is soon shown to be horrifyingly misplaced ('The scene is truly dreadful. Mothers hanging in agonies over their helpless infants... Wives clinging round their husbands, daughters round their fathers', 128).

[49] *A Warning to Britons against French Perfidy and Cruelty* (London: T. Cadell etc., 1798), 12, 29. Abridgements were published in London and Newcastle, and the most lurid passages appeared in newspapers throughout the country. The threatened cottage became an integral part of political rhetoric. See especially John Barrell, 'Cottage Politics', in *The Spirit of Despotism: Invasions of Privacy in the 1790s* (Oxford: Oxford University Press, 2006), 210–46. See also Ann Bermingham, 'The Simple Life: Cottages and Gainsborough's Cottage Doors', in Peter de Bolla, Nigel Leask, and David Simpson (eds), *Land, Nation and Culture, 1740–1810: Thinking the Republic of Taste* (Basingstoke: Palgrave Macmillan, 2004), 37–62 (56–7); also Sarah Lloyd, 'Cottage Conversations: Poverty and Manly Independence in Eighteenth-Century England', *Past and Present*, 184 (August 2004), 69–108 (94).

At the poem's conclusion, Coleridge's anxious look homeward to 'my own lowly cottage, where my babe | And my babe's mother dwell in peace!', and his 'light and quicken'd footsteps thitherward' (224), suggest he is less a likely collaborator than a potential victim of the invasion to come.

But the tactics of Sheridan's move into anti-French rhetoric are also thoughtfully judged. He insists that an invasion would mean the utter destruction of the country; but in doing so he is careful to frame his words with an insistence that he remains in principle a supporter of the French Revolution:

Sir, without retracting any one opinion which I have ever held, I do not conceive that there ever was any period of our history, in which the conquest of the kingdom by a foreign power would bring such total ruin upon it, as the conquest of Great-Britain by the present French Republic. And when I say this, I do not retract any thing I have ever maintained upon the French Revolution, or the establishment of a Republic in France.

Sheridan makes it clear that republicanism is irrelevant. 'Though I dread the Republic of France, I should not dread less the Monarchy of France.' His anti-French rhetoric should not be construed as *retracting* his long-held views on the revolution.

He also insists on another telling point about national responsibility; it is one that Coleridge also makes when he urges Britons not to be triumphalist, but to take their share of blame for the war, to respond 'with fear, | Repenting of the wrongs, with which we stung | So fierce a foe to frenzy' (148–50). Nicholas Roe has drawn attention to the way 'Fears in Solitude' casts the invasion 'as a consequence of British "offence" and "tyranny" in provoking revolutionary violence'.[50] Sheridan agrees with him:

I say we have provoked and insulted them beyond all human patience. I will not now discuss whether we were the aggressors or not; but the more I think we were so ... the more must I give them credit for the sincerity of their revenge against this country.

In 'Fears in Solitude' Coleridge is in no doubt that the French promise of freedom is entirely hollow and hypocritical. They are, he says, 'a light yet cruel race, | That laugh away all virtue, mingling mirth | With deeds of murder; and still promising | Freedom, themselves too sensual to be free' (137–40). In a similar way, with his caveats in place, Sheridan can launch with mounting irony into the hypocrisy of the French promising Freedom:

'Right restored, Freedom regained; Peace to Commerce; Peace to Cottages. He will come for the humane and liberal purpose of establishing Liberty.' Can any thing be more glorious, I had almost said more godlike, than this? But is there any Englishman so absurd, so besotted and befooled as to give credit to one word of it? ... What do they want? Glory? They are gorged with it. Territory? They have more, perhaps, than

---

[50] Roe, *Wordsworth and Coleridge: The Radical Years*, 264.

they will be able to retain—*What is it they want? Ships, Commerce, Manufactures, Cash, Capital and Credit*; or in other words, they *only* want the *sinews, bones, marrow, and heart's blood of Great Britain.*—(*Loud and universal cries of hear! hear! accompanied with clapping of hands.*) Give them that, and they will give you as much liberty in return as you please ... We know how little real liberty they have at home.

As Bowles's footnote confirms, Sheridan's speech was widely welcomed as manly and principled, and for catching the patriotic mood without slipping into what he called 'that spirit of invective and personality'. On 20 April 1798 it showed how to incorporate yourself into the nation without oath-taking and subscribing. Sheridan (whom Coleridge had previously likened to St Michael[51]) stubbornly refuses to 'sign up'. He shuns the letter, and instead puts his faith in the spirit, locating himself carefully in relation to the rhetoric of war. His St Michael is also aware of the nation's sins.

But the extraordinary events of 20 April did not end there. Things moved quickly, and shortly after Sheridan finished speaking it was confirmed that the House would immediately be asked to approve a bill suspending the Habeas Corpus Act. With minimal debate, this guarantee of British liberties was duly suspended, and the bill passed through all its stages that same evening, with Sheridan and just four other members opposing it. The next day, a fresh round of arrests began.

I want to suggest that in subscribing 'Fears in Solitude', *Nether Stowey, April 20th, 1798*, Coleridge was locating its patriotic spirit in the events of that date, and that Sheridan's speech in particular was both an encourage-ment and a direct stimulus to his poem. 'Fears in Solitude' shows how Sheridan's appeal for a *rising zeal* across the country could stir a response in one remote spot of England. It was exactly what was required at this moment: a local pledge, which did not attempt to redeem the nation (it could hardly do that) but hinted that values and commitments were being sus-tained independently in quieter and more hidden places throughout the kingdom. Out of these, it is intimated, a national integrity might be restored, but only when the abuses of the state could be confronted. Both Bowles's *St Michael's Mount* and Coleridge's 'Fears in Solitude' speak for the country in this powerfully qualified fashion. In their different ways, they suggest (what Dundas and the war cabinet also recognised) that the mere *Idea* of Britain could no longer command unquestioning allegiance. In its place was a Burkean acknowledgment that 'to be attached to the subdivision, to love the little platoon we belong to in society, is the first principle (the germ as it were) of public affections'.[52] A rooted and permanent reform had to be on

[51] In the last of his 'Sonnets on Eminent Characters' (Dec. 1794) Coleridge celebrates Sheridan's oratorical ability to transfix his enemy, 'As erst that elder Fiend beneath great Michael's sword' (Mays, i.169).
[52] Edmund Burke, *Reflections on the Revolution in France* [1790], ed. Conor Cruise O'Brien (Harmondsworth: Penguin, 1986), 135.

the basis of trusting the individual and local. As if to make this point, by what appears a 'natural' transition, the poem's language of combat and engagement modulates back into the quietness of the dell:

> May the vaunts
> And menace of the vengeful enemy
> Pass like a gust, that roar'd and died away
> In the distant tree, which heard, and only heard;
> In this low dell bow'd not the delicate grass.
> But now the gentle dew-fall sends abroad
> The fruitlike perfume of the golden furze: (195–201)

Coleridge entrusts this crucial move to a simile (*like a gust*).[53] The threat of invasion and the roar of the wind are not metaphorically fused, but remain separate, held in an intimate, potentially ethical, tension. The power of these lines is in their refusing of the symbolic Idea. It remains a landscape where a distant boom or crash might indeed be French artillery. Coleridge's finely chosen words realise that the outrageousness of war is its fundamental contempt for life, its system of death, a negation that destroys a person's freedom to hear, see, touch, and smell. This dell is no retreat, but a moral charge. It asserts natural, not prescribed, rights, and an autonomy that refuses to be served by murderers, under whatever banner they might enlist. To read these lines as some kind of evasion is extraordinary, as if peace were an evasion of war.

When Coleridge conceives of Britain it is as an infusion, something he has *drunk in*. There is no subscribing to an Idea, just the commitment to a rich accumulation of experience (the word *prove* is important), which seems to articulate for him a whole network of *dear and holy* relationships:

> O my mother Isle!
> Needs must thou prove a name most dear and holy
> To me, a son, a brother, and a friend,
> A husband and a father! who revere
> All bonds of natural love, and find them all
> Within the limits of thy rocky shores. (173–8)

The concept of a *tabula rasa*, pristine and untouched by the events of history, disturbs him; and as if to emphasise the threat of vacancy he repeats, re-imprints his own words:

> O my mother Isle!
> How should'st thou prove aught else but dear and holy
> To me, who from thy lakes and mountain-hills,
> Thy clouds, thy quiet dales, thy rocks, and seas,
> Have drunk in all my intellectual life (179–83)

---

[53] On the power of Coleridge's uses of simile, see Susan J. Wolfson, *Formal Charges: The Shaping of Poetry in British Romanticism* (Stanford: Stanford University Press, 1997), 63–99.

These two echoing passages are from the same matrix of meaning and value. The critical moment becomes a revisiting; and he plants himself, intellectually and emotionally, within a context of memory and experience he cannot afford to lose. In their respective poems, both Bowles and Coleridge suggest that at this time of immediate crisis it is not symbols that are the repositories of value, and that the more durable meanings are embedded ones. In Bowles's Cornwall, the symbolic chair of St Michael stands empty. In the Quantocks, Coleridge turns to notice his own neighbourhood hill overlooking the Bristol Channel. Historically, it is part of the same national system of local warning beacons; but thankfully it is lit, as yet, only by a natural glow:

> The light has left the summit of the hill,
> Tho' still a sunny gleam lies beautiful
> On the long-ivied beacon ...   (202–4)[54]

Viewed in these terms, a nation is held together not by a spurious unity, but by a network of locally sustained values. It is an uneasy, perhaps only temporary, peace.

---

[54] Although my emphasis is different, I'm indebted to Roe's discussion of the 'uneasy rest' of this passage and what follows, *Wordsworth and Coleridge: The Radical Years*, 265–8.

Postscript

DURING FEBRUARY 1801 Coleridge was deeply immersed in 'metaphysical Speculation' and the world of Idea. He was projecting a major book on the pleasures of poetry which, he told Humphry Davy, 'would supersede all the Books of Metaphysics hitherto written'.[1] Recovering from a protracted illness and in a period of increased opium intake, 'wild Dreams' and 'long long wakeful nights' (668, 672), he was also making a thorough study of Locke's *Essay Concerning Human Understanding*. The result was a series of letters during that month addressed to Josiah Wedgwood (677–703) in which he angrily refuted Lockean empiricism, attacked Locke's 'system', its terminology, its logic, and its argumentative basis in the rejection of 'innate ideas'. It was, Coleridge told Wedgwood, the first time he had read the *Essay* 'attentively'; and it was, of course, being read for the first time since his studies in Germany during 1798–9. On 9 February 1801 he humorously bombarded poor Dorothy Wordsworth with a complex passage he had been reading from Fichte's *Der Begriff des Wissenschaftslehre*:

'the I . . . is abstracted from the Proposition in the Science of absolute Knowledge, I am I—the substance therefore or sum total of every Thing, to which it may be legitimately applied, must lie in the I, and be comprehended under it. No A therefore can be aught else than something established in the I, and now therefore the Proposition may stand thus: What is established in the I, is established—if therefore A is established in the I, then it is established (that is to say in so far as it is established, whether as only possible, or as real, or necessary) and then the Proposition is true without possibility of contradiction, if the I is to be I . . .[2]

And so on, and on. Four days later he wrote to Poole that he was immersed in philosophy and had become 'a purus putus Metaphysicus' (an undefiled metaphysical boy).[3] His progress was such that on 16 March he was able to report excitedly to Tom Poole that he had 'overthrown' Hartley's 'doctrine of Association' and more, and was now on the brink of achieving a great synthesis:

This I have *done*; but I trust, that I am about to do more—namely, that I shall be able to evolve all the five senses, that is, to deduce them from *one sense*, & to state their growth, & the causes of their difference——& in this evolvement to solve the process of Life & Consciousness.——I write this to you only; & I pray you, mention what I have written to no one.——At Wordsworth's advice or rather fervent intreaty I have intermitted the pursuit—the intensity of thought, & the multitude of minute experi-

---

[1] Griggs, 671.   [2] Ibid. 673–4.   [3] Ibid. 676.

ments with Light & Figure, have made me so nervous & feverish, that I cannot sleep as long as I ought & have been used to do.[4]

It is a euphoric but guarded letter announcing, in a sublime whisper, the possibility of an extraordinary smoothing out of all experience into a single line of *evolvement*. Here, to *evolve* is to *solve*. The secret of life and consciousness, sense and thought, is about to be explained in a unified theory. But there is an interruption: he has *intermitted* his *pursuit*, and his sleep has also been interrupted. Along with the big Idea goes a language of intensity and minuteness. The whole paragraph builds into a disturbing paradox of confident ease and disruptive complication, an incoherent expression of the possibility of total coherence. Wordsworth was clearly worried; and Poole was being asked to tell no one.

Three years earlier, before he left for Germany in September 1798, Coleridge wrote 'Frost at Midnight', a poem that inhabits this same potentially fraught area of sleeplessness, vacancy, lonely concentration, secrecy, and intermission, but which makes out of these materials an entirely positive experience. The poem takes for its subject that same 'process of Life & Consciousness', but not as something that in any way demands a 'solution'. It is easy to say that one text is philosophical, the other poetic; but this distinction is false, given that it is in the poem that the profound thinking is being done, albeit of an empirical rather than metaphysical kind. Unconcerned with any need to unify, this 1798 'Frost at Midnight' develops as a series of sense experiences and thoughts, with things being noticed, recollected, anticipated, and associated. Rather than seeking for a unifying mind it seems content to register gaps of time and space across which the consciousness plays. The poem is very simple in its ingredients, which throughout are juxtaposed rather than compounded or fused. It is aware that many 'lives' of different kinds are continuing simultaneously ('all the numberless goings on of life, | Inaudible as dreams', 12–13). However, within the confined space of the text, two particular human lives are being lived side by side—intimately connected, but separate—and at this moment one has consciousness, the other not. Almost within reach of them is a living fire burnt low in the grate; and a few yards away shut out from the warm space of human intimacy is a different 'life', that of the active frost; and well beyond is the distant moon, soon to be replaced by the morning sun. The poem is alert to relative location and potential dialogue, so that the spaces and intervals between things come alive. In my Introduction I remarked that this book assumes that organic poetic meaning is not inherent in a unifying Idea but is 'a form of intricate interconnection, of reading across and between', and the 1798 text of 'Frost at Midnight' offers itself to us in these terms.

The poem unfolds like a philosophical case-study for a seminar on identity and consciousness. It is happy to accommodate a variety of concurrent relationships, so that we are conscious of how the 'thin blue flame' might,

---

[4] Griggs, 706–7.

from different perspectives, be detached from, responsive to, dependent on, or integral with, the fire:

> The thin blue flame
> Lies on my low-burnt fire, and quivers not:
> Only that film, which flutter'd on the grate,
> Still flutters there, the sole unquiet thing[5]   (*1798*: 13–16)

'Things' in the poem remain in this way separate but intimately related, almost erotically adjacent. Here the word *on*, used twice, is teasing, so that the 'film' that flutters 'on the grate' plays like a gossamer thread over the surface, or as a layer across it. It is part of something else, yet has its own identity. Somehow we feel that the 'life' is not in the individual thing but in the play between, in the connections.

The poem's images are repeatedly responsive and animating in this way, like the thatch that 'smokes in the sun-thaw' (75), or 'the eave-drops fall | Heard only in the *trances* of the blast' (75–6, my italics), an eloquent idea, as if the wind itself were a *suspended consciousness*. Here and elsewhere we find that the intermittent (like the owlet's repeated cry at the beginning) develops a special power:

> Dear babe, that sleepest cradled by my side,
> Whose gentle breathings, heard in this dead calm,
> Fill up the interspersed vacancies
> And momentary pauses of the thought!   (*1798*: 49–52)

'Interspersed vacancies' could be a chilling idea, but here it has the reassurance of life being continually confirmed through the repeated breathing. The thought is enriched by its 'momentary pauses', the mind's capacity to ponder and sidle.

The key fireside idea in 1798 is the 'idle thought', the sense of a mind playing over, around, and between things, which is conscious not so much of 'a self' (a term that seems in context too defined and static) as of its own self-consciousness, its potential to be aware of its activities:

> Idle thought!
> But still the living spirit in our frame,
> That loves not to behold a lifeless thing,
> Transfuses into all it's own delights
> It's own volition, sometimes with deep faith,
> And sometimes with fantastic playfulness.
> Ah me! amus'd by no such curious toys
> Of the self-watching subtilizing mind...   (*1798*: 20–7)

---

[5] S. T. Coleridge, 'Frost at Midnight', in *Fears in Solitude, Written in 1798, During the Alarm of an Invasion, To which are added, France, An Ode; and Frost at Midnight* (London: J. Johnson, 1798), 19–20.

The poet of 1798 has a multifaceted consciousness, one that is not searching for Truth, but is capable of being surprised by meaning. It might emerge equally from a humorous fancy or a deep conviction. He is 'amus'd' by the 'curious toys | Of the self-watching subtilizing mind', and in this alert, ironic mode he is always ready to shift his position and see things from various perspectives.

Revising 'Frost at Midnight' nine years later, Coleridge removed the 'idle thought', and the playfulness became 'wilful';[6] and for his *Poetical Works* in 1829 the poem underwent further alteration to produce the text familiar today. We need to remember that it was thirty years after the 1798 version that Coleridge added the following much admired lines, which develop the playfulness of the 'film' on the grate, but in a way that takes the poem into a new area. Here this 'companionable form' is one

> Whose puny flaps and freaks the idling Spirit
> By its own moods interprets, every where
> Echo or mirror seeking of itself,
> And makes a toy of Thought.   (*1829*: 20–3)

This later version introduces an egoistic element of teasing frustration. The line 'Echo or mirror seeking of itself', even if we allow 'itself' to mean 'companion', suggests a restless search, a longing for completion, but one that will prove impossible. Were this to be achieved, the result, far from bringing unity, would be a solipsistic endless replication: eternally mimicked sounds and infinitely receding images. The effect would be a Platonic trick. There is no spatial juxtaposition and accommodation here. In the 1798 passage, by contrast, Coleridge had allowed himself a fuller and more varied response, in which identity is expressive activity ('Transfuses into all it's own delights'): it is not something out there to be sought for and confirmed. The result is the possibility of a game rather than the need for a search. The verbal power of the later version, with its 'puny flaps and freaks', is undeniable, but the meaning has changed. In 1829, to 'make a toy of Thought' (now capitalised) is not to allow thought to toy with a possibility, but to let Thought become a mere 'toy', or 'fancy' (now a more negative idea). The Coleridge of 1798, however, was able to balance the alternatives of 'deep faith' and 'fantastic playfulness'.

At his first revision of the poem c. 1807 Coleridge removed the original six-line ending, so that the familiar version closes memorably with those 'silent icicles, | Quietly shining to the quiet moon'. It is a rapt phrase that gains intensity through its surreptitious move from 'silent' to 'quiet', from something perfect that hints at secrecy and enigma, to something potentially audible and communicative that assumes an ambient world of sense.

---

[6] See Mays, i.1311–12, ii.570–1.

The 1798 text, however, at this point takes us back to that world. It chooses to end by unwinding the enigma and finally bringing the baby into its own consciousness:

> Like those, my babe! which, ere to-morrow's warmth
> Have capp'd their sharp keen points with pendulous drops,
> Will catch thine eye, and with their novelty
> Suspend thy little soul; then make thee shout,
> And stretch and flutter from thy mother's arms
> As thou would'st fly for very eagerness.   (*1798*: 80–5)

Pensive contemplation is transformed to infant wonder, which breaks the cold platonic communion of the frost and moon. We are reminded too that things melt, and identities shift: daggers of ice can turn into pearl earrings. Here in 1798 the philosophical voice of the poem finally modulates into the tones of a fond and amused father, watching his child transfixed in play. In the child, notions of Idea and sense can be brought together—not synthesised, but accommodated.

It is the young man who could make that poetic move, the Coleridge of the 1790s, which has been the foremost subject of this book. I have tried to extricate his early poems from the critical template that has traditionally accompanied them thanks to his own brilliant theoretical analyses post-1801. A largely anachronistic vocabulary has tended to blur the distinctive features of the eighteenth-century Coleridge. By placing the younger poet among his friends during a decade when everything was being brought into question, it has perhaps been possible to see what meanings and values these men felt they needed to hold on to. The move to Germany by Coleridge and the Wordsworths in the Autumn of 1798 is an appropriate point to leave them, though the story continues: the context changes; new pressures arise, and new possibilities open up.

I realise there are many gaps in my account, but I hope many connections too. Rather than being driven by a single 'Idea' or a notion of unity, the book has aimed to engage with the more mixed, varied, localised, and adaptive elements of these poets' work. From the beginning I have urged that an empirical and historicised concept of the 'organic', which can be traced back through the eighteenth century, is a more appropriate and generous guide to their poetry at this time than the German 'organic form' of the idealist critical tradition. With this in mind I have tried to set them in a fresh light as late eighteenth-century poets caught up in various situations, dialogues, and quarrels, responding to different contexts, and creating new ones. There is a great deal left to say about the poems I have discussed, all of which will continue to respond to new critical trajectories.

Throughout I have tried to insist on 'richness' of meaning, as something contingent, mediated, layered, and faceted; and in the 1798 text of 'Frost at

Midnight' there is fresh meaning of this kind when we read it sequentially in the slim quarto, as the third and final item following 'Fears in Solitude' and 'France. An Ode'. In this volume largely given over to war and invasion, what becomes striking about the final poem is how, within the cottage, *peace* is continually being reaffirmed, not as a unified concept or ideal, but as an experience conveyed more three-dimensionally. The meaning grows richer as each word turns the idea round on itself ('rest', 'peacefully', 'calm', 'silentness', 'inaudible', 'hush', 'dead calm', 'silent', 'quiet'). Effectively, peace in this poem is no mere capitalised Idea, but something palpable that suffuses the scene. The state of being at peace is just too real and valuable to be a symbol. It becomes in the end more than the subject of the poem, rather its living medium.

Bibliography

PRIMARY SOURCES (SELECTED)

Adams, John, *A Defence of the Constitutions of Government of the United States of America* (London: C. Dilly, 1787).

Addison, Joseph, and Sir Richard Steele, *The Spectator*, ed. Donald F. Bond, 5 vols (Oxford: Clarendon Press, 1965).

Akenside, Mark, *The Poetical Works of Mark Akenside*, ed. Robin Dix (Madison/ Teaneck: Fairleigh Dickinson University Press; London: Associated University Presses, 1996).

Anon., *Authentic Copies of the Instructions Given by Gen. Hoche to Colonel Tate, Previous to His Landing on the Coast of South Wales, in the Beginning of 1797* (London: J. Wright, 1798).

—— *The Invasion; or, What Might have Been. A Novel*, 2 vols (London: H. D. Symonds, 1798).

—— *A Plan for Driving the Livestock of such Parts of the Country as may become Exposed to the Inroads of the Enemy in Case of an Invasion . . . and for Rendering the Body of the People Instrumental in the General Defence* (London, 1798).

Aufrère, Anthony (trans.), *A Warning to Britons against French Perfidy and Cruelty* (London: T. Cadell etc., 1798).

Bacon, Francis, *The Advancement of Learning*, ed. Michael Kiernan (Oxford: Clarendon Press, 2000).

Bampfylde, John, *The Poems of John Bampfylde*, ed. Roger Lonsdale (Oxford: Perpetua Press, 1988).

Barbauld, Anna Letitia, *The Poems of Anna Letitia Barbauld*, ed. William McCarthy and Elizabeth Kraft (Athens/London: University of Georgia Press, 1994).

Berkeley, George, *An Essay Towards a New Theory of Vision* (Dublin: Jeremy Pepyat, 1709).

—— *The Theory of Vision, or Visual Language . . . Vindicated and Explained* (London: J. Tonson, 1733).

Biographia Britannica, 2nd edn, ed. Andrew Kippis, 5 vols (London: W. and A. Strahan, 1778–93).

Bowles, William Lisle, *Sonnets, Written Chiefly on Picturesque Spots, During a Tour*, 2nd edn (Bath: R. Cruttwell, 1789).

—— *Elegy Written at the Hot-Wells, Bristol* (Bath: R. Cruttwell, 1791).

—— *Sonnets, with Other Poems* (Bath: R. Cruttwell, 1794).

—— *St. Michael's Mount, A Poem* (Salisbury: Adams and Dilly, 1798).

—— *Poems, by the Reverend Wm. Lisle Bowles*, vol. ii (London: T. Cadell; Bath: R. Cruttwell, 1801).

—— *Scenes and Shadows of Days Departed* (London: W. Pickering, 1837).

Bowles, William Lisle, *A Wiltshire Parson and his Friends: The Correspondence of William Lisle Bowles*, ed. Garland Greever (London: Constable, 1926).

Burke, Edmund, *Reflections on the Revolution in France* [1790], ed. Conor Cruise O'Brien (Harmondsworth: Penguin, 1986).

—— *A Letter from Mr Burke, to a Member of the National Assembly* (London: J. Dodsley, 1791).

—— *The Writings and Speeches of Edmund Burke*, ed. Paul Langford, 12 vols (Oxford: Clarendon Press, 1981–).

Chambers, Ephraim, *Cyclopaedia: or, An Universal Dictionary of Arts and Sciences*, 2 vols (London: James and John Knapton, etc., 1728).

Chatterton, Thomas, *Miscellanies in Prose and Verse; by Thomas Chatterton, the supposed author of the poems published under the names of Rowley, Canning, &c*, ed. John Broughton (London: Fielding and Walker, 1778).

—— *Poems, Supposed to have been written at Bristol, in the Fifteenth Century by Thomas Rowley, Priest, &c. With a Commentary, in which the Antiquity of them is Considered, and Defended*, ed. Jeremiah Milles (London: T. Payne, 1782).

—— *The Complete Works of Thomas Chatterton*, ed. Donald S. Taylor and Benjamin B. Hoover, 2 vols (Oxford: Clarendon Press, 1971).

Cheyne, George, *The Natural Method of Cureing the Diseases of the Body, and the Disorders of the Mind Depending on the Body* (London: Geo. Strahan, and John and Paul Knapton, 1742).

Clarke, Samuel, *A Third Defense of an Argument Made use of in a Letter to Mr Dodwel, to prove the Immateriality and Natural Immortality of the Soul* (London: James Knapton, 1708).

Coleridge, S. T., *Poems on Various Subjects* (London: G.G. and J. Robinson; Bristol: J. Cottle, 1796).

—— (ed.) *Sonnets from Various Authors* (1796).

—— *Poems, by S. T. Coleridge, Second Edition. To which are now added Poems by Charles Lamb, and Charles Lloyd* (Bristol: J. Cottle, and London: Messrs. Robinsons, 1797).

—— *Fears in Solitude, Written in 1798, During the Alarm of an Invasion, To which are added, France, An Ode; and Frost at Midnight. By S.T. Coleridge* (London: J. Johnson, 1798).

—— *Coleridge's Shakespearean Criticism*, ed. T. M. Raysor, 2 vols (London: Constable and Co, 1930).

—— *Collected Letters of Samuel Taylor Coleridge*, vols i–ii (1785–1806), ed. Earl Leslie Griggs (Oxford: Clarendon, 1956).

—— *The Notebooks of Samuel Taylor Coleridge*, vols i–iii, ed. Kathleen Coburn (London: Routledge and Kegan Paul, 1957–73).

—— *Coleridge: The Critical Heritage*, ed. J. R. de J. Jackson (London: Routledge and Kegan Paul, 1970).

—— *The Collected Works of Samuel Taylor Coleridge*, gen. ed. Kathleen Coburn. Bollingen Series LXXV, 16 vols (London: Routledge and Kegan Paul; Princeton: Princeton University Press, 1969–2002).

—— *Lectures 1795: On Politics and Religion*, ed. Lewis Patton and Peter Mann (Princeton: Princeton University Press, 1971). [*Collected Works*, vol. i]

——*The Watchman*, ed. Lewis Patton (Princeton: Princeton University Press, 1970). [*Collected Works*, vol. ii]

——*The Friend*, ed. Barbara E. Rooke (Princeton: Princeton University Press, 1969). [*Collected Works*, vol. iv]

——*Lay Sermons*, ed. R. J. White (Princeton: Princeton University Press, 1972). [*Collected Works*, vol. vi]

——*Biographia Literaria*, ed. James Engell and W. Jackson Bate (London: Routledge and Kegan Paul, 1983). [*Collected Works*, vol. vii]

——*Aids to Reflection*, ed. John Beer (Princeton: Princeton University Press, 1993). [*Collected Works*, vol. ix]

——*Poetical Works*, ed. J. C. C. Mays (Princeton: Princeton University Press, 2001). [*Collected Works*, vol. xvi]

Condorcet, Marquis de, *Sketch for a Historical Picture of the Progress of the Human Mind*, trans. June Barraclough (London: Weidenfeld and Nicolson, 1955).

Cottle, Joseph, *Early Recollections; Chiefly Relating to the Late Samuel Taylor Coleridge*, 2 vols (London: Longman, etc., 1837).

Cowper, William, *The Poems of William Cowper*, ed. John D. Baird and Charles Ryskamp, 3 vols (Oxford: Clarendon Press, 1980–95).

De Quincey, Thomas, *The Works of Thomas De Quincey*, ed. Grevel Lindop et al., 21 vols (London: Pickering and Chatto, 2000–3).

Dodsley, Robert (ed.), *A Collection of Poems*, 2nd edn, 3 vols (London, 1748).

Dyer, John, *Selected Poetry and Prose*, ed. John Goodridge (Nottingham: Trent Editions, 2000).

Gardner, Edward, *Miscellanies, in Prose and Verse*, 2 vols (Bristol: Biggs and Cottle, 1798).

Godwin, William, *Collected Novels and Memoirs of William Godwin*, ed. Mark Philp, 8 vols (London: Pickering and Chatto, 1992).

——*Political and Philosophical Writings of William Godwin*, ed. Mark Philp, 7 vols (London: William Pickering, 1993), vol. iii (*An Enquiry Concerning Political Justice*).

Goethe, Johann Wolfgang von, *Goethe's Botanical Writings*, trans. Bertha Mueller, intro. Charles J. Engard (Woodbridge, CT: Ox Bow Press, 1989).

Goldsmith, Oliver, *The Deserted Village, A Poem*, 2nd edn (London: W. Griffin, 1770).

Gray, Thomas, *Correspondence*, ed. Paget Toynbee and Leonard Whibley, 3 vols (Oxford: Clarendon Press, 1935).

Gregory, George, *The Life of Thomas Chatterton, with Criticisms on his Genius and Writings, and a Concise View of the Controversy concerning Rowley's Poems* (London: G. Kearsley, 1789).

Hardinge, George, *Rowley and Chatterton in the Shades: Or, Nugæ Antiquæ et Novæ. A New Elysian Interlude, in Prose and Verse* (London: T. Becket, 1782).

Hartley, David, *Observations on Man, his Frame, his Duty, and his Expectations. In Two Parts* (London: S. Richardson, 1749).

——*Observations on Man, his Frame, his Duty, and his Expectations*, 3 vols (London: J. Johnson, 1791).

Hayley, William, *An Essay on Epic Poetry* (London: J. Dodsley, 1782).

Hazlitt, William, *An Essay on the Principles of Human Action* (London: J. Johnson, 1805).

—— *The Complete Works of William Hazlitt*, ed. P. P. Howe, 21 vols (London/Toronto: J. M. Dent and Sons, 1930–4).

Headley, Henry, *Fugitive Pieces* (London: C. Dilly, 1785).

—— *An Invocation to Melancholy: A Fragment* (Oxford: Fletcher, 1785).

—— *Poems and Other Pieces* (London: J. Robson, 1786).

—— *Select Beauties of Ancient English Poetry*, 2 vols (London: T. Cadell, 1787).

—— *Select Beauties of Ancient English Poetry*, ed. Henry Kett, 2 vols (London: John Sharpe, 1810).

Hesiod, *Theogony and Works and Days*, trans. M. L. West (Oxford: Oxford University Press, 1988).

Hume, David, *A Treatise of Human Nature*, ed. L. A. Selby-Bigge, rev. P. H. Nidditch, 2nd edn (Oxford: Clarendon Press, 1978).

—— *Enquiries Concerning Human Understanding and Concerning the Principles of Morals*, ed. L. A. Selby-Bigge, rev. P. H. Nidditch, 6th edn (Oxford: Clarendon Press, 1997).

Johnson, Samuel, *Lives of the English Poets*, ed. Roger Lonsdale, 4 vols (Oxford: Clarendon Press, 2006).

Kant, Immanuel, *The Critique of Judgement*, trans. J. C. Meredith (Oxford: Clarendon Press, 1964).

Keats, John, *The Letters of John Keats 1814–1821*, ed. Hyder Edward Rollins, 2 vols (Cambridge MA: Harvard University Press, 1958).

Kett, Henry, *Juvenile Poems* (Oxford: J. Fletcher, 1793).

Knox, Vicesimus, *Essays Moral and Literary*, 2 vols (London: Charles Dilly, 1782).

Lamb, Charles, *The Letters of Charles and Mary Anne Lamb*, vol. i: *Letters of Charles Lamb, 1796–1801*, ed. Edwin W. Marrs, Jr. (Ithaca/London: Cornell University Press. 1975).

—— and Charles Lloyd. *Blank Verse, by Charles Lloyd and Charles Lamb* (London: T. Bensley, 1798).

Law, Edmund, *A Defence of Mr. Locke's Opinion concerning Personal Identity* (Cambridge: J. Archdeacon, 1769).

Leapor, Mary, *Poems upon Several Occasions* (London: J. Roberts, 1751).

Lloyd, Charles, *Poems on Various Subjects* (Carlisle: F. Jollie, 1795).

—— *Poems on the Death of Priscilla Farmer, by her Grandson* (Bristol: N. Biggs, 1796).

—— *Edmund Oliver* (Bristol: J. Cottle, 1798).

Lloyd, Henry, *A Political and Military Rhapsody, on the Invasion and Defence of Great Britain and Ireland*, 5th edn (London: Egerton and Debrett, 1798).

Locke, John, *An Essay Concerning Human Understanding*, ed. Peter Nidditch (Oxford: Clarendon Press, 1975).

—— *Two Treatises of Government*, ed. Peter Laslett (Cambridge: Cambridge University Press, 1988).

Lovell, Robert, and Robert Southey, *Poems: Containing the Retrospect, Odes, Elegies, Sonnets, &c* (Bath: R. Cruttwell, 1795).

Lyttelton, George, *Letters from a Persian in England, to his Friend at Ispahan*, 2nd edn (London: J. Millan, 1735).

Milton, John, *The Poetical Works of John Milton*, ed. Helen Darbishire, 2 vols (Oxford: Clarendon Press, 1952–5).

Nichols, John, *Literary Anecdotes of the Eighteenth Century*, 9 vols (London: Nichols, Son, and Bentley, 1812–15).

Paine, Thomas, *Rights of Man*, ed. Henry Collins (Harmondsworth: Penguin, 1976).

——*Common Sense; Addressed to the Inhabitants of America ... A New Edition, with several Additions* (London: J. Ridgway, 1791).

Park, Thomas, *Sonnets and Other Small Poems* (London: G. Sael, 1797).

Philips, John, *Cyder. A Poem. In Two Books* (London: Tonson, 1708).

Priestley, Joseph, *A Description of a New Chart of History, Containing a View of the principal Revolutions of Empire, That have taken Place in the World*, 2nd edn (London: J. Johnson, 1770).

——*The History and Present State of Discoveries relating to Vision, Light, and Colours*, 2 vols (London: J. Johnson, 1772).

——*Disquisitions Relating to Matter and Spirit* (London: J. Johnson, 1777).

——*A Free Discussion of the Doctrines of Materialism, and Philosophical Necessity, in a Correspondence between Dr. Price, and Dr. Priestley* (London: J. Johnson and T. Cadell, 1778).

Pye, Henry James, *The Progress of Refinement. A Poem. In Three Parts* (Oxford: Clarendon Press, 1783).

Radcliffe, Ann, *The Romance of the Forest*, ed. Chloe Chard (Oxford: Oxford University Press, 1986).

Rannie, John, *Poems*, 2nd edn (Aberdeen: J. Chalmers, 1791).

Richards, George, *Poems*, 2 vols (Oxford: University Press, 1804).

Robinson, Mary, *Poems by Mrs. M. Robinson* (London: J. Bell, 1791).

Rogers, Samuel, *The Pleasures of Memory* (London: T. Cadell, 1792).

Rousseau, Jean-Jacques, *The Social Contract*, trans. Maurice Cranston (London: Penguin Books, 1968).

Rushton, Edward, *Neglected Genius: or, Tributary Stanzas to the Memory of the Unfortunate Chatterton* (London: J. Philips, 1787).

Russell, Thomas, *Sonnets and Miscellaneous Poems* (Oxford: D. Prince, etc., 1789).

Sandford, Elizabeth, *Thomas Poole and His Friends* (1888), introd. Reginald Watters (Over Stowey: Friarn Press, 1996).

Schlegel, Friedrich, *Philosophical Fragments*, trans. Peter Firchow (Minneapolis/Oxford: University of Minnesota Press, 1991).

Smith, Charlotte, *Elegiac Sonnets*, 5th edn (London: T. Cadell, 1789).

Smith, William, *A Dissertation upon the Nerves* (London: W. Owen, 1768).

Sotheby, William, *Poems: Consisting of a Tour through Parts of North and South Wales, Sonnets, Odes, and an Epistle to a Friend on Physiognomy* (Bath: R. Cruttwell, 1790).

Southey, Robert, *Poems* (Bristol: Biggs and Cottle; London: G.G. and J. Robinson, 1797).

——(ed.) *Specimens of the Later English Poets*, 3 vols (London: Longman, 1807).

——(ed.) *The Life and Works of William Cowper ... with a Life of the Author*, 15 vols (London: Baldwin and Cradock, 1835–7).

——*The Life and Correspondence of Robert Southey*, ed. C. C. Southey, 6 vols (London: Longman, 1849–50).

Southey, Robert, *Selections from the Letters of Robert Southey*, ed. John Wood Warter, 4 vols (London: Longman, 1856).

—— *New Letters of Robert Southey*, ed. Kenneth Curry, 2 vols (New York/London: Columbia University Press, 1965).

—— *Poetical Works 1793–1810*, gen. ed. Lynda Pratt, 5 vols (London: Pickering and Chatto, 2004).

Sterne, Laurence, *Tristram Shandy*, ed. Melvyn New et al., 3 vols (Gainesville, FL: University Presses of Florida, 1978–84).

Stewart, John, *The Revolution of Reason: or the Establishment of the Constitution of Things in Nature* (London: J. Ridgway, [1794]).

Swift, Jonathan, *A Tale of a Tub, etc.*, ed. Frank Ellis (Frankfurt etc.: Peter Lang, 2006).

Thelwall, John, *An Essay, Towards a Definition of Animal Vitality* (London: T. Rickaby, 1793).

—— *Poems Written in Close Confinement in the Tower and Newgate, Under a Charge of High Treason* (London: Printed for the Author, 1795).

—— *The Natural and Constitutional Right of Britons* (London: For the Author, 1795).

—— *The Peripatetic*, ed. Judith Thompson (Detroit: Wayne State University Press, 2001).

—— *The Rights of Nature, Against the Usurpations of Establishments. A Series of Letters to the People of Britain* [published in two parts] (Norwich: H. D. Symonds and J. March, 1796).

—— *Poems chiefly written in Retirement* (Hereford: W. H. Parker, 1801).

—— *The Politics of English Jacobinism: Writings of John Thelwall*, ed. Gregory Claeys (University Park: Pennsylvania State University Press, 1995).

Virgil, *The Georgics*, trans. L. P. Wilkinson (Harmondsworth: Penguin, 1982).

Volney, C. F., *Lectures on History, delivered in The Normal School of Paris, by C.F. Volney... Translated from the French* (London: J. Ridgway, 1800).

Warton, Thomas, *Poems: A New Edition, with Additions* (London: T. Becket, 1777).

—— *The History of English Poetry, from the Close of the Eleventh to the Commencement of the Eighteenth Century*, 3 vols (London: J. Dodsley, etc., 1774–81).

—— *The Poetical Works of the Late Thomas Warton, B.D.*, 2 vols, ed. Richard Mant (Oxford: University Press, 1802).

—— *The Correspondence of Thomas Warton*, ed. David Fairer (Athens/London: University of Georgia Press, 1995).

—— *Thomas Warton's History of English Poetry* (facsimile edition), introd. David Fairer, 4 vols (Routledge/Thoemmes Press, 1998).

Warton, Thomas (the Elder), *Poems on Several Occasions* (London: R. Manby and H. S. Cox, 1748).

Watts, Isaac, *Reliquiae Juveniles: Miscellaneous Thoughts in Prose and Verse* (London: Richard Ford and Richard Hett, 1734).

Williams, Helen Maria, *Letters Written in France, in the Summer 1790, to a Friend in England* (London: T. Cadell, 1790).

Wollstonecraft, Mary, *An Historical and Moral View of the Origin and Progress of the French Revolution* (London: J. Johnson, 1794).

—— *The Works of Mary Wollstonecraft*, ed. Janet Todd and Marilyn Butler, 7 vols (London: Pickering and Chatto, 1989).

Wordsworth, William, *Lyrical Ballads, with A Few Other Poems* (Bristol: Biggs and Cottle; London: Longman, 1798).

—— *Lyrical Ballads, with Other Poems*, 2 vols (London: Longman and Rees; Bristol: Biggs and Co., 1800).

—— *Poems, in Two Volumes* (London: Longman etc.,1807).

—— *The River Duddon, A Series of Sonnets* (London, 1820).

—— *The Prose Works*, ed. W. J. B. Owen and Jane Worthington Smyser, 3 vols (Oxford: Clarendon Press, 1974).

—— *The Ruined Cottage and The Pedlar*, ed. James Butler (Ithaca: Cornell University Press, 1979).

—— *Poems, in Two Volumes, and Other Poems, 1800–1807*, ed. Jared Curtis (Ithaca: Cornell University Press, 1983).

Yearsley, Anne, *Poems on Various Subjects* (London: Printed for the Author, 1787).

SECONDARY SOURCES

Abrams, M. H., 'Archetypal Analogies in the Language of Criticism', *UTQ*, 18 (1948–9), 313–27.

—— *The Mirror and the Lamp: Romantic Theory and the Critical Tradition* (New York: Oxford University Press, 1953).

Allen, Richard C., 'Charles Lloyd, Coleridge, and *Edmund Oliver*', *SiR*, 35 (1996), 245–94.

Armstrong, Charles I., *Romantic Organicism: From Idealist Origins to Ambivalent Afterlife* (Houndmills: Palgrave Macmillan, 2003).

Axcelson, John, 'Timing the Apocalypse: The Career of *Religious Musings*', *European Romantic Review*, 16 (2005), 439–54.

Ayers, Michael, *Locke. Volume II: Ontology* (London/New York: Routledge, 1991).

Baker, Keith Michael, *Condorcet: From Natural Philosophy to Social Mathematics* (Chicago/London: University of Chicago Press, 1975).

—— *Inventing the French Revolution: Essays on French Political Culture in the Eighteenth Century* (Cambridge: Cambridge University Press, 1990).

Bamborough, J. B., 'William Lisle Bowles and the Riparian Muse', in W. W. Robson (ed.), *Essays and Poems Presented to Lord David Cecil* (London: Constable, 1970).

Barker-Benfield, G. J., *The Culture of Sensibility: Sex and Society in Eighteenth-Century Britain* (Chicago: University of Chicago Press, 1992).

Barrell, John, *The Spirit of Despotism: Invasions of Privacy in the 1790s* (Oxford: Oxford University Press, 2006).

Barry, Jonathan, 'Chatterton in Bristol', *Angelaki*, 1:2 (1993–4), 55–81.

Bate, Jonathan, *Romantic Ecology: Wordsworth and the Environmental Tradition* (London: Routledge, 1991).

Bate, Walter Jackson, 'The Sympathetic Imagination in Eighteenth-Century English Criticism', *ELH*, 12 (1945), 144–64.

Battelle, John, *The Search: How Google and Its Rivals Rewrote the Rules of Business and Transformed Our Culture* (London: Nicholas Brealey, 2005).

Benjamin, Walter, *Theses on the Philosophy of History*, in *Illuminations*, ed. Hannah Arendt (London: Fontana/Collins, 1973).

Bennett, Jonathan, 'Locke's Philosophy of Mind', in Vere Chappell (ed.), *The Cambridge Companion to Locke* (Cambridge: Cambridge University Press, 1994), 89–114.

Benziger, James, 'Organic Unity: Leibnitz to Coleridge', *PMLA*, 66 (1951), 24–48.

Bermingham, Ann, 'The Simple Life: Cottages and Gainsborough's Cottage Doors', in Peter de Bolla, Nigel Leask, and David Simpson (eds), *Land, Nation and Culture, 1740–1810: Thinking the Republic of Taste* (Basingstoke: Palgrave Macmillan, 2004), 37–62.

Bewell, Alan, *Wordsworth and the Enlightenment: Nature, Man, and Society in the Experimental Poetry* (New Haven: Yale University Press, 1989).

Blakemore, Steven, *Burke and the Fall of Language: The French Revolution as Linguistic Event* (Hanover, NH/London: University Press of New England, 1988).

Bonnard, G., 'The Invasion of Switzerland and English Public Opinion (January to April 1798): The Background to S.T. Coleridge's *France: An Ode*', *English Studies*, 22 (1940), 1–26.

Bromwich, David, *Hazlitt: The Mind of a Critic* (New York/Oxford: Oxford University Press, 1983).

Brown, Marshall, 'The Pre-Romantic Discovery of Consciousness', *SiR*, 17 (Fall 1978), 387–412.

—— *Preromanticism* (Stanford: Stanford University Press, 1991).

Buell, Lawrence, *The Environmental Imagination: Thoreau, Nature Writing, and the Formation of American Culture* (Cambridge, MA: Belknap Press of Harvard University Press, 1995).

Burwick, Frederick (ed.), *Approaches to Organic Form: Permutations in Science and Culture* (Dordrecht: D. Reidel, 1987).

Bygrave, Stephen, *Coleridge and the Self: Romantic Egotism* (Houndmills: Macmillan, 1986).

Caruth, Cathy, *Empirical Truths and Critical Fictions: Locke, Wordsworth, Kant, Freud* (Baltimore/London: Johns Hopkins University Press, 1991).

Chandler, James K., 'Wordsworth and Burke', *ELH*, 47 (1980), 741–71.

—— 'The Pope Controversy: Romantic Politics and the English Canon', *Critical Inquiry*, 10 (1984), 481–509.

—— *Wordsworth's Second Nature: A Study of the Poetry and the Politics* (Chicago: Chicago University Press, 1984).

Chappell, Vere (ed.), *The Cambridge Companion to Locke* (Cambridge: Cambridge University Press, 1994).

Chase, Cynthia (ed.), *Romanticism* (London: Longman, 1993).

Christensen, Jerome, *Coleridge's Blessed Machine of Language* (Ithaca: Cornell University Press, 1981).

—— *Romanticism at the End of History* (Baltimore: Johns Hopkins University Press, 2004).

Christie, Ian R., *Stress and Stability in Late Eighteenth-Century Britain: Reflections on the British Avoidance of Revolution* (Oxford: Clarendon Press, 1984).

—— 'Conservatism and Stability in British Society', in Mark Philp (ed.), *The French Revolution and British Popular Politics* (Cambridge: Cambridge University Press, 2002), 169–87.

Clark, Steve, '"Between Self and Self's Book": Locke and the Poetry of the Early Romantics', in Thomas Woodman (ed.), *Early Romantics: Perspectives in British Poetry from Pope to Wordsworth* (Houndmills: Macmillan; New York: St Martin's Press, 1998), 30–54.

Coburn, Kathleen, *The Self Conscious Imagination* (London: Oxford University Press, 1974).

Colley, Linda, *Britons: Forging the Nation 1707–1837* (New Haven, NH/London: Yale University Press, 1992).

Connell, Philip, *Romanticism, Economics, and the Question of 'Culture'* (Oxford: Oxford University Press, 2001).

Conrad, Peter, *Shandyism: The Character of Romantic Irony* (New York: Barnes and Noble, 1978).

Cookson, J. E., 'The English Volunteer Movement of the French Wars, 1793–1815: Some Contexts', *Historical Journal*, 32 (1989), 867–91.

—— *The British Armed Nation, 1793–1815* (Oxford: Clarendon Press, 1997).

Cox, Stephen D., *'The Stranger within Thee': Concepts of the Self in Late-Eighteenth-Century Literature* (Pittsburgh: University of Pittsburgh Press, 1980).

Craig, David M., *Robert Southey and Romantic Apostasy: Political Argument in Britain, 1780–1840* (Woodbridge: Royal Historical Society and Boydell Press, 2007).

Cronin, Richard (ed.), *1798: The Year of the* Lyrical Ballads (Basingstoke: Macmillan; New York: St Martin's Press, 1998).

—— *The Politics of Romantic Poetry: In Search of the Pure Commonwealth* (Basingstoke: Macmillan; New York: St Martin's Press, 2000).

Cummings, R. M. (ed.), *Spenser: The Critical Heritage* (London: Routledge, 1971).

Curry, Kenneth, and Robert Dedmon, 'Southey's Contributions to *The Quarterly Review*', WC, 6 (1975), 261–72.

Davidson, Graham, *Coleridge's Career* (Houndmills: Macmillan, 1990).

Davies, Damian Walford, *Presences that Disturb: Models of Romantic Identity in the Literature and Culture of the 1790s* (Cardiff: University of Wales Press, 2002).

Dekker, George, *Coleridge and the Literature of Sensibility* (London: Vision, 1978).

De Man, Paul, *Blindness and Insight: Essays in the Rhetoric of Contemporary Criticism*, 2nd edn (London: Methuen, 1983).

DePorte, Michael V., *Nightmares and Hobbyhorses: Swift, Sterne, and Augustan Ideas of Madness* (San Marino: Huntington Library, 1974).

Dickinson, H. T., *British Radicalism and the French Revolution, 1789–1815* (Oxford: Blackwell, 1985).

Dilley, Frank B., 'Resurrection and the "Replica Objection"', *Religious Studies*, 19 (1983), 459–74.

Doolittle, Ian, *William Blackstone: A Biography* (Haslemere: I. Doolittle, 2001).

Douglas, David C., *English Scholars, 1660–1730*, 2nd rev. edn (London: Eyre and Spottiswoode, 1951).

Dunn, John, 'The Politics of Locke in England and America in the Eighteenth Century', in John Yolton (ed.), *John Locke: Problems and Perspectives* (London: Cambridge University Press, 1969), 45–80.

Edwards, Pamela, *The Statesman's Science: History, Nature, and Law in the Political Thought of Samuel Taylor Coleridge* (New York: Columbia University Press, 2004).

Eichner, Hans, 'The Rise of Modern Science and the Genesis of Romanticism', *PMLA*, 97 (1982), 8–30.

Emsley, Clive, *British Society and the French Wars, 1793–1815* (London/Basingstoke: Macmillan, 1979).

Everest, Kelvin, *Coleridge's Secret Ministry: The Context of the Conversation Poems 1795–1798* (Hassocks: Harvester Press; New York: Barnes and Noble, 1979).

Fairer, David, 'The Origins of Warton's *History of English Poetry*', *RES*, 32 (1981), 37–63.

—— 'Baby Language and Revolution: The Early Poetry of Charles Lloyd and Charles Lamb', *CLB*, 74 (April 1991), 33–52.

—— 'Thomas Warton, Thomas Gray, and the Recovery of the Past', in W. B. Hutchings and William Ruddick (eds), *Thomas Gray: Contemporary Essays* (Liverpool: Liverpool University Press, 1993), 146–70.

—— 'The Formation of Warton's *History*', in *Thomas Warton's History of English Poetry* (facsimile edn), introd. David Fairer, 4 vols (London: Routledge/Thoemmes Press, 1998), 1–70.

—— 'Sentimental Translation in Mackenzie and Sterne', *EC*, 49 (1999), 132–51.

—— 'Creating a National Poetry: The Tradition of Spenser and Milton', in John Sitter (ed.), *The Cambridge Companion to Eighteenth-Century Poetry* (Cambridge: Cambridge University Press, 2001), 177–201.

—— *English Poetry of the Eighteenth Century, 1700–1789* (London: Longman, 2003).

Ferguson, Frances, 'Organic Form and its Consequences', in Peter de Bolla, Nigel Leask, and David Simpson (eds), *Land, Nation and Culture, 1740–1810: Thinking the Republic of Taste* (Basingstoke: Palgrave Macmillan, 2004), 223–40.

Fosso, Kurt, 'Community and Mourning in William Wordsworth's *The Ruined Cottage*, 1797–1798', *SP*, 92 (1995), 329–45.

Fox, Christopher, *Locke and the Scriblerians: Identity and Consciousness in Early Eighteenth-Century Britain* (Berkeley, etc.: University of California Press, 1988).

Freeman, Arthur, and Theodore Hofmann, 'The Ghost of Coleridge's First Effort: "A Monody on the Death of Chatterton"', *The Library*, 11 (1989), 328–35.

Fruman, Norman, *Coleridge, The Damaged Archangel* (London: George Allen & Unwin, 1972).

Frye, Northrop, 'Towards Defining an Age of Sensibility', *ELH*, 23 (1956), 144–52.

Gallant, Christine (ed.), *Coleridge's Theory of Imagination Today* (New York: AMS Press, 1989).

Gee, Austin, *The British Volunteer Movement, 1794–1814* (Oxford: Clarendon Press, 2003).

Gérard, Albert, 'The Systolic Rhythm: The Structure of Coleridge's Conversation Poems', *EC*, 10 (1960), 307–19.

Gibbs, Lewis, *Sheridan* (London: J. M. Dent and Sons, 1947).

Gibbs, Warren E., 'An Unpublished Letter from John Thelwall to S.T. Coleridge', *MLR*, 25 (1930), 85–90.

Goodman, Kevis, *Georgic Modernity and British Romanticism: Poetry and the Mediation of History* (Cambridge: Cambridge University Press, 2004).

Goodridge, John, 'Rowley's Ghost: A Checklist of Creative Works Inspired by Thomas Chatterton's Life and Writings', in Nick Groom (ed.), *Thomas Chatterton and Romantic Culture* (Houndmills: Macmillan; New York: St Martin's Press, 1999), 262–92.

Gordon, I. A., 'The Case-History of Coleridge's *Monody on the Death of Chatterton*', *RES*, 18 (1942), 49–71.

Gravil, Richard, 'The Somerset Sound; or, the Darling Child of Speech', *CB*, 26 (Winter 2005), 1–21.

Greene, Richard, *Mary Leapor: A Study in Eighteenth-Century Women's Poetry* (Oxford: Clarendon Press, 1993).

Griffin, Robert J., *Wordsworth's Pope: A Study in Literary Historiography* (Cambridge: Cambridge University Press, 1995).

Grob, Alan, *The Philosophic Mind: A Study of Wordsworth's Poetry and Thought, 1797–1805* (Columbus: Ohio State University Press, 1973).

Groom, Nick (ed.), *Thomas Chatterton and Romantic Culture* (Houndmills: Macmillan; New York: St Martin's Press, 1999).

Grovier, Kelly, ' "Shades of the Prison-House": "Walking" Stewart, Michel Foucault and the Making of Wordsworth's "Two Consciousnesses" ', *SiR*, 44 (Fall 2005), 341–66.

—— 'Dream Walker: A Wordsworth Mystery Solved', *Romanticism*, 13 (2007), 156–63.

Hamilton, Paul, *Coleridge's Poetics* (Oxford: Basil Blackwell, 1983).

—— 'The New Romanticism: Philosophical Stand-ins in English Romantic Discourse', in *Metaromanticism: Aesthetics, Literature, Theory* (Chicago: University of Chicago Press, 2003).

Harvey, A. D., 'The Cult of Chatterton amongst English Poets *c.* 1770–*c.* 1820', *Zeitschrift für Anglistik und Amerikanistik*, 39 (1991), 124–33.

Havens, Raymond D., 'Southey's *Specimens of the Later English Poets*', *PMLA*, 60 (1945), 1066–79.

Herzog, Don, *Poisoning the Minds of the Lower Orders* (Princeton: Princeton University Press, 1998).

Hewitt, Regina, *Wordsworth and the Empirical Dilemma* (New York: Peter Lang, 1990).

Holmes, Richard, *Coleridge: Early Visions* (London: Hodder, 1989).

—— 'Forging the Poet: Some Early Pictures of Thomas Chatterton', in Nick Groom (ed.), *Thomas Chatterton and Romantic Culture* (Houndmills: Macmillan; New York: St Martin's Press, 1999), 253–8.

Hospers, John, 'Problems of Aesthetics', in Paul Edwards (ed.), *Encyclopaedia of Philosophy*, 8 vols (New York: Macmillan/Free Press, 1967), i.35–56.

Hutchings, P. Æ., 'Organic Unity Revindicated?', *JAAC*, 23 (1965), 323–7.

Ingold, Tim, *Lines: A Brief History* (London/New York: Routledge, 2007).

Jacobus, Mary, *Tradition and Experiment in Wordsworth's Lyrical Ballads, 1798* (Oxford: Clarendon Press, 1976).

James, Felicity, 'Agreement, Dissonance, Dissent: The Many Conversations of "This Lime-Tree Bower"', *CB*, 26 (Winter 2005), 37–57.

—— *Charles Lamb, Coleridge and Wordsworth: Reading Friendship in the 1790s* (Basingstoke: Palgrave Macmillan, 2008).

Janowitz, Anne, 'The Romantic Fragment', in Duncan Wu (ed.), *A Companion to Romanticism* (Oxford and Malden, MA: Blackwell, 1999), 442–51.

Johnston, Arthur, *Enchanted Ground: The Study of Medieval Romance in the Eighteenth Century* (London: Athlone Press, 1964).

Johnston, Kenneth R., *Wordsworth and the Recluse* (New Haven: Yale University Press, 1984).

Jones, Myrddin, 'Gray, Jaques, and the Man of Feeling', *RES*, 25 (1974), 39–48.

Keegan, Bridget, 'Nostalgic Chatterton: Fictions of Poetic Identity and the Forging of a Self-Taught Tradition', in Nick Groom (ed.), *Thomas Chatterton and Romantic Culture* (Houndmills: Macmillan; New York: St Martin's Press, 1999), 210–27.

Keller, Evelyn Fox, *Refiguring Life: Metaphors of Twentieth-Century Biology* (New York: Columbia University Press, 1995).

Kerrigan, John, 'Wordsworth and the Sonnet: Building, Dwelling, Thinking', *EC*, 35 (1985), 45–75.

Kharbutli, Mahmoud K., 'Locke and Wordsworth', *Forum for Modern Language Studies*, 25 (1989), 225–37.

Kipperman, Mark, *Beyond Enchantment: German Idealism and English Romantic Poetry* (Philadelphia: University of Pennsylvania Press, 1986).

Krieger, Murray, *A Reopening of Closure: Organicism against Itself* (New York: Columbia University Press, 1989).

Kroeber, Karl, *Ecological Literary Criticism: Romantic Imagining and the Biology of Mind* (New York: Columbia University Press, 1994).

Kucich, Greg, *Keats, Shelley, and Romantic Spenserianism* (University Park: Pennsylvania State University Press, 1991).

Lacoue-Labarthe, Philippe, and Jean-Luc Nancy, *The Literary Absolute: The Theory of Literature in German Romanticism* (Albany: SUNY Press, 1988).

Landry, Donna, *The Muses of Resistance: Labouring-Class Women's Poetry in Britain, 1739–1796* (Cambridge: Cambridge University Press, 1990).

Langbaum, Robert, *The Mysteries of Identity: A Theme in Modern Literature* (New York: Oxford University Press, 1977).

Larkin, Peter, '*Fears in Solitude*: Reading from the Dell', *WC*, 22 (1991), 11–14.

—— 'Relations of Scarcity: Ecology and Eschatology in *The Ruined Cottage*', *SiR*, 39 (2000), 345–64.

Law, Jules David, *The Rhetoric of Empiricism: Language and Perception from Locke to I. A. Richards* (Ithaca/London: Cornell University Press, 1993).

Lawrence, Christopher, 'The Nervous System and Society in the Scottish Enlightenment', in Barry Barnes and Steven Shapin (eds), *Natural Order: Historical Studies of Scientific Culture* (Beverly Hills/London: Sage Publications, 1979), 19–40.

Levinson, Marjorie, *Wordsworth's Great Period Poems: Four Essays* (Cambridge: Cambridge University Press, 1986).

—— 'Romantic Criticism: The State of the Art', in Mary A. Favret and Nicola J. Watson (eds), *At the Limits of Romanticism: Essays in Cultural, Feminist, and*

Materialist Criticism (Bloomington/Indianapolis: Indiana University Press, 1994), 269–81.

Lipking, Lawrence, *The Ordering of the Arts in Eighteenth-Century England* (Princeton: Princeton University Press, 1970).

Liu, Alan, *Wordsworth: The Sense of History* (Stanford: Stanford University Press, 1989).

Lloyd, Sarah, 'Cottage Conversations: Poverty and Manly Independence in Eighteenth-Century England', *Past and Present*, 184 (August 2004), 69–108.

Lockridge, Laurence S., *Coleridge the Moralist* (Ithaca/London: Cornell University Press, 1977).

Lord, Catherine, 'Organic Unity Reconsidered', *JAAC*, 22 (1964), 263–8.

Lucas, E. V. (ed.), *Charles Lamb and the Lloyds* (London: Smith, Elder, 1898).

Lussier, Mark S., *Romantic Dynamics: The Poetics of Physicality* (Houndmills: Macmillan; New York: St Martin's Press, 2000).

McKenzie, Gordon, *Organic Unity in Coleridge* (Berkeley: University of California Press, 1939; New York: AMS Press rpt, 1977).

McKusick, James C., *Coleridge's Philosophy of Language* (New Haven, NH/London: Yale University Press, 1986).

—— *Green Writing: Romanticism and Ecology* (New York: St Martin's Press, 2000).

McLane, Maureen N., *Romanticism and the Human Sciences: Poetry, Population, and the Discourse of the Species* (Cambridge: Cambridge University Press, 2000).

McPherson, Thomas, *The Argument from Design* (London: Macmillan, 1972).

Magnuson, Paul, *Reading Public Romanticism* (Princeton: Princeton University Press, 1998).

Manly, Susan, *Language, Custom and Nation in the 1790s: Locke, Tooke, Wordsworth, Edgeworth* (Aldershot/Burlington VT: Ashgate, 2007).

Marshall, John, 'Locke, Socinianism, "Socinianism", and Unitarianism', in M. A. Stewart (ed.), *English Philosophy in the Age of Locke* (Oxford: Clarendon Press, 2000), 111–82.

Martin, Raymond and John Barresi, *Naturalization of the Soul: Self and Personal Identity in the Eighteenth Century* (London/New York: Routledge, 2000).

Maturana, Humberto R. and Francisco J. Varela, *Autopoiesis and Cognition: The Realization of the Living*, Boston Studies in the Philosophy of Science 42 (Dordrecht/Boston/London: D. Reidel, 1980).

Mayberry, Tom, *Coleridge and Wordsworth in the West Country* (Stroud: Alan Sutton, 1992).

Meyerstein, E. H. W., *A Life of Thomas Chatterton* (London: Ingpen and Grant, 1930).

—— 'An Elegy on Chatterton', *TLS*, 8 Feb. 1934, 92.

Modiano, Raimonda, *Coleridge and the Concept of Nature* (Tallahassee: Florida State University Press, 1985).

Newlyn, Lucy, 'Parodic Allusion: Coleridge and the 'Nehemiah Higginbottom' Sonnets, 1797', *CLB*, 56 (1986), 255–9.

—— 'Coleridge and the Anxiety of Reception', *Romanticism*, 1 (1995), 206–38.

—— *Reading, Writing and Romanticism: The Anxiety of Reception* (Oxford: Oxford University Press, 2000).

Olson, Richard, 'On the Nature of God's Existence, Wisdom and Power: The Interplay between Organic and Mechanistic Imagery in Anglican Natural Theology, 1640–1740', in Frederick Burwick (ed.), *Approaches to Organic Form: Permutations in Science and Culture* (Dordrecht: D. Reidel, 1987), 1–48.

O'Neill, Michael, *Romanticism and the Self-Conscious Poem* (Oxford: Clarendon Press; New York: Oxford University Press, 1997).

Orsini, G. N. G., 'Coleridge and Schlegel Reconsidered', *CL*, 16 (1964), 97–118.

—— 'The Organic Concepts in Aesthetics', *CL*, 21 (1969), 1–30.

Paley, Morton, *Apocalypse and Millennium in English Romantic Poetry* (Oxford: Clarendon Press, 1999).

Peckham, Morse, 'Toward a Theory of Romanticism', *PMLA*, 66 (1951), 5–23.

Pellicer, Juan Christian, 'The Georgic at Mid-Eighteenth Century and the Case of Dodsley's "Agriculture"', *RES*, 54 (2003), 67–93.

Perkins, David, *Is Literary History Possible?* (Baltimore: Johns Hopkins University Press, 1992).

—— 'Compassion for Animals and Radical Politics: Coleridge's "To a Young Ass"', *ELH*, 65 (1998), 929–44.

Perry, Seamus, *Coleridge and the Uses of Division* (Oxford: Oxford University Press, 1999).

Pfau, Thomas, *Romantic Moods: Paranoia, Trauma, and Melancholy, 1790–1840* (Baltimore: Johns Hopkins University Press, 2005).

Philp, Mark, *Godwin's Political Justice* (London: Duckworth, 1986).

—— (ed.), *The French Revolution and British Popular Politics* (Cambridge: Cambridge University Press, 2002).

—— (ed.), *Resisting Napoleon: The British Response to the Threat of Invasion, 1797–1815* (Aldershot: Ashgate, 2006).

Piper, H. W., *The Active Universe: Pantheism and the Concept of Imagination in the English Romantic Poets* (London: Athlone Press, 1962).

Plug, Jan, 'Romanticism and the Invention of Literature', in Tilottama Rajan and Arkady Plotnitsky (eds), *Idealism without Absolutes: Philosophy and Romantic Culture* (Albany: SUNY Press, 2004), 15–37.

Pocock, J. G. A., 'Burke and the Ancient Constitution—A Problem in the History of Ideas', *Historical Journal*, 3 (1960), 125–43.

Pollin, Burton R. (assist. Redmond Burke), 'John Thelwall's Marginalia in a Copy of Coleridge's *Biographia Literaria*', *Bulletin of the New York Public Library*, 74 (1970), 73–94.

—— 'Charles Lamb and Charles Lloyd as Jacobins and Anti-Jacobins', *SiR*, 12 (1973), 633–47.

Poovey, Mary, 'The Model System of Contemporary Literary Criticism', *Critical Inquiry*, 27 (Spring 2001), 408–38.

Pratt, Lynda, '"Perilous Acquaintance"? Lloyd, Coleridge and Southey in the 1790s: Five Unpublished Letters', *Romanticism*, 6 (2000), 98–115.

Purton, Valerie, *A Coleridge Chronology* (Houndmills: Macmillan, 1993).

Radcliffe, Evan, '"In Dreams Begins Responsibility": Wordsworth's Ruined Cottage Story', *SiR*, 23 (1984), 101–19.

Rajan, Tilottama, 'Organicism', *English Studies in Canada*, 30 (2004), 46–50.

——and Arkady Plotnitsky (eds), *Idealism without Absolutes: Philosophy and Romantic Culture* (Albany: SUNY Press, 2004).

Rauber, D. F., 'The Fragment as Romantic Form', *MLQ*, 30 (1969), 212–21.

Rawlinson, Mark, 'Invasion! Coleridge, the Defence of Britain and the Cultivation of the Public's Fear', in Philip Shaw (ed.), *Romantic Wars: Studies in Culture and Conflict, 1793–1822* (Aldershot: Ashgate, 2000), 110–37.

Ritterbush, Philip C., *The Art of Organic Forms* (Washington, DC: Smithsonian Institute Press, 1968).

Roe, Nicholas, 'Coleridge, Wordsworth, and the French Invasion Scare', *WC*, 17 (1986), 142–7.

——*Wordsworth and Coleridge: The Radical Years* (Oxford: Clarendon Press, 1988).

——'Coleridge and John Thelwall: The Road to Nether Stowey', in Richard Gravil and Molly Lefebure (eds), *The Coleridge Connection: Essays for Thomas McFarland* (Basingstoke: Macmillan, 1990), 60–80.

——*John Keats and the Culture of Dissent* (Oxford: Clarendon Press, 1997).

——(ed.), *Samuel Taylor Coleridge and the Sciences of Life* (Oxford: Oxford University Press, 2001).

——*The Politics of Nature: William Wordsworth and Some Contemporaries*. 2nd edn (Houndmills: Palgrave, 2002).

——*Fiery Heart: The First Life of Leigh Hunt* (London: Pimlico, 2005).

Rosenberg, Daniel, 'Joseph Priestley and the Graphic Invention of Modern Time', *Studies in Eighteenth-Century Culture*, 36 (2007), 55–103.

Ross, Trevor, *The Making of the English Literary Canon: From the Middle Ages to the Late Eighteenth Century* (Montreal/Kingston: McGill-Queen's University Press, 1998).

Rousseau, G. S. (ed.), *Organic Form: The Life of an Idea* (London/Boston: Routledge and Kegan Paul, 1972).

Royle, Edward, *Revolutionary Britannia? Reflections on the Threat of Revolution in Britain, 1789–1848* (Manchester: Manchester University Press, 2001).

Schlick, Moritz, 'Philosophy of Organic Life', in Herbert Feigl and May Brodbeck (eds), *Readings in the Philosophy of Science* (New York: Appleton-Century-Crofts, 1953), 523–36.

Shaffer, Eleanor, 'Myths of Community in the *Lyrical Ballads* 1798–1998: The Commonwealth and the Constitution', in Nicholas Roe (ed.), *Samuel Taylor Coleridge and the Sciences of Life* (Oxford: Oxford University Press, 2001), 25–46.

Sheats, Paul D., 'Cultivating Margaret's Garden: Wordsworthian "Nature" and the Quest for Historical "Difference"', in Peter Kitson (ed.), *Placing and Displacing Romanticism* (Aldershot: Ashgate, 2001), 16–32.

Sheps, Arthur, 'Joseph Priestley's Time *Charts*: The Use and Teaching of History by Rational Dissent in late Eighteenth-Century England', *Lumen*, 18 (1999), 135–54.

Simmons, A. John, *The Lockean Theory of Rights* (Princeton: Princeton University Press, 1992).

Simpson, David, *Irony and Authority in Romantic Poetry* (London/Basingstoke: Macmillan, 1979).

Simpson, David, *Wordsworth's Historical Imagination: The Poetry of Displacement* (New York/London: Methuen, 1987).

—— 'Coleridge on Wordsworth and the Form of Poetry', in Christine Gallant (ed.), *Coleridge's Theory of Imagination Today* (New York: AMS Press, 1989), 211–25.

Simpson, Michael, 'The Morning (Post) After: Apocalypse and Bathos in Coleridge's "Fears in Solitude"', in Tim Fulford (ed.), *Romanticism and Millenarianism* (New York/Houndmills: Palgrave, 2002), 71–86.

Siskin, Clifford, *The Historicity of Romantic Discourse* (New York/Oxford: Oxford University Press, 1988).

Smith, Christopher J. P., *A Quest for Home: Reading Robert Southey* (Liverpool: Liverpool University Press, 1997).

Smith, D. Nichol, 'Warton's *History of English Poetry*', *Proceedings of the British Academy*, 15 (1929), 73–99.

Stabler, Jane, 'Guardians and Watchful Powers: Literary Satire and *Lyrical Ballads* in 1798', in Richard Cronin (ed.), *1798: The Year of the* Lyrical Ballads (Basingstoke: Macmillan; New York: St Martin's Press, 1998), 203–30.

—— 'Space for Speculation: Coleridge, Barbauld, and the Poetics of Priestley', in Nicholas Roe (ed.), *Samuel Taylor Coleridge and the Sciences of Life* (Oxford: Oxford University Press, 2001), 175–204.

Stempel, Daniel, 'Coleridge and Organic Form: The English Tradition', *SiR*, 6 (1967), 89–97.

Stones, Graeme, 'Charles Lloyd and *Edmund Oliver*: A Demonology', *CLB*, 95 (1996), 110–21.

—— 'The Ragged-Trousered Philanthropist: Coleridge and Self-exposure in the Higginbottom Sonnets', *CLB*, 100 (1997), 122–32.

Storey, Mark, *Robert Southey: A Life* (Oxford: Oxford University Press, 1997).

Suarez, Michael F., SJ, 'What Thomas Knew: Chatterton and the Business of Getting into Print', *Angelaki*, 1.2 (1993–4), 83–94.

—— '"This Necessary Knowledge": Thomas Chatterton and the Ways of the London Book Trade', in Nick Groom (ed.), *Thomas Chatterton and Romantic Culture* (Houndmills: Macmillan; New York: St Martin's Press, 1999), 96–113.

Swann, Karen, 'Suffering and Sensation in *The Ruined Cottage*', *PMLA*, 106 (1991), 83–95.

Swift, Simon, *Romanticism, Literature and Philosophy: Expressive Rationality in Rousseau, Kant, Wollstonecraft and Contemporary Theory* (London/New York: Continuum, 2006).

Taussig, Gurion, '"Lavish Promises": Coleridge, Charles Lamb and Charles Lloyd, 1794–1798', *Romanticism*, 6 (2000), 78–97.

—— *Coleridge and the Idea of Friendship, 1789–1804* (Newark: University of Delaware Press; London: Associated University Presses, 2002).

Taylor, Anya, 'Coleridge and the Pleasures of Verse', *SiR*, 40 (2001), 547–69.

Taylor, Charles, *Sources of the Self: The Making of the Modern Identity* (Cambridge: Cambridge University Press, 1989).

Taylor, Donald S., *Thomas Chatterton's Art: Experiments in Imagined History* (Princeton: Princeton University Press, 1978).

Terry, Richard, 'Transitions and Digressions in the Eighteenth-Century Long Poem', *SEL*, 32 (1992), 495–510.

Thomas, Sophie, 'Assembling History: Fragments and Ruins', *European Romantic Review*, 14 (2003), 177–86.
—— 'The Fragment', in Nicholas Roe (ed.), *Romanticism: An Oxford Guide* (Oxford: Oxford University Press, 2005), 502–20.
Thompson, C. Bradley, 'John Adams and the Coming of the French Revolution', *Journal of the Early Republic*, 16 (1996), 361–87.
Thompson, E. P., 'Disenchantment or Default? A Lay Sermon', in C. C. O'Brien and W. D. Vanech (eds), *Power and Consciousness* (London: University of London Press: New York: New York University Press, 1969), 149–81.
Thompson, Judith, 'An Autumnal Blast, a Killing Frost: Coleridge's Poetic Conversation with John Thelwall', *SiR*, 36 (1997), 427–56.
Trott, Nicola, 'The Coleridge Circle and the "Answer to Godwin"', *RES*, 41 (1990), 212–29.
Ulmer, William, A., 'Wordsworth, the One Life, and *The Ruined Cottage*', *SP*, 93 (1996), 304–31.
—— 'The Rhetorical Occasion of "This Lime-Tree Bower my Prison"', *Romanticism*, 13 (2007), 15–27.
Watson, Jeanie, *Risking Enchantment: Coleridge's Symbolic World of Faery* (Lincoln, NE/London: University of Nebraska Press, 1990).
Watters, C.R., 'A Distant "Boum" among the Hills: Some Notes on "Fears in Solitude"', *CLB*, 59 (July 1987), 85–96.
Wayne, Valerie, '*Cymbeline*: Patriotism and Performance', in Richard Dutton and Jean E. Howard (eds), *A Companion to Shakespeare's Works*, vol. iv (Oxford: Blackwell, 2003), 389–407.
Wellek, René, *The Rise of English Literary History* (Chapel Hill: University of North Carolina Press, 1941).
Wells, Roger, 'English Society and Revolutionary Politics in the 1790s: The Case for Insurrection', in Mark Philp (ed.), *The French Revolution and British Popular Politics* (Cambridge: Cambridge University Press, 2002), 188–226.
Wesling, Donald, *The Chances of Rhyme: Device and Modernity* (Berkeley: University of California Press, 1980).
Westfall, Richard S., *Science and Religion in Seventeenth-Century England* (New Haven: Yale University Press, 1958).
Whale, John, 'The Limits of Paine's Revolutionary Literalism', in Kelvin Everest (ed.), *Revolution in Writing: British Literary Responses to the French Revolution* (Milton Keynes: Open University Press, 1991), 121–37.
—— 'Literal and Symbolic Representations: Burke, Paine and the French Revolution', *History of European Ideas*, 16 (1993), 343–9.
—— *Imagination under Pressure, 1789–1832: Aesthetics, Politics and Utility* (Cambridge: Cambridge University Press, 2000).
Whalley, George, 'The Bristol Library Borrowings of Southey and Coleridge, 1793–8', *The Library*, 5th ser., 4 (1950), 114–32.
Wheeler, Kathleen M., *The Creative Mind in Coleridge's Poetry* (London: Heinemann, 1981).
—— *Romanticism, Pragmatism and Deconstruction* (Oxford: Blackwell, 1993).
Wilbur, Earl Morse, *A History of Unitarianism: In Transylvania, England, and America* (Cambridge, MA: Harvard University Press, 1952).

Williams, Iolo M., 'An Identification of Some Early Drawings by Flaxman', *Burlington Magazine*, 102 (June 1960), 246–51.

Williams, John R., *The Life of Goethe: A Critical Biography* (Oxford: Blackwell, 1998).

Williams, Raymond, *Keywords: A Vocabulary of Culture and Society*, rev. edn (New York: Oxford University Press, 1983).

Wilson, Jack, *Biological Individuality: The Identity and Persistence of Living Entities* (Cambridge: Cambridge University Press, 1999).

Wimsatt, W. K., 'Organic Form: Some Questions about a Metaphor', in David Thorburn and Geoffrey Hartman (eds), *Romanticism: Vistas, Instances, Continuities* (Ithaca/London: Cornell University Press, 1973), 13–37.

Winchester, Simon, *The Map that Changed the World: The Tale of William Smith and the Birth of a Science* (London: Viking, 2001).

Wolfson, Susan J., *Formal Charges: The Shaping of Poetry in British Romanticism* (Stanford: Stanford University Press, 1997).

Woodring, Carl R., *Politics in the Poetry of Coleridge* (Madison: University of Wisconsin Press, 1961).

Wordsworth, Jonathan, *The Music of Humanity: A Critical Study of Wordsworth's 'Ruined Cottage' incorporating texts from a manuscript of 1799–1800* (New York/Evanston: Harper and Row, 1969).

—— *William Wordsworth: The Borders of Vision* (Oxford: Clarendon Press, 1982).

Wu, Duncan, 'Wordsworth's Reading of Bowles', *N&Q*, 234 (1989), 166–7.

—— 'Coleridge, Thelwall, and the Politics of Poetry', *CB*, 4 (1994), 23–44.

Wylie, Ian, *Young Coleridge and the Philosophers of Nature* (Oxford: Clarendon Press, 1989).

Yolton, John, *Locke and the Compass of Human Understanding* (Cambridge: Cambridge University Press, 1970).

—— (ed.), *John Locke: Problems and Perspectives* (London: Cambridge University Press, 1969).

Zall, Paul M. (ed.), *Coleridge's 'Sonnets from Various Authors' bound with Rev. W.L. Bowles' 'Sonnets', annotated by Paul M. Zall* (Glendale: La Siesta Press, 1968).

Index

Lightning Source UK Ltd.
Milton Keynes UK
UKHW010642130223
416869UK00003B/209